# Alice 19th 1

story and art by **Yû Watase**

*volume 1*

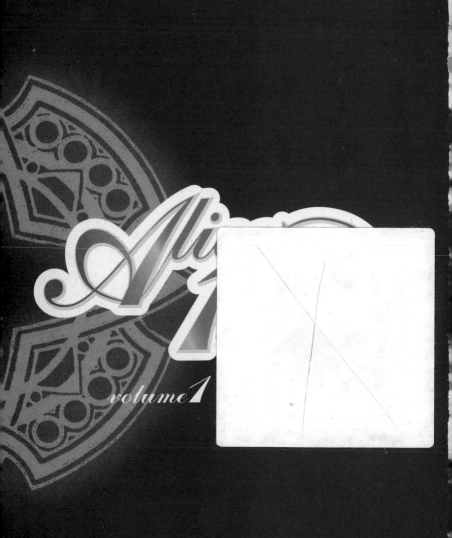

# *Alice 19th*
## *volume 1* *Lotis Master*

### STORY & ART BY
# Yû Watase

English Adaptation/Lance Caselman
Translaton/JN Productions
Touch-Up Art & Lettering/Walden Wong
Cover Design & Layout/Izumi Evers
Editor/Frances Wall

Managing Editor/Annette Roman
Editor in Chief/Alvin Lu
Production Manager/Noboru Watanabe
Sr. Director of Licensing & Acquisitions/Rika Inouye
Vice President of Marketing/Liza Coppola
V.P. of Sale/Joe Morici
Publisher/Seiji Horibuchi

Printed in Canada

Published by VIZ, LLC
P.O. Box 77010 · San Francisco, CA 94107

10 9 8 7 6 5 4 3 2
Second printing, December 2003
Third printing, August 2004

www.viz.com   storeviz.com   ANIMERICA
ANIME & MANGA MONTHLY

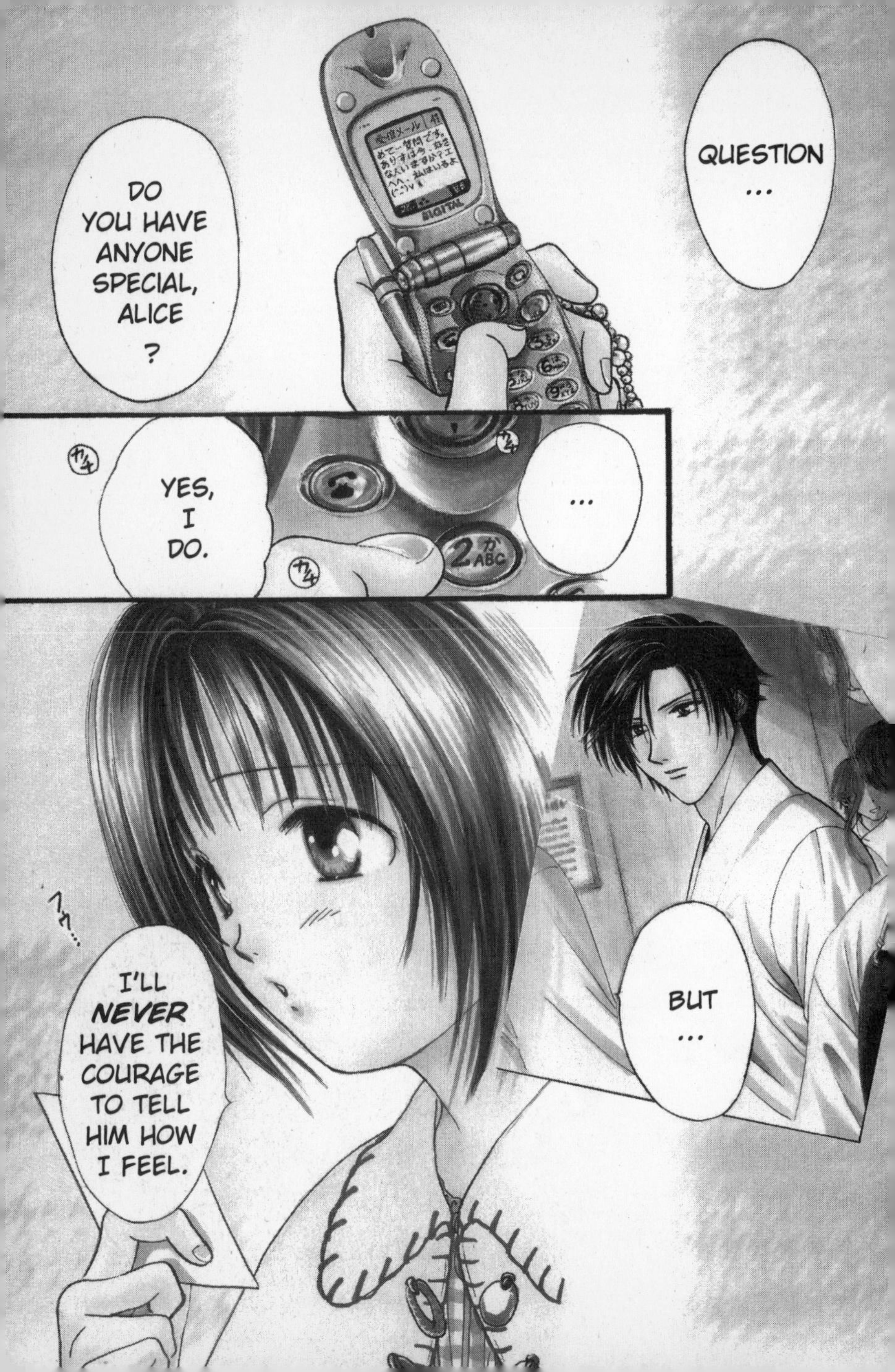
QUESTION...
DO YOU HAVE ANYONE SPECIAL, ALICE?
...
YES, I DO.
BUT...
I'LL **NEVER** HAVE THE COURAGE TO TELL HIM HOW I FEEL.

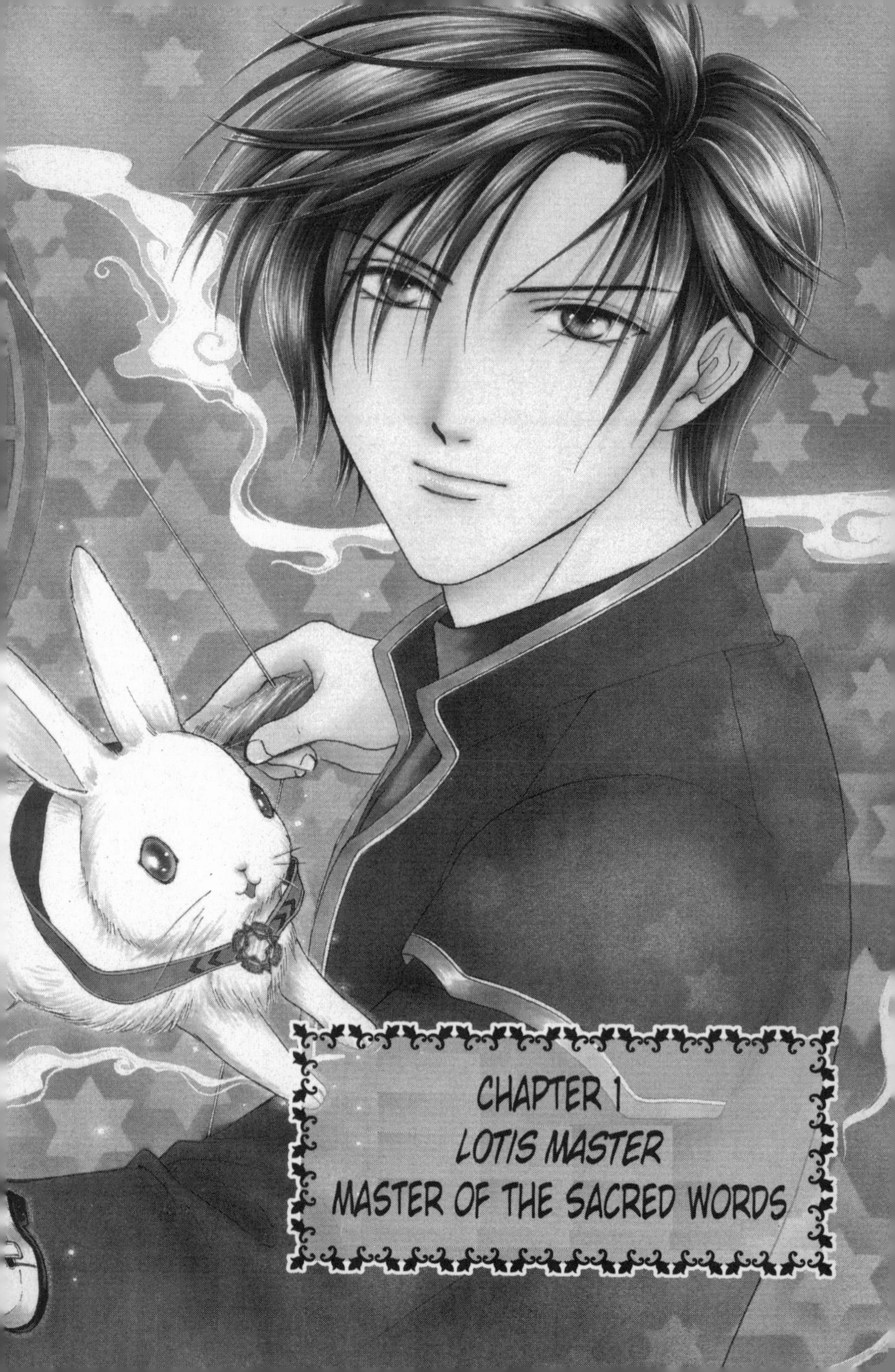
CHAPTER 1
LOTIS MASTER
MASTER OF THE SACRED WORDS

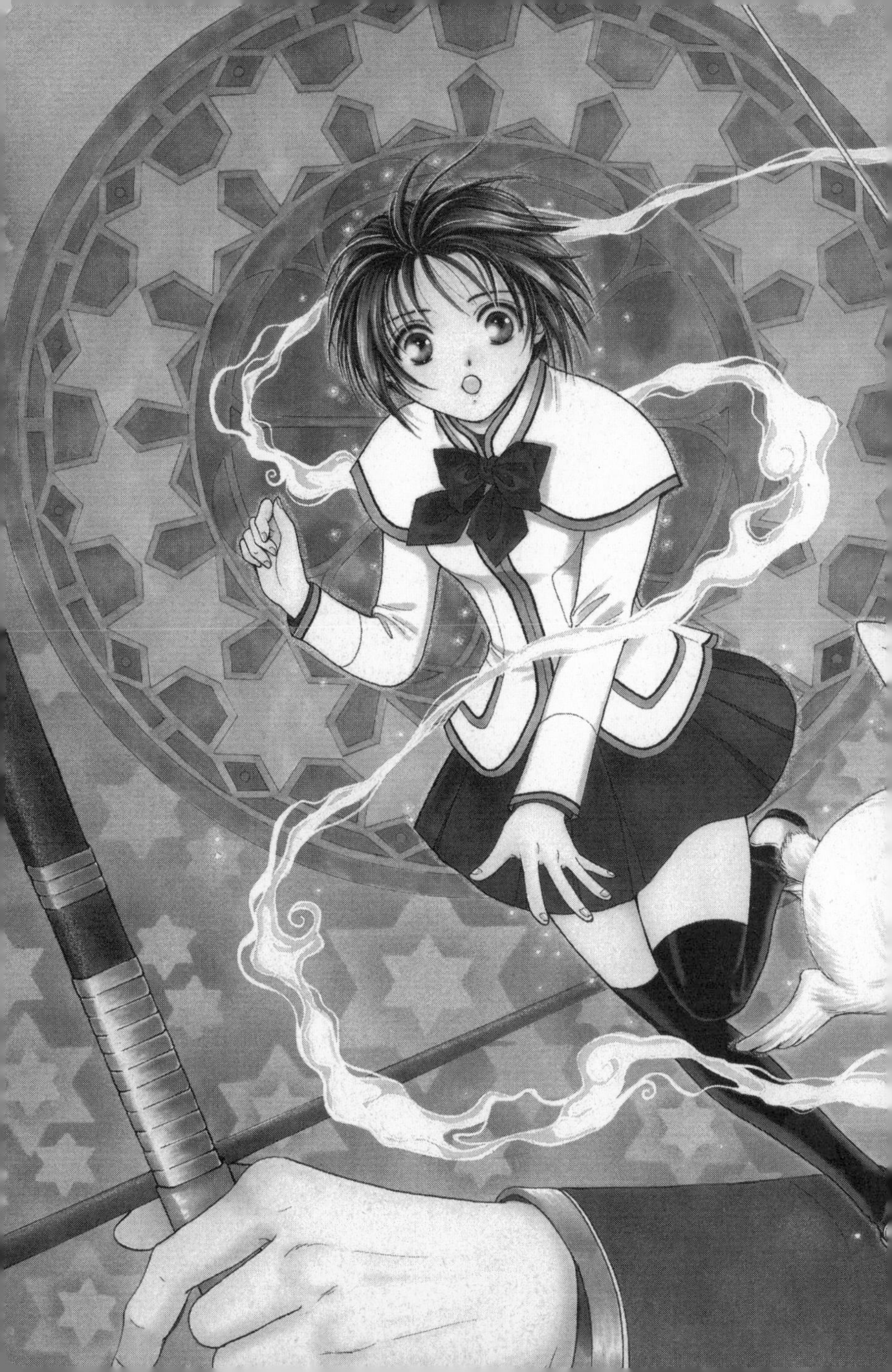

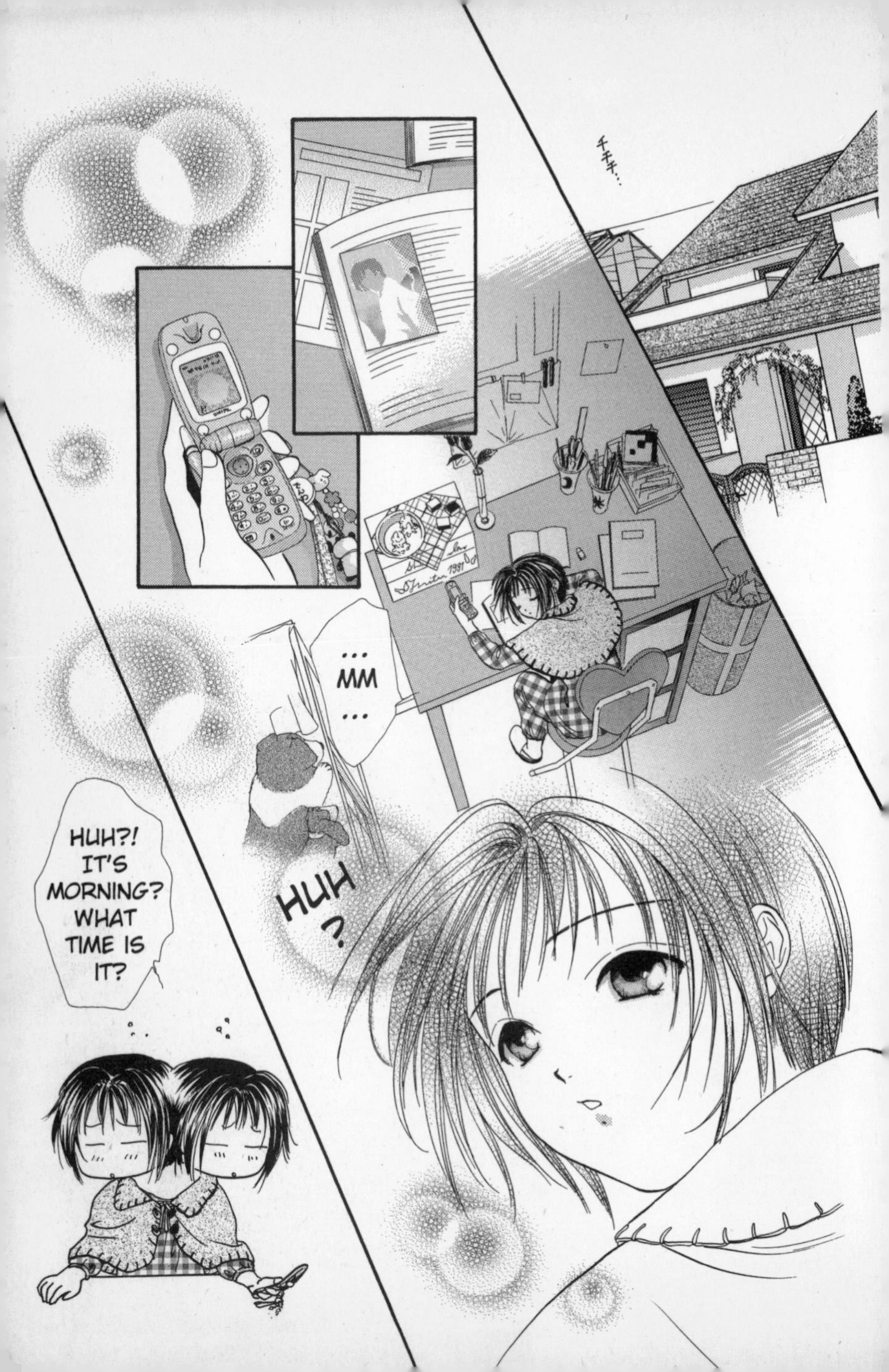
チチチ…
... MM ...
HUH ?
HUH?! IT'S MORNING? WHAT TIME IS IT?

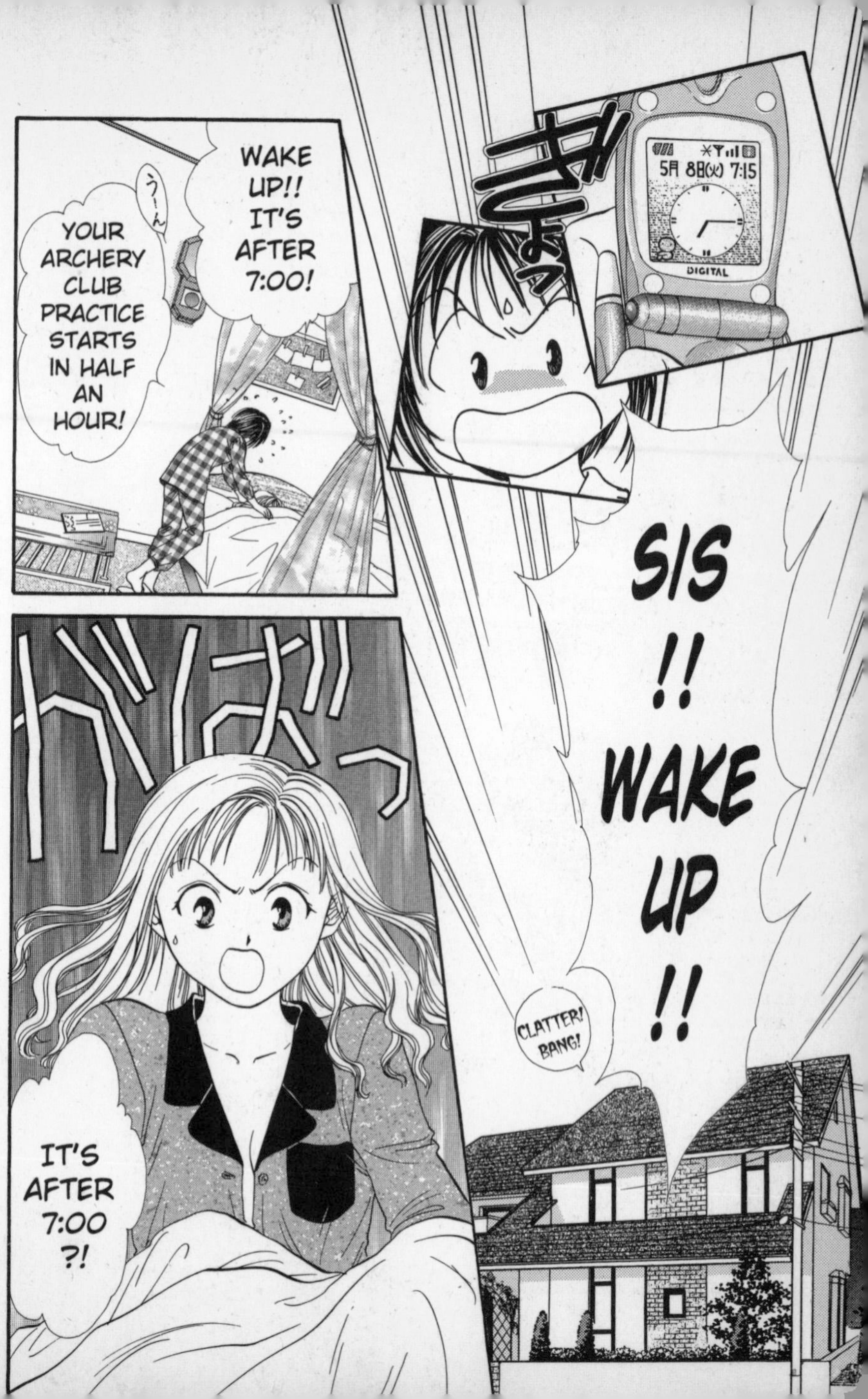

5月 8日(火) 7:15
DIGITAL
ぎょっ
WAKE UP!! IT'S AFTER 7:00!
う～ん
YOUR ARCHERY CLUB PRACTICE STARTS IN HALF AN HOUR!
SIS!! WAKE UP!!
CLATTER! BANG!
がばっ
IT'S AFTER 7:00?!

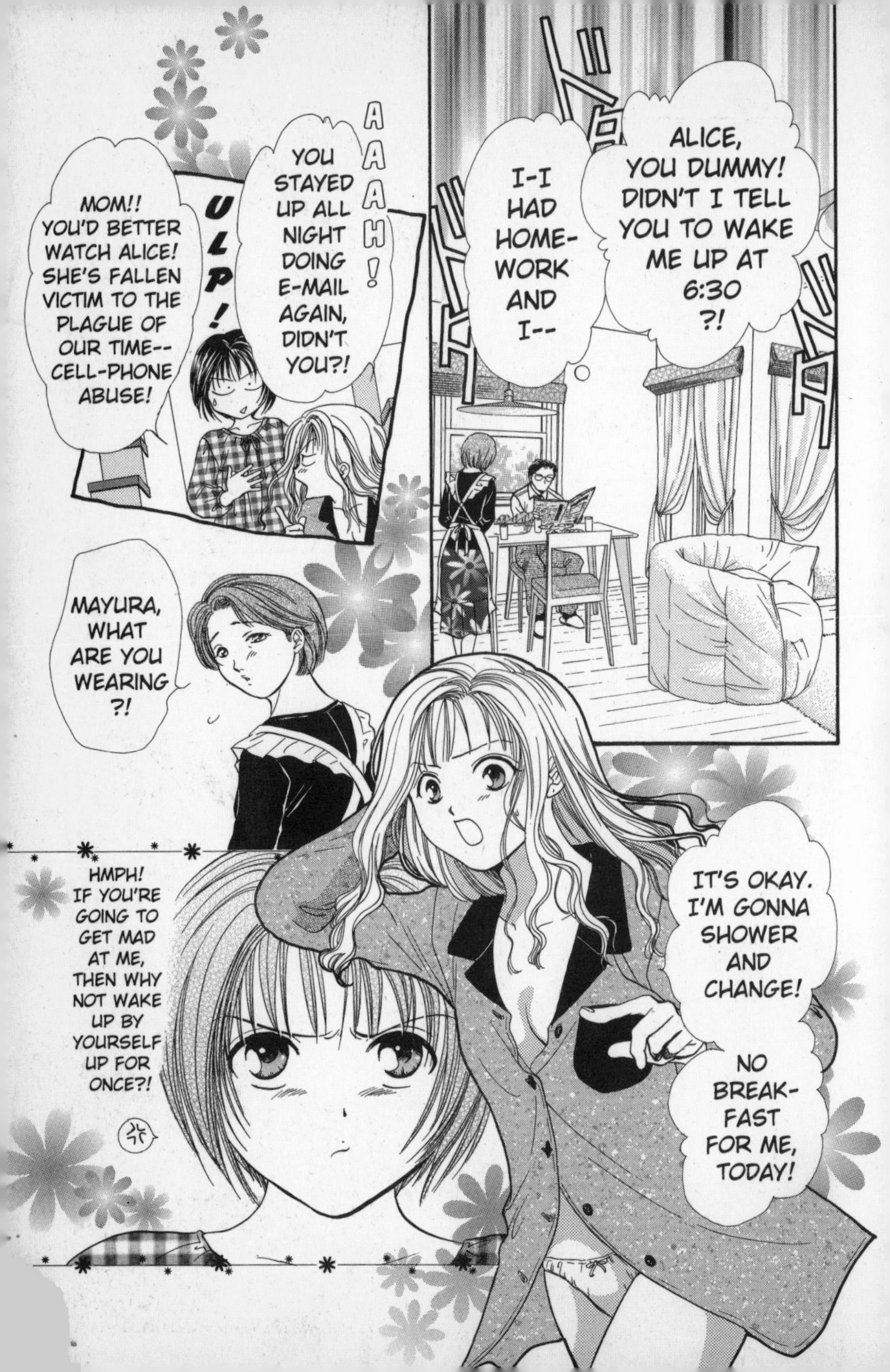
ALICE, YOU DUMMY! DIDN'T I TELL YOU TO WAKE ME UP AT 6:30 ?!
I-I HAD HOME-WORK AND I--
AAAAH!
YOU STAYED UP ALL NIGHT DOING E-MAIL AGAIN, DIDN'T YOU?!
ULP!
MOM!! YOU'D BETTER WATCH ALICE! SHE'S FALLEN VICTIM TO THE PLAGUE OF OUR TIME-- CELL-PHONE ABUSE!
MAYURA, WHAT ARE YOU WEARING ?!
IT'S OKAY. I'M GONNA SHOWER AND CHANGE!
NO BREAK-FAST FOR ME, TODAY!
HMPH! IF YOU'RE GOING TO GET MAD AT ME, THEN WHY NOT WAKE UP BY YOURSELF UP FOR ONCE?!

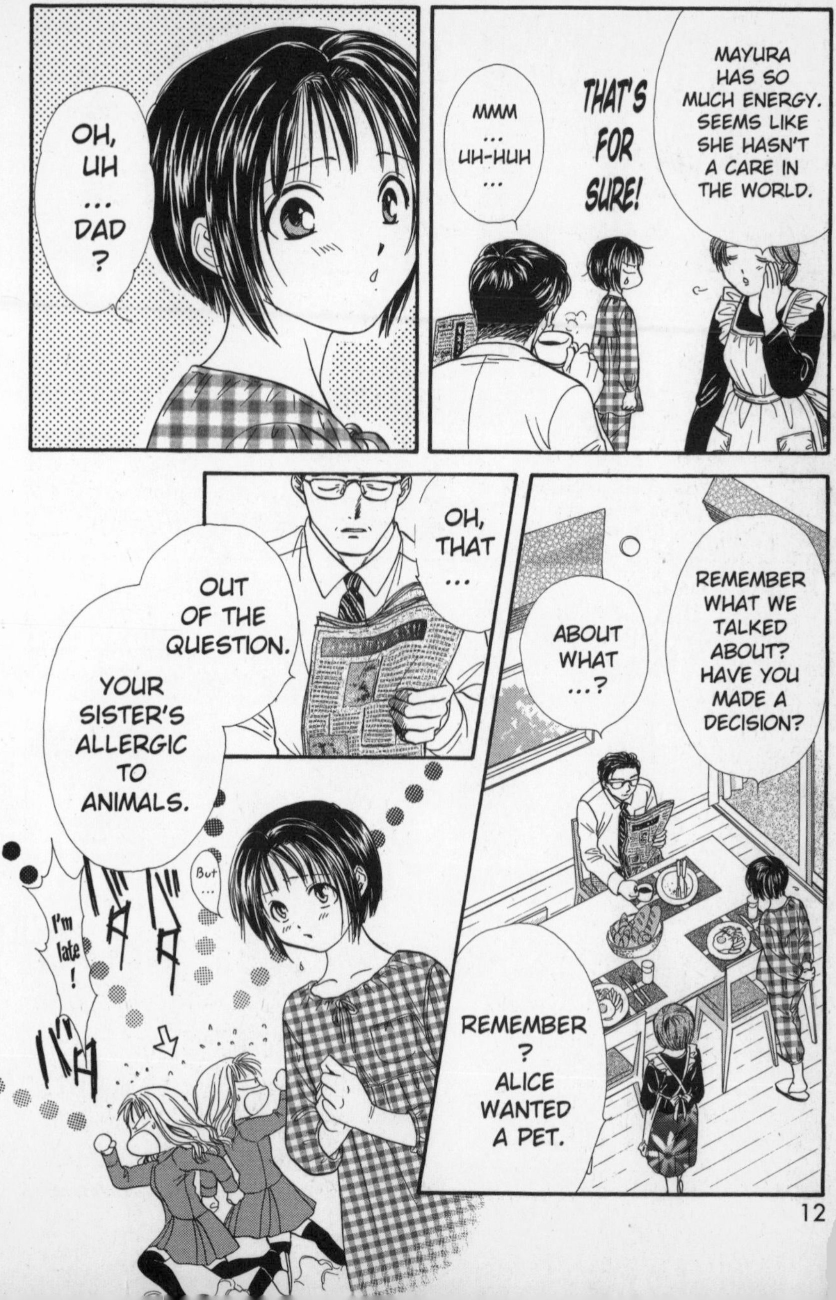
MAYURA HAS SO MUCH ENERGY. SEEMS LIKE SHE HASN'T A CARE IN THE WORLD.
THAT'S FOR SURE!
MMM ... UH-HUH ...
OH, UH ... DAD ?
REMEMBER WHAT WE TALKED ABOUT? HAVE YOU MADE A DECISION?
ABOUT WHAT ...?
REMEMBER ? ALICE WANTED A PET.
OH, THAT ...
OUT OF THE QUESTION.
YOUR SISTER'S ALLERGIC TO ANIMALS.
But ...
I'm late !

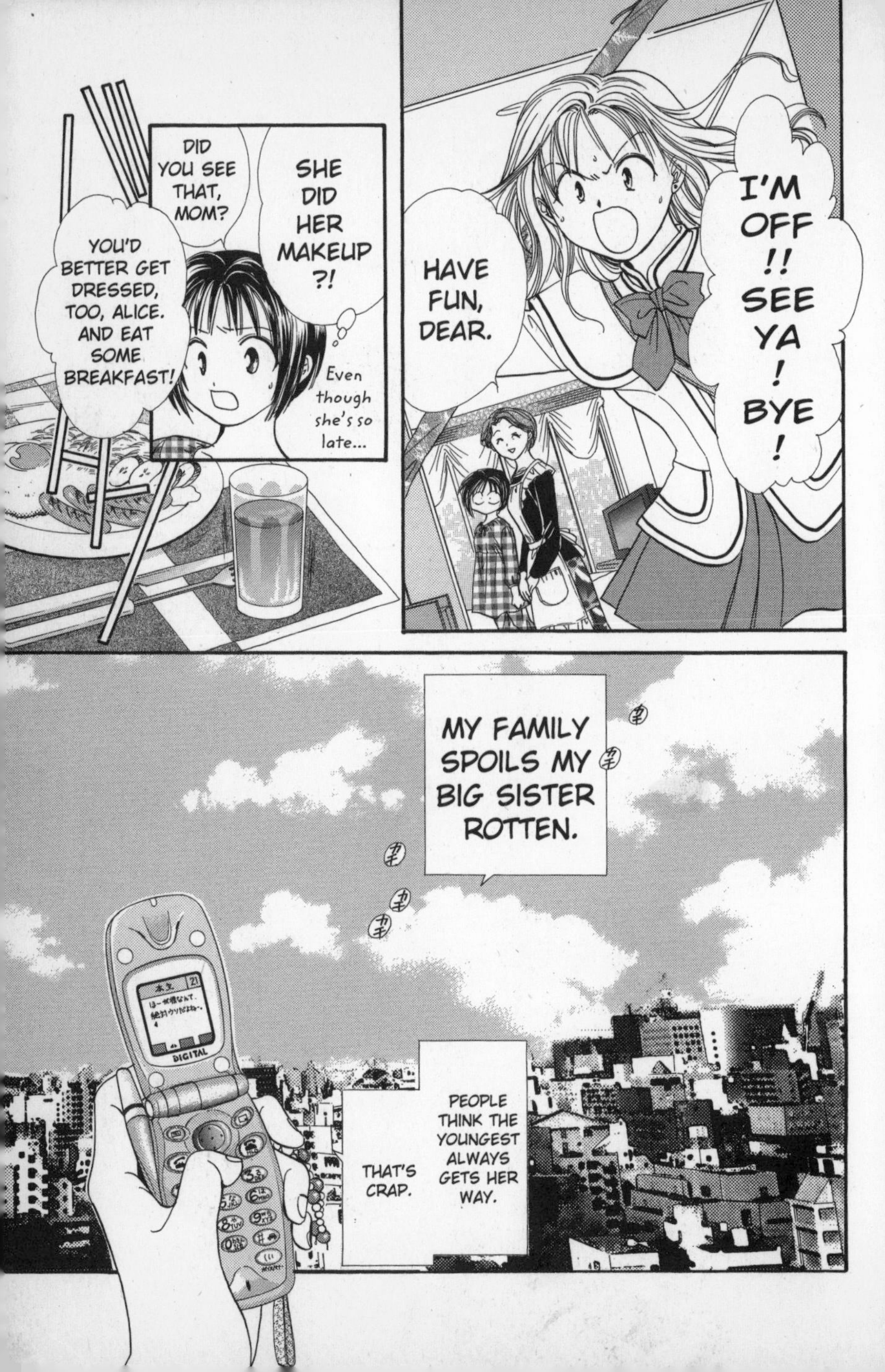

I'M OFF!! SEE YA! BYE!
HAVE FUN, DEAR.
DID YOU SEE THAT, MOM?
SHE DID HER MAKEUP?!
Even though she's so late...
YOU'D BETTER GET DRESSED, TOO, ALICE. AND EAT SOME BREAKFAST!
MY FAMILY SPOILS MY BIG SISTER ROTTEN.
PEOPLE THINK THE YOUNGEST ALWAYS GETS HER WAY.
THAT'S CRAP.

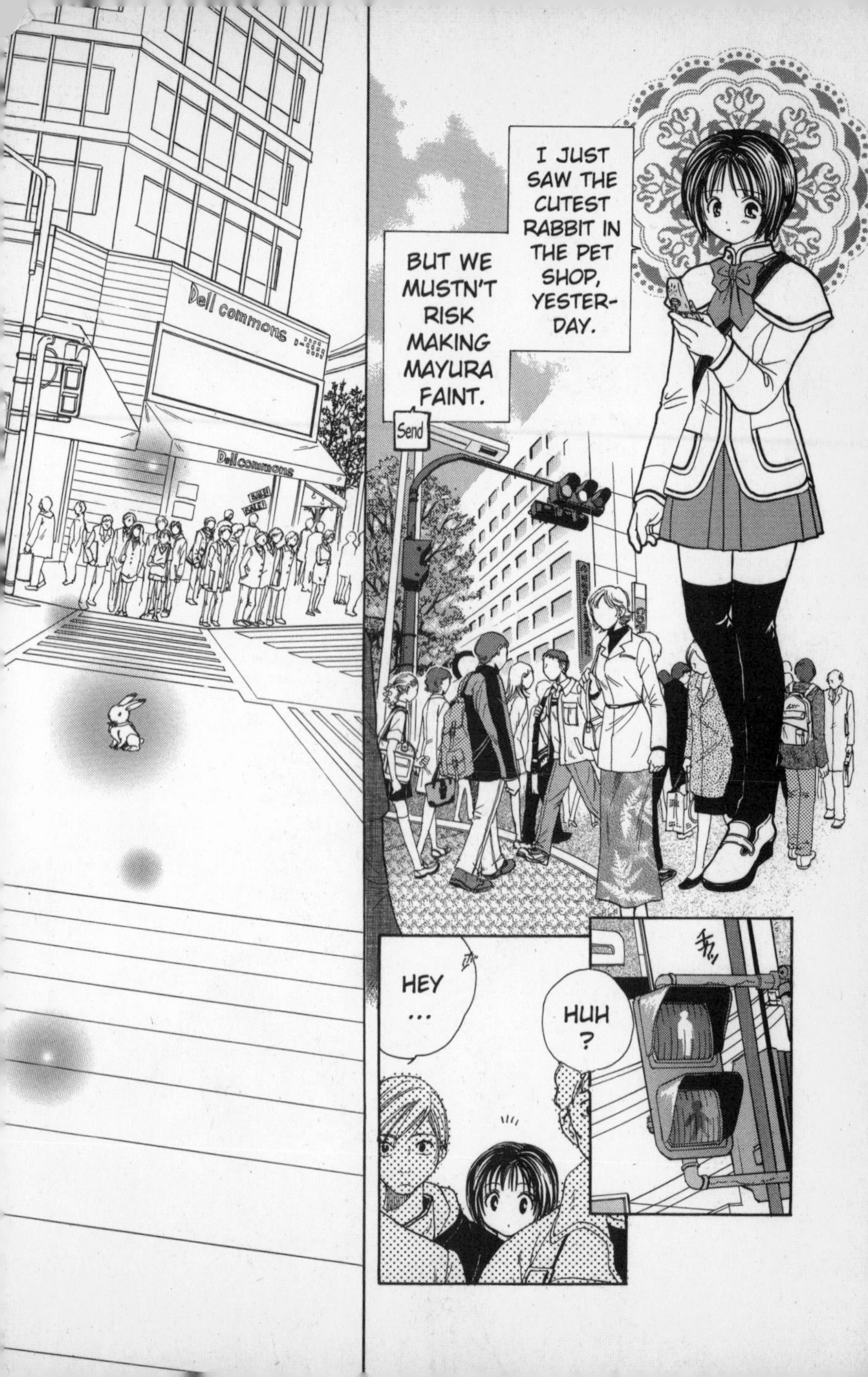
I JUST SAW THE CUTEST RABBIT IN THE PET SHOP, YESTER-DAY.
BUT WE MUSTN'T RISK MAKING MAYURA FAINT.
Send
HUH ?
HEY ...
Dell commons
Dell commons

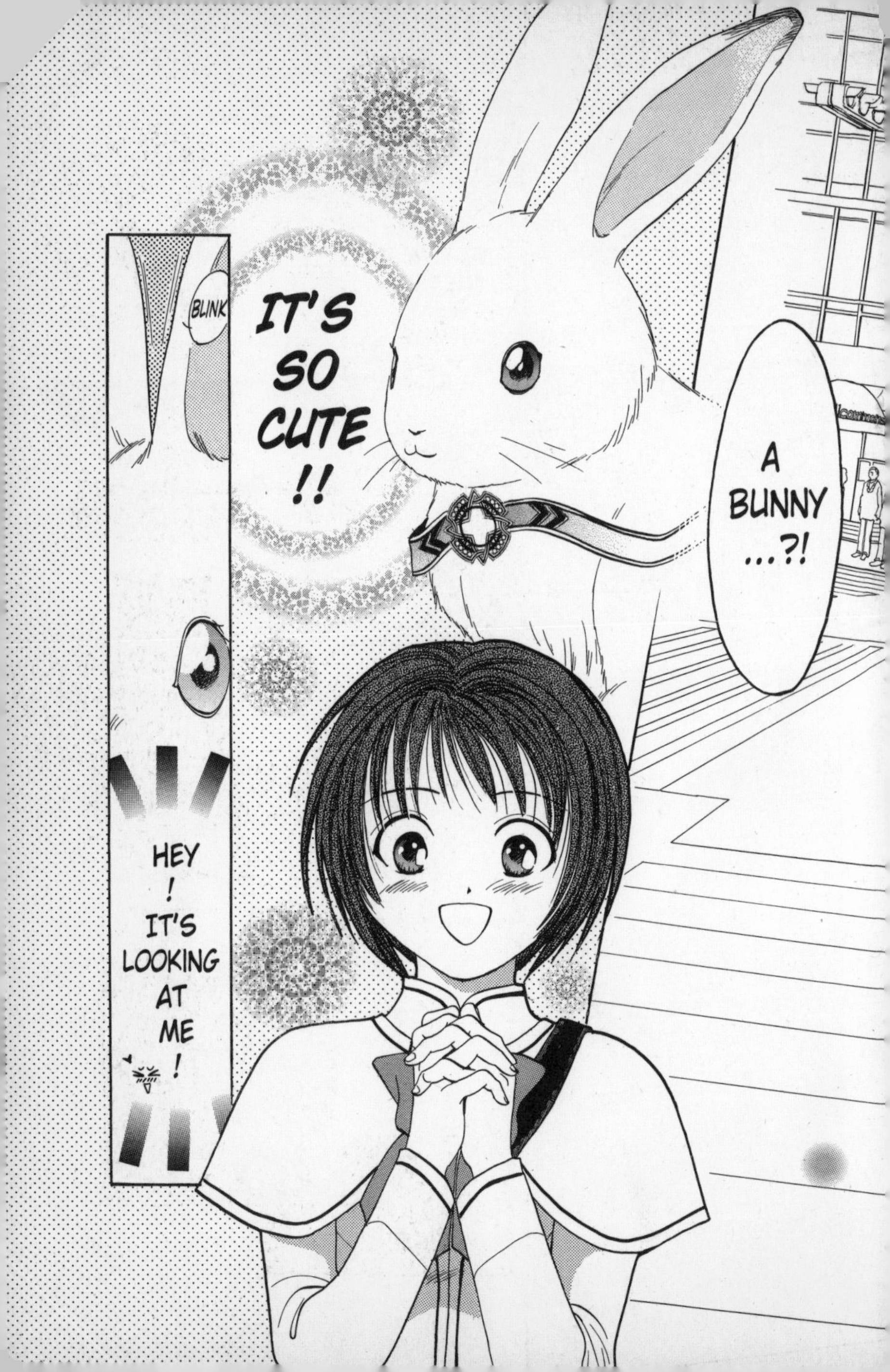
A BUNNY ...?!
IT'S SO CUTE !!
BLINK
HEY ! IT'S LOOKING AT ME !

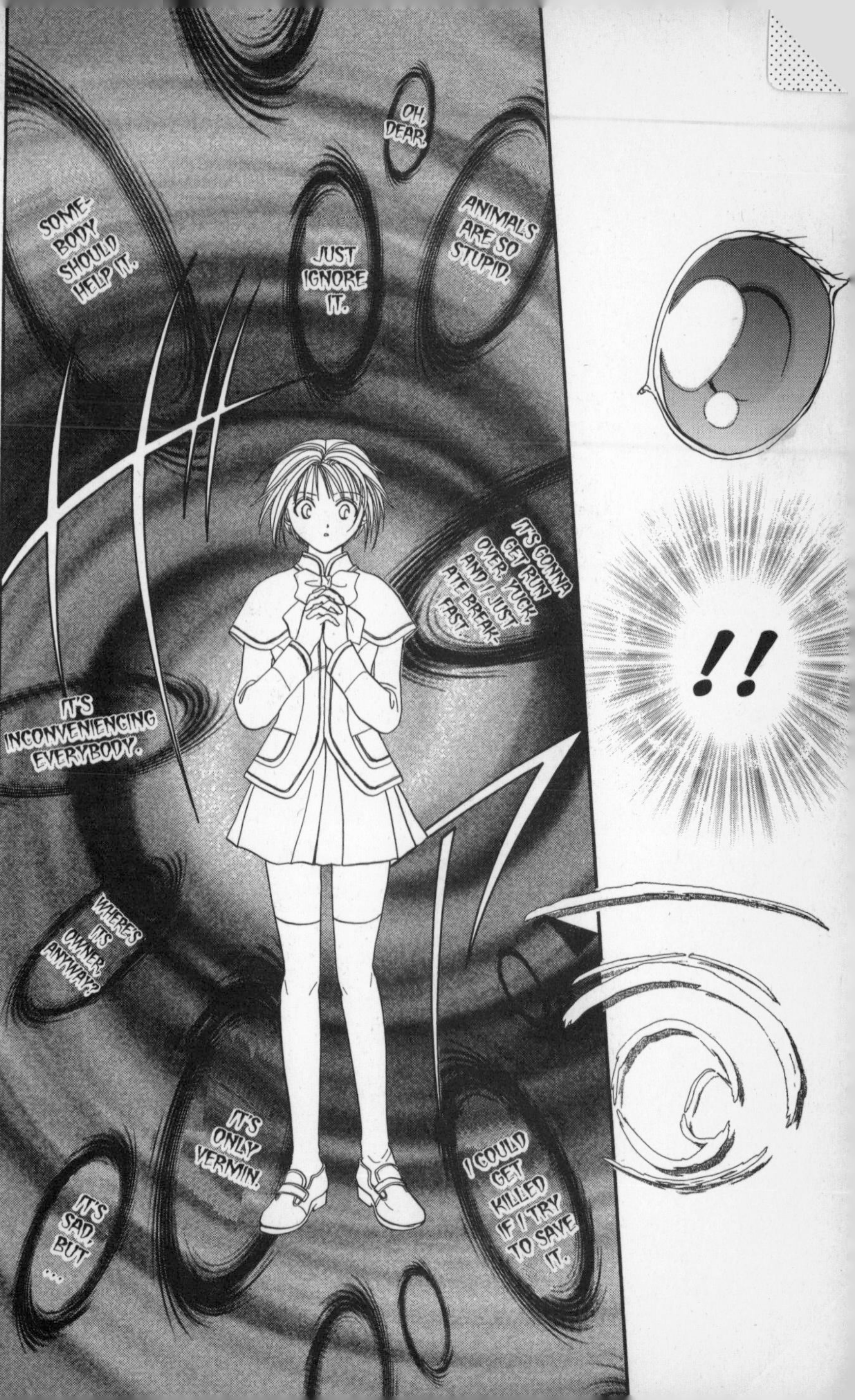
!!
OH, DEAR.
ANIMALS ARE SO STUPID.
JUST IGNORE IT.
SOME-BODY SHOULD HELP IT.
IT'S GONNA GET RUN OVER. YUCK, AND I JUST ATE BREAK-FAST.
IT'S INCONVENIENCING EVERYBODY.
WHERE'S ITS OWNER, ANYWAY?
I COULD GET KILLED IF I TRY TO SAVE IT.
IT'S ONLY VERMIN.
IT'S SAD, BUT...

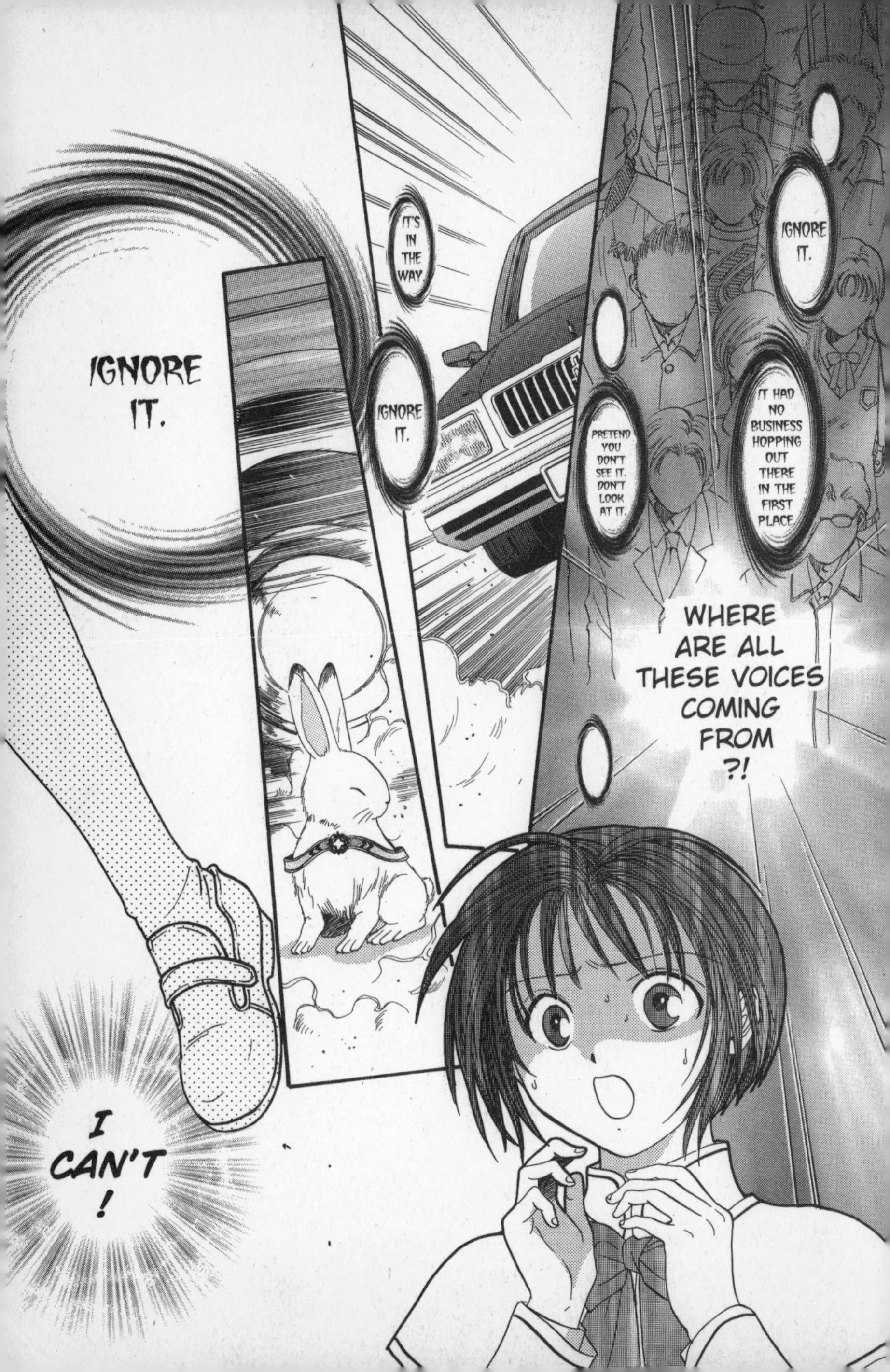
IGNORE IT.
IT HAD NO BUSINESS HOPPING OUT THERE IN THE FIRST PLACE
PRETEND YOU DON'T SEE IT. DON'T LOOK AT IT.
WHERE ARE ALL THESE VOICES COMING FROM ?!
IT'S IN THE WAY.
IGNORE IT.
IGNORE IT.
I CAN'T !

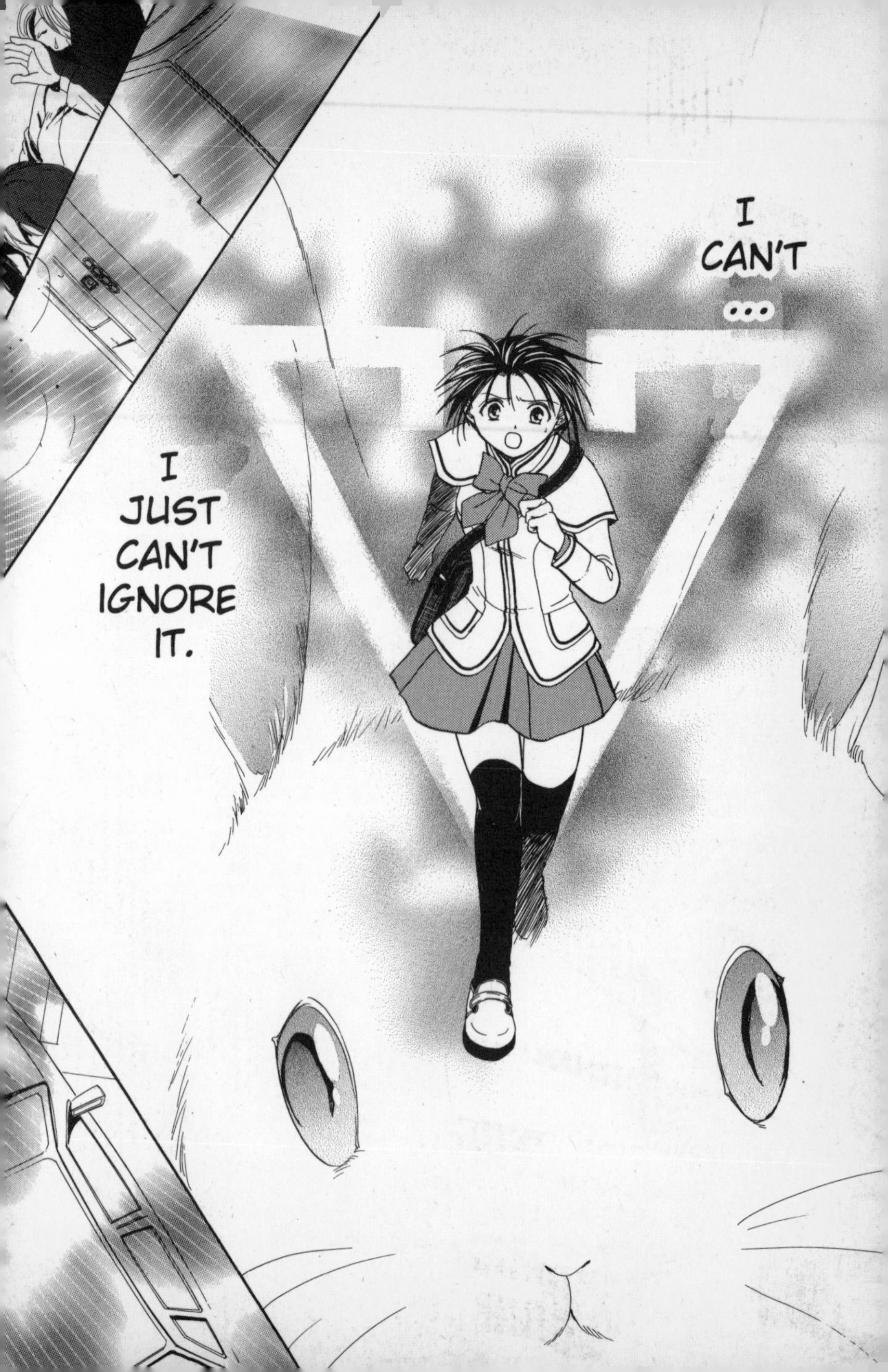
I CAN'T ...
I JUST CAN'T IGNORE IT.

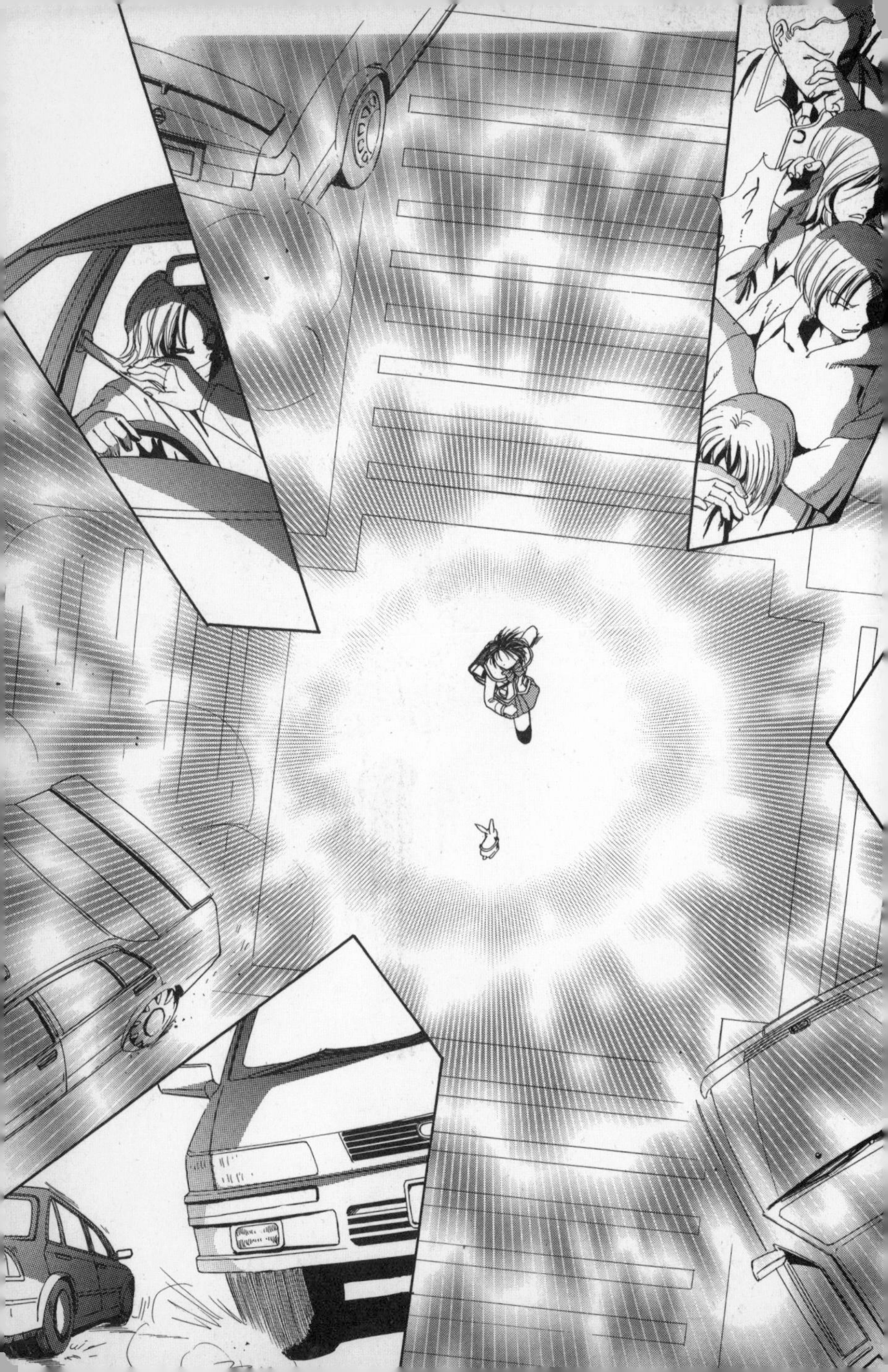

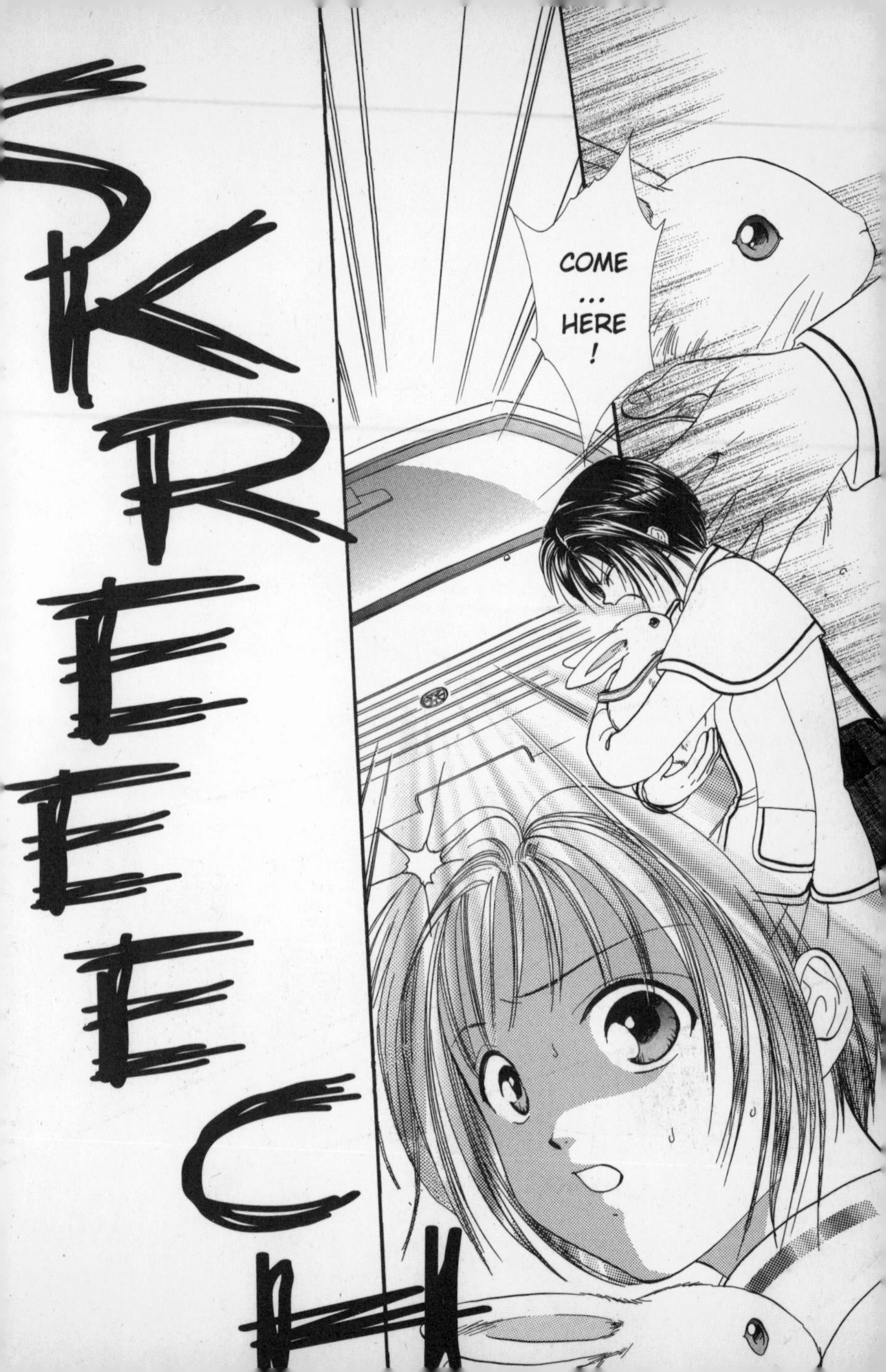
COME ... HERE !
SKREEECH

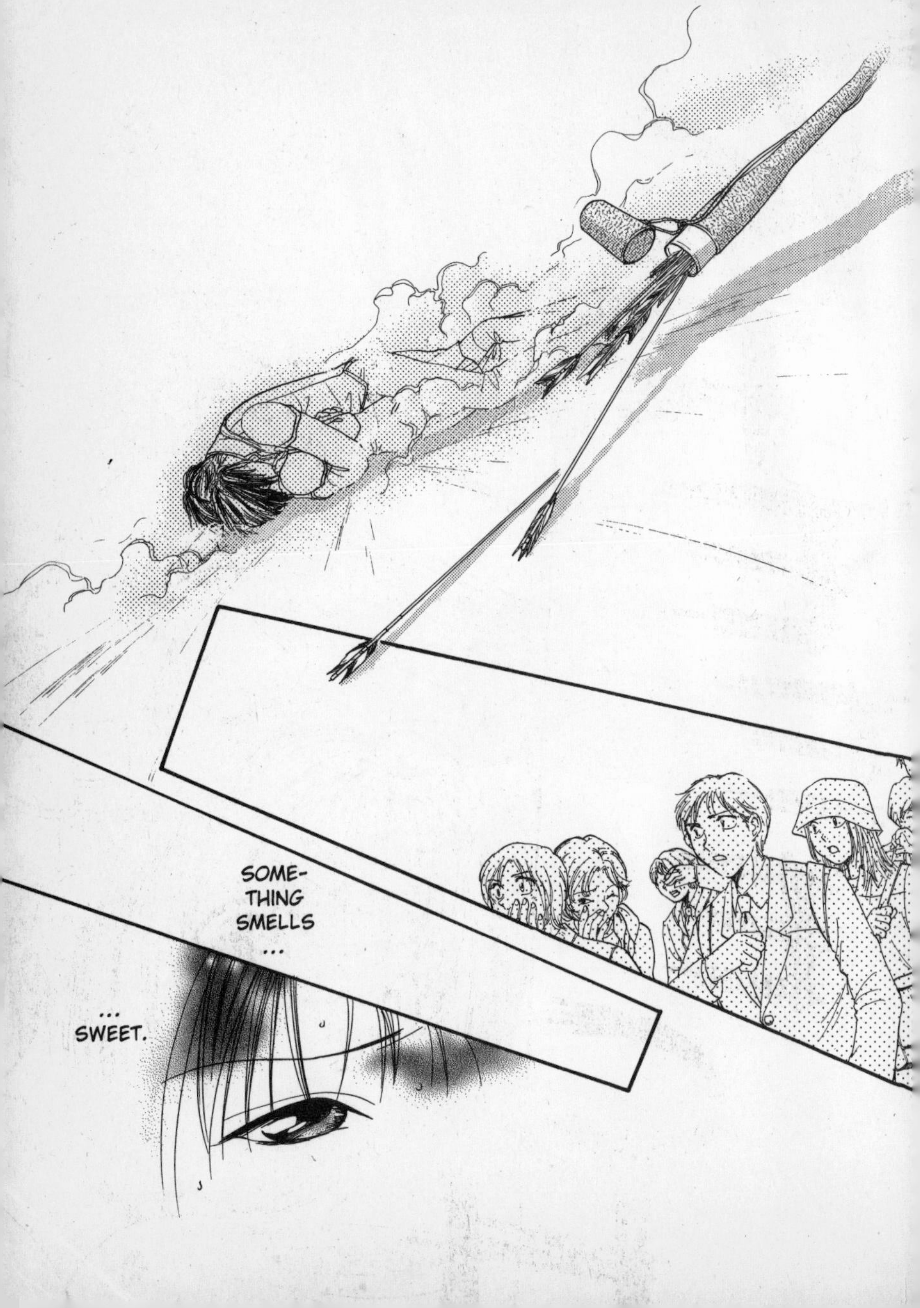
SOME-
THING
SMELLS
...
... SWEET.

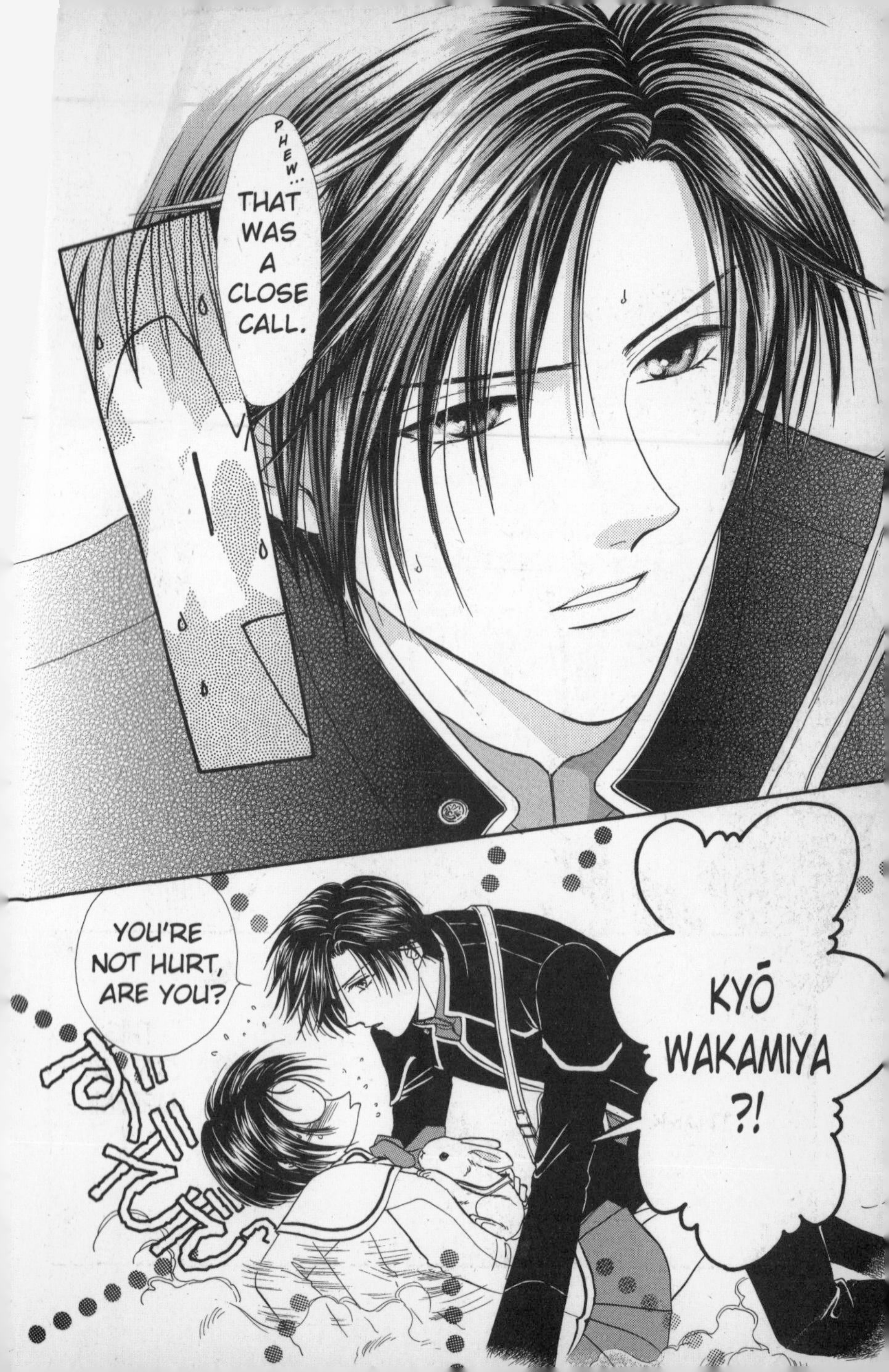
PHEW... THAT WAS A CLOSE CALL.
KYŌ WAKAMIYA ?!
YOU'RE NOT HURT, ARE YOU?

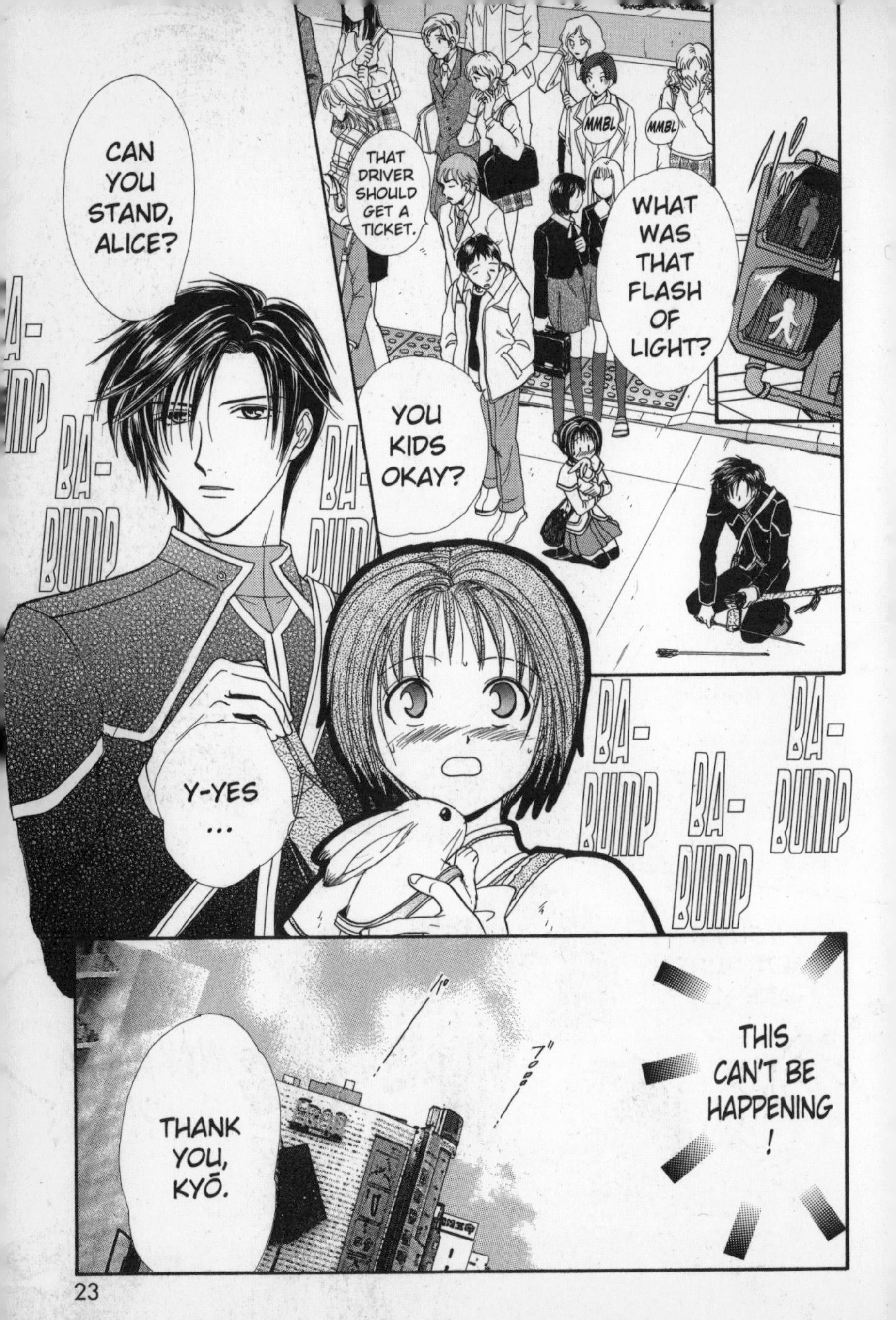
MMBL
MMBL
WHAT WAS THAT FLASH OF LIGHT?
THAT DRIVER SHOULD GET A TICKET.
YOU KIDS OKAY?
CAN YOU STAND, ALICE?
BA-BUMP
BA-BUMP
BA-BUMP
BA-BUMP
BA-BUMP
BA-BUMP
BA-BUMP
Y-YES ...
THIS CAN'T BE HAPPENING!
THANK YOU, KYŌ.

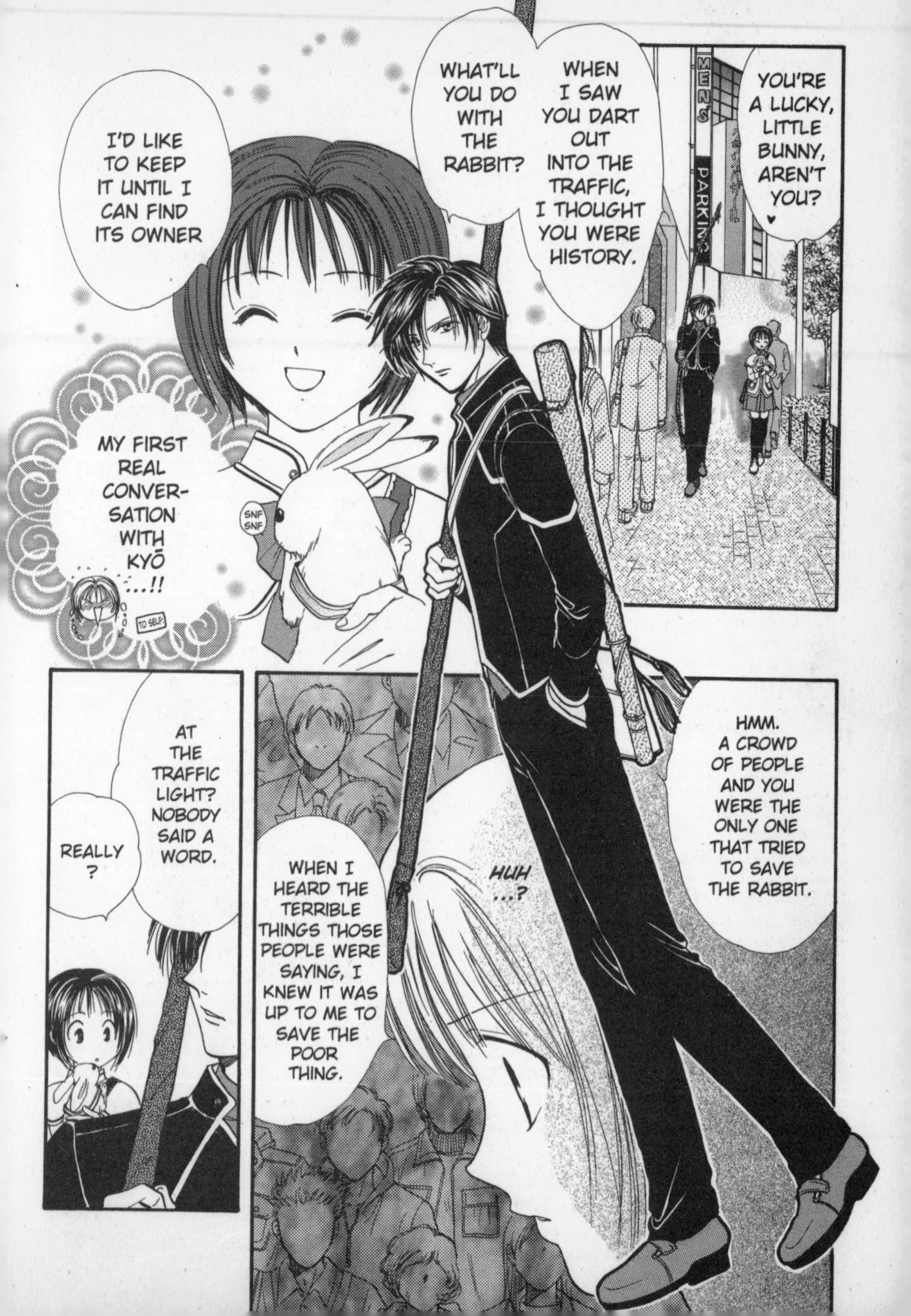
YOU'RE A LUCKY, LITTLE BUNNY, AREN'T YOU? ♥
WHEN I SAW YOU DART OUT INTO THE TRAFFIC, I THOUGHT YOU WERE HISTORY.
WHAT'LL YOU DO WITH THE RABBIT?
I'D LIKE TO KEEP IT UNTIL I CAN FIND ITS OWNER
SNF SNF
MY FIRST REAL CONVERSATION WITH KYŌ ...!!
TO SELF:
HMM. A CROWD OF PEOPLE AND YOU WERE THE ONLY ONE THAT TRIED TO SAVE THE RABBIT.
HUH ...?
WHEN I HEARD THE TERRIBLE THINGS THOSE PEOPLE WERE SAYING, I KNEW IT WAS UP TO ME TO SAVE THE POOR THING.
AT THE TRAFFIC LIGHT? NOBODY SAID A WORD.
REALLY ?

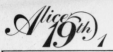

Hi, everyone! Watase here, and this is my new comic! Thanks for reading it!
Well, the world is in a pretty sorry state (since September 11, 2001). There's no telling what will happen, so we'll just have to wait and see. But war is wrong! That much I can say with certainty! Dialogue was never more important than now. We should take a lesson from Gandhi's non-violent approach!
Actually, maybe this is pretty relevant... Even in the context of Alice 19th, I'm trying to express this, and I'm thinking, "Wow..." This "dialogue" I'm talking about is when people exchange words.
In nations, ideologies, and even one's own classroom or family, everybody is different, and we "talk things over" for the purpose of understanding. Force and violence are very bad. Well, in the comics of yesterday, two rival kids would duke it out (one-on-one, of course), until one smiled and said, "You're pretty good." And the other one would smile back and said, "So are you." Then they'd kick back, watch the sun set, and laugh. That's how things used to be. Kids were more innocent. That's why a story like that worked, I suppose.
These days, maybe people aren't so good at communicating or maybe they just refuse to! People can't communicate without computers or cell phones! That's the kind of age this is (of course, sometimes it's good).
But I still believe it's important for people to sit down and talk to each other in the flesh.

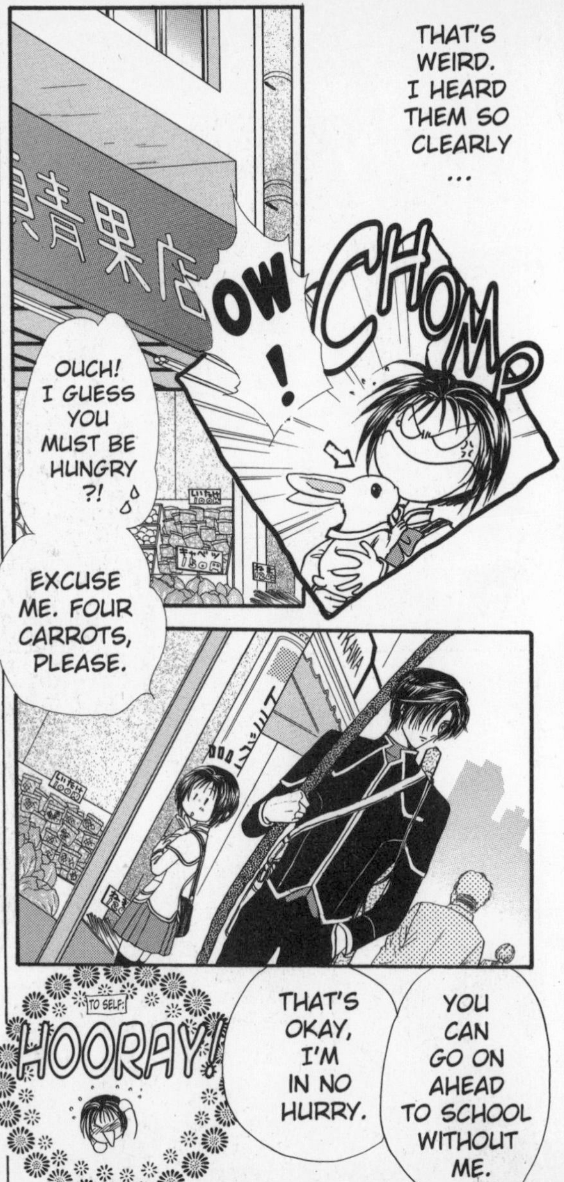
THAT'S WEIRD. I HEARD THEM SO CLEARLY ...
CHOMP
OW!
OUCH! I GUESS YOU MUST BE HUNGRY?!
EXCUSE ME. FOUR CARROTS, PLEASE.
YOU CAN GO ON AHEAD TO SCHOOL WITHOUT ME.
THAT'S OKAY, I'M IN NO HURRY.
TO SELF:
HOORAY!

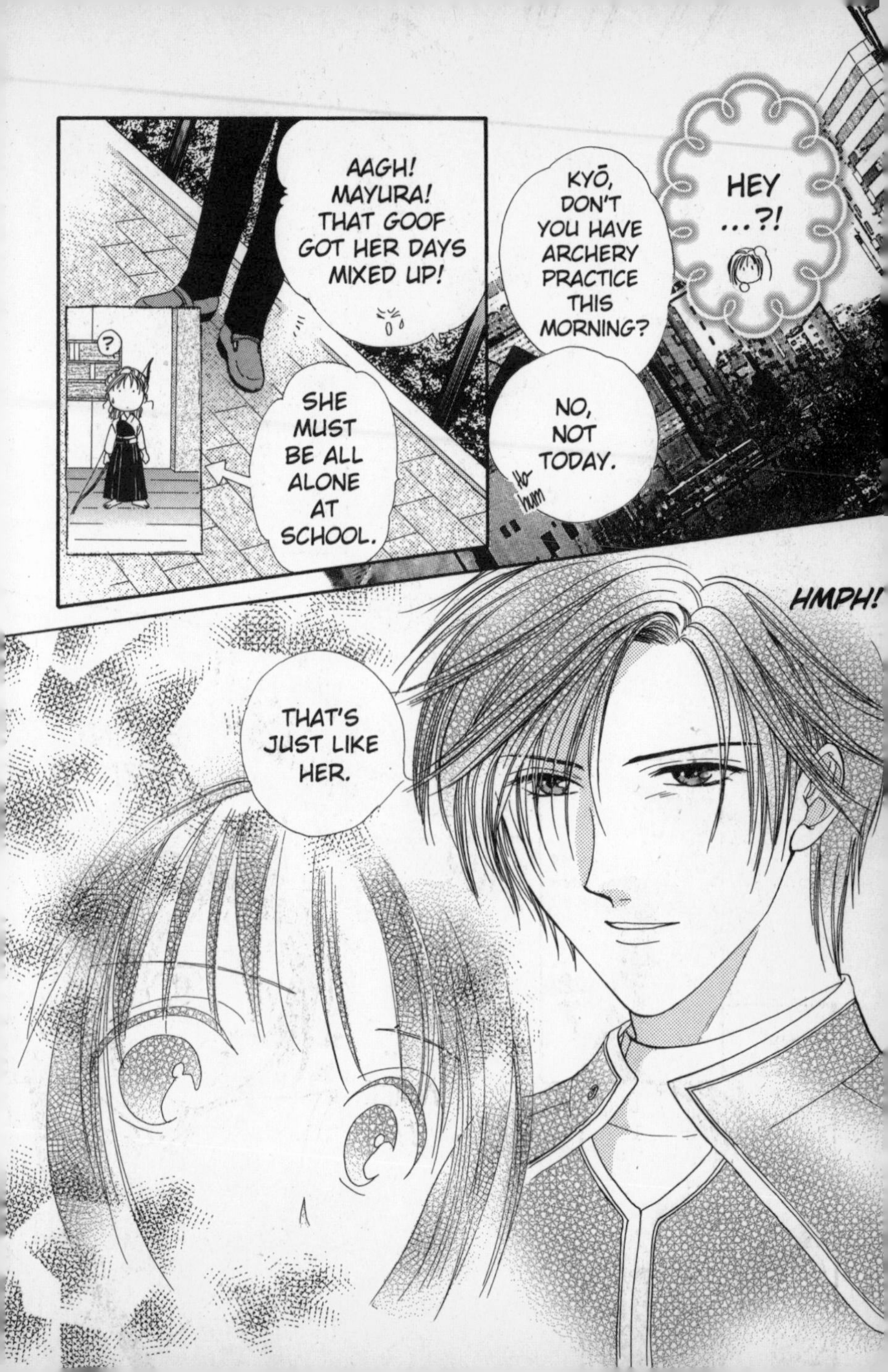
HEY ...?!
KYŌ, DON'T YOU HAVE ARCHERY PRACTICE THIS MORNING?
NO, NOT TODAY.
Ho-hum
AAGH! MAYURA! THAT GOOF GOT HER DAYS MIXED UP!
?
SHE MUST BE ALL ALONE AT SCHOOL.
HMPH!
THAT'S JUST LIKE HER.

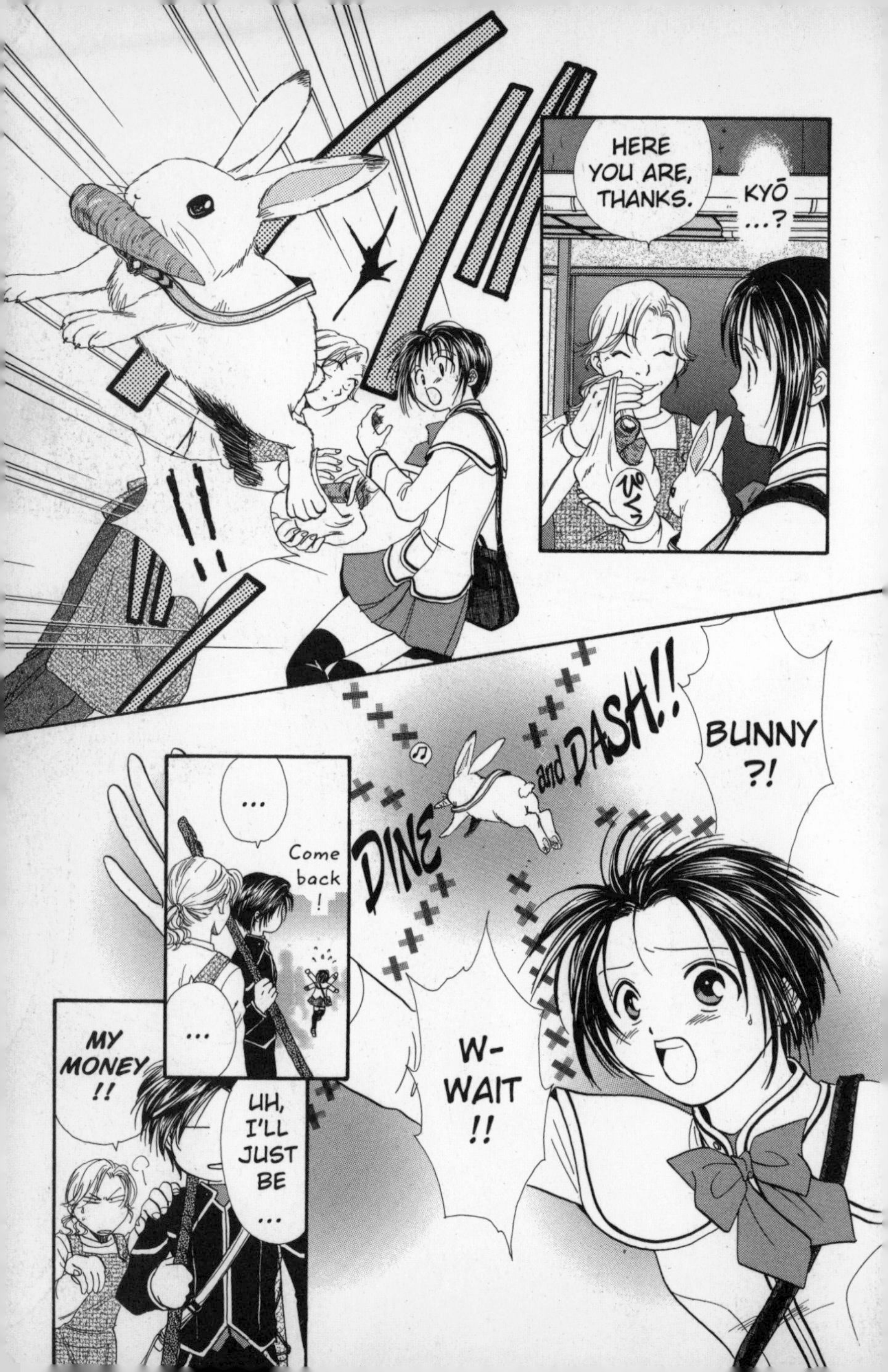
HERE YOU ARE, THANKS.
KYŌ ...?
!!
BUNNY ?!
DINE and DASH!!
W- WAIT !!
...
Come back !
...
MY MONEY !!
UH, I'LL JUST BE ...

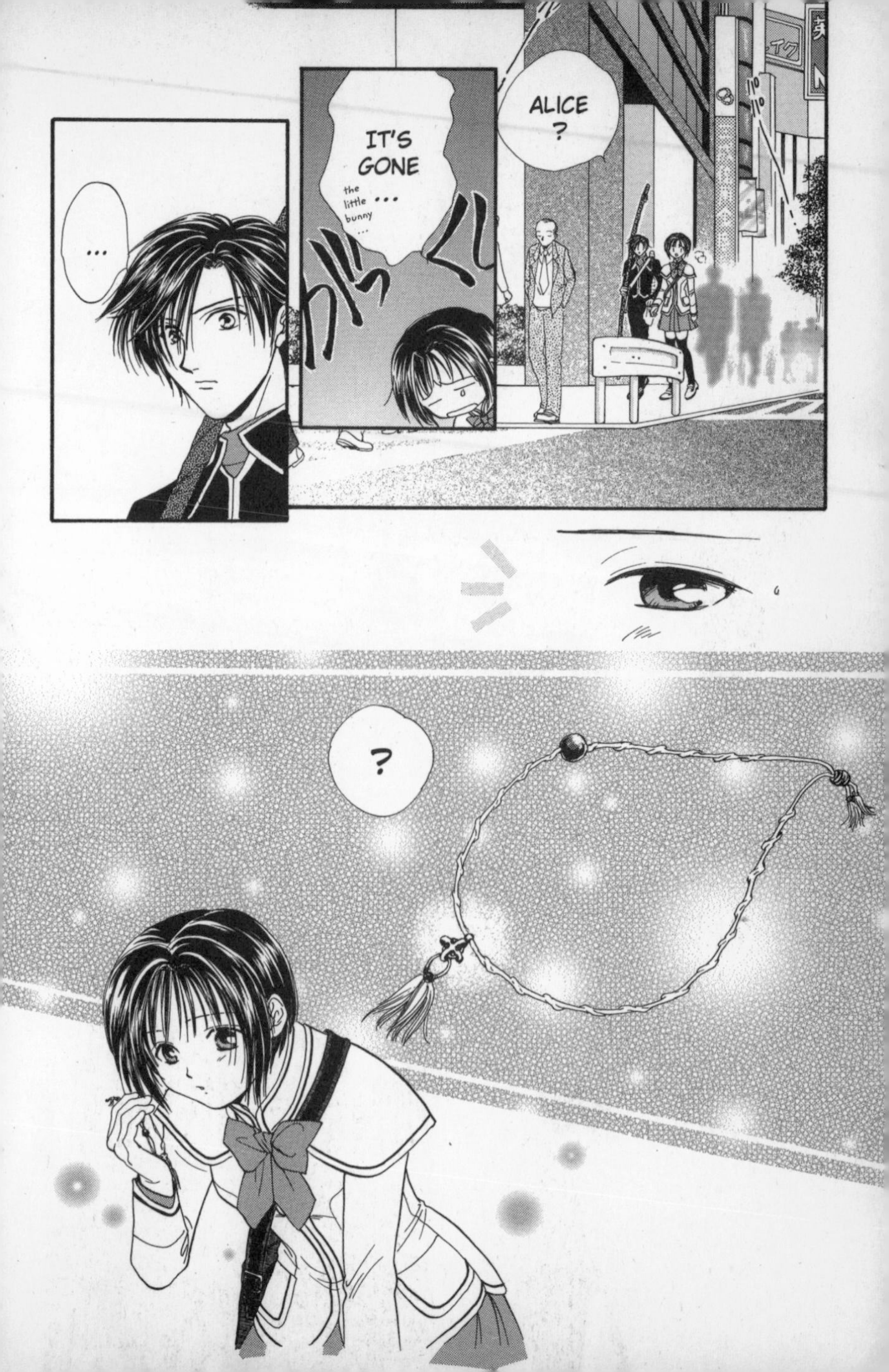
ALICE ?
IT'S GONE
the little bunny ...
...
がっくし
...
?

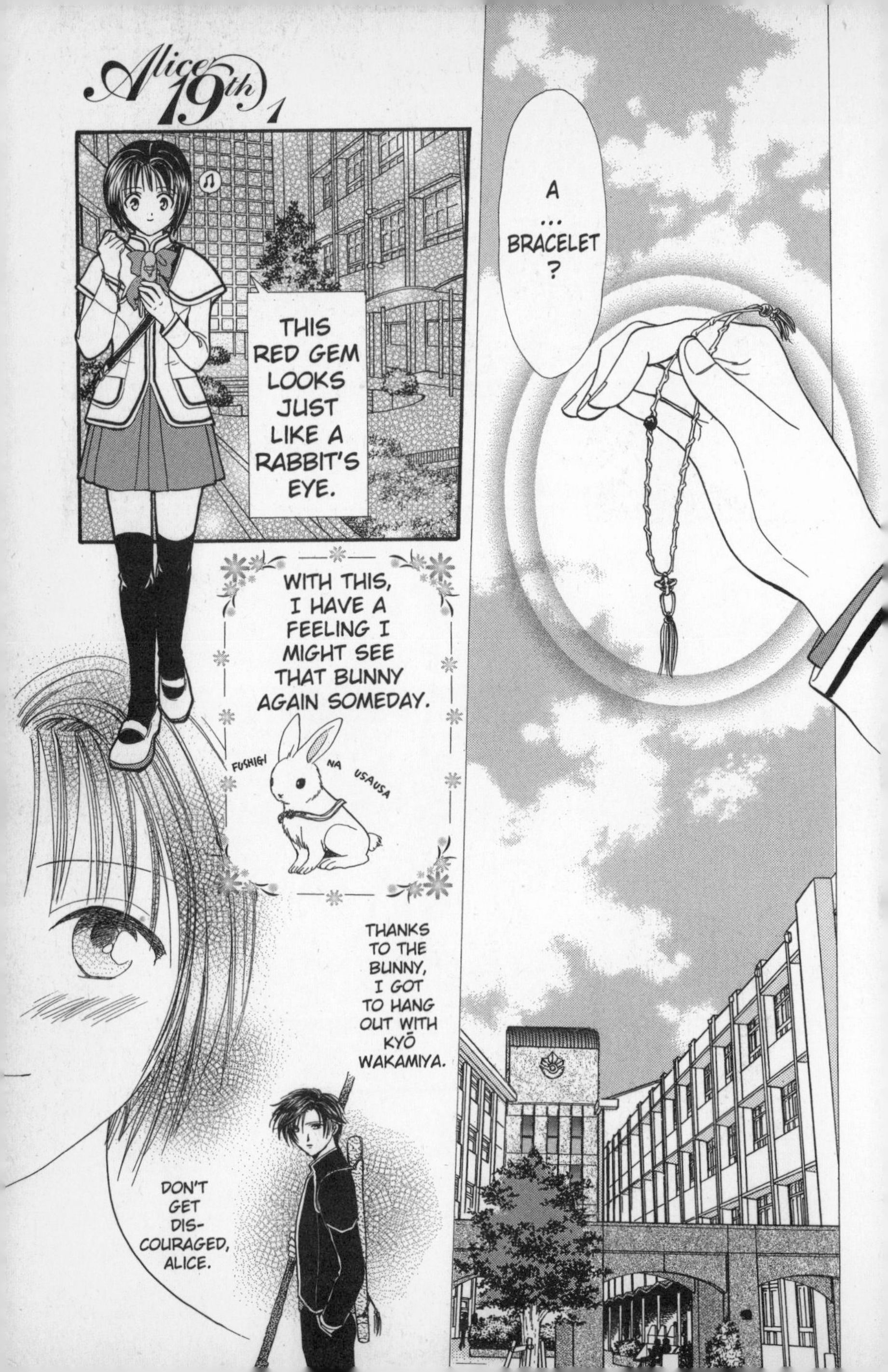
A ... BRACELET ?
THIS RED GEM LOOKS JUST LIKE A RABBIT'S EYE.
WITH THIS, I HAVE A FEELING I MIGHT SEE THAT BUNNY AGAIN SOMEDAY.
FUSHIGI NA USAUSA
THANKS TO THE BUNNY, I GOT TO HANG OUT WITH KYŌ WAKAMIYA.
DON'T GET DIS- COURAGED, ALICE.

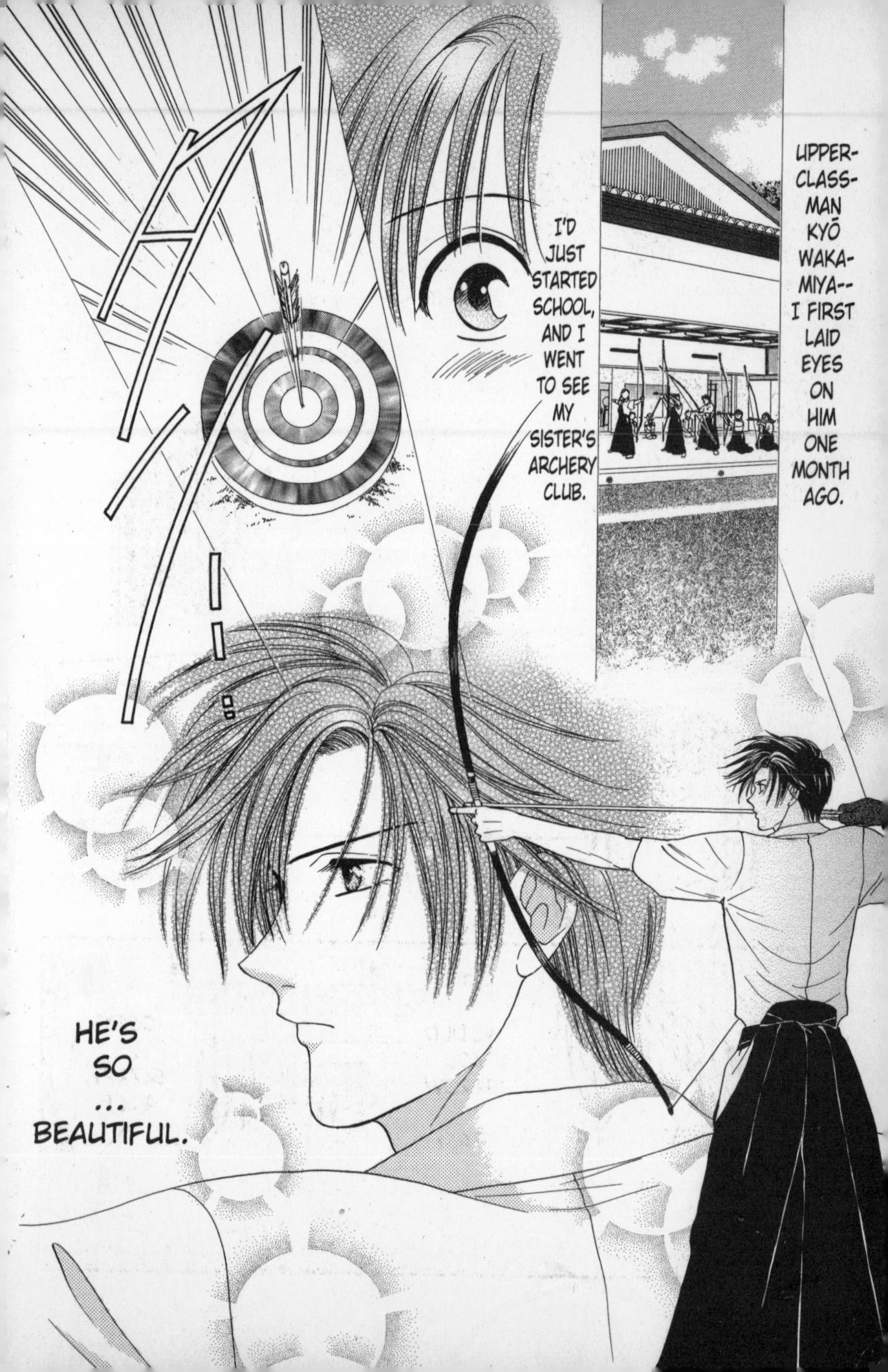

UPPER-CLASSMAN KYŌ WAKA-MIYA-- I FIRST LAID EYES ON HIM ONE MONTH AGO.
I'D JUST STARTED SCHOOL, AND I WENT TO SEE MY SISTER'S ARCHERY CLUB.
HE'S SO ... BEAUTIFUL.

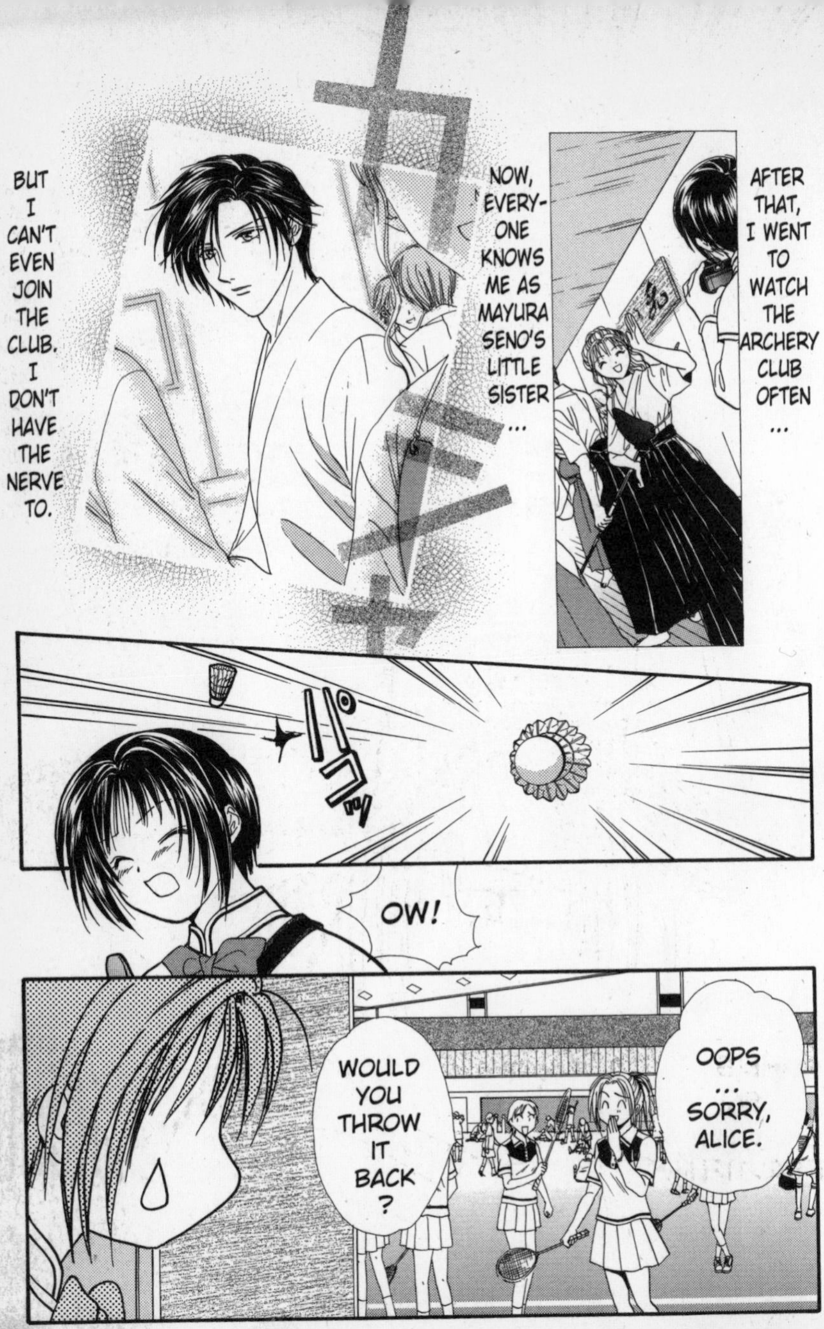
AFTER THAT, I WENT TO WATCH THE ARCHERY CLUB OFTEN...
NOW, EVERYONE KNOWS ME AS MAYURA SENO'S LITTLE SISTER...
BUT I CAN'T EVEN JOIN THE CLUB. I DON'T HAVE THE NERVE TO.
OW!
OOPS... SORRY, ALICE.
WOULD YOU THROW IT BACK?

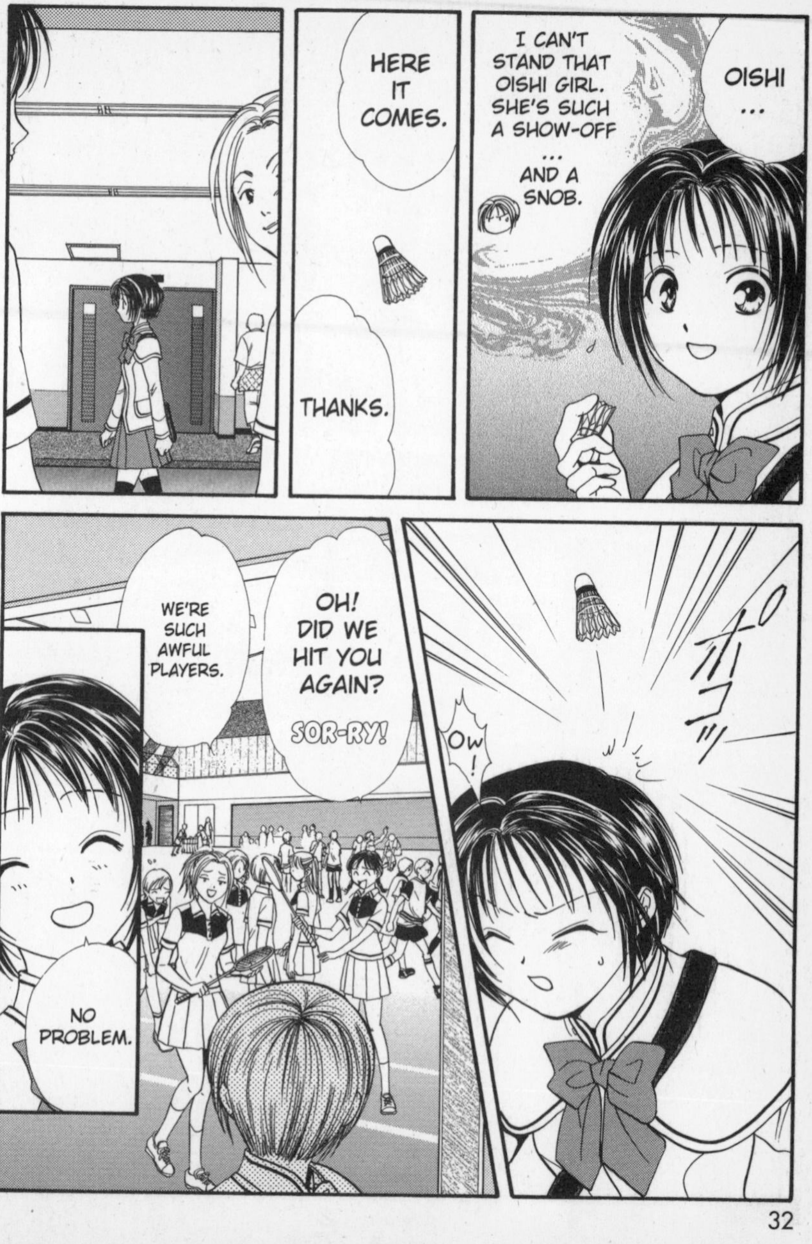
OISHI ...
I CAN'T STAND THAT OISHI GIRL. SHE'S SUCH A SHOW-OFF ... AND A SNOB.
HERE IT COMES.
THANKS.
OW!
OH! DID WE HIT YOU AGAIN?
SOR-RY!
WE'RE SUCH AWFUL PLAYERS.
NO PROBLEM.

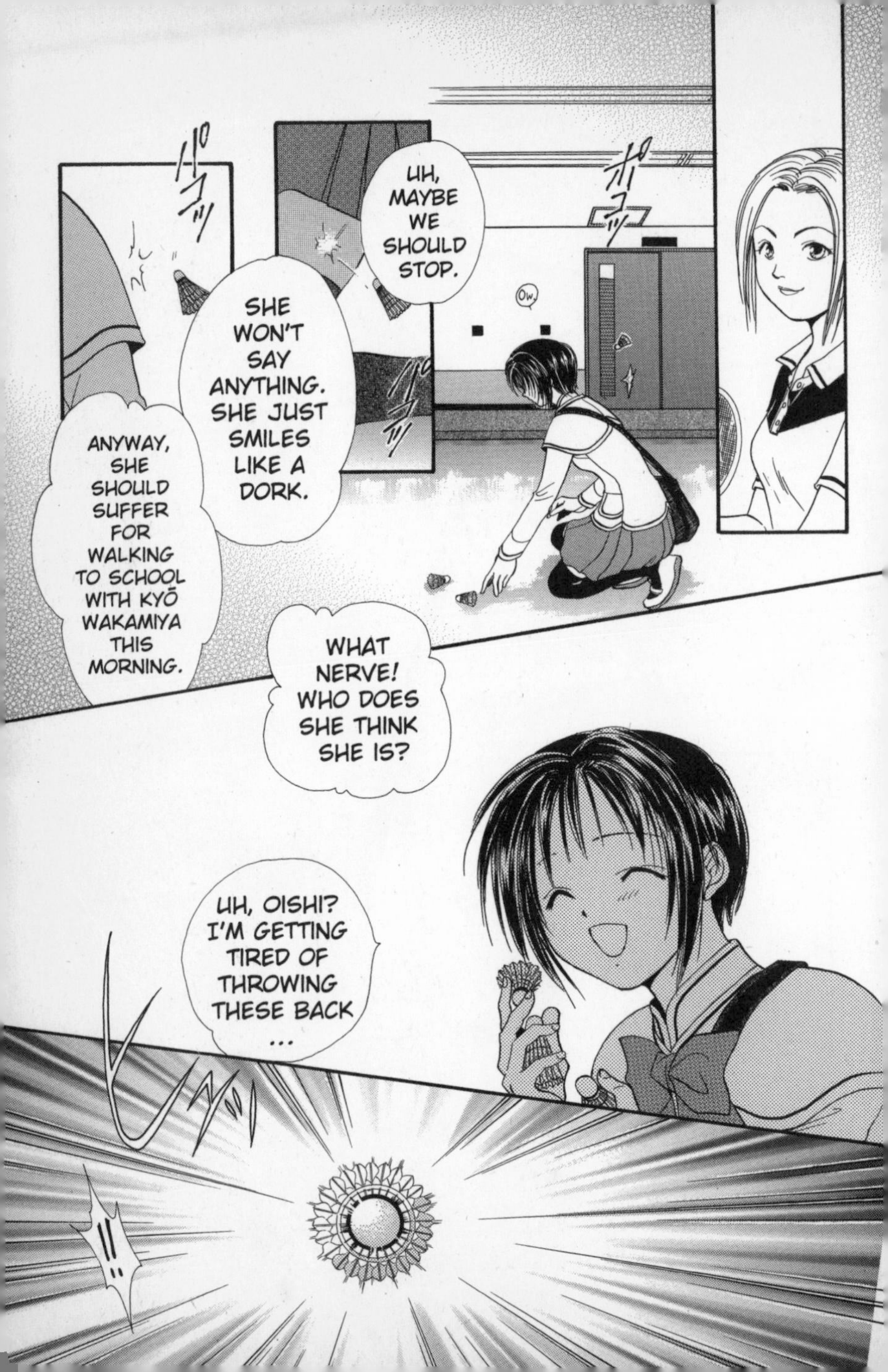
Ow.
UH, MAYBE WE SHOULD STOP.
SHE WON'T SAY ANYTHING. SHE JUST SMILES LIKE A DORK.
ANYWAY, SHE SHOULD SUFFER FOR WALKING TO SCHOOL WITH KYŌ WAKAMIYA THIS MORNING.
WHAT NERVE! WHO DOES SHE THINK SHE IS?
UH, OISHI? I'M GETTING TIRED OF THROWING THESE BACK ...
!!

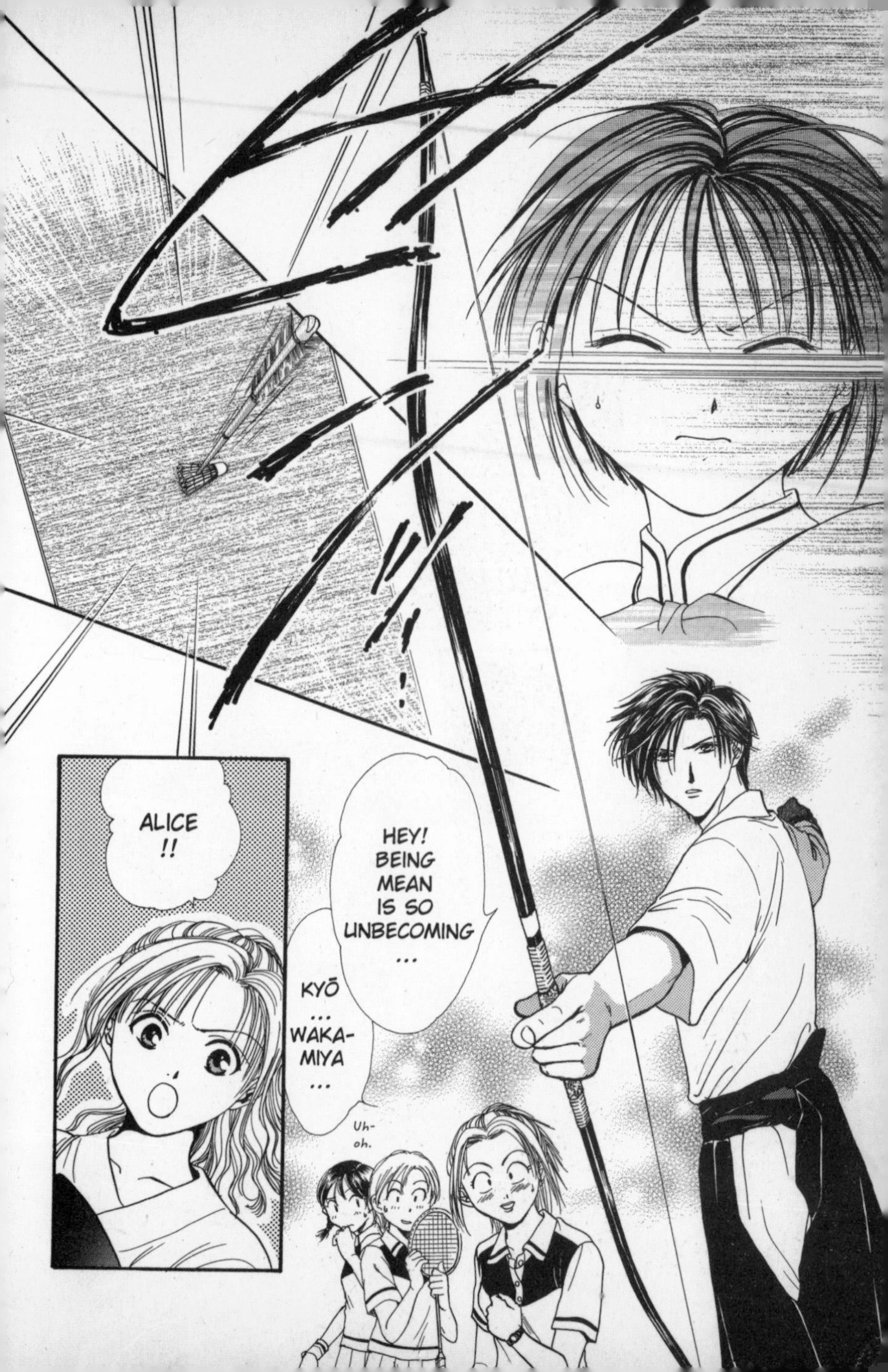
HEY! BEING MEAN IS SO UNBECOMING ...
KYŌ ... WAKA-MIYA ...
Uh-oh.
ALICE !!

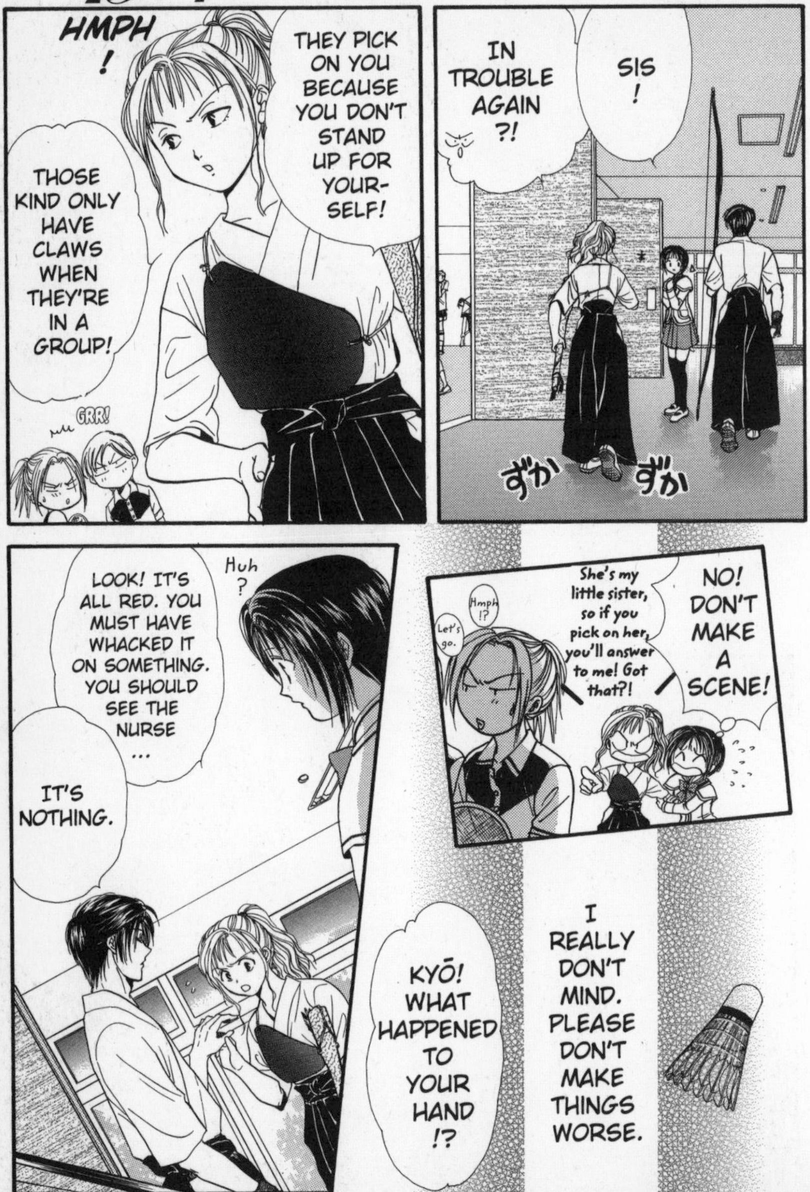
SIS!
IN TROUBLE AGAIN ?!
ずか ずか
THEY PICK ON YOU BECAUSE YOU DON'T STAND UP FOR YOUR-SELF!
HMPH!
THOSE KIND ONLY HAVE CLAWS WHEN THEY'RE IN A GROUP!
GRR!
NO! DON'T MAKE A SCENE!
She's my little sister, so if you pick on her, you'll answer to me! Got that?!
Hmph !?
Let's go.
I REALLY DON'T MIND. PLEASE DON'T MAKE THINGS WORSE.
KYŌ! WHAT HAPPENED TO YOUR HAND !?
Huh ?
LOOK! IT'S ALL RED. YOU MUST HAVE WHACKED IT ON SOMETHING. YOU SHOULD SEE THE NURSE ...
IT'S NOTHING.

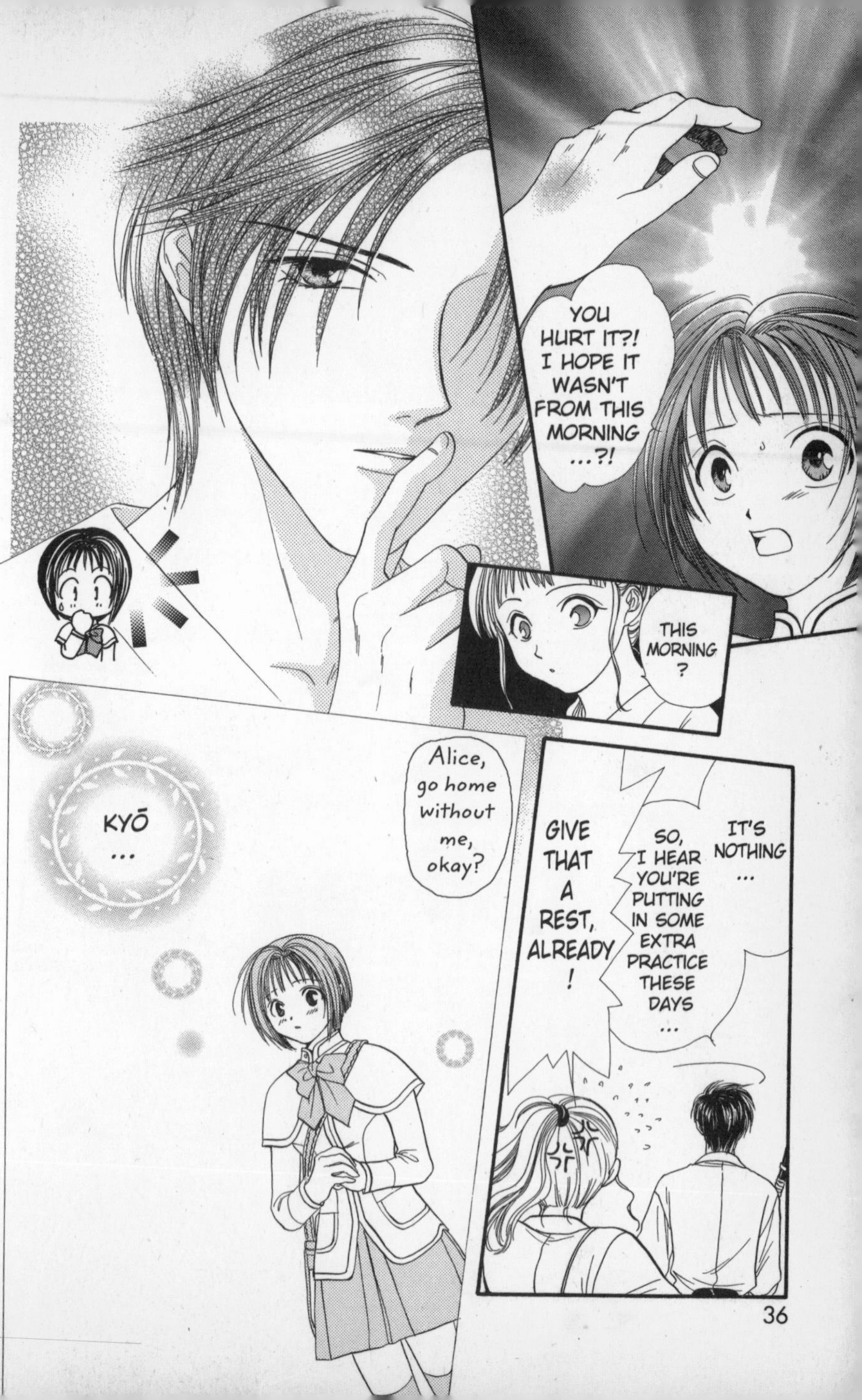
YOU HURT IT?! I HOPE IT WASN'T FROM THIS MORNING ...?!
THIS MORNING ?
IT'S NOTHING ...
SO, I HEAR YOU'RE PUTTING IN SOME EXTRA PRACTICE THESE DAYS ...
GIVE THAT A REST, ALREADY !
Alice, go home without me, okay?
KYŌ ...

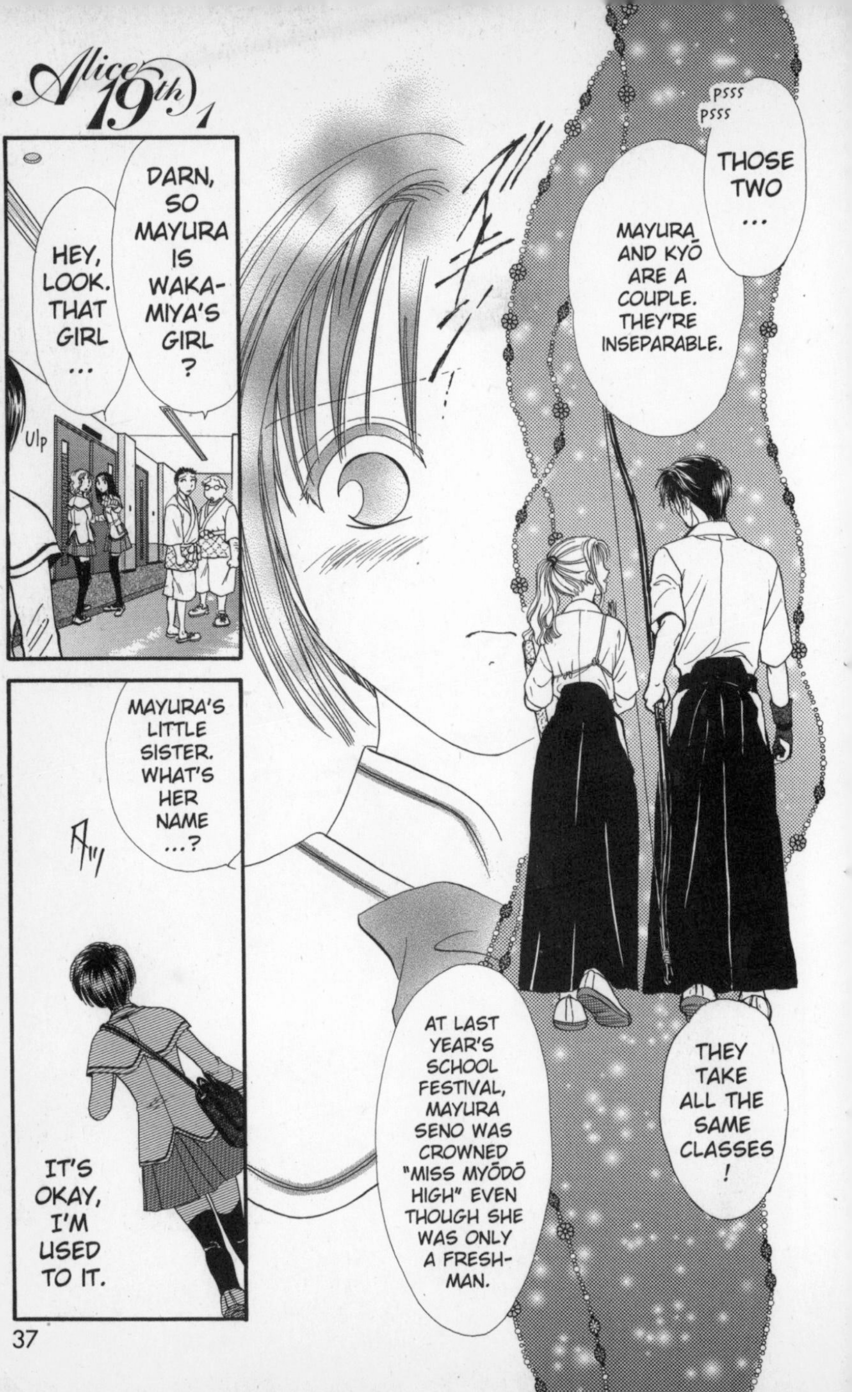
PSSS
PSSS
THOSE TWO ...
MAYURA AND KYŌ ARE A COUPLE. THEY'RE INSEPARABLE.
THEY TAKE ALL THE SAME CLASSES !
AT LAST YEAR'S SCHOOL FESTIVAL, MAYURA SENO WAS CROWNED "MISS MYŌDŌ HIGH" EVEN THOUGH SHE WAS ONLY A FRESH-MAN.
DARN, SO MAYURA IS WAKA-MIYA'S GIRL ?
HEY, LOOK. THAT GIRL ...
Ulp
MAYURA'S LITTLE SISTER. WHAT'S HER NAME ...?
IT'S OKAY, I'M USED TO IT.

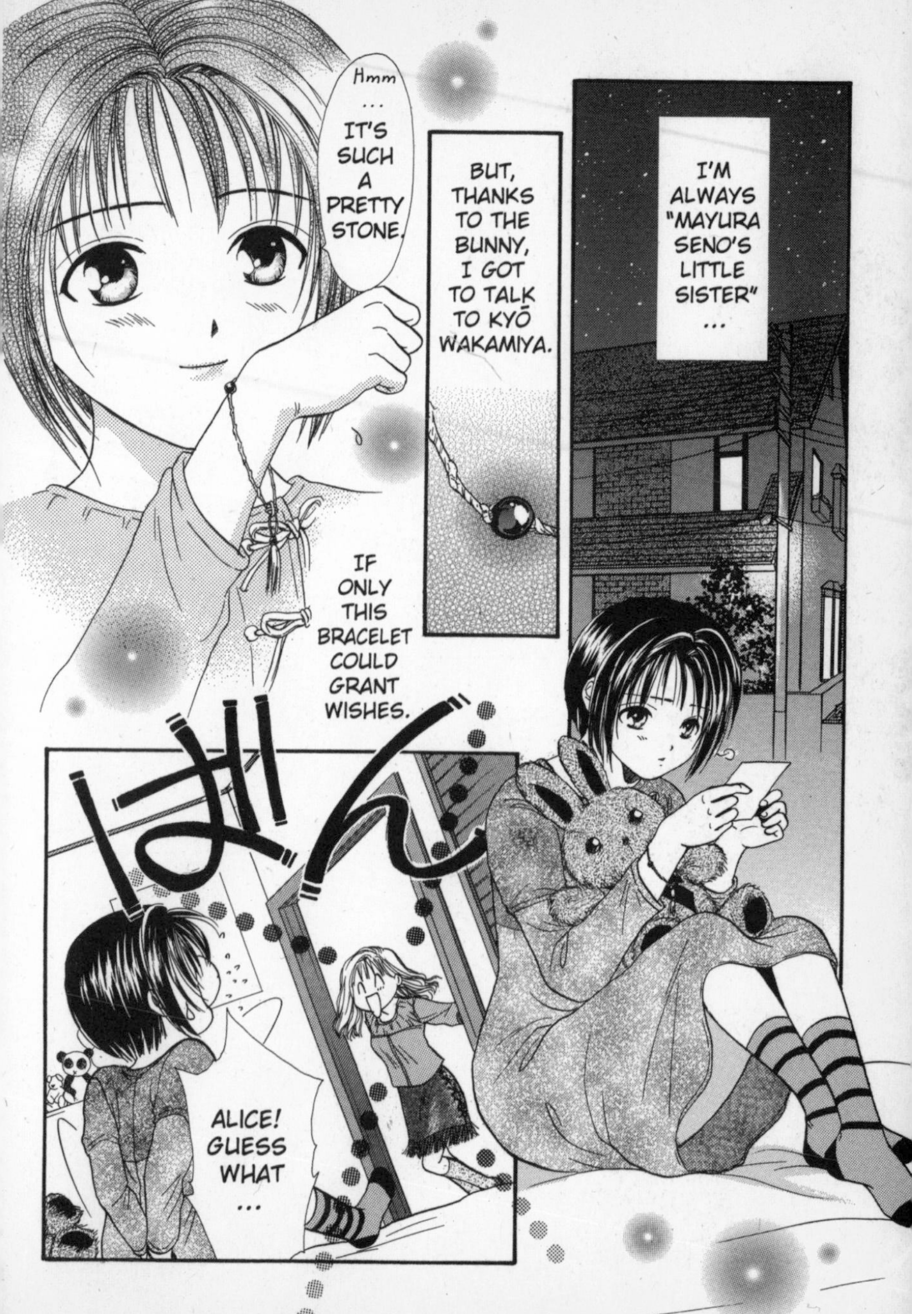
I'M ALWAYS "MAYURA SENO'S LITTLE SISTER" ...
BUT, THANKS TO THE BUNNY, I GOT TO TALK TO KYŌ WAKAMIYA.
Hmm ... IT'S SUCH A PRETTY STONE.
IF ONLY THIS BRACELET COULD GRANT WISHES.
ばん
ALICE! GUESS WHAT ...

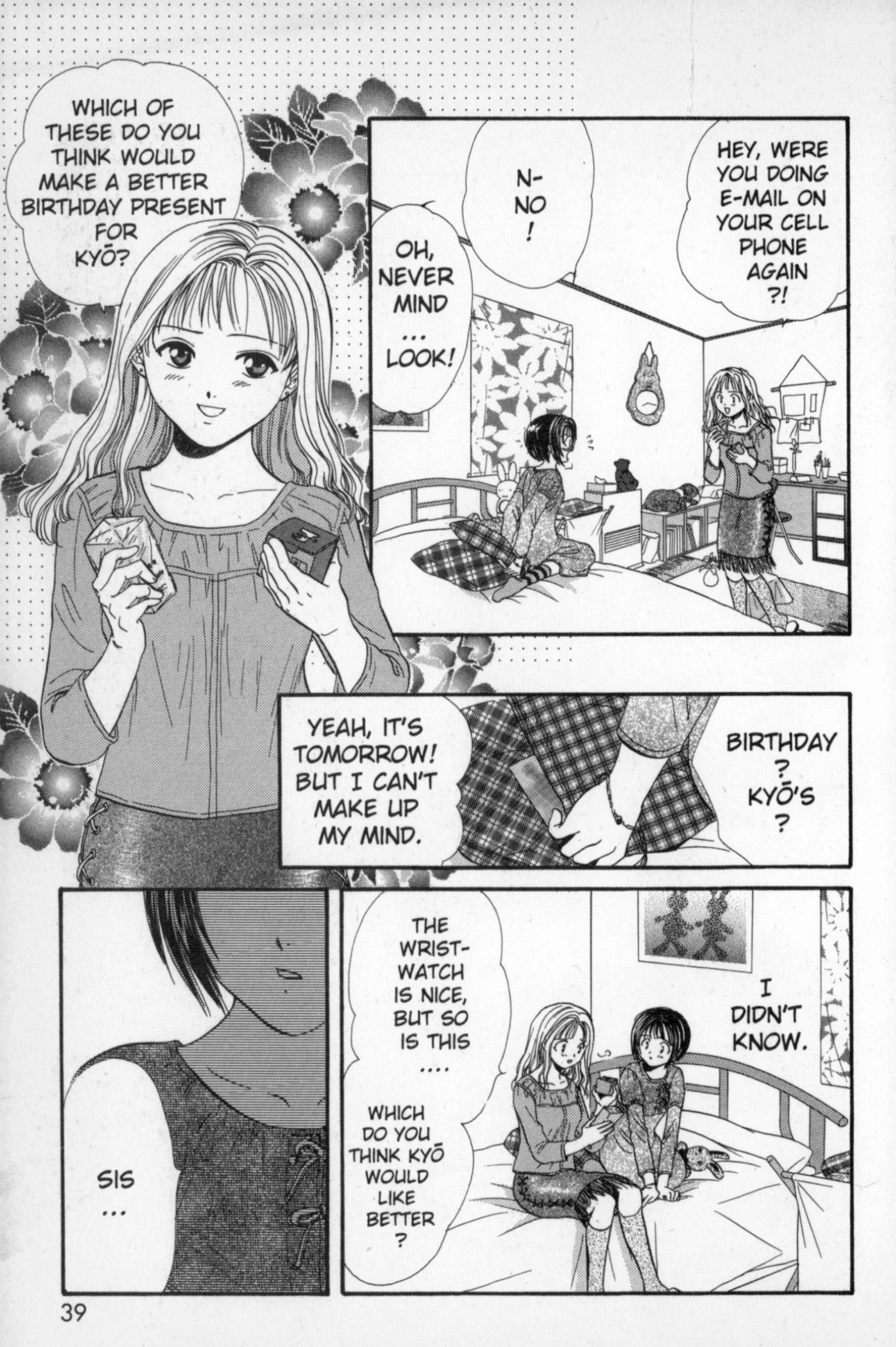
HEY, WERE YOU DOING E-MAIL ON YOUR CELL PHONE AGAIN ?!
N- NO !
OH, NEVER MIND ... LOOK!
WHICH OF THESE DO YOU THINK WOULD MAKE A BETTER BIRTHDAY PRESENT FOR KYŌ?
BIRTHDAY ? KYŌ'S ?
YEAH, IT'S TOMORROW! BUT I CAN'T MAKE UP MY MIND.
I DIDN'T KNOW.
THE WRIST-WATCH IS NICE, BUT SO IS THIS ....
WHICH DO YOU THINK KYŌ WOULD LIKE BETTER ?
SIS ...

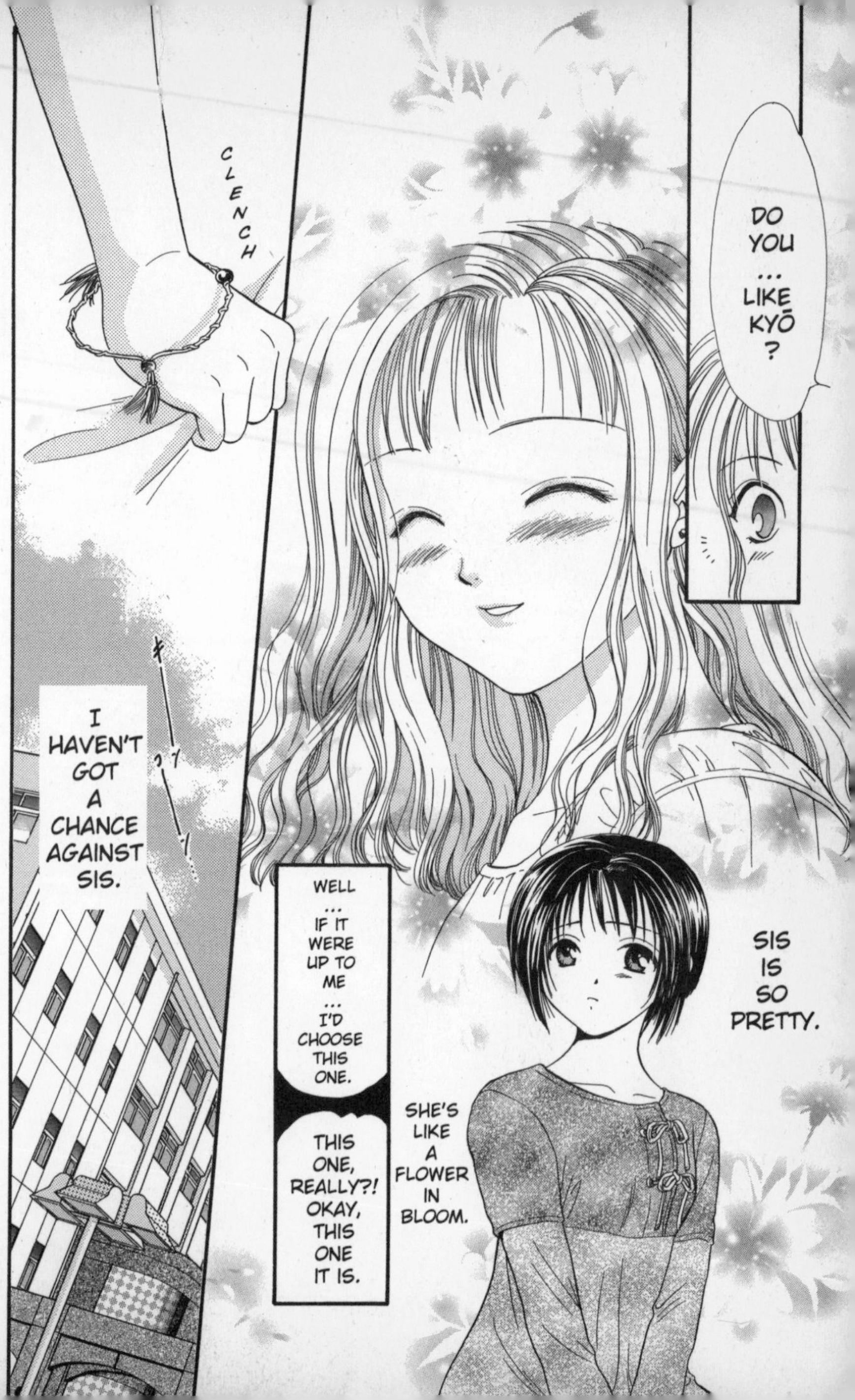
DO YOU ... LIKE KYŌ?
WELL ... IF IT WERE UP TO ME ... I'D CHOOSE THIS ONE.
SIS IS SO PRETTY.
THIS ONE, REALLY?! OKAY, THIS ONE IT IS.
SHE'S LIKE A FLOWER IN BLOOM.
CLENCH
I HAVEN'T GOT A CHANCE AGAINST SIS.

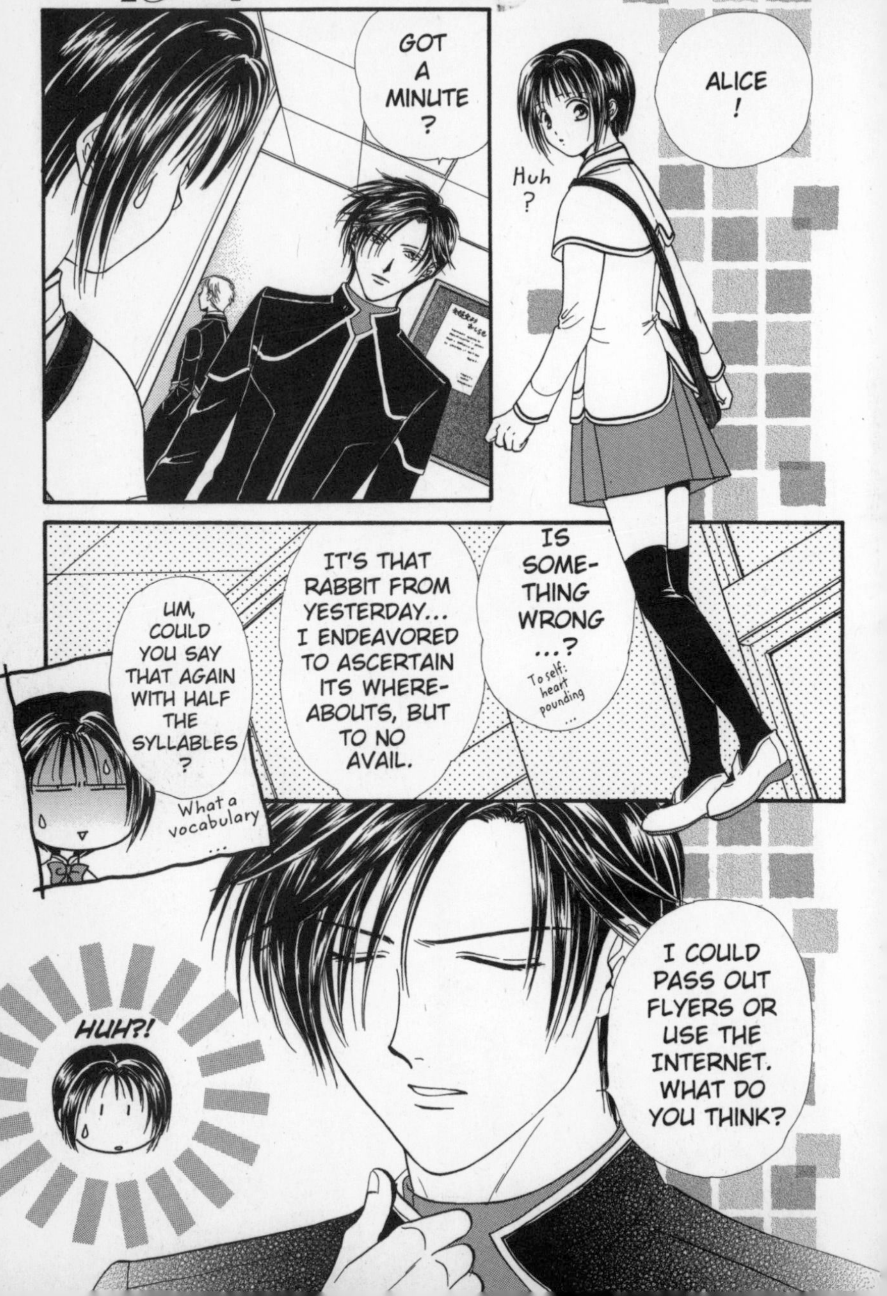
ALICE !
Huh ?
GOT A MINUTE ?
IS SOMETHING WRONG ...?
To self: heart pounding ...
IT'S THAT RABBIT FROM YESTERDAY... I ENDEAVORED TO ASCERTAIN ITS WHEREABOUTS, BUT TO NO AVAIL.
UM, COULD YOU SAY THAT AGAIN WITH HALF THE SYLLABLES ?
What a vocabulary ...
I COULD PASS OUT FLYERS OR USE THE INTERNET. WHAT DO YOU THINK?
HUH?!

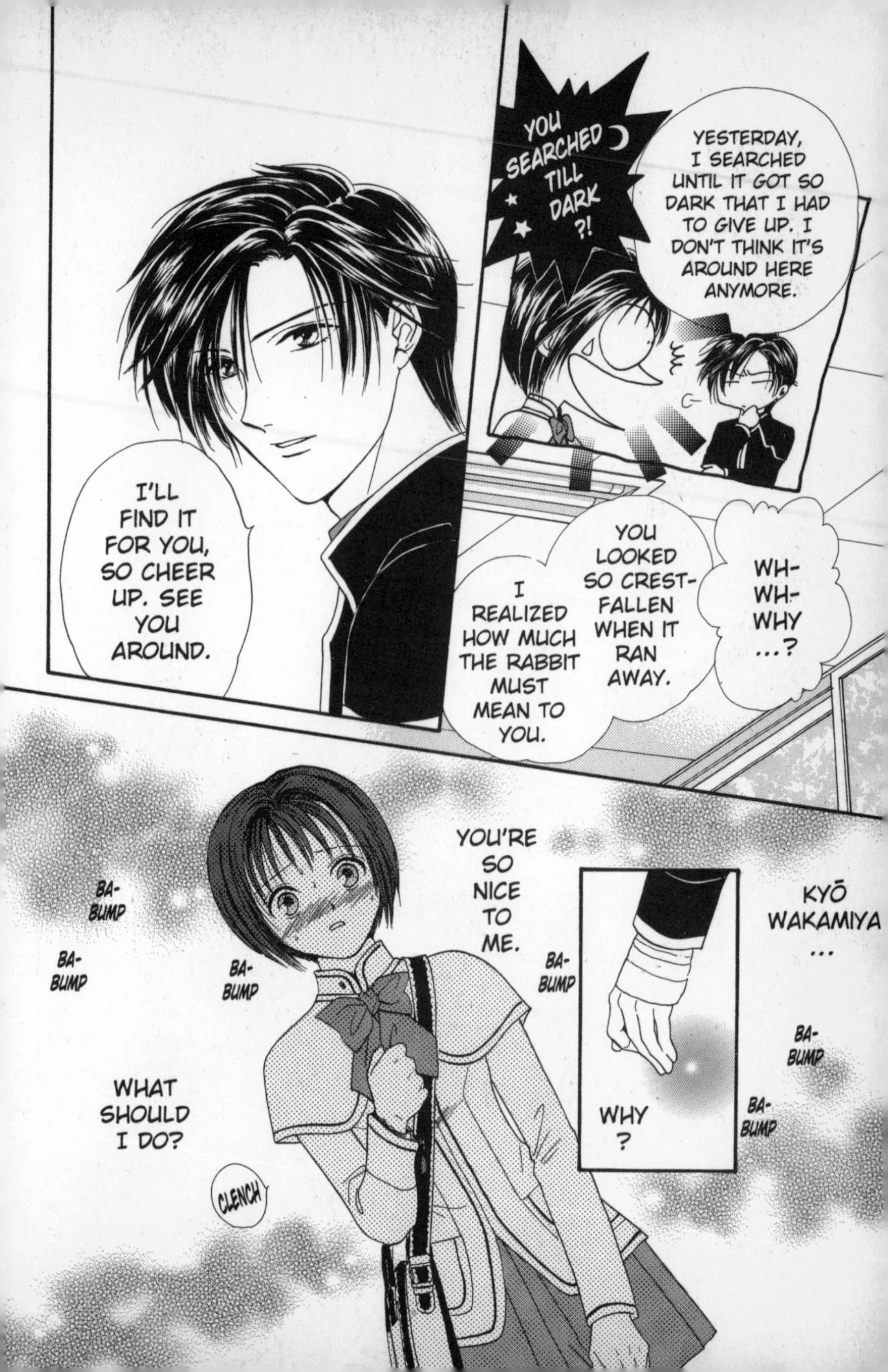

YESTERDAY, I SEARCHED UNTIL IT GOT SO DARK THAT I HAD TO GIVE UP. I DON'T THINK IT'S AROUND HERE ANYMORE.
YOU SEARCHED TILL DARK ?!
WH-WH-WHY ...?
YOU LOOKED SO CREST-FALLEN WHEN IT RAN AWAY.
I REALIZED HOW MUCH THE RABBIT MUST MEAN TO YOU.
I'LL FIND IT FOR YOU, SO CHEER UP. SEE YOU AROUND.
KYŌ WAKAMIYA ...
BA-BUMP
BA-BUMP
WHY ?
BA-BUMP
YOU'RE SO NICE TO ME.
BA-BUMP
BA-BUMP
BA-BUMP
WHAT SHOULD I DO?
CLENCH

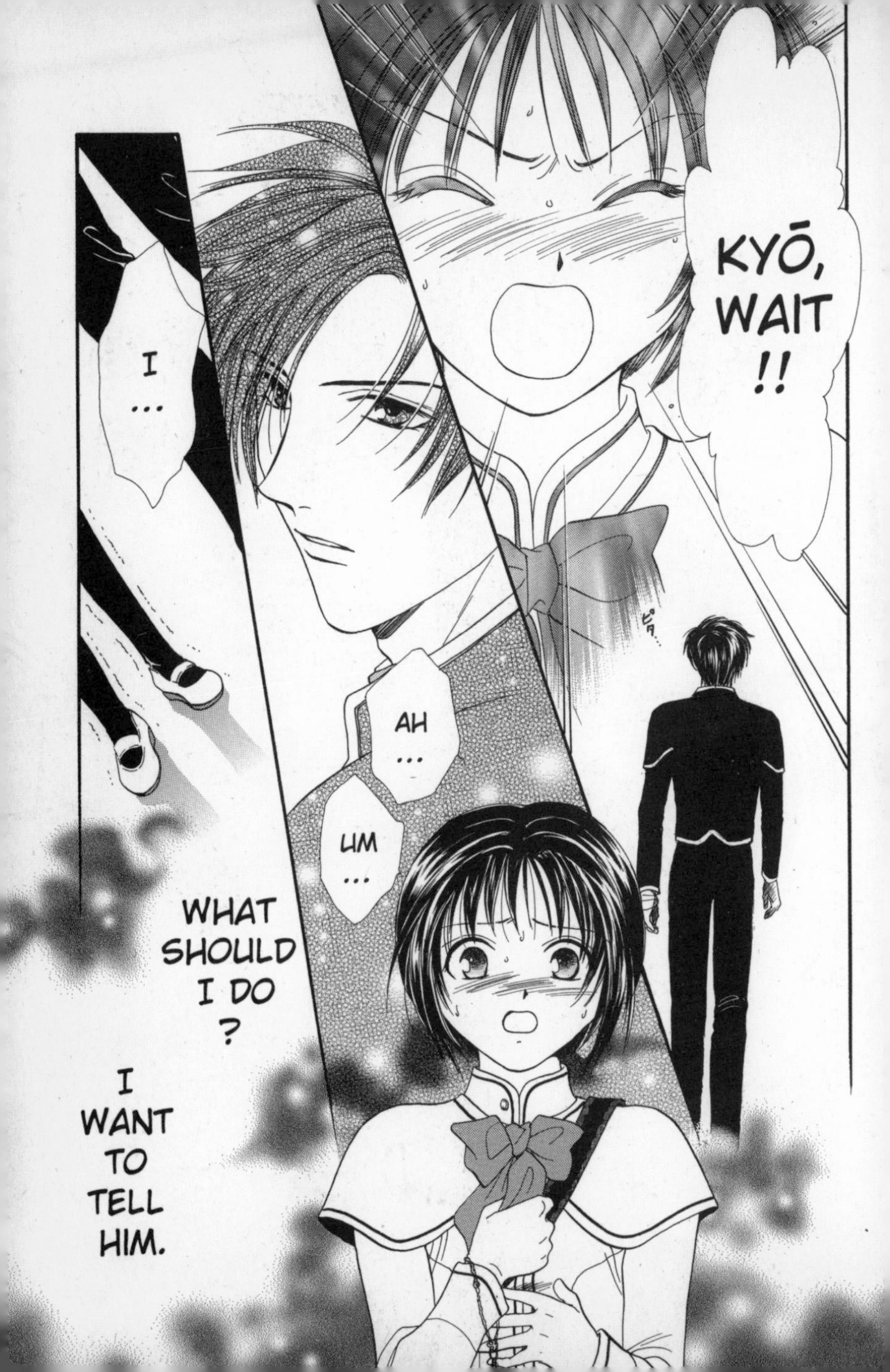
KYŌ, WAIT !!
ピタ…
AH ...
UM ...
I ...
WHAT SHOULD I DO ?
I WANT TO TELL HIM.

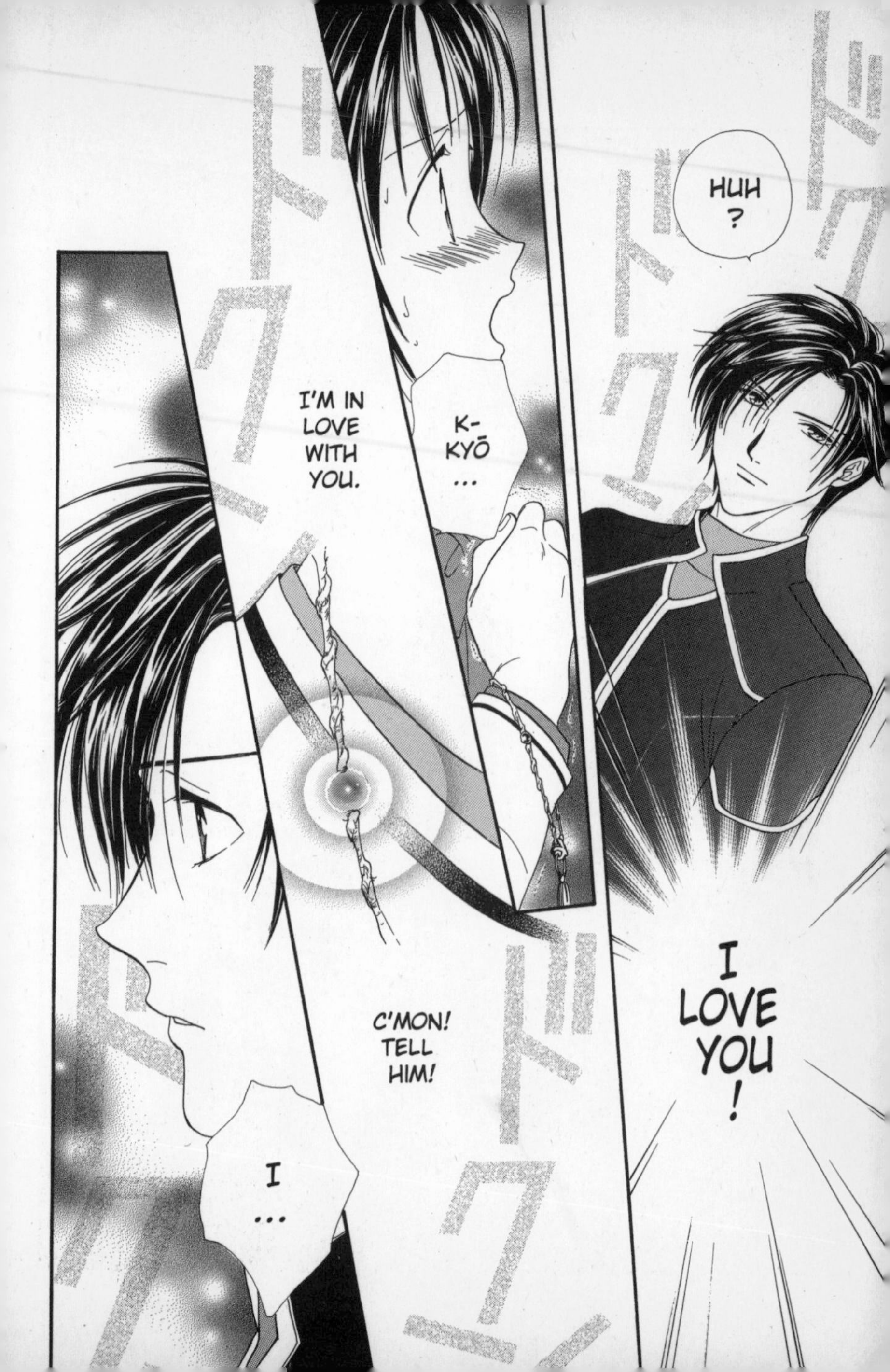
HUH?
I LOVE YOU!
K-KYŌ...
I'M IN LOVE WITH YOU.
C'MON! TELL HIM!
I...

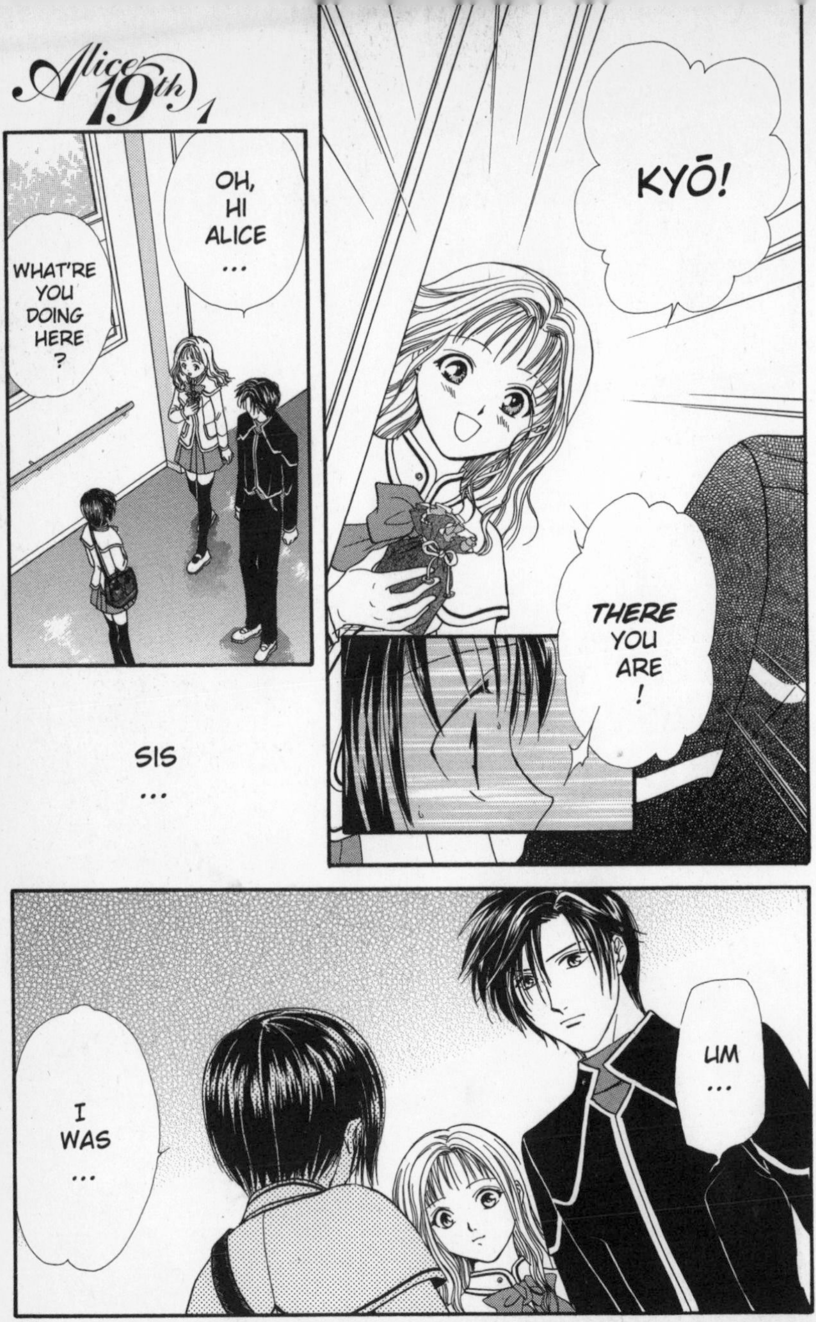
KYŌ!
THERE YOU ARE!
OH, HI ALICE ...
WHAT'RE YOU DOING HERE?
SIS ...
UM ...
I WAS ...

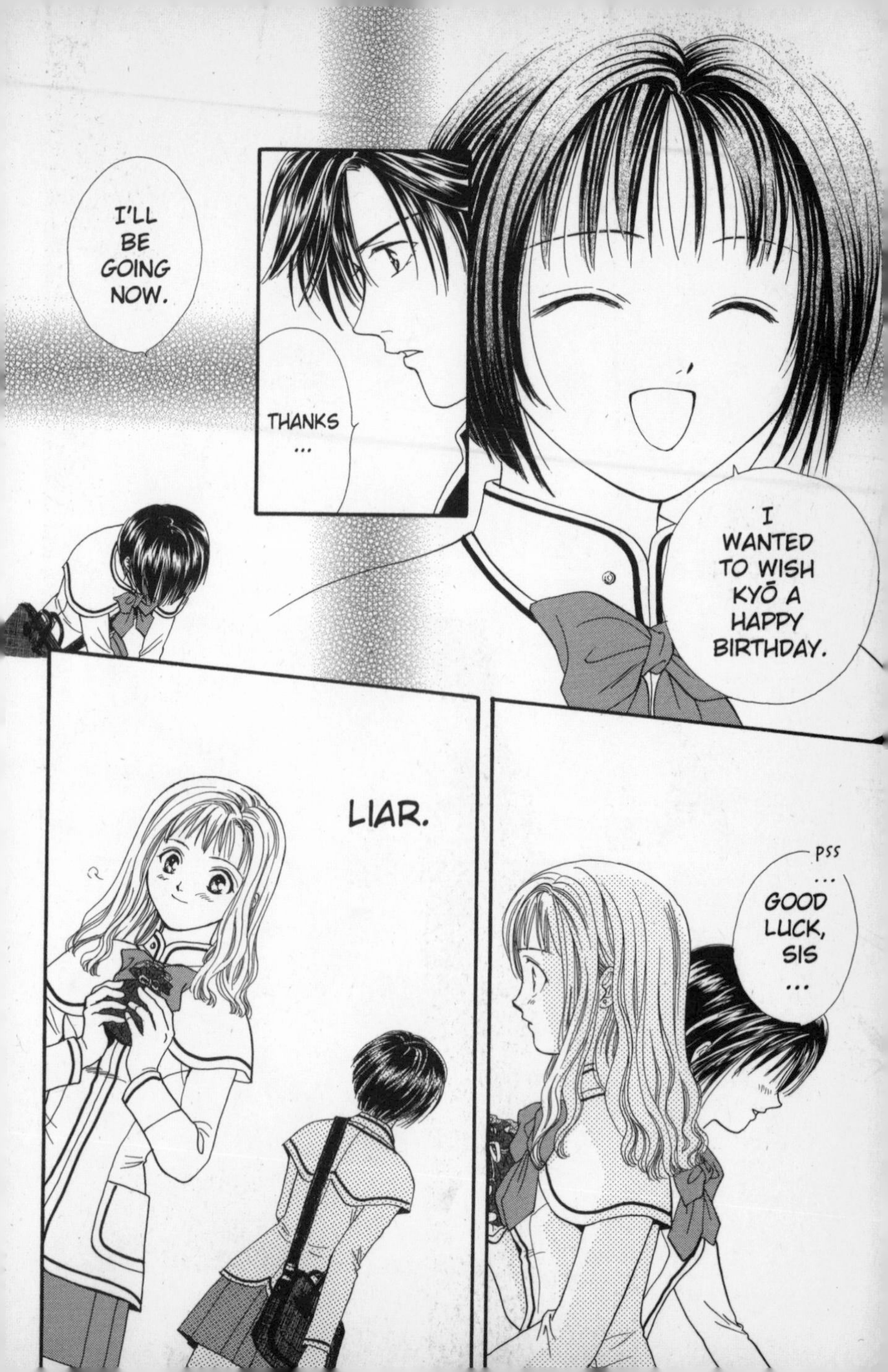
I WANTED TO WISH KYŌ A HAPPY BIRTHDAY.
THANKS ...
I'LL BE GOING NOW.
PSS ... GOOD LUCK, SIS ...
LIAR.

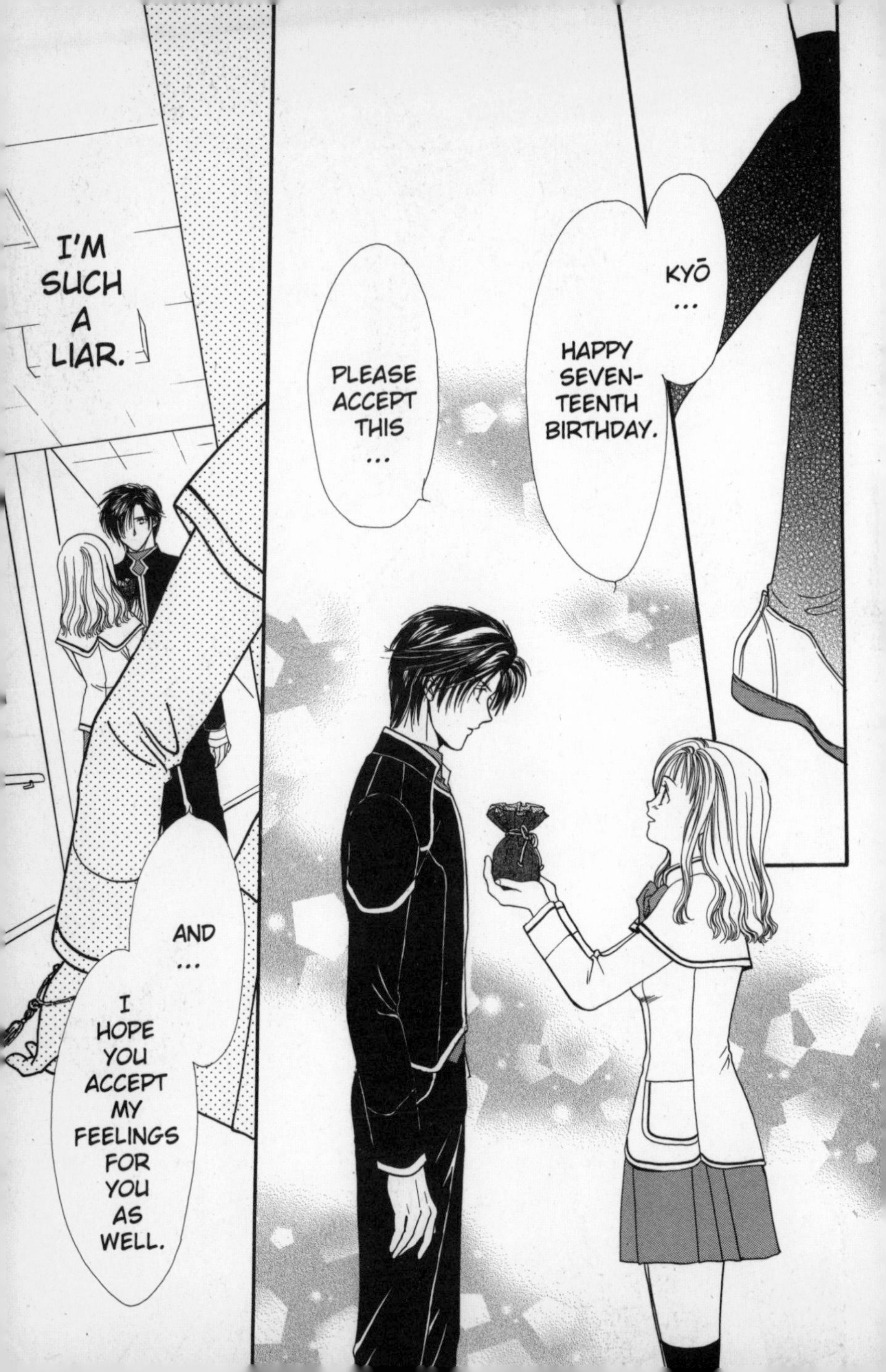
KYŌ ... HAPPY SEVEN-TEENTH BIRTHDAY.
PLEASE ACCEPT THIS ...
I'M SUCH A LIAR.
AND ... I HOPE YOU ACCEPT MY FEELINGS FOR YOU AS WELL.

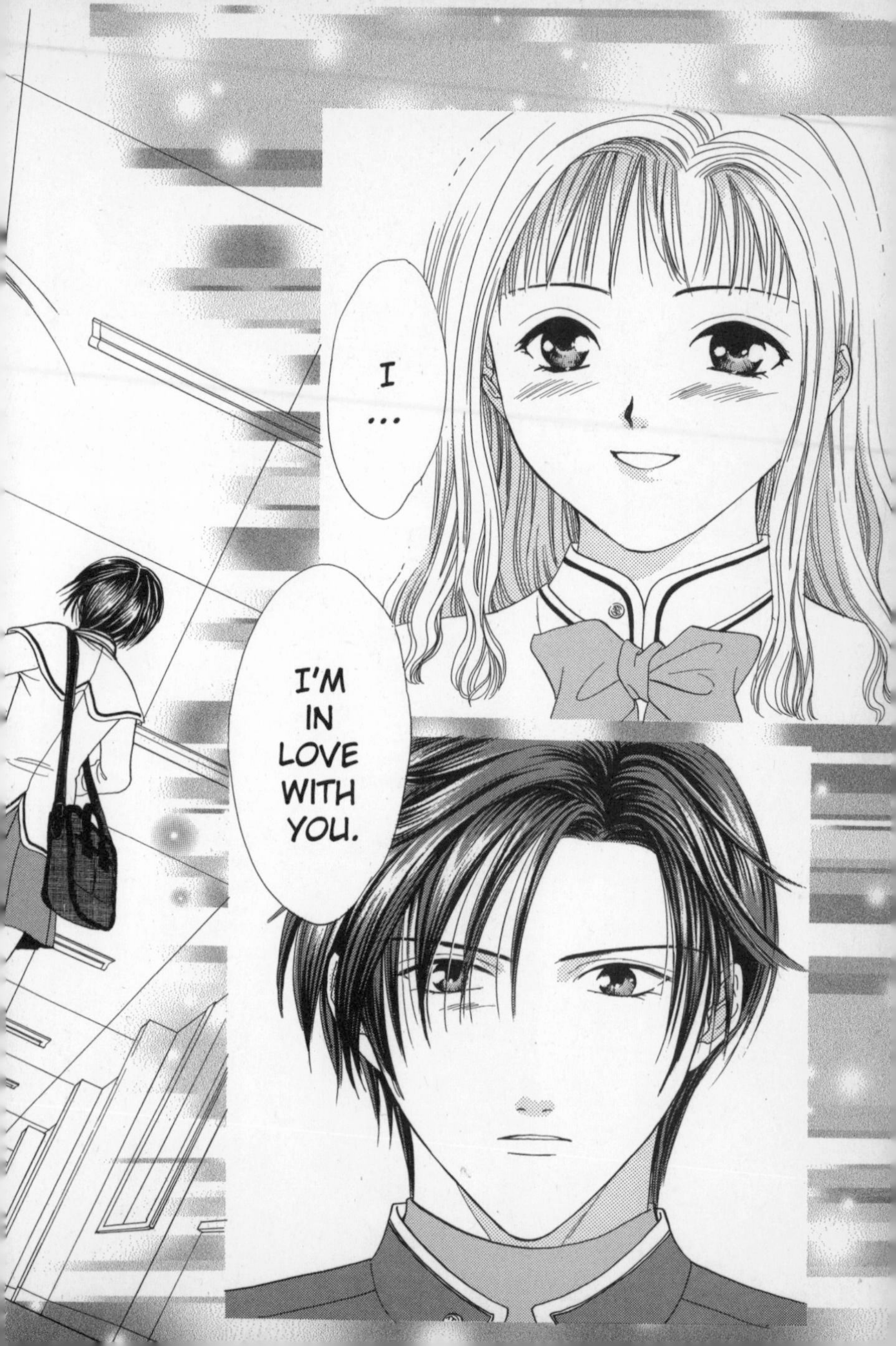
I ...
I'M IN LOVE WITH YOU.

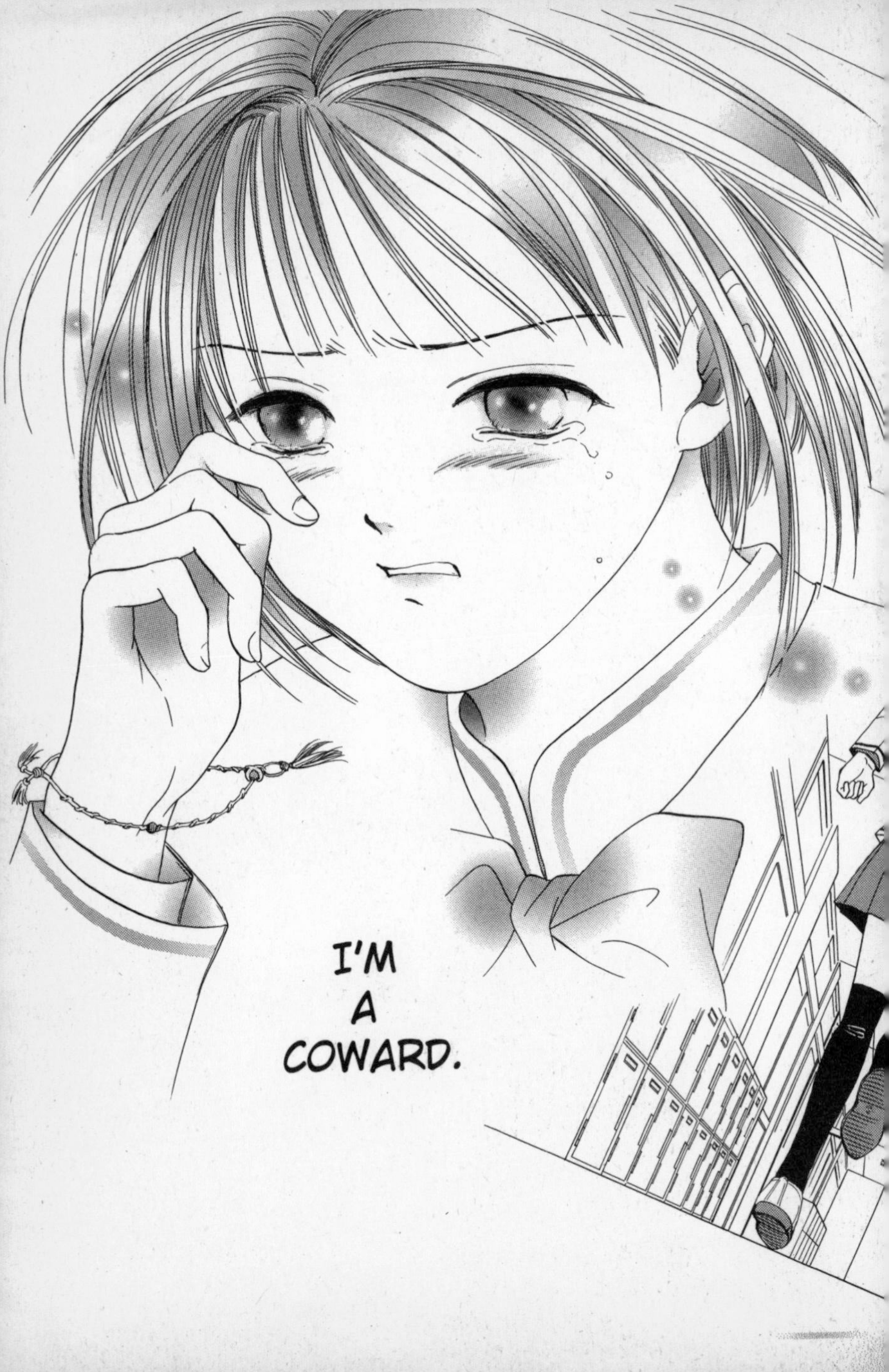
I'M A COWARD.

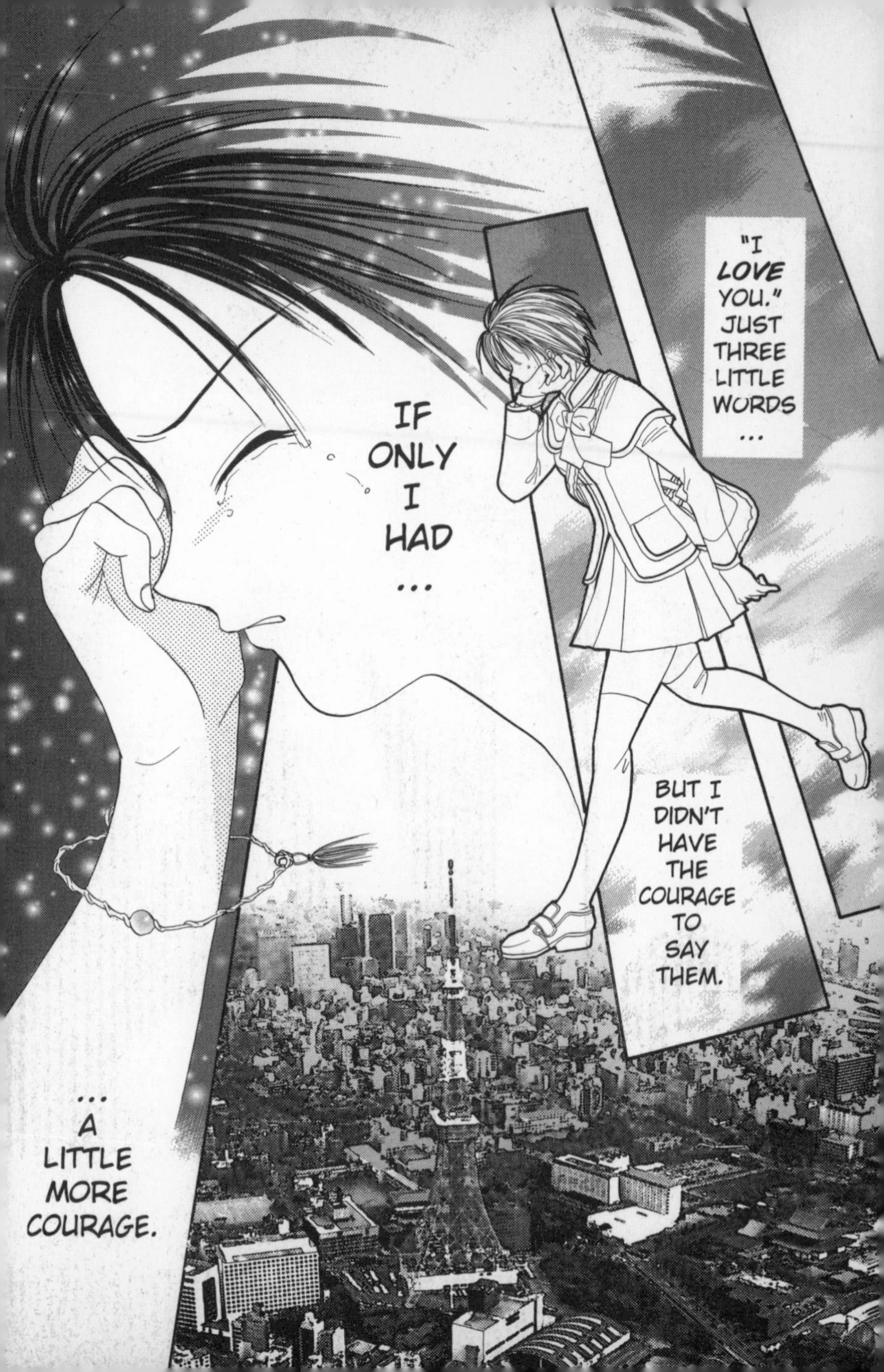
"I *LOVE* YOU." JUST THREE LITTLE WORDS ...
BUT I DIDN'T HAVE THE COURAGE TO SAY THEM.
IF ONLY I HAD ...
... A LITTLE MORE COURAGE.

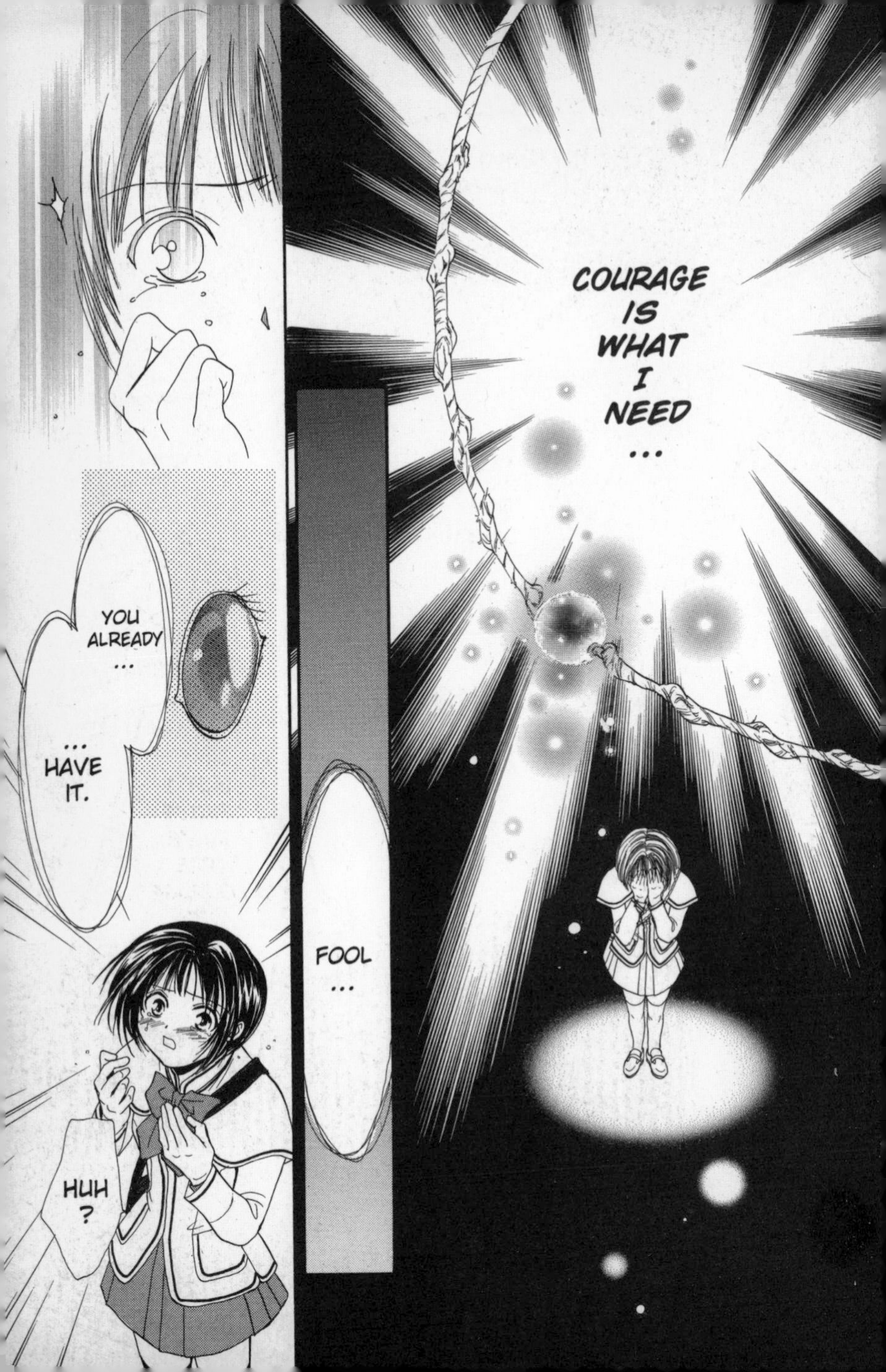
COURAGE IS WHAT I NEED...
FOOL...
YOU ALREADY...
...HAVE IT.
HUH?

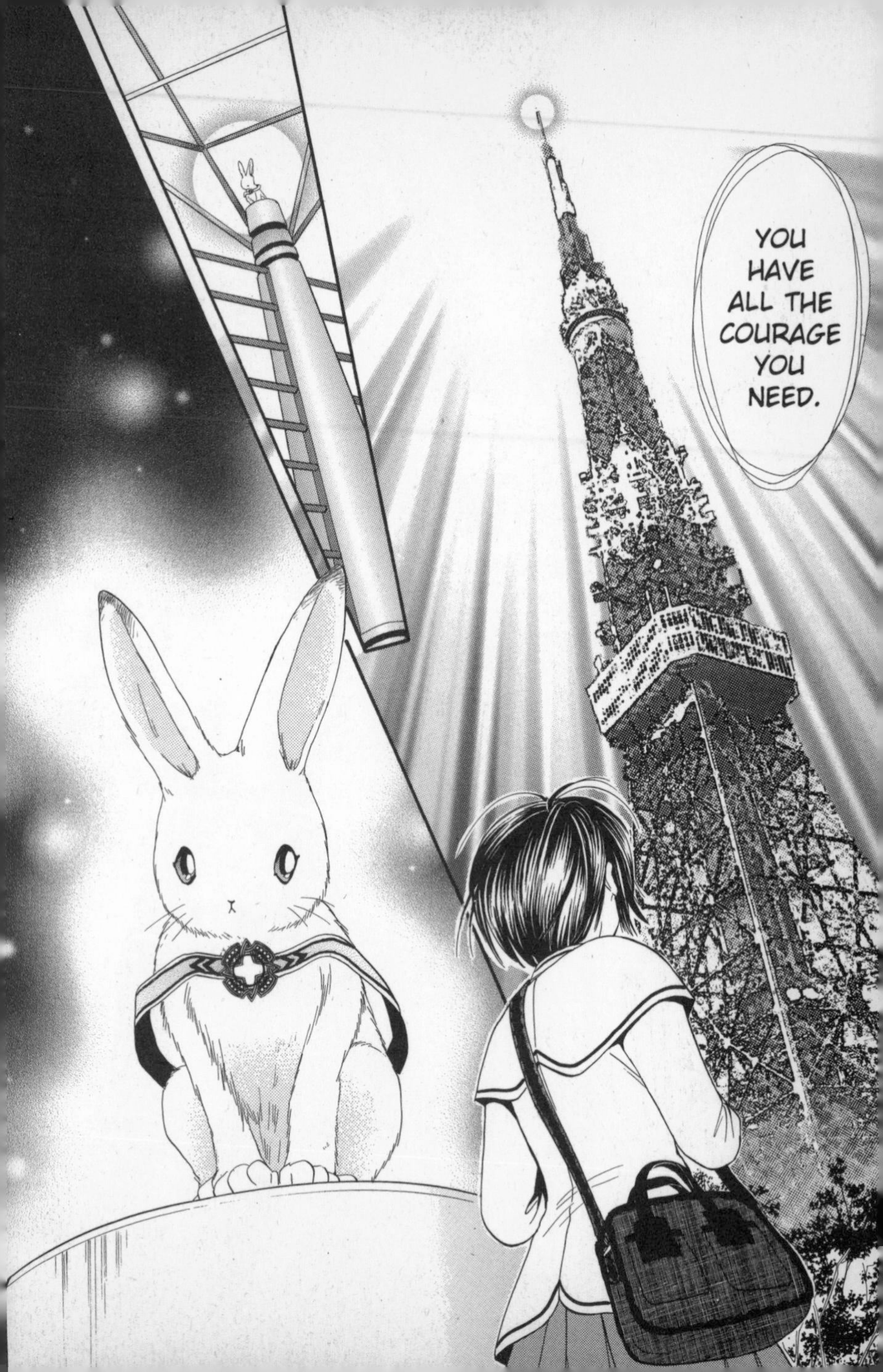
YOU HAVE ALL THE COURAGE YOU NEED.

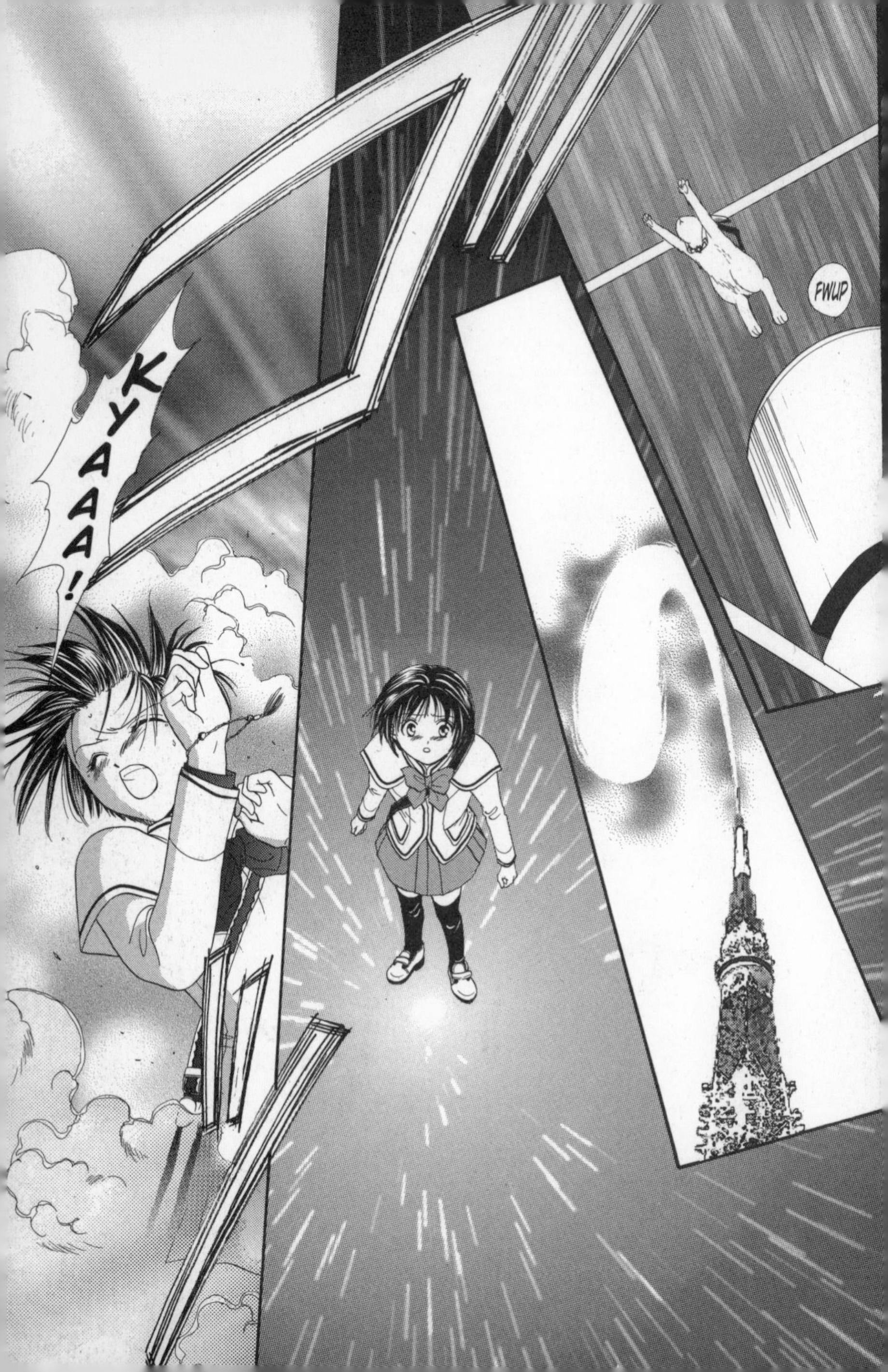
FWUP
KYAAAA!

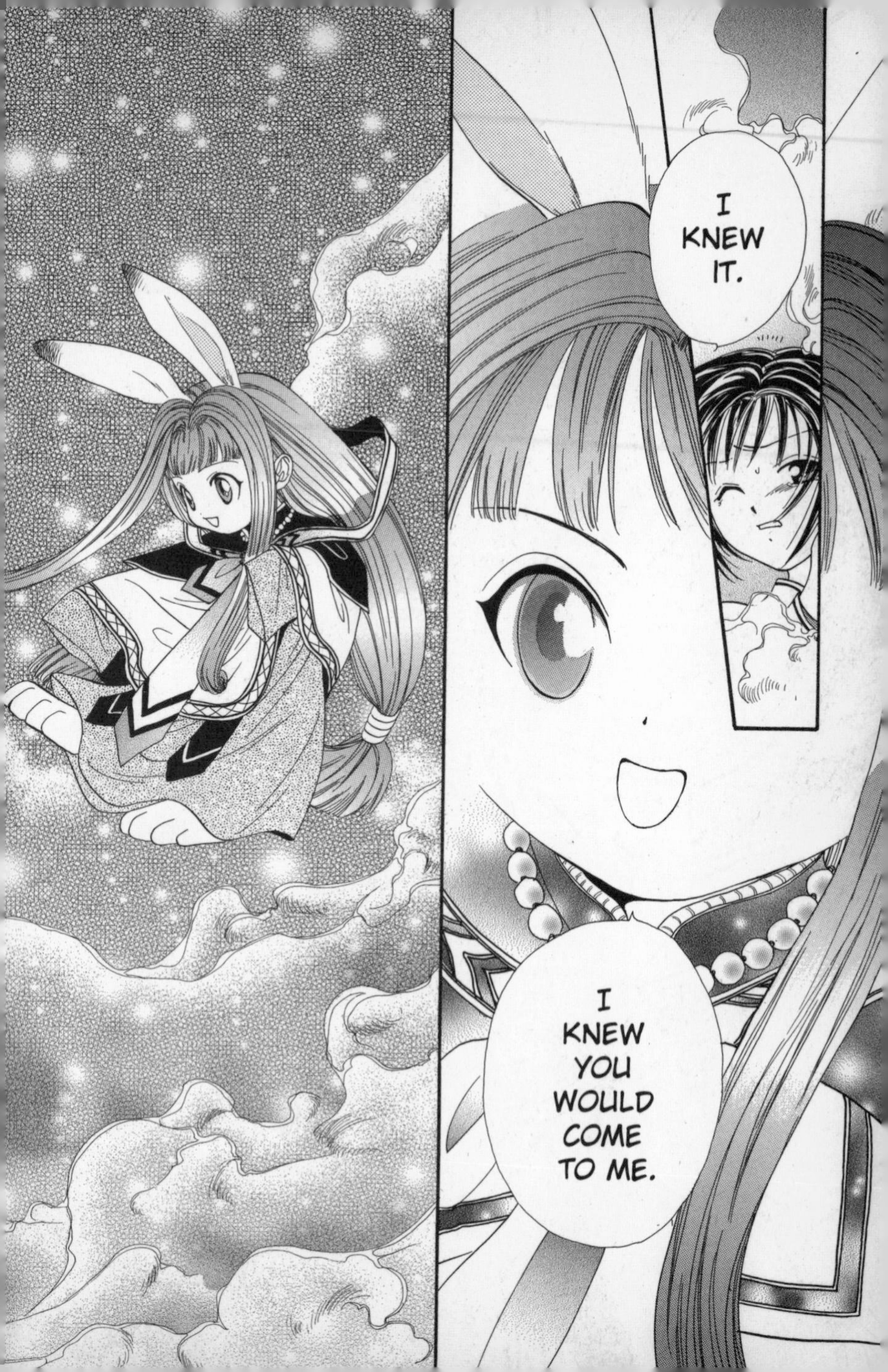
I KNEW IT.
I KNEW YOU WOULD COME TO ME.

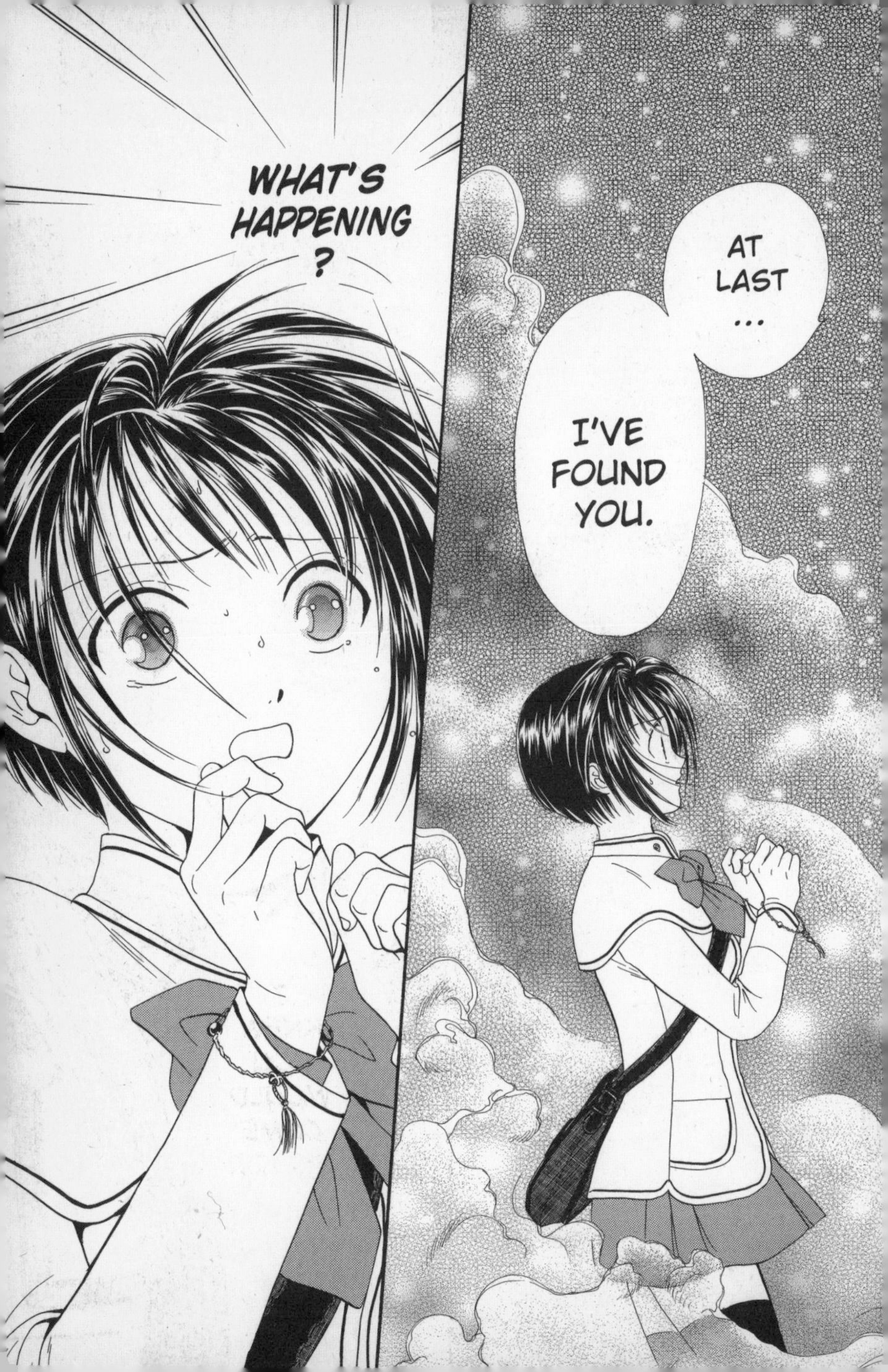
AT LAST ...
I'VE FOUND YOU.
WHAT'S HAPPENING ?

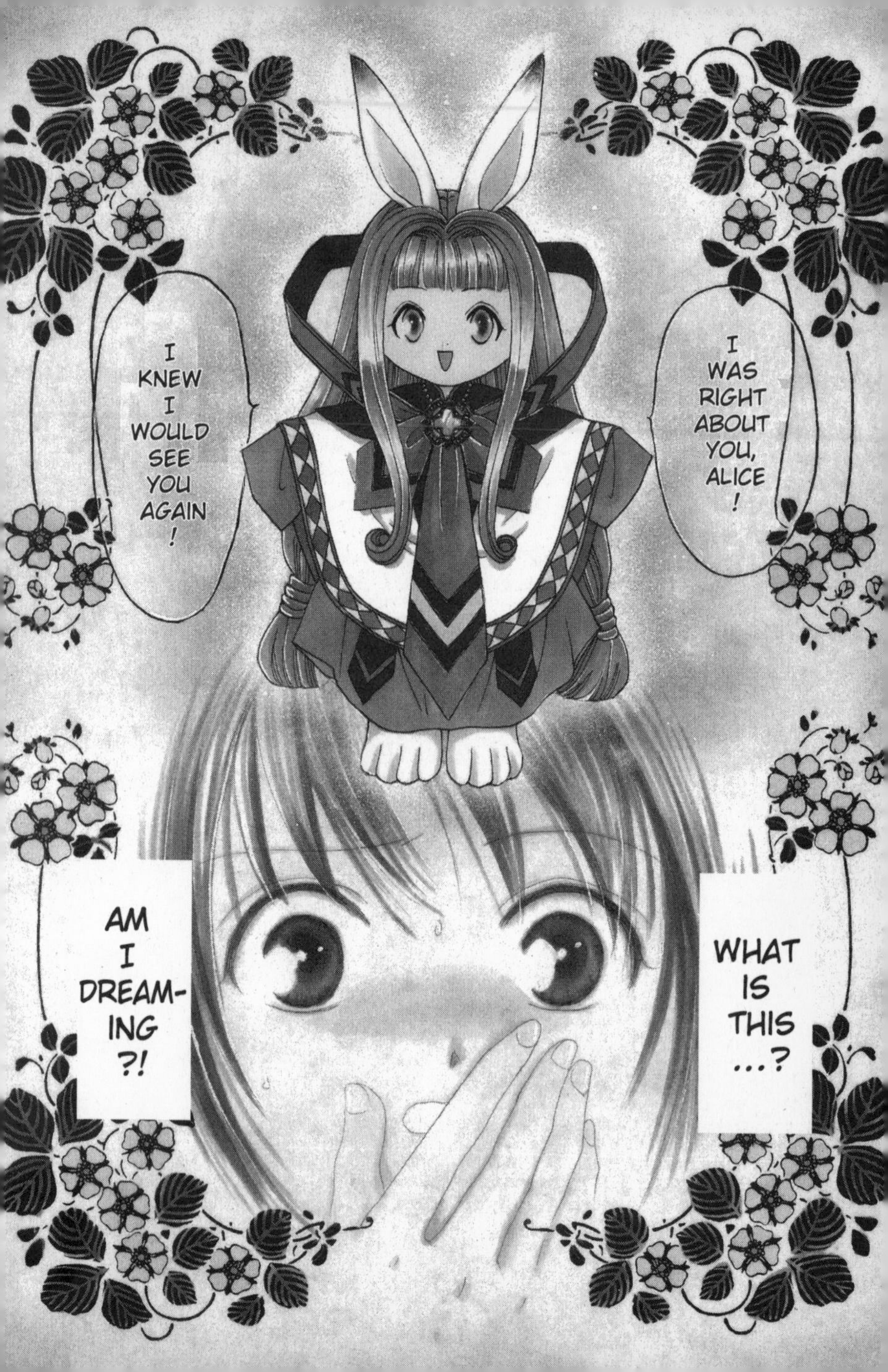
I WAS RIGHT ABOUT YOU, ALICE!
I KNEW I WOULD SEE YOU AGAIN!
WHAT IS THIS ...?
AM I DREAMING?!

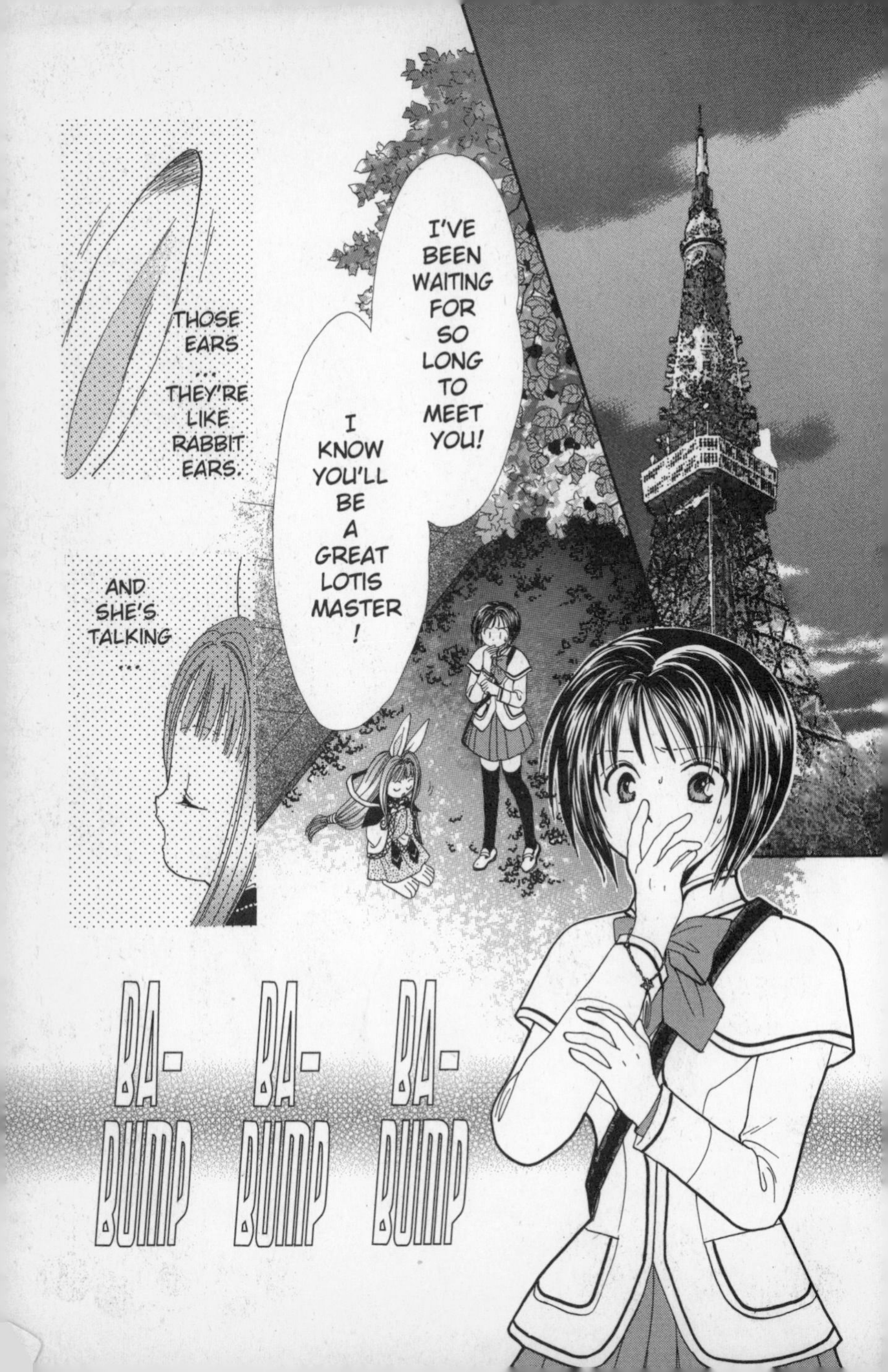
I'VE BEEN WAITING FOR SO LONG TO MEET YOU!
I KNOW YOU'LL BE A GREAT LOTIS MASTER!
THOSE EARS ... THEY'RE LIKE RABBIT EARS.
AND SHE'S TALKING ...
BA-BUMP BA-BUMP BA-BUMP

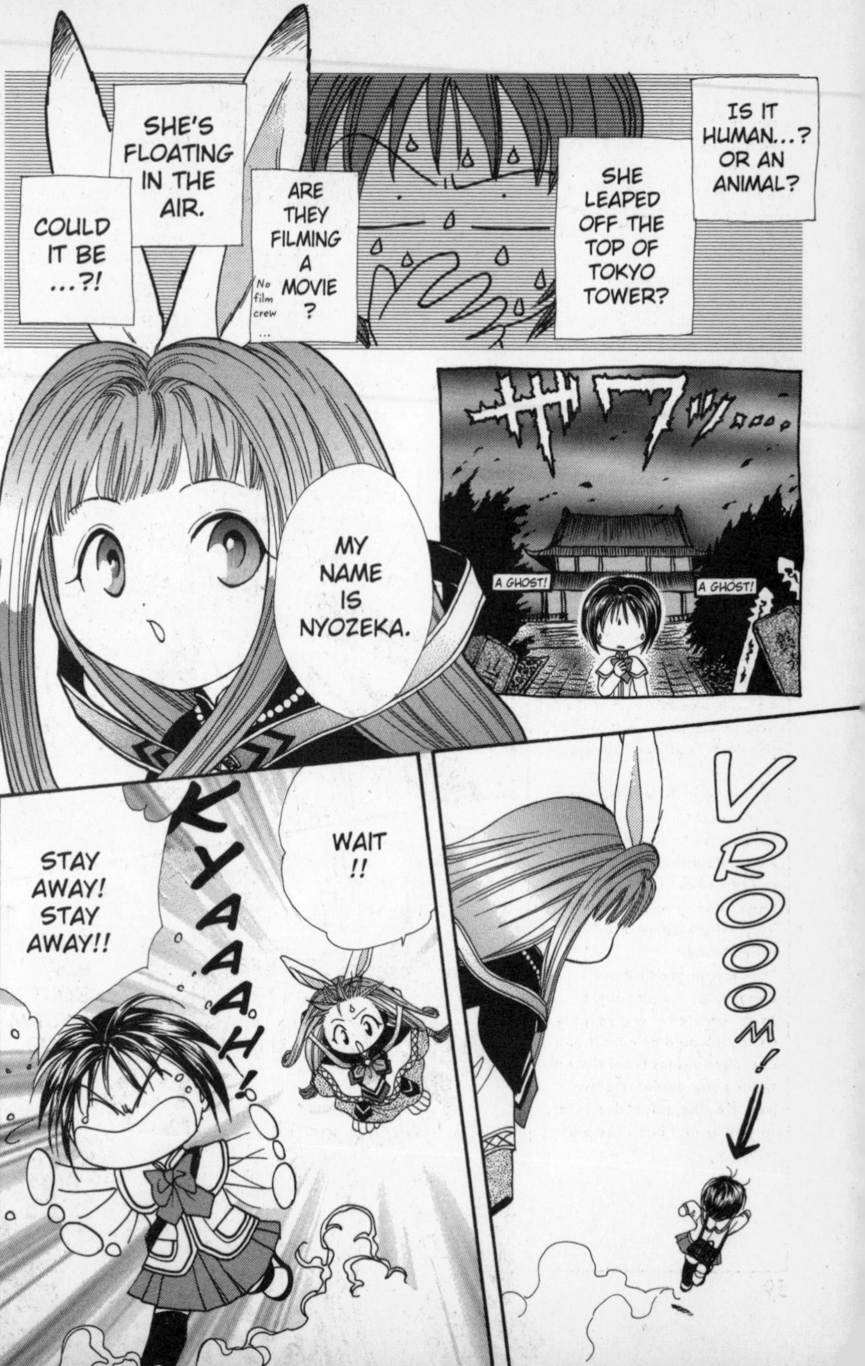
IS IT HUMAN...? OR AN ANIMAL?
SHE LEAPED OFF THE TOP OF TOKYO TOWER?
ARE THEY FILMING A MOVIE?
No film crew...
SHE'S FLOATING IN THE AIR.
COULD IT BE ...?!
A GHOST!
A GHOST!
MY NAME IS NYOZEKA.
VROOOOM!
WAIT !!
KYAAAAH!
STAY AWAY! STAY AWAY!!

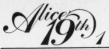

So now, in Alice 19th, I'm emphasizing the power of words. And at the same time, communication is also included in the theme of the story. Since this is only the first episode, you'll just have to keep reading. Alice, the heroine, is a girl who always holds back from saying what she feels. Is she just shy? Actually, no. Alice builds relationships by adjusting her actions to accommodate others. Even when people are mean to her, she just smiles so that things don't get out of control. It's her way of keeping herself from getting hurt. That's one of the ways in which Alice is different from the other heroines I've drawn. Many of my past heroines have been feisty and worked to solve their problems aggressively. Frankly, they were my ideal. But I came to wonder if more girls weren't actually like Alice. Are those super-vivacious types really so sincere? That's not always the case.
So I was a little worried that Alice might be too meek for a heroine, but once the serial went into publication, many readers said, "I like Alice," and "I can sympathize with her," which came as a relief to me.
"I'm a younger sister, so I can relate," some people said, but even if you're a big sister, it would be nice if you could see things from the kid sister's standpoint. By the way, I'm the eldest daughter, so I've always been the big sister, myself.

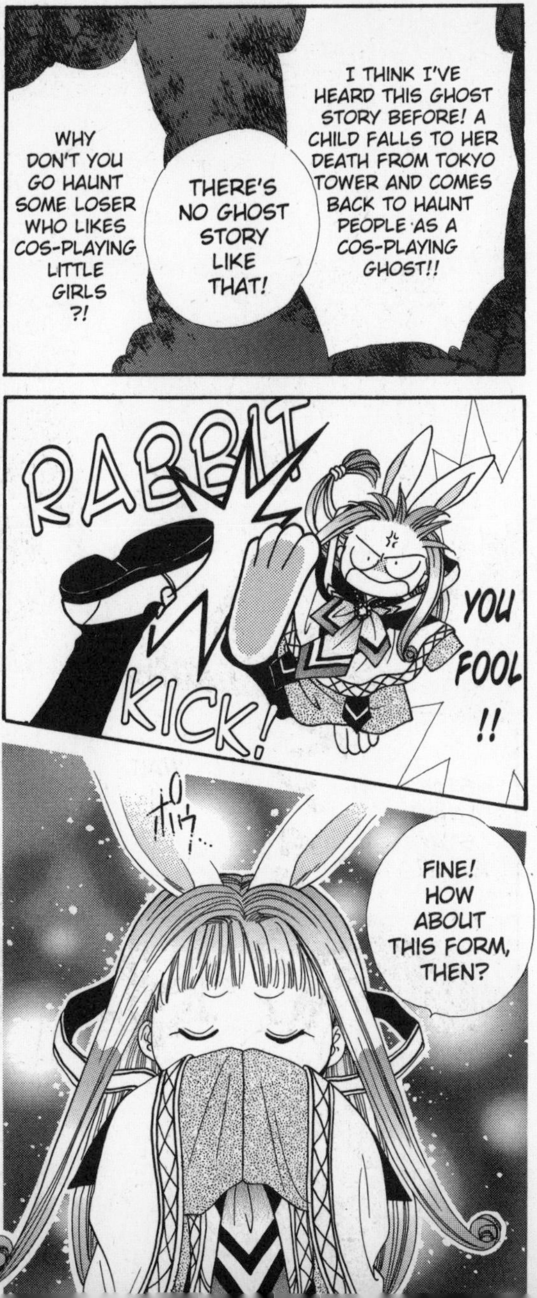
I THINK I'VE HEARD THIS GHOST STORY BEFORE! A CHILD FALLS TO HER DEATH FROM TOKYO TOWER AND COMES BACK TO HAUNT PEOPLE AS A COS-PLAYING GHOST!!
THERE'S NO GHOST STORY LIKE THAT!
WHY DON'T YOU GO HAUNT SOME LOSER WHO LIKES COS-PLAYING LITTLE GIRLS ?!
YOU FOOL !!
RABBIT KICK!
FINE! HOW ABOUT THIS FORM, THEN?

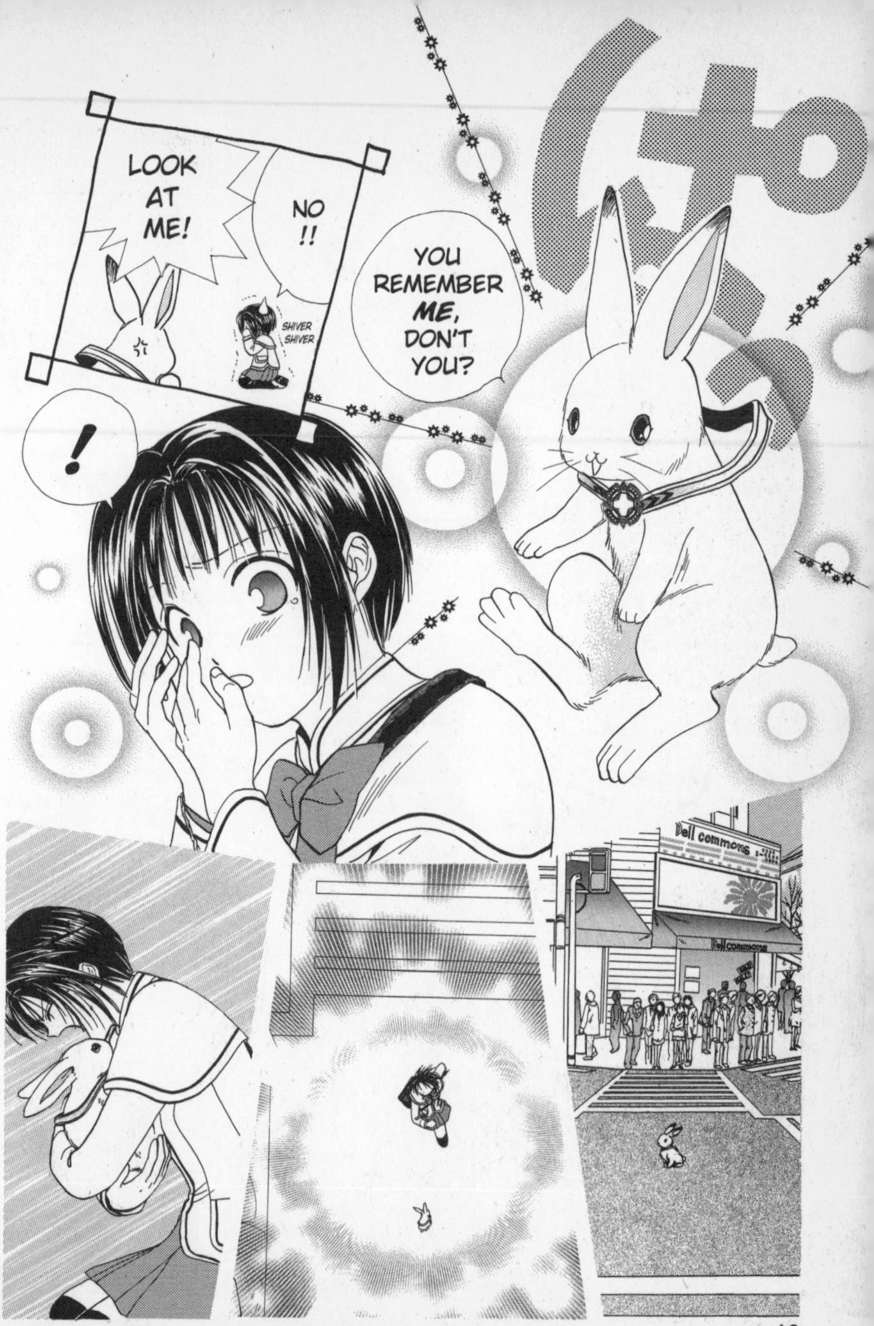
YOU REMEMBER *ME*, DON'T YOU?
NO !!
LOOK AT ME!
SHIVER SHIVER
!
Dell commons
Dell commons

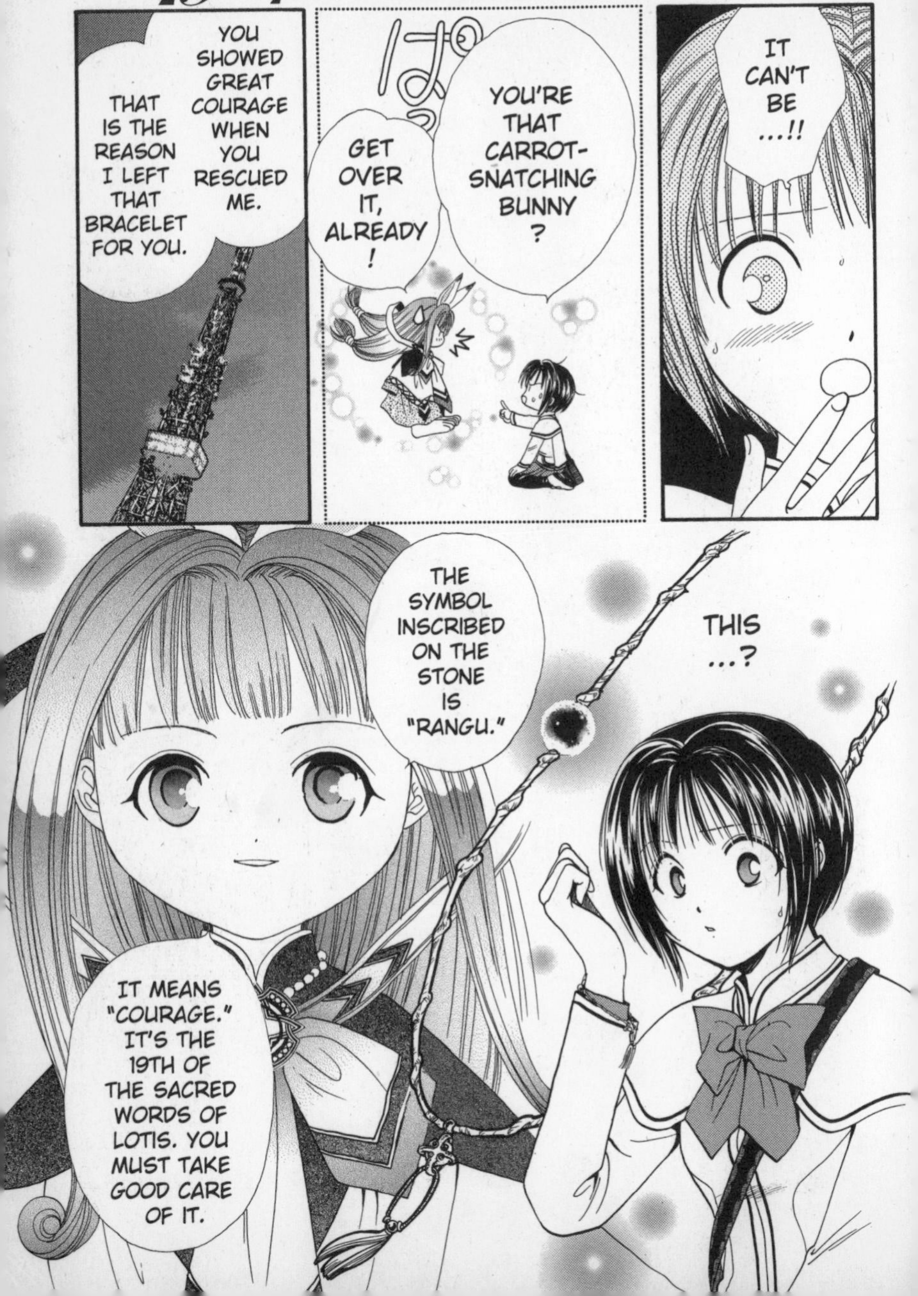
IT CAN'T BE ...!!
YOU'RE THAT CARROT-SNATCHING BUNNY?
ぱっ
GET OVER IT, ALREADY!
YOU SHOWED GREAT COURAGE WHEN YOU RESCUED ME.
THAT IS THE REASON I LEFT THAT BRACELET FOR YOU.
THIS ...?
THE SYMBOL INSCRIBED ON THE STONE IS "RANGU."
IT MEANS "COURAGE." IT'S THE 19TH OF THE SACRED WORDS OF LOTIS. YOU MUST TAKE GOOD CARE OF IT.

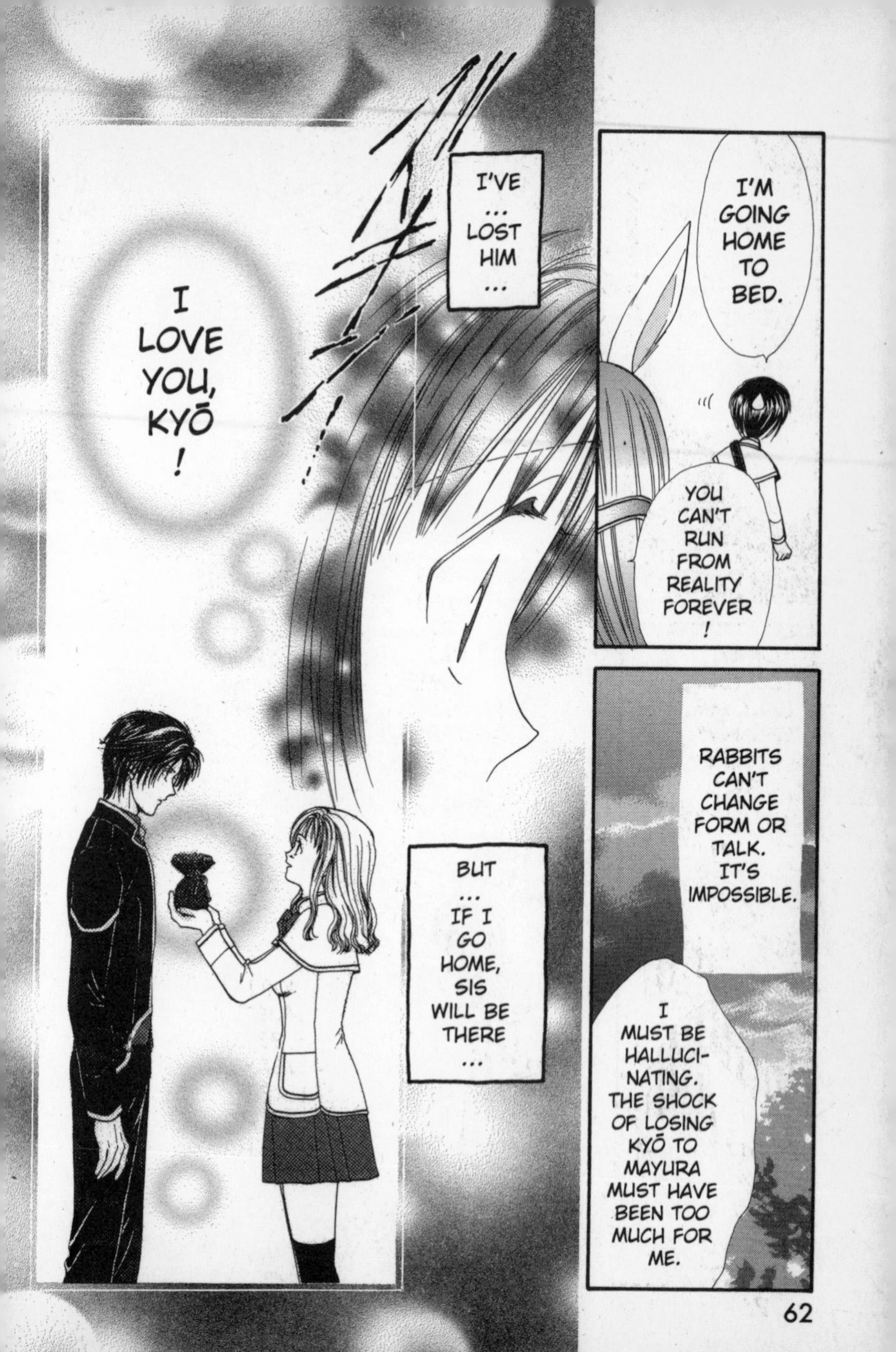
I'M GOING HOME TO BED.
YOU CAN'T RUN FROM REALITY FOREVER!
RABBITS CAN'T CHANGE FORM OR TALK. IT'S IMPOSSIBLE.
I MUST BE HALLUCINATING. THE SHOCK OF LOSING KYŌ TO MAYURA MUST HAVE BEEN TOO MUCH FOR ME.
I'VE ... LOST HIM ...
BUT ... IF I GO HOME, SIS WILL BE THERE ...
I LOVE YOU, KYŌ!

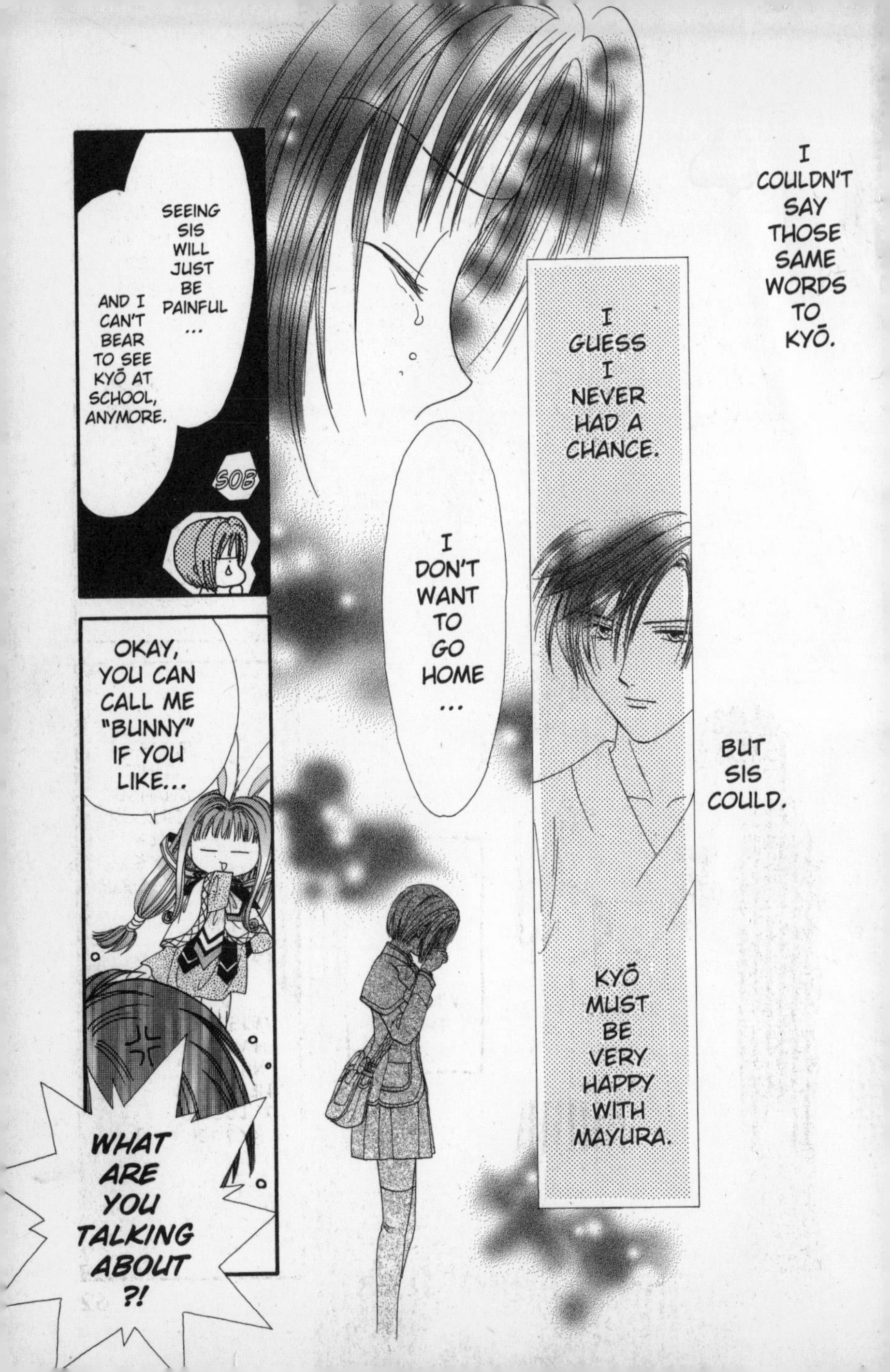
I COULDN'T SAY THOSE SAME WORDS TO KYŌ.
I GUESS I NEVER HAD A CHANCE.
BUT SIS COULD.
KYŌ MUST BE VERY HAPPY WITH MAYURA.
I DON'T WANT TO GO HOME...
SEEING SIS WILL JUST BE PAINFUL...
AND I CAN'T BEAR TO SEE KYŌ AT SCHOOL, ANYMORE.
SOB
OKAY, YOU CAN CALL ME "BUNNY" IF YOU LIKE...
WHAT ARE YOU TALKING ABOUT?!

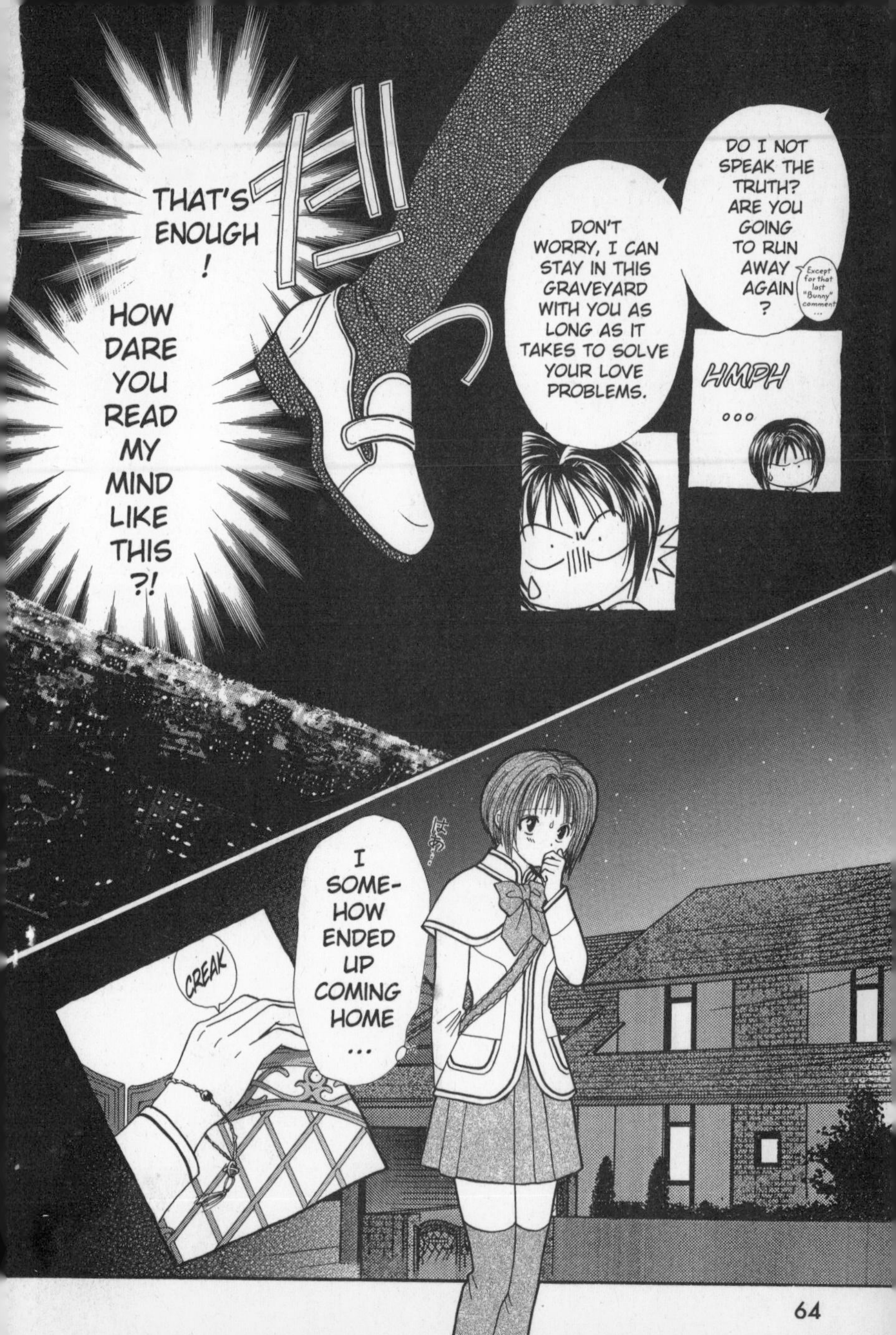

DO I NOT SPEAK THE TRUTH? ARE YOU GOING TO RUN AWAY AGAIN?
Except for that last "Bunny" comment...
HMPH
...
DON'T WORRY, I CAN STAY IN THIS GRAVEYARD WITH YOU AS LONG AS IT TAKES TO SOLVE YOUR LOVE PROBLEMS.
THAT'S ENOUGH!
HOW DARE YOU READ MY MIND LIKE THIS?!
I SOME-HOW ENDED UP COMING HOME...
CREAK

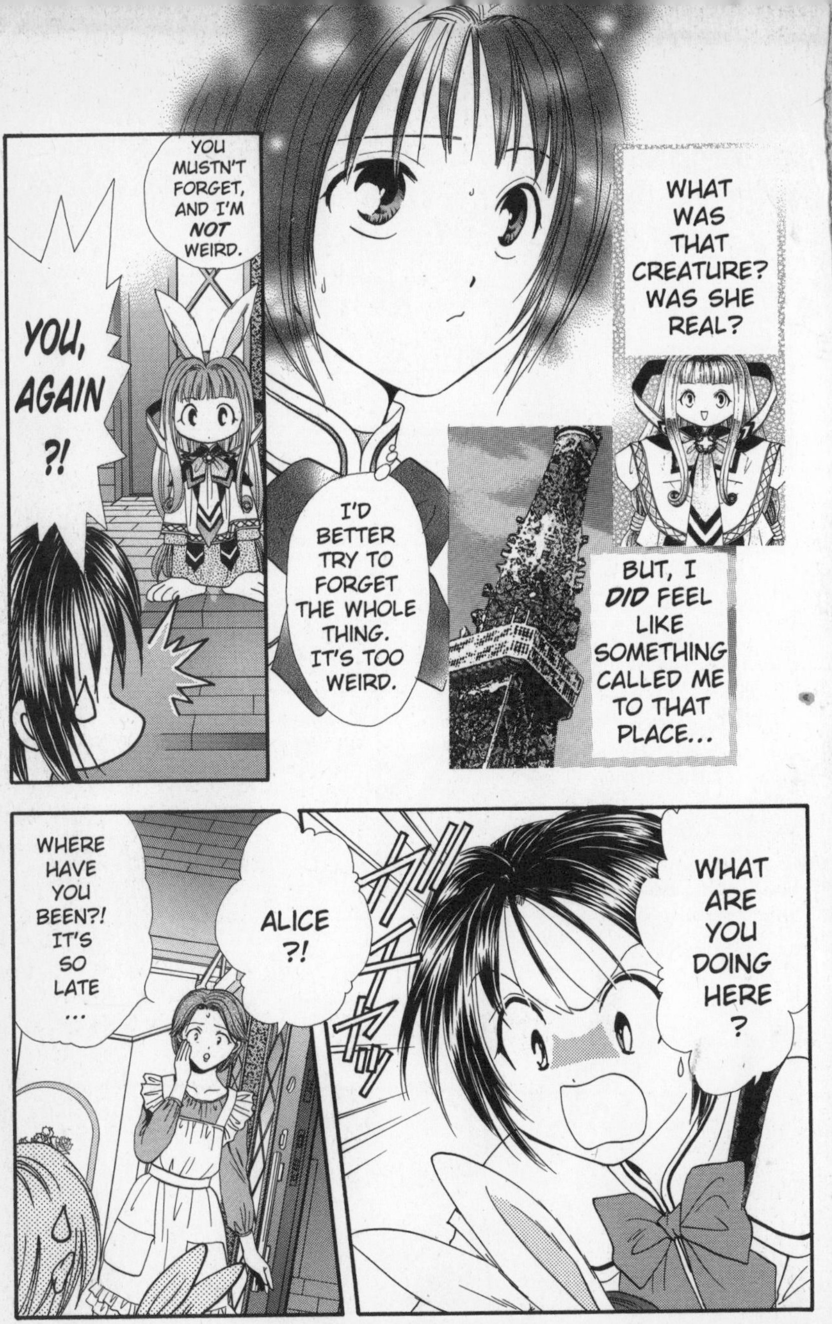
WHAT WAS THAT CREATURE? WAS SHE REAL?
BUT, I *DID* FEEL LIKE SOMETHING CALLED ME TO THAT PLACE...
I'D BETTER TRY TO FORGET THE WHOLE THING. IT'S TOO WEIRD.
YOU MUSTN'T FORGET, AND I'M *NOT* WEIRD.
YOU, AGAIN ?!
WHAT ARE YOU DOING HERE ?
ALICE ?!
WHERE HAVE YOU BEEN?! IT'S SO LATE ...

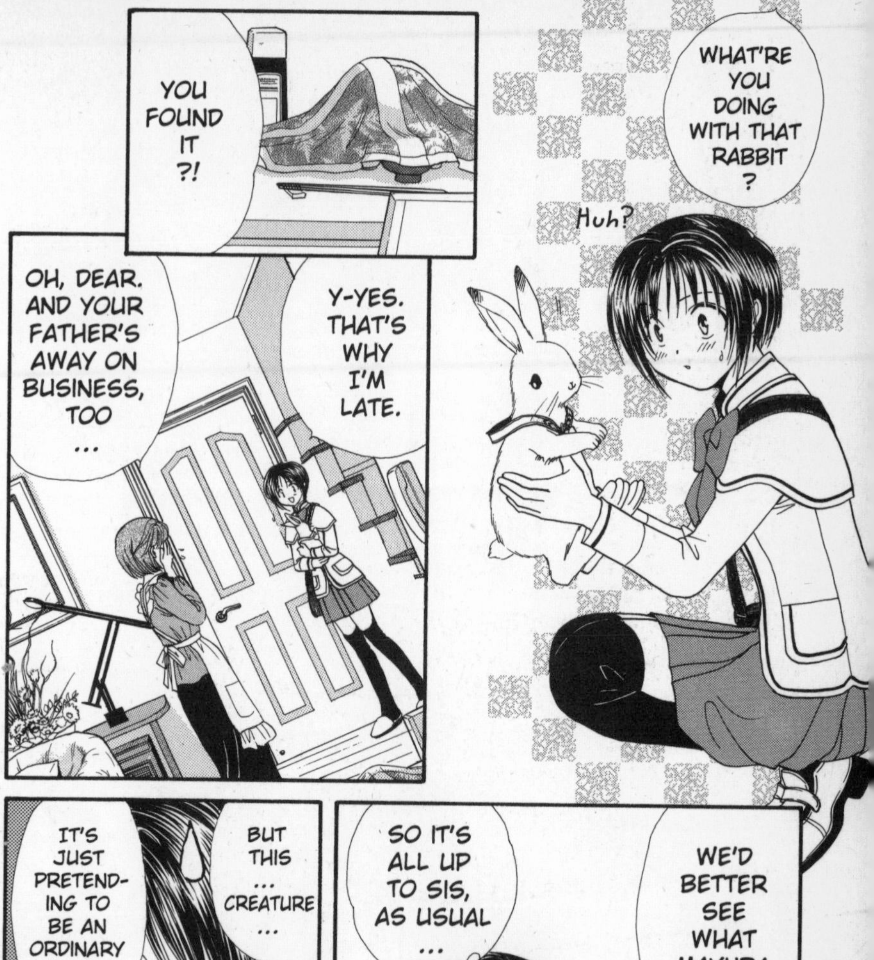
WHAT'RE YOU DOING WITH THAT RABBIT ?
Huh?
YOU FOUND IT ?!
Y-YES. THAT'S WHY I'M LATE.
OH, DEAR. AND YOUR FATHER'S AWAY ON BUSINESS, TOO ...
WE'D BETTER SEE WHAT MAYURA THINKS.
SO IT'S ALL UP TO SIS, AS USUAL ...
BUT THIS ... CREATURE ...
IT'S JUST PRETEND-ING TO BE AN ORDINARY RABBIT ...

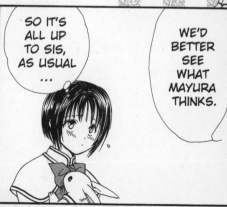

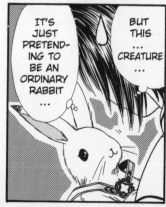

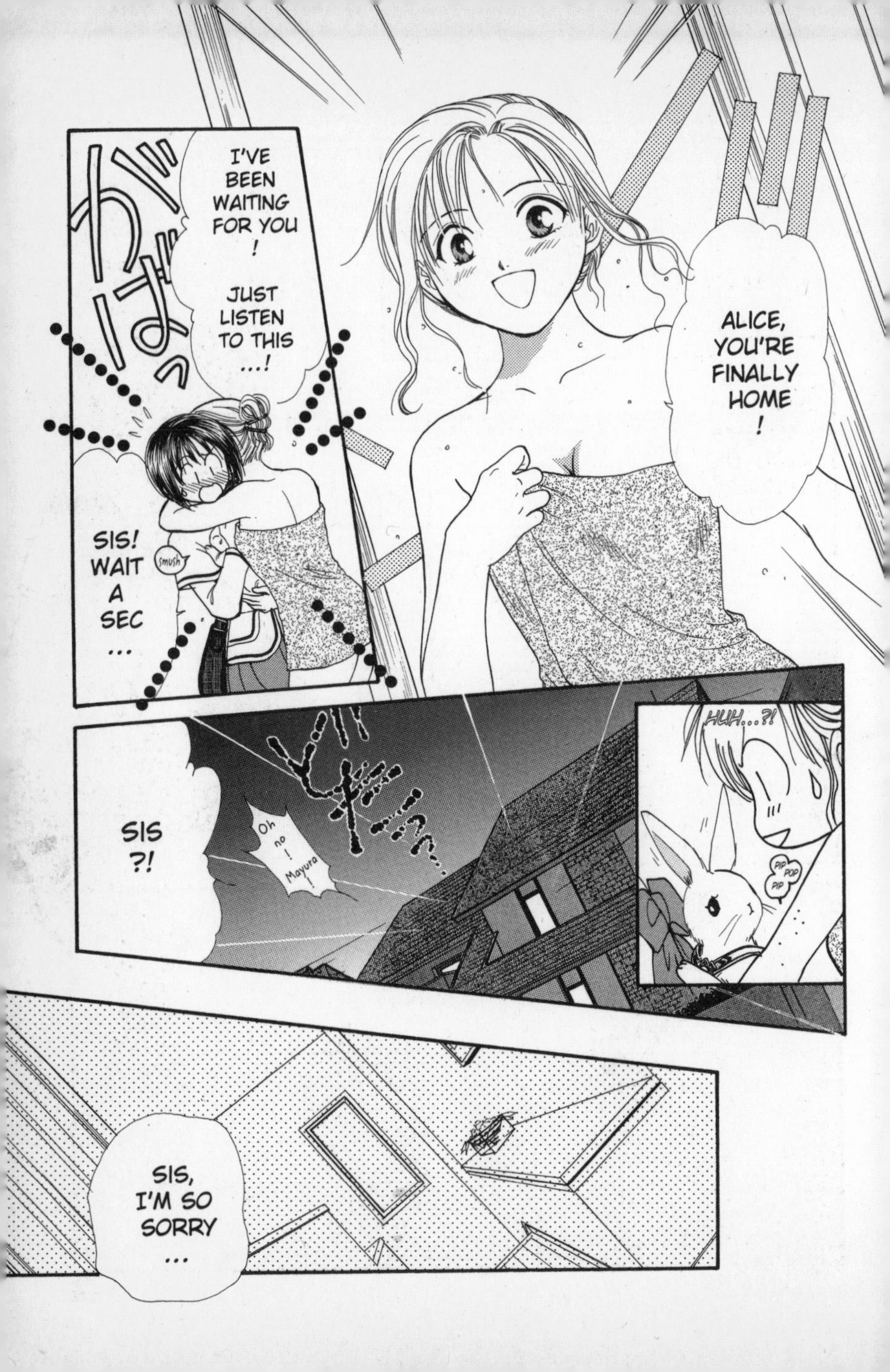
ALICE, YOU'RE FINALLY HOME!
I'VE BEEN WAITING FOR YOU! JUST LISTEN TO THIS...!
SIS! WAIT A SEC...
smush
HUH...?!
PIP POP PIP
SIS?!
Oh no! Mayura!
SIS, I'M SO SORRY...

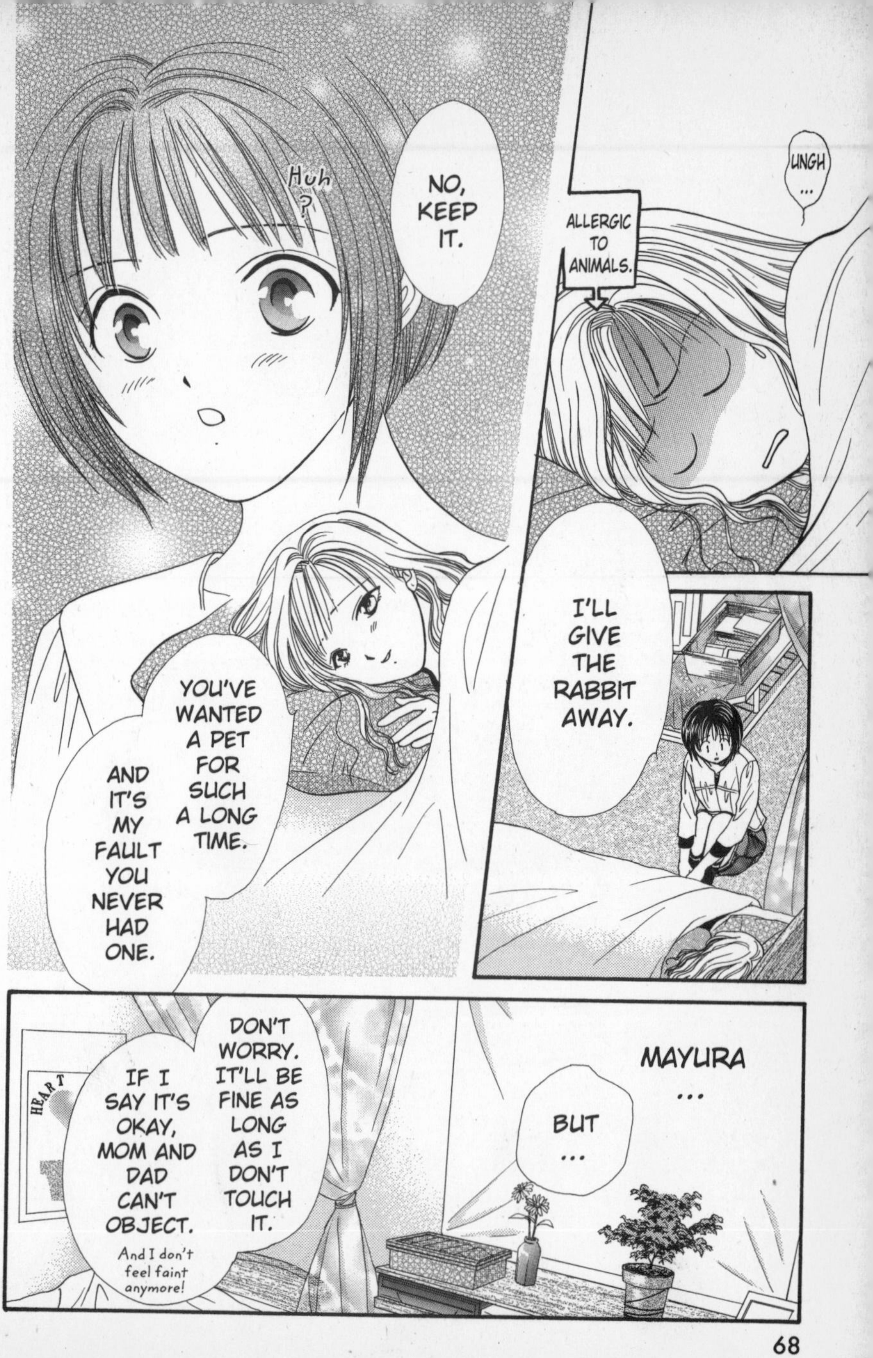
UNGH ...
ALLERGIC TO ANIMALS.
I'LL GIVE THE RABBIT AWAY.
NO, KEEP IT.
Huh ?
YOU'VE WANTED A PET FOR SUCH A LONG TIME.
AND IT'S MY FAULT YOU NEVER HAD ONE.
MAYURA ...
BUT ...
DON'T WORRY. IT'LL BE FINE AS LONG AS I DON'T TOUCH IT.
IF I SAY IT'S OKAY, MOM AND DAD CAN'T OBJECT.
And I don't feel faint anymore!
HEART

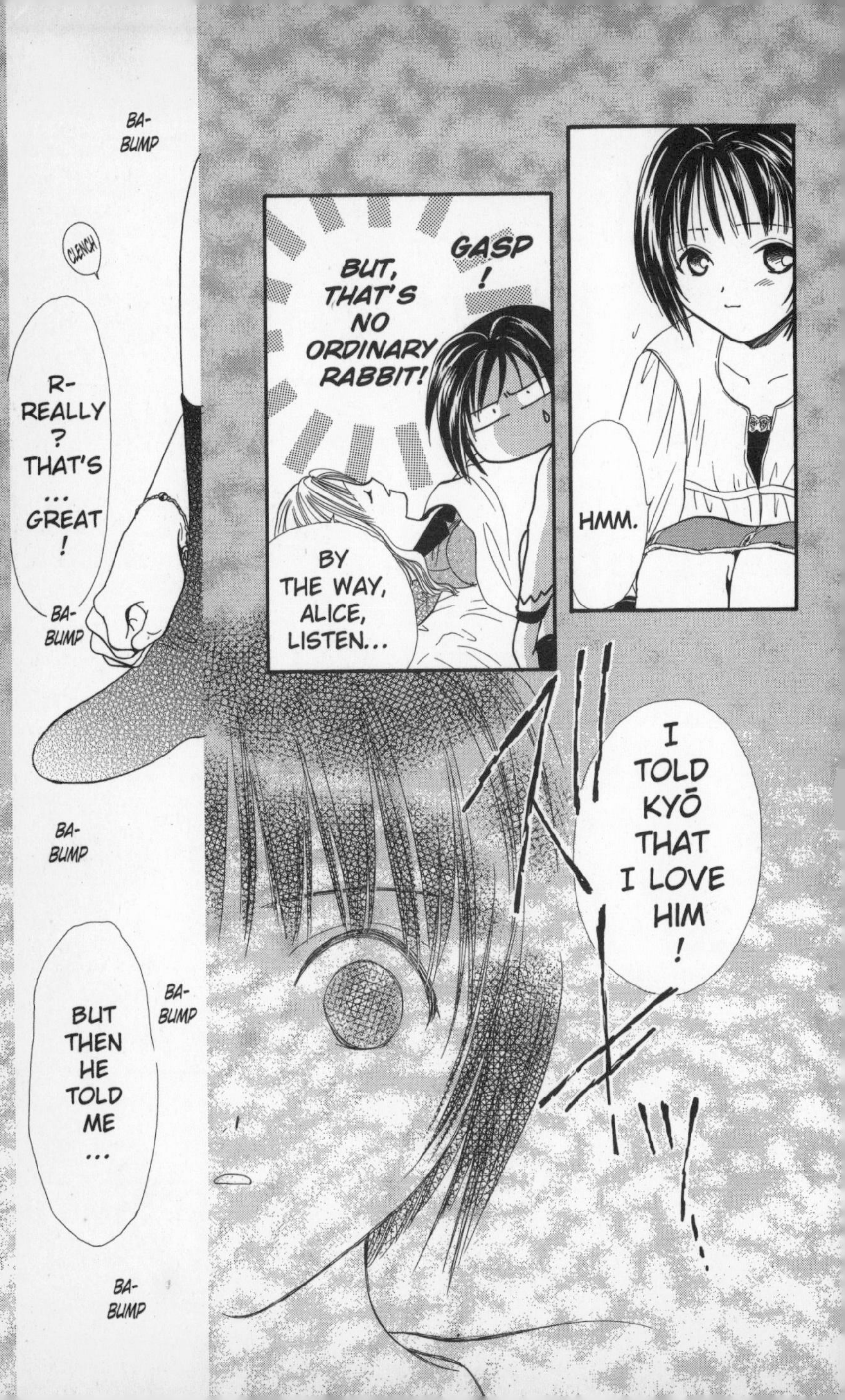
HMM.
GASP!
BUT, THAT'S NO ORDINARY RABBIT!
BY THE WAY, ALICE, LISTEN...
I TOLD KYŌ THAT I LOVE HIM!
BA-BUMP
CLENCH
R-REALLY? THAT'S... GREAT!
BA-BUMP
BA-BUMP
BUT THEN HE TOLD ME...
BA-BUMP
BA-BUMP

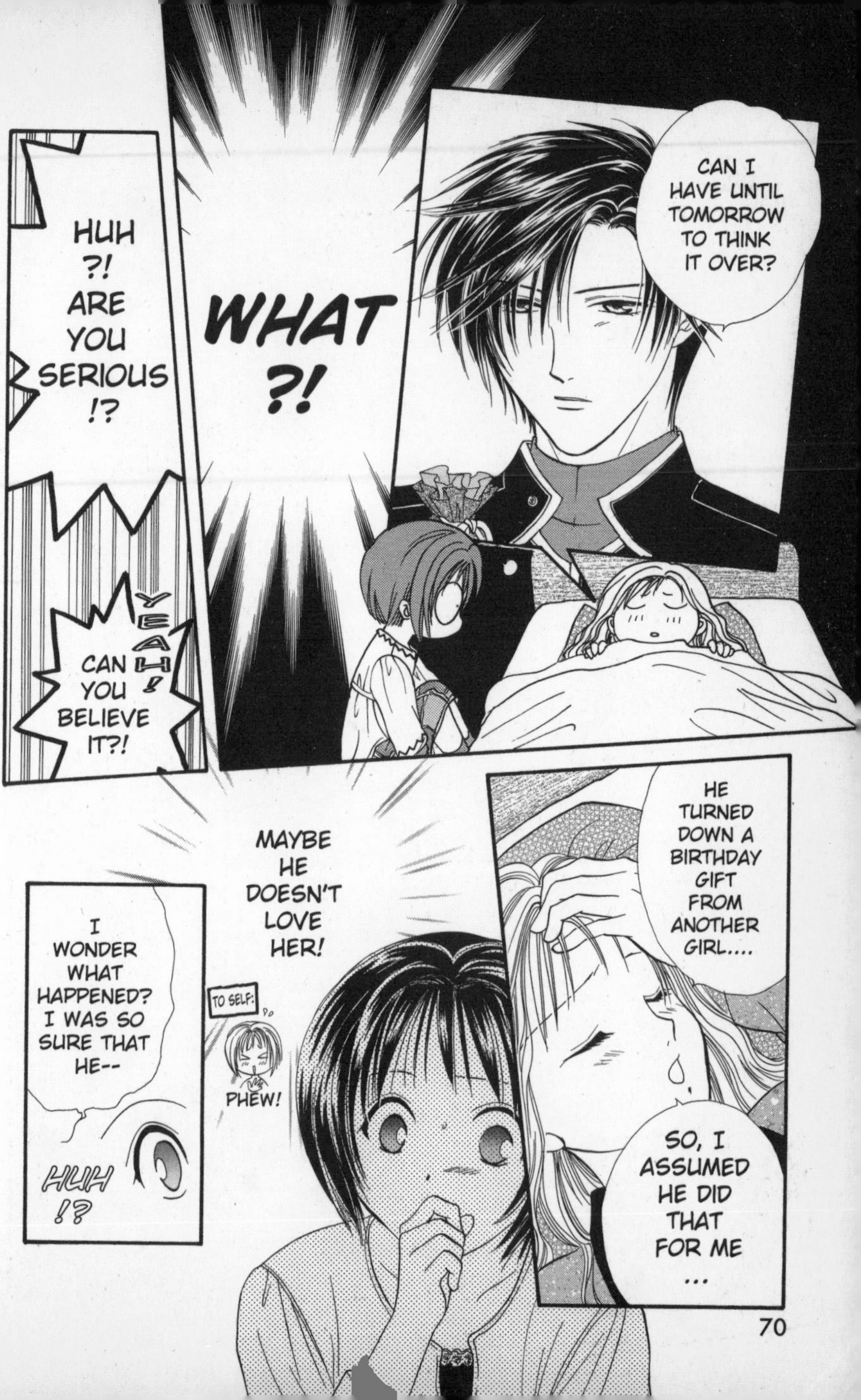
CAN I HAVE UNTIL TOMORROW TO THINK IT OVER?
WHAT ?!
HUH ?! ARE YOU SERIOUS !?
YEAH!
CAN YOU BELIEVE IT?!
HE TURNED DOWN A BIRTHDAY GIFT FROM ANOTHER GIRL....
SO, I ASSUMED HE DID THAT FOR ME ...
MAYBE HE DOESN'T LOVE HER!
TO SELF:
PHEW!
I WONDER WHAT HAPPENED? I WAS SO SURE THAT HE--
HUH !?

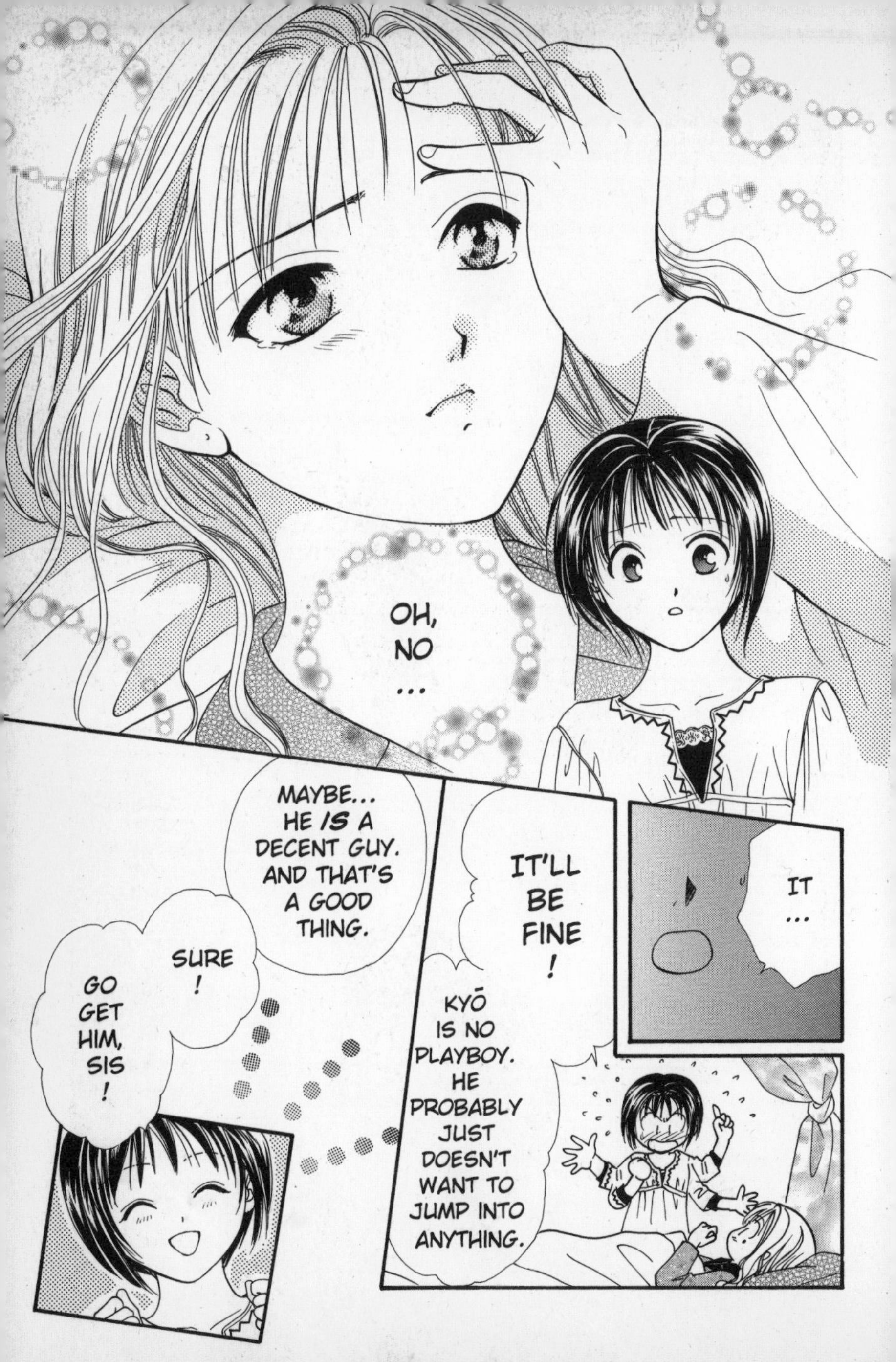
OH, NO ...
IT ...
IT'LL BE FINE!
KYŌ IS NO PLAYBOY. HE PROBABLY JUST DOESN'T WANT TO JUMP INTO ANYTHING.
MAYBE... HE *IS* A DECENT GUY. AND THAT'S A GOOD THING.
SURE!
GO GET HIM, SIS!

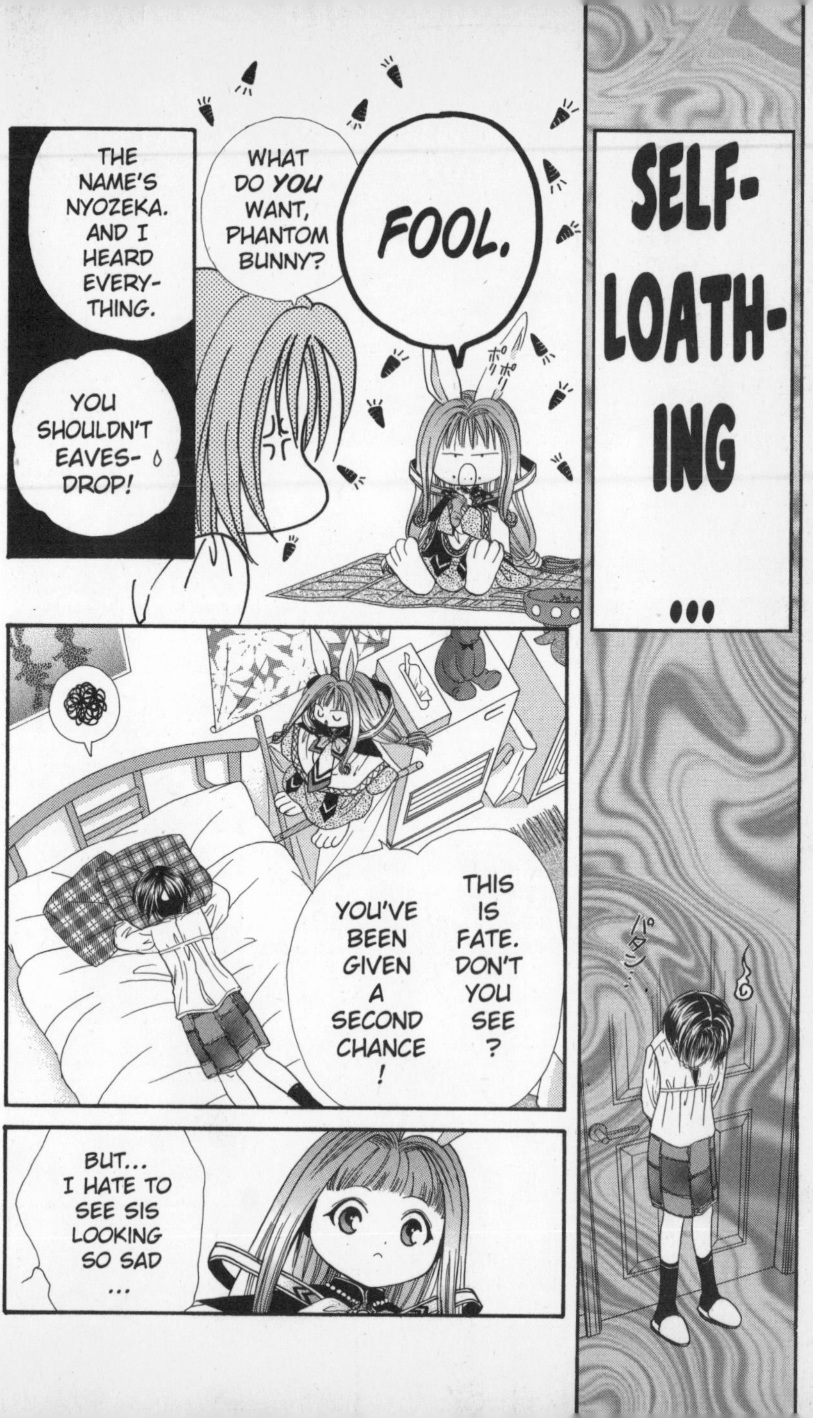
SELF-LOATHING...
FOOL.
WHAT DO *YOU* WANT, PHANTOM BUNNY?
THE NAME'S NYOZEKA. AND I HEARD EVERYTHING.
YOU SHOULDN'T EAVESDROP!
THIS IS FATE. DON'T YOU SEE?
YOU'VE BEEN GIVEN A SECOND CHANCE!
BUT... I HATE TO SEE SIS LOOKING SO SAD...

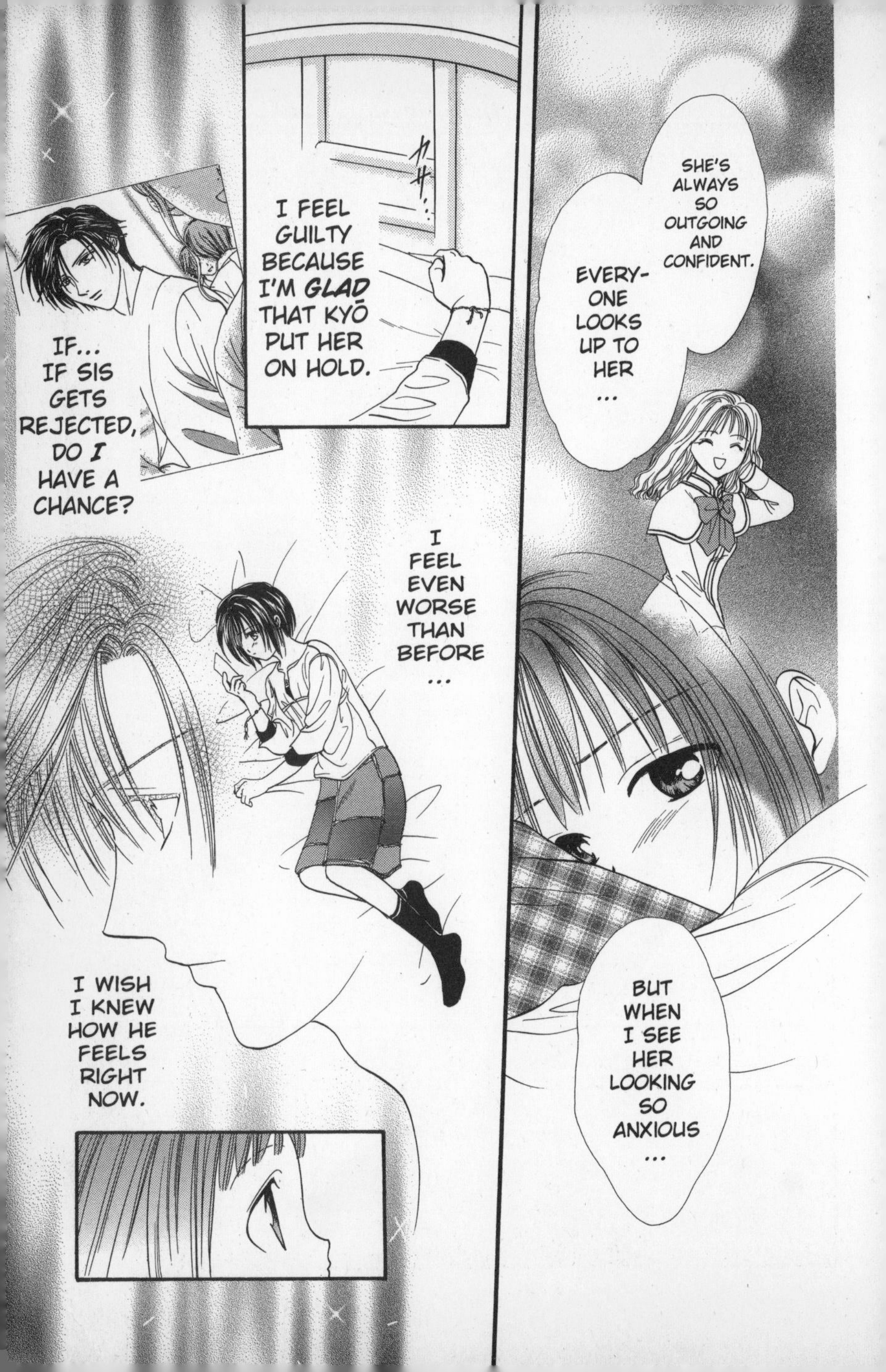
SHE'S ALWAYS SO OUTGOING AND CONFIDENT.
EVERY-ONE LOOKS UP TO HER ...
BUT WHEN I SEE HER LOOKING SO ANXIOUS ...
I FEEL GUILTY BECAUSE I'M GLAD THAT KYŌ PUT HER ON HOLD.
IF... IF SIS GETS REJECTED, DO I HAVE A CHANCE?
I FEEL EVEN WORSE THAN BEFORE ...
I WISH I KNEW HOW HE FEELS RIGHT NOW.

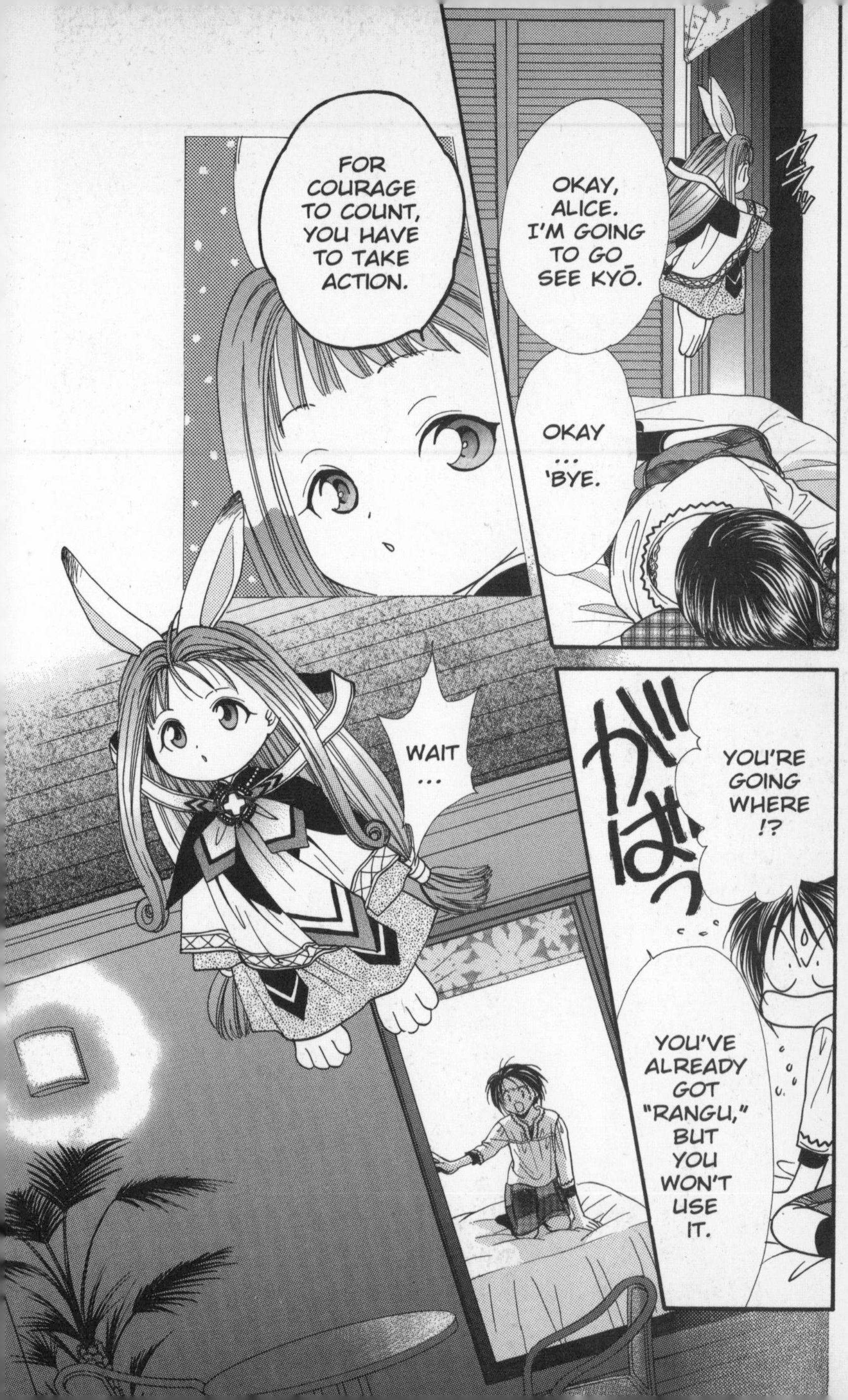
OKAY, ALICE. I'M GOING TO GO SEE KYŌ.
OKAY ... 'BYE.
FOR COURAGE TO COUNT, YOU HAVE TO TAKE ACTION.
がばっ
YOU'RE GOING WHERE !?
YOU'VE ALREADY GOT "RANGU," BUT YOU WON'T USE IT.
WAIT ...

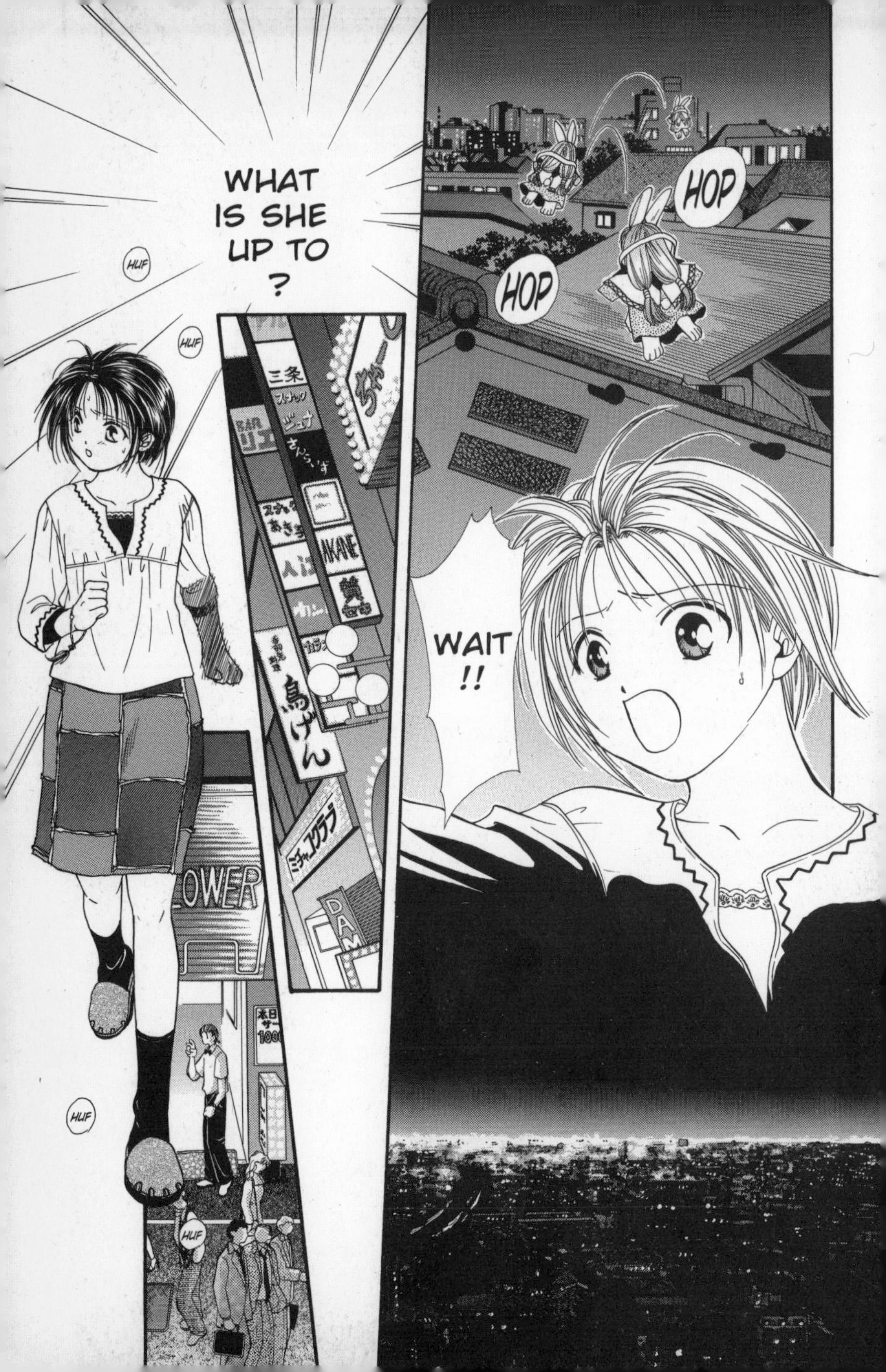
HOP
HOP
WAIT !!
WHAT IS SHE UP TO ?
HUF
HUF
HUF
HUF

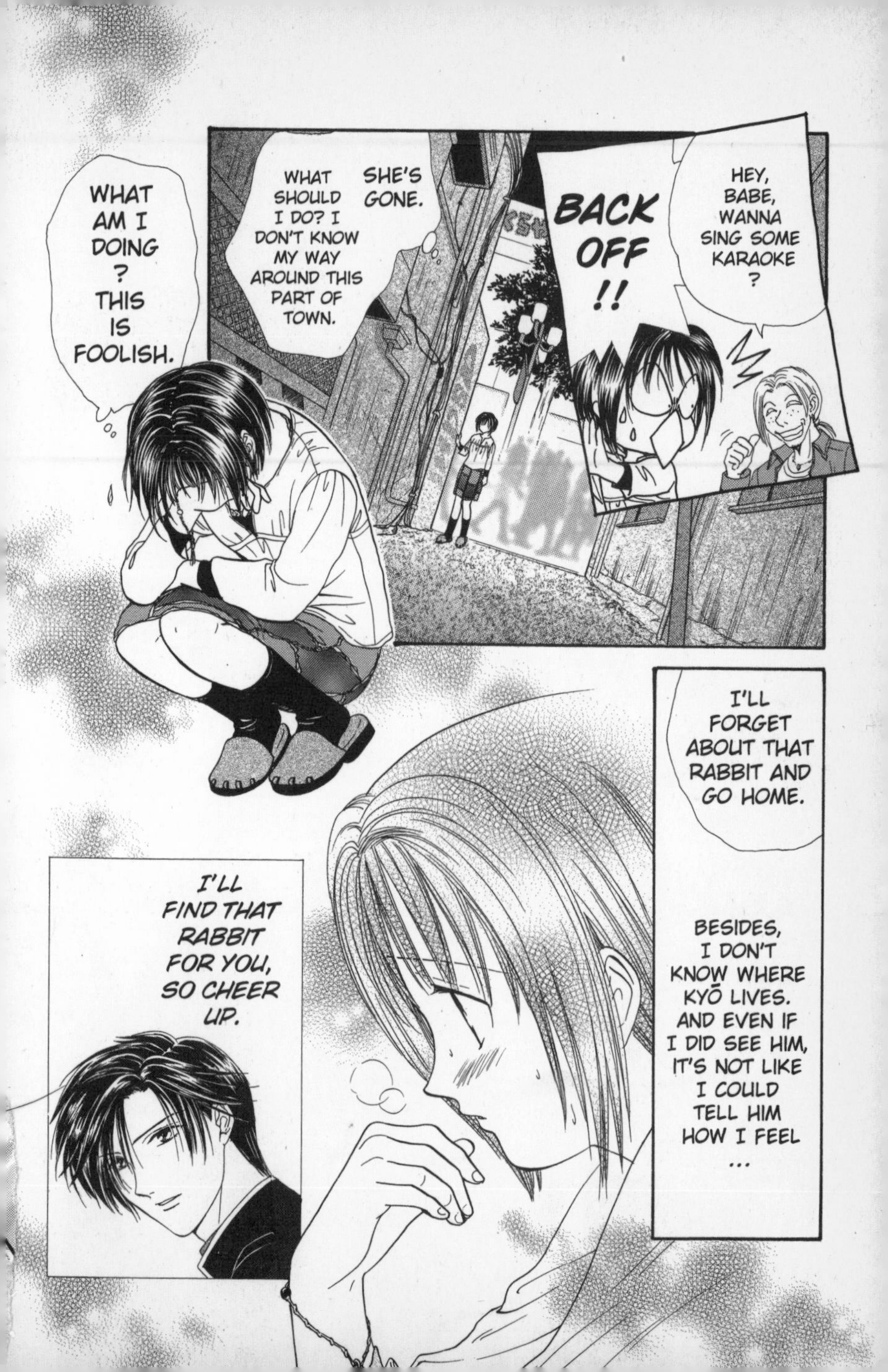
HEY, BABE, WANNA SING SOME KARAOKE?
BACK OFF!!
SHE'S GONE.
WHAT SHOULD I DO? I DON'T KNOW MY WAY AROUND THIS PART OF TOWN.
WHAT AM I DOING? THIS IS FOOLISH.
I'LL FORGET ABOUT THAT RABBIT AND GO HOME.
BESIDES, I DON'T KNOW WHERE KYŌ LIVES. AND EVEN IF I DID SEE HIM, IT'S NOT LIKE I COULD TELL HIM HOW I FEEL...
I'LL FIND THAT RABBIT FOR YOU, SO CHEER UP.

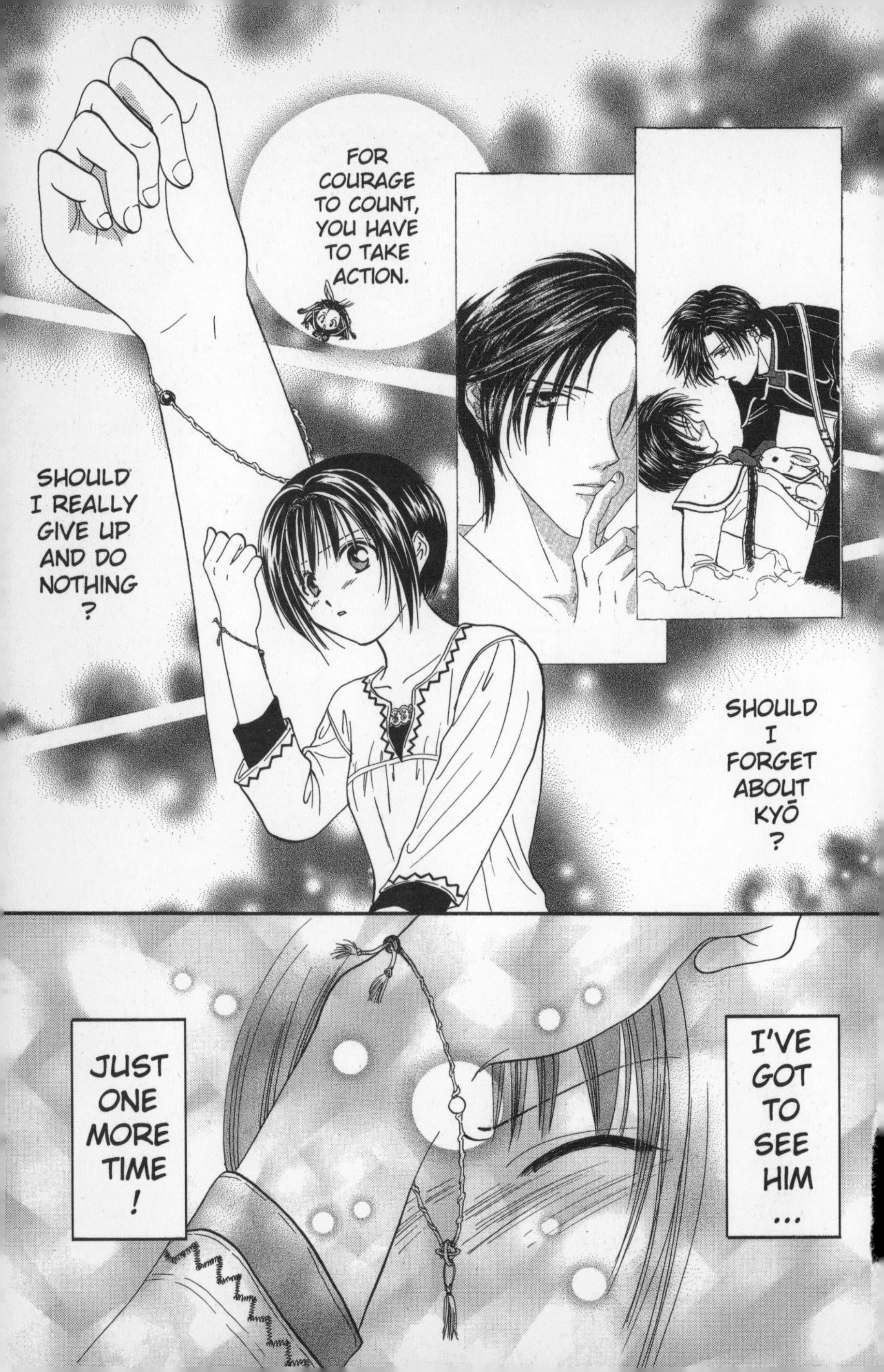
FOR COURAGE TO COUNT, YOU HAVE TO TAKE ACTION.
SHOULD I REALLY GIVE UP AND DO NOTHING?
SHOULD I FORGET ABOUT KYŌ?
I'VE GOT TO SEE HIM...
JUST ONE MORE TIME!

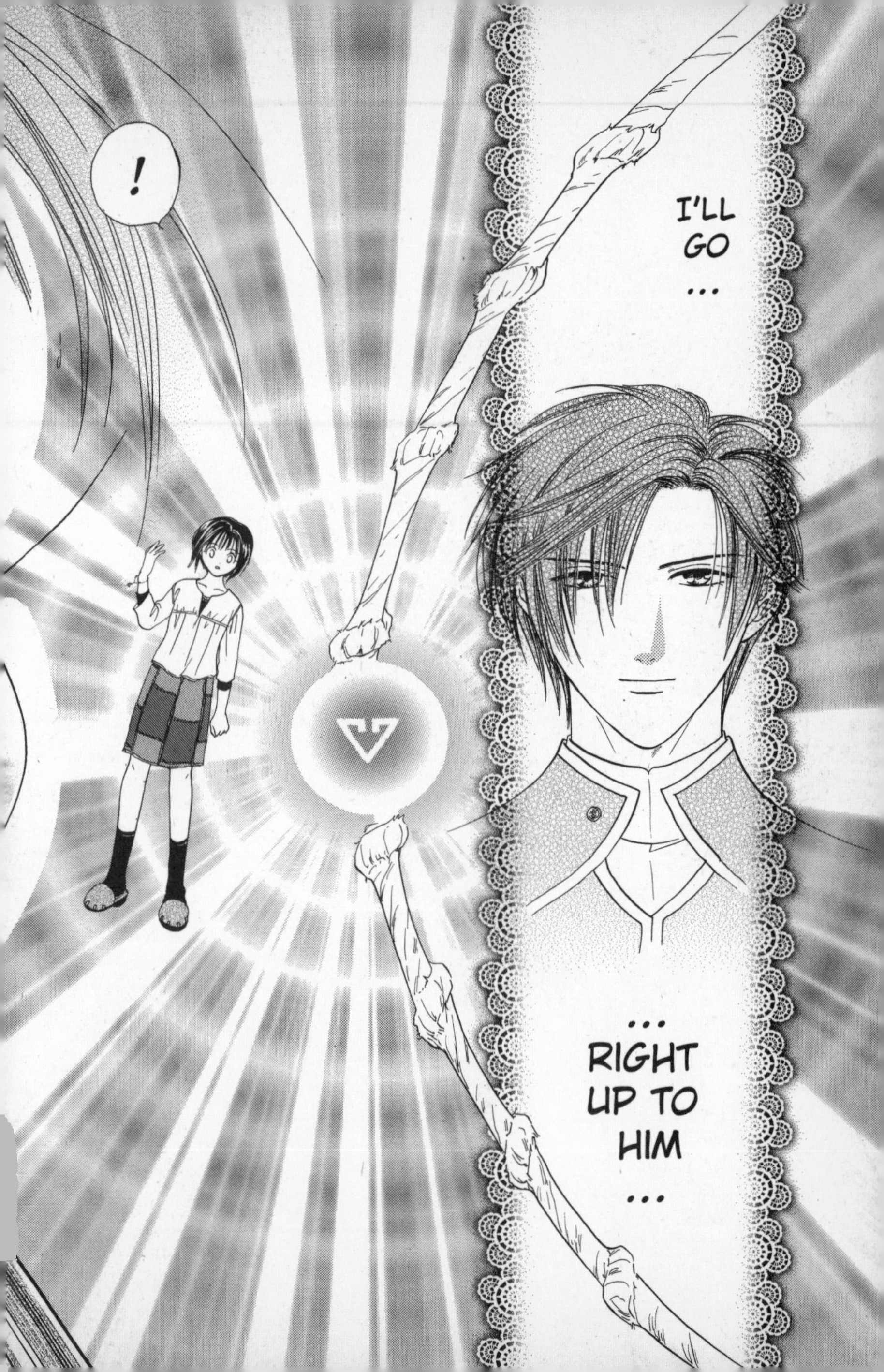
I'LL GO ...
... RIGHT UP TO HIM ...
!

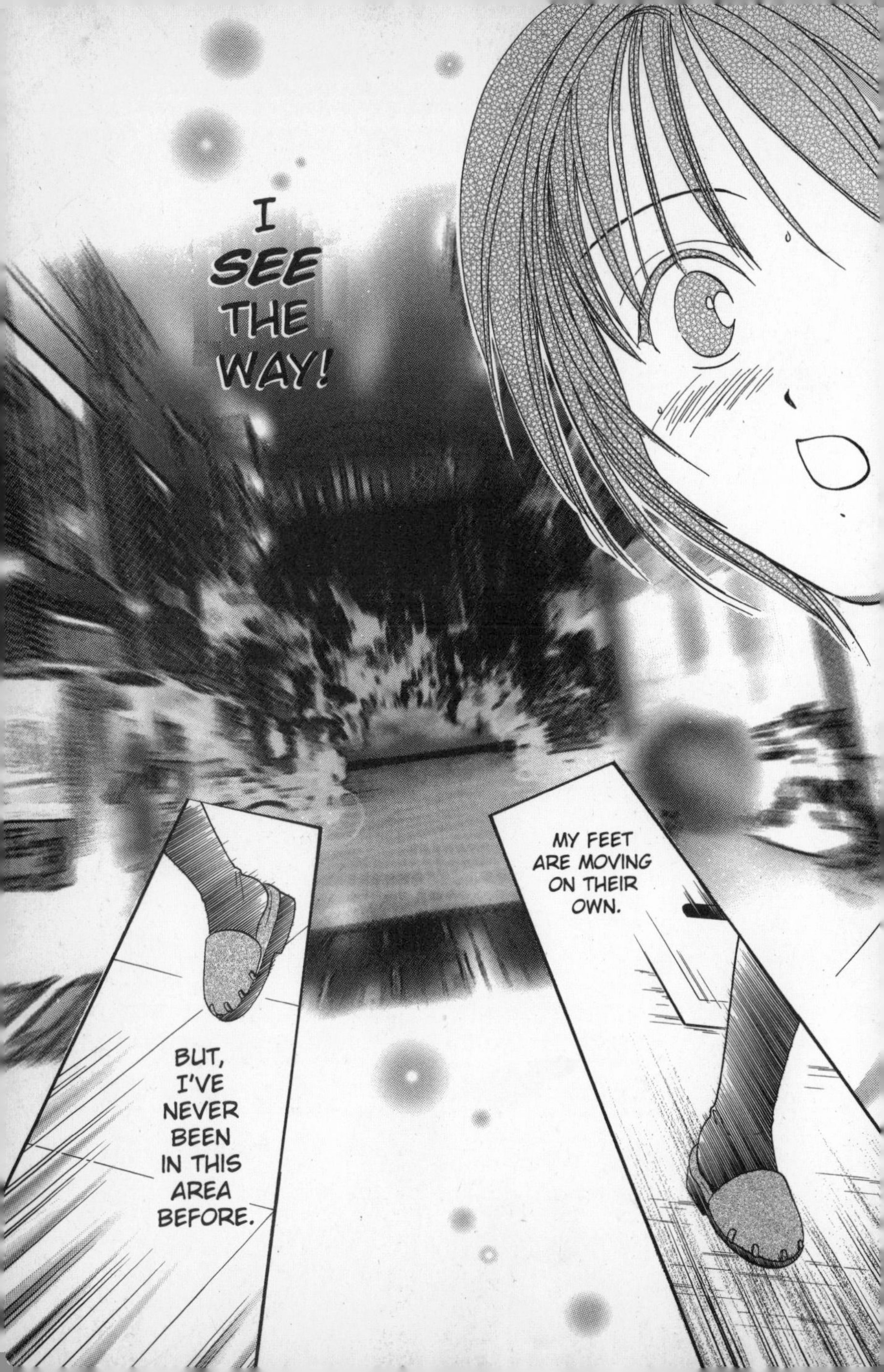
I SEE THE WAY!
MY FEET ARE MOVING ON THEIR OWN.
BUT, I'VE NEVER BEEN IN THIS AREA BEFORE.

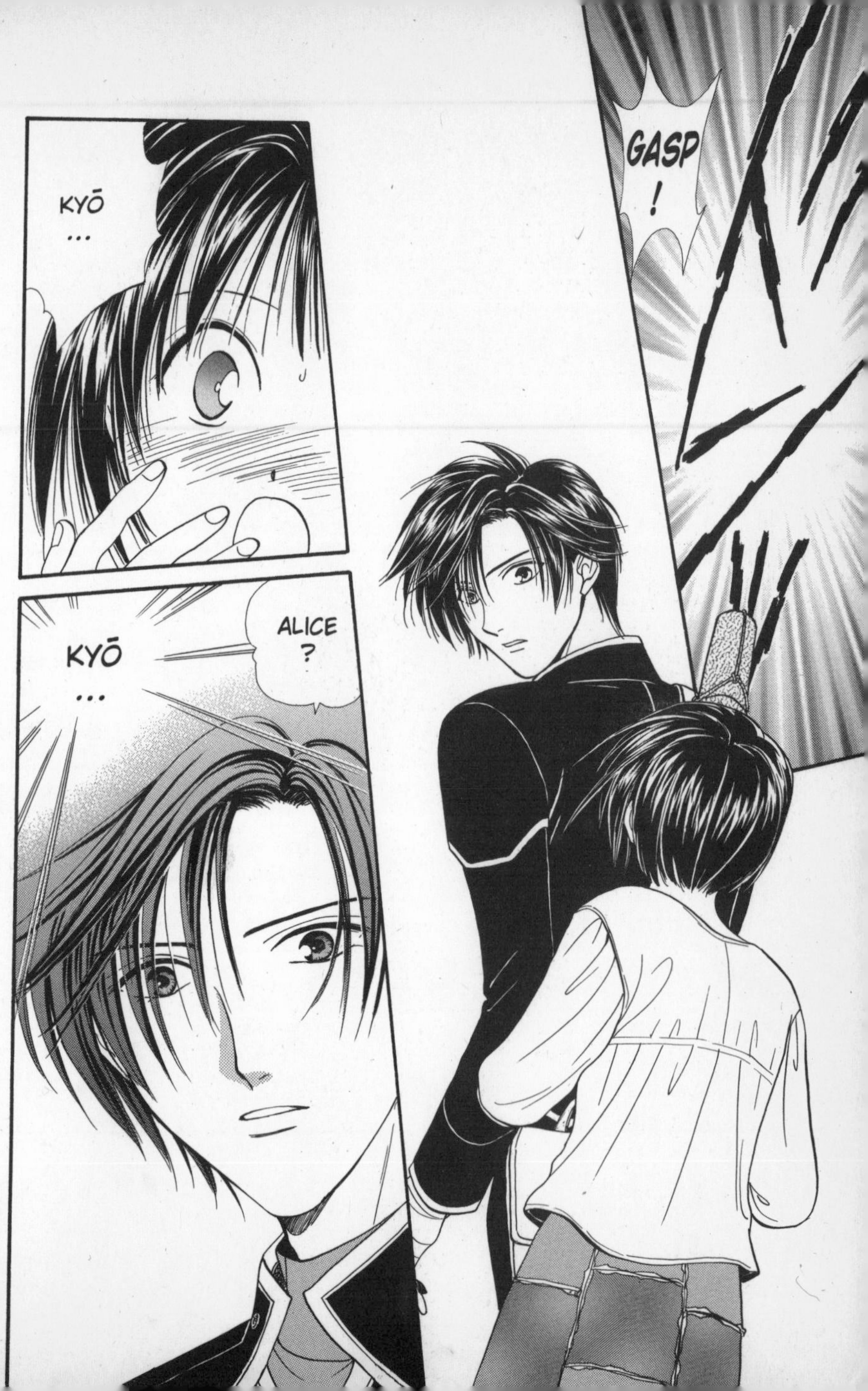
GASP!
KYŌ...
ALICE?
KYŌ...

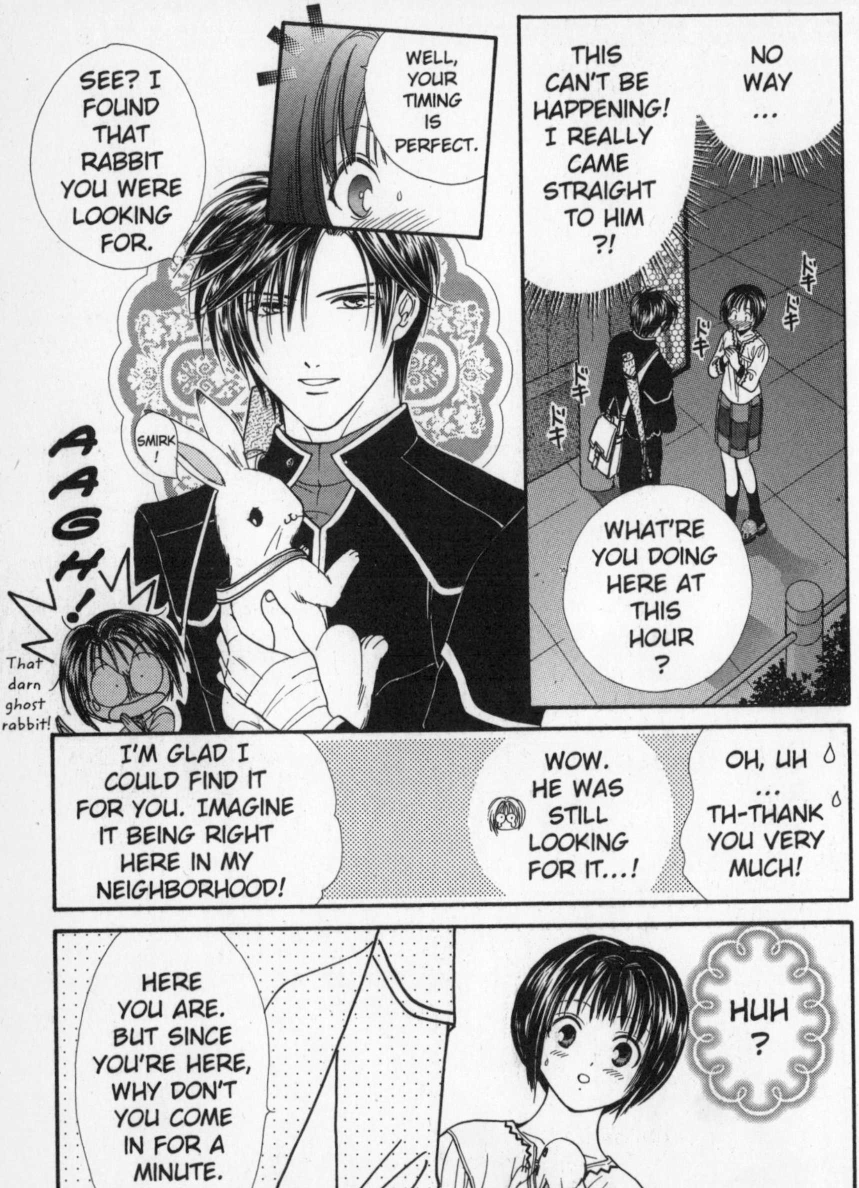
NO WAY ...
THIS CAN'T BE HAPPENING! I REALLY CAME STRAIGHT TO HIM ?!
WHAT'RE YOU DOING HERE AT THIS HOUR ?
WELL, YOUR TIMING IS PERFECT.
SEE? I FOUND THAT RABBIT YOU WERE LOOKING FOR.
SMIRK !
AAGH!
That darn ghost rabbit!
OH, UH ... TH-THANK YOU VERY MUCH!
WOW. HE WAS STILL LOOKING FOR IT...!
I'M GLAD I COULD FIND IT FOR YOU. IMAGINE IT BEING RIGHT HERE IN MY NEIGHBORHOOD!
HUH ?
HERE YOU ARE. BUT SINCE YOU'RE HERE, WHY DON'T YOU COME IN FOR A MINUTE.

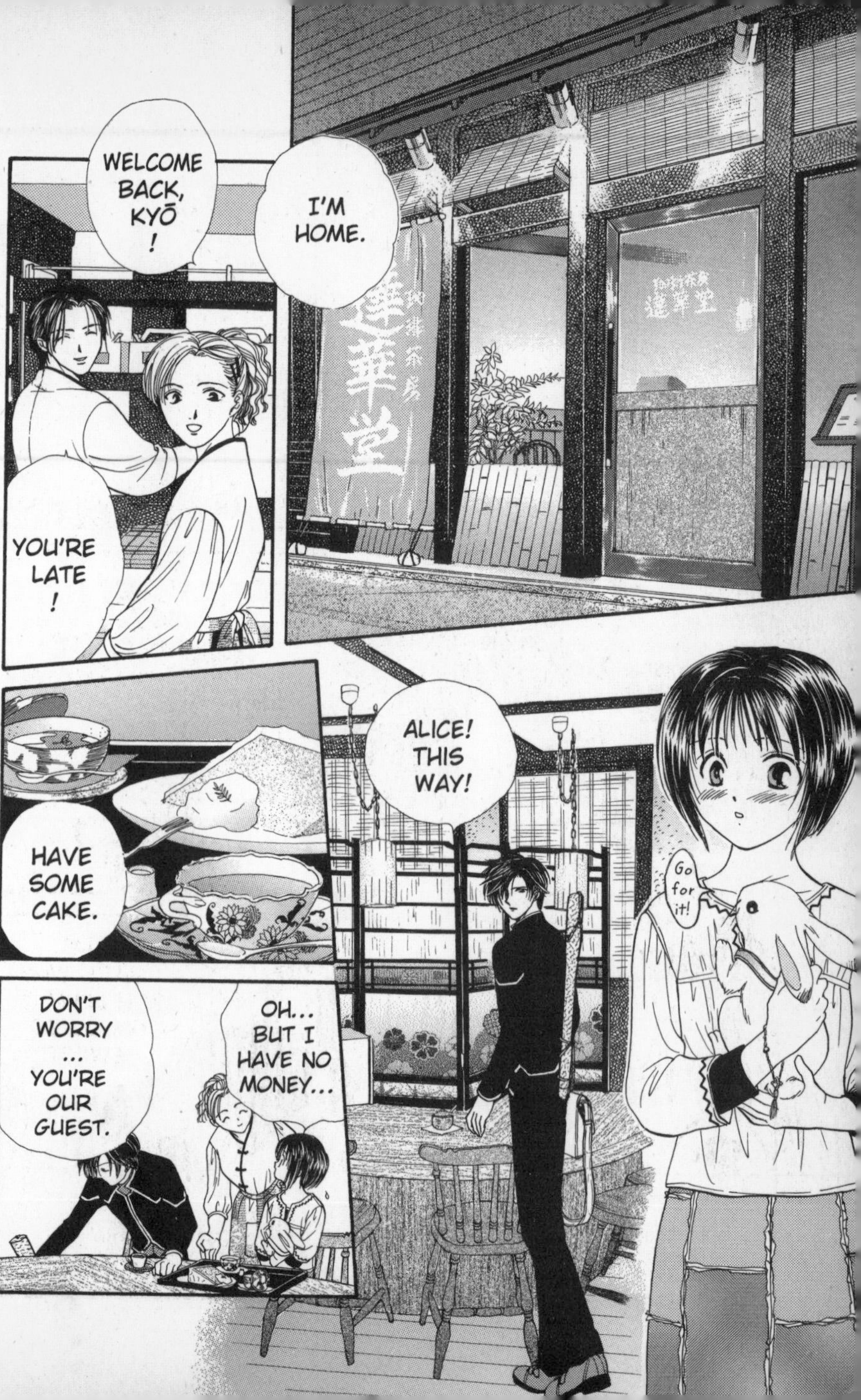
I'M HOME.
WELCOME BACK, KYŌ!
YOU'RE LATE!
ALICE! THIS WAY!
Go for it!
HAVE SOME CAKE.
OH... BUT I HAVE NO MONEY...
DON'T WORRY ... YOU'RE OUR GUEST.

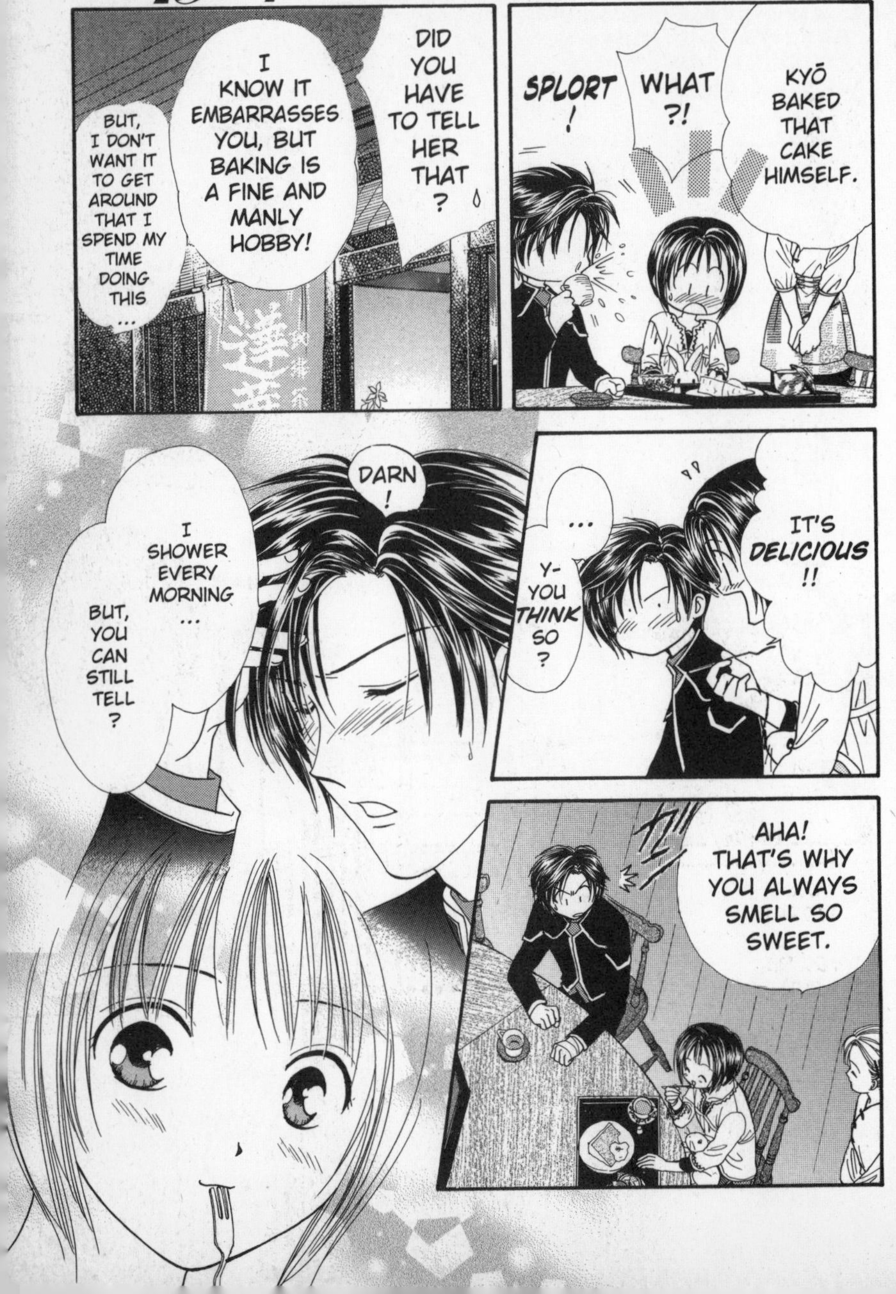
KYŌ BAKED THAT CAKE HIMSELF.
WHAT?!
SPLORT!
DID YOU HAVE TO TELL HER THAT?
I KNOW IT EMBARRASSES YOU, BUT BAKING IS A FINE AND MANLY HOBBY!
BUT, I DON'T WANT IT TO GET AROUND THAT I SPEND MY TIME DOING THIS...
IT'S DELICIOUS!!
...
Y-YOU THINK SO?
AHA! THAT'S WHY YOU ALWAYS SMELL SO SWEET.
DARN!
I SHOWER EVERY MORNING...
BUT, YOU CAN STILL TELL?

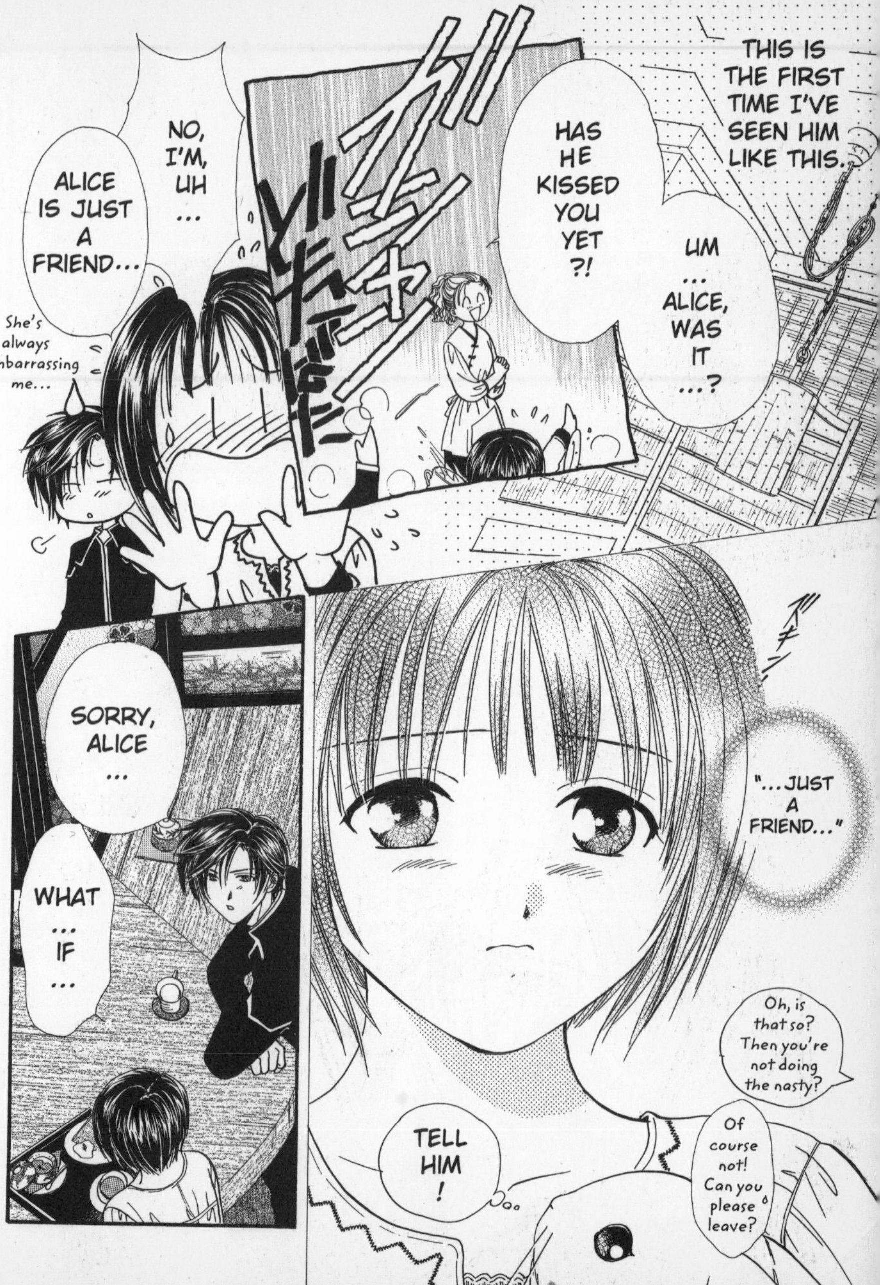
THIS IS THE FIRST TIME I'VE SEEN HIM LIKE THIS.
UM ... ALICE, WAS IT ...?
HAS HE KISSED YOU YET ?!
NO, I'M, UH ...
ALICE IS JUST A FRIEND...
She's always embarrassing me...
"...JUST A FRIEND..."
Oh, is that so? Then you're not doing the nasty?
Of course not! Can you please leave?
TELL HIM!
SORRY, ALICE ...
WHAT ... IF ...

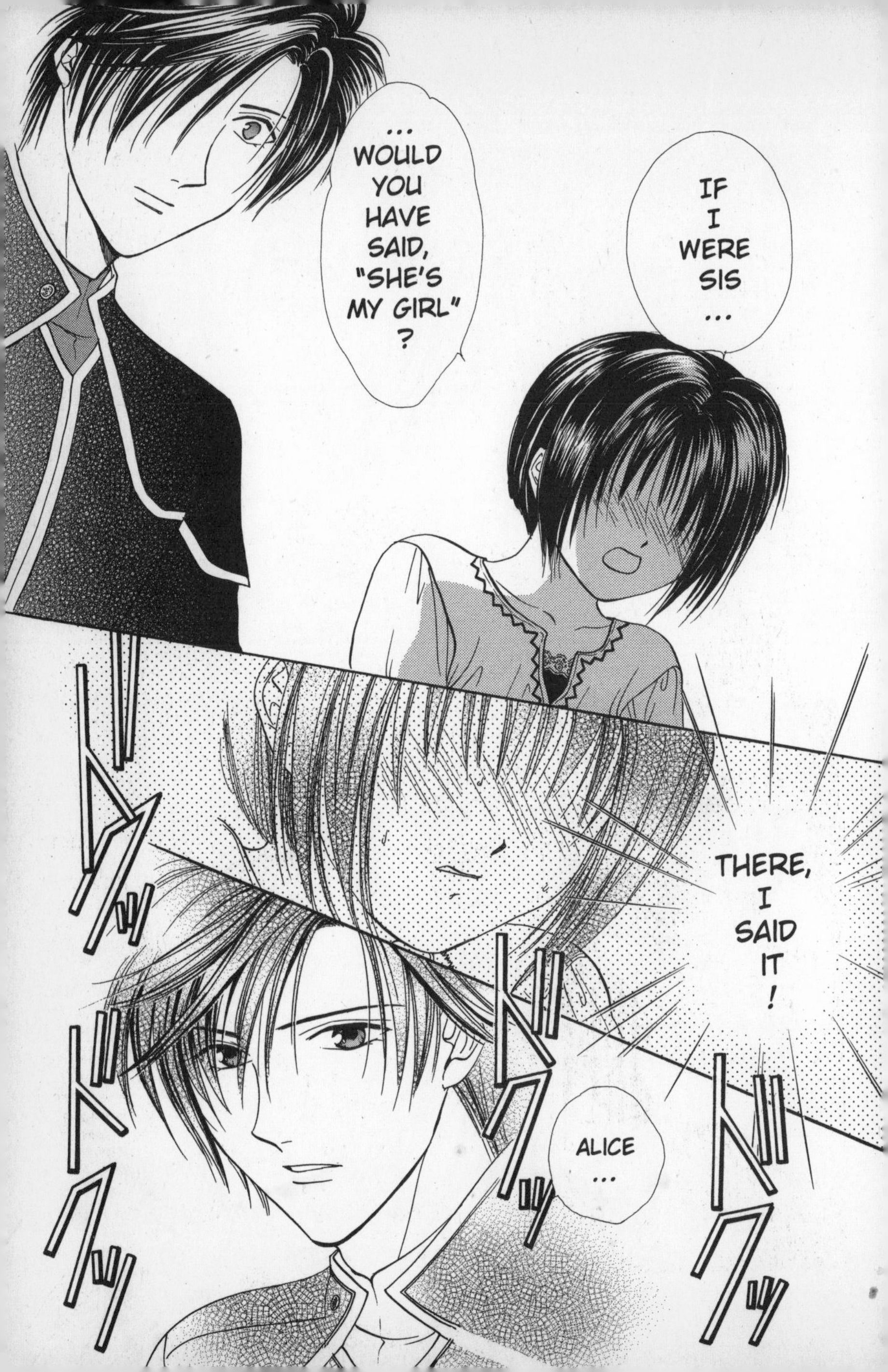
IF I WERE SIS ...
... WOULD YOU HAVE SAID, "SHE'S MY GIRL" ?
THERE, I SAID IT !
ALICE ...

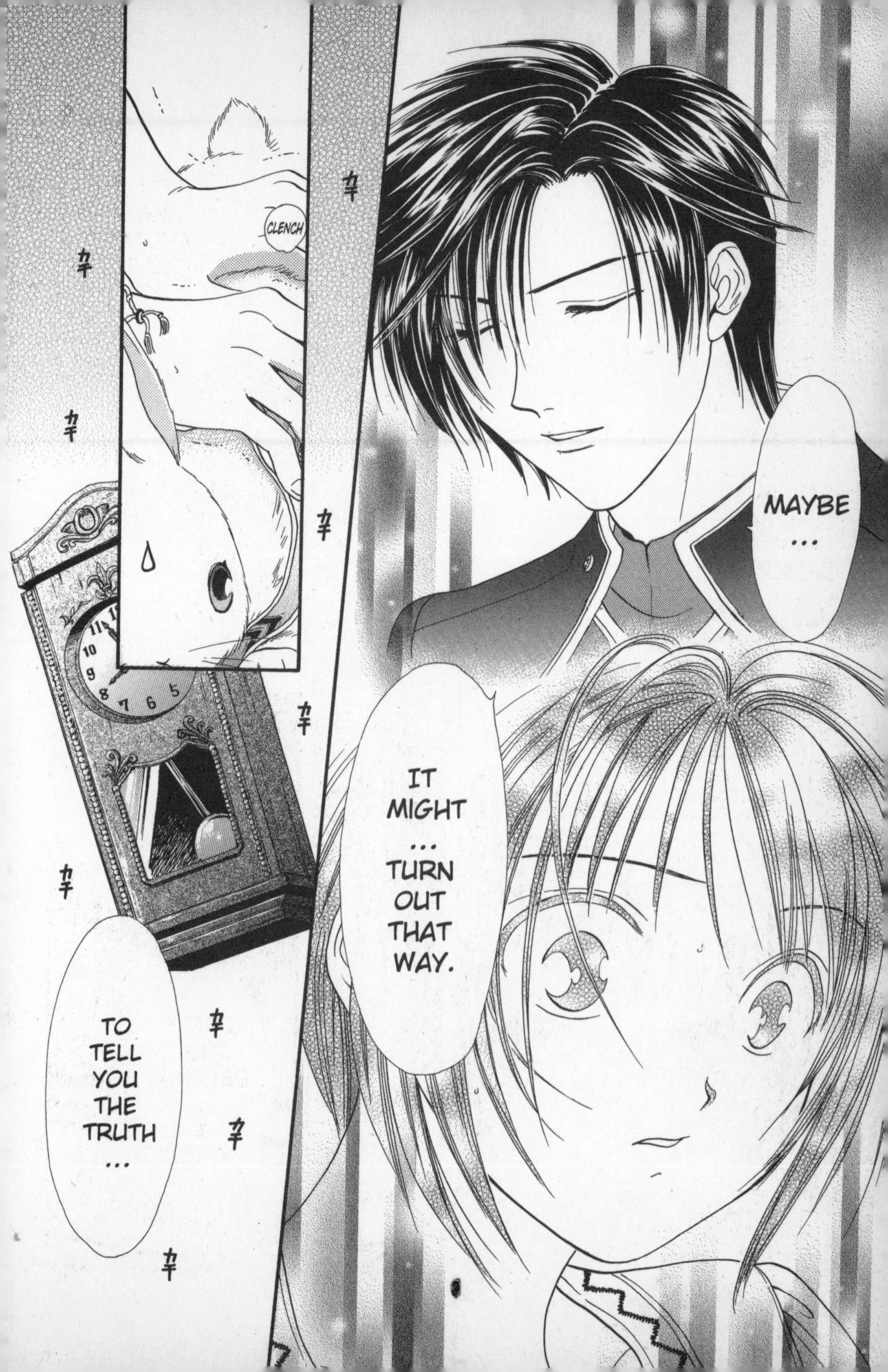
MAYBE ...
IT MIGHT ... TURN OUT THAT WAY.
CLENCH
TO TELL YOU THE TRUTH ...

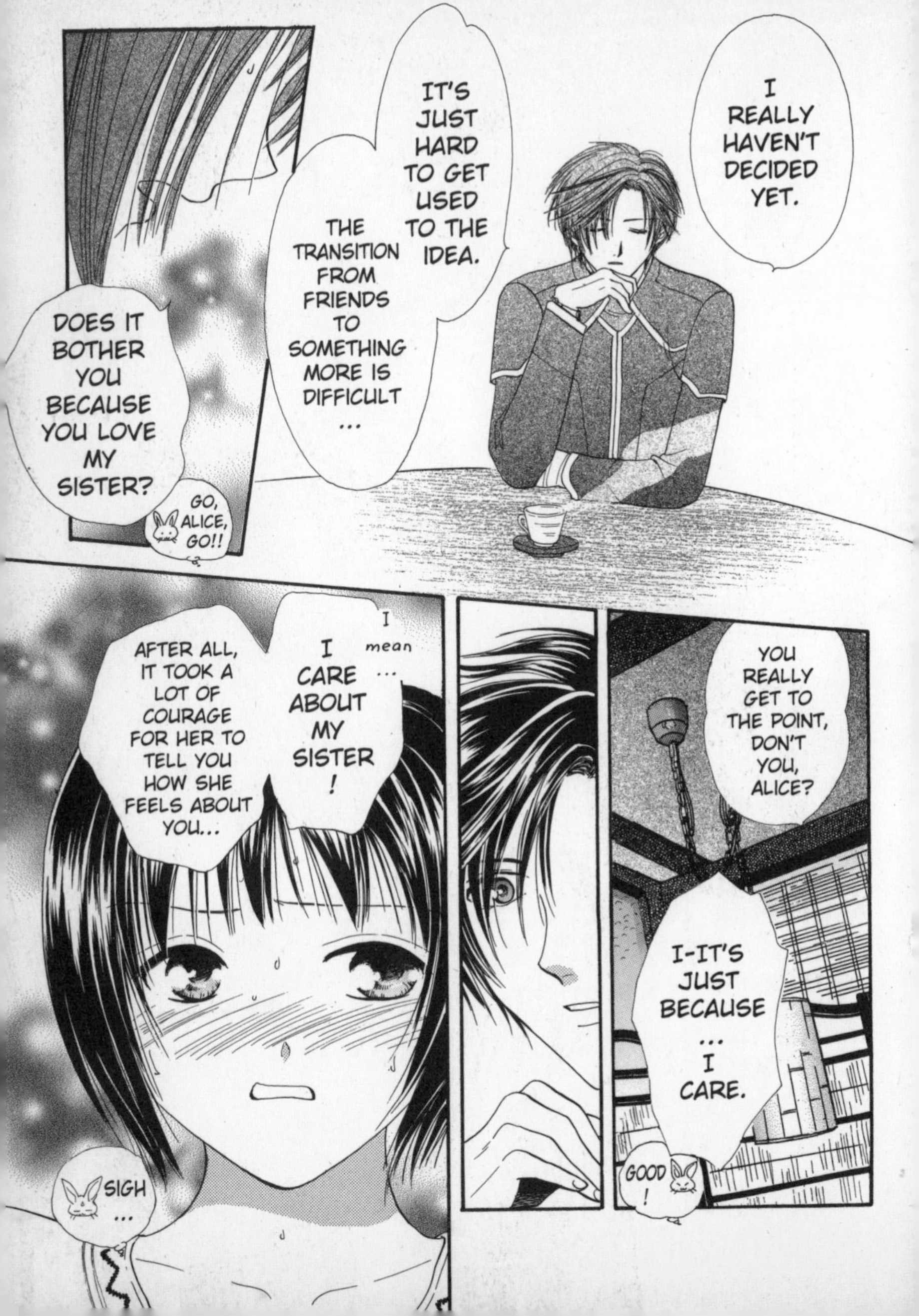
I REALLY HAVEN'T DECIDED YET.
IT'S JUST HARD TO GET USED TO THE IDEA.
THE TRANSITION FROM FRIENDS TO SOMETHING MORE IS DIFFICULT...
DOES IT BOTHER YOU BECAUSE YOU LOVE MY SISTER?
GO, ALICE, GO!!
YOU REALLY GET TO THE POINT, DON'T YOU, ALICE?
I-IT'S JUST BECAUSE... I CARE.
GOOD!
I mean...
I CARE ABOUT MY SISTER!
AFTER ALL, IT TOOK A LOT OF COURAGE FOR HER TO TELL YOU HOW SHE FEELS ABOUT YOU...
SIGH...

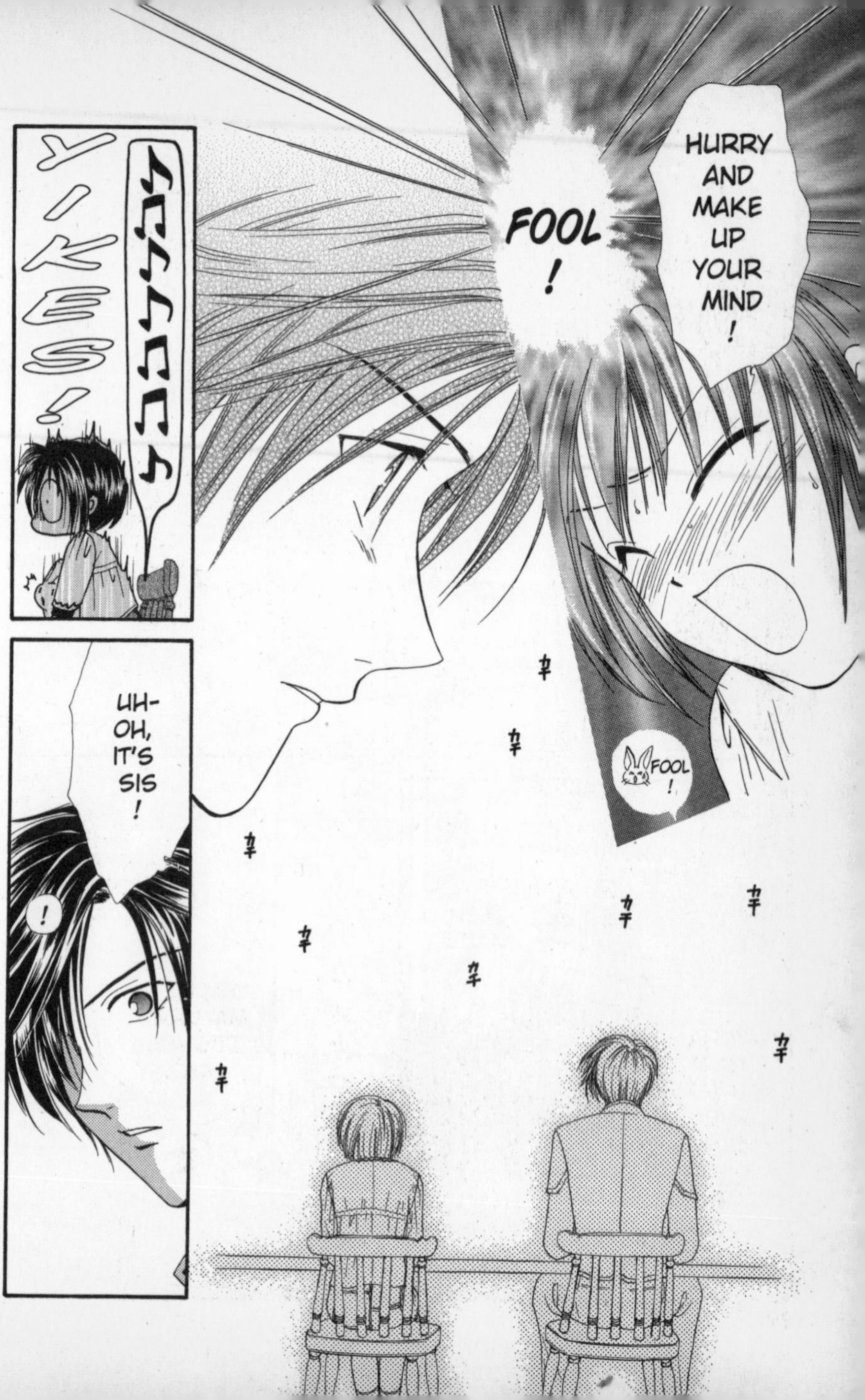
HURRY AND MAKE UP YOUR MIND!
FOOL!
FOOL!
YIKES!
UH-OH, IT'S SIS!

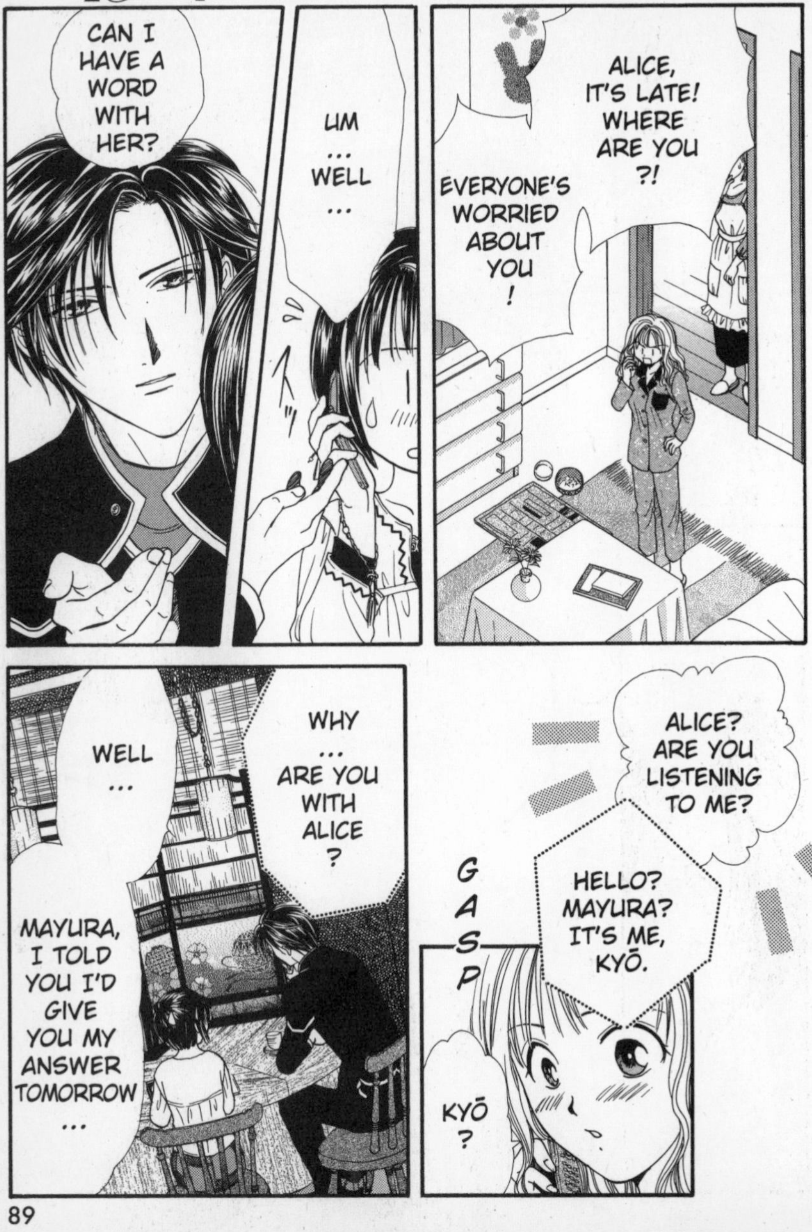
ALICE, IT'S LATE! WHERE ARE YOU ?!
EVERYONE'S WORRIED ABOUT YOU !
UM ... WELL ...
CAN I HAVE A WORD WITH HER?
ALICE? ARE YOU LISTENING TO ME?
HELLO? MAYURA? IT'S ME, KYŌ.
GASP
KYŌ ?
WHY ... ARE YOU WITH ALICE ?
WELL ...
MAYURA, I TOLD YOU I'D GIVE YOU MY ANSWER TOMORROW ...

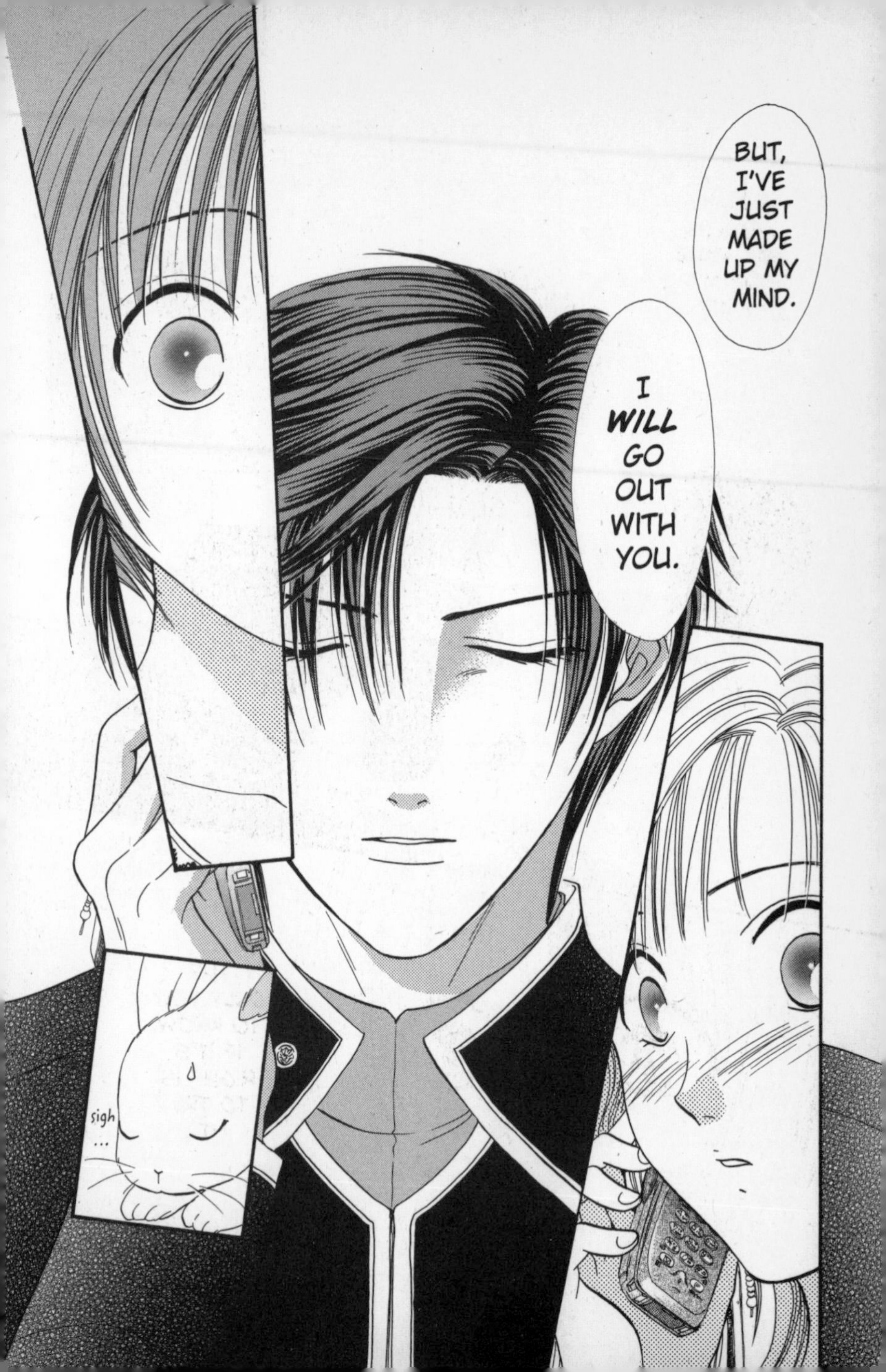
BUT, I'VE JUST MADE UP MY MIND.
I *WILL* GO OUT WITH YOU.
sigh ...

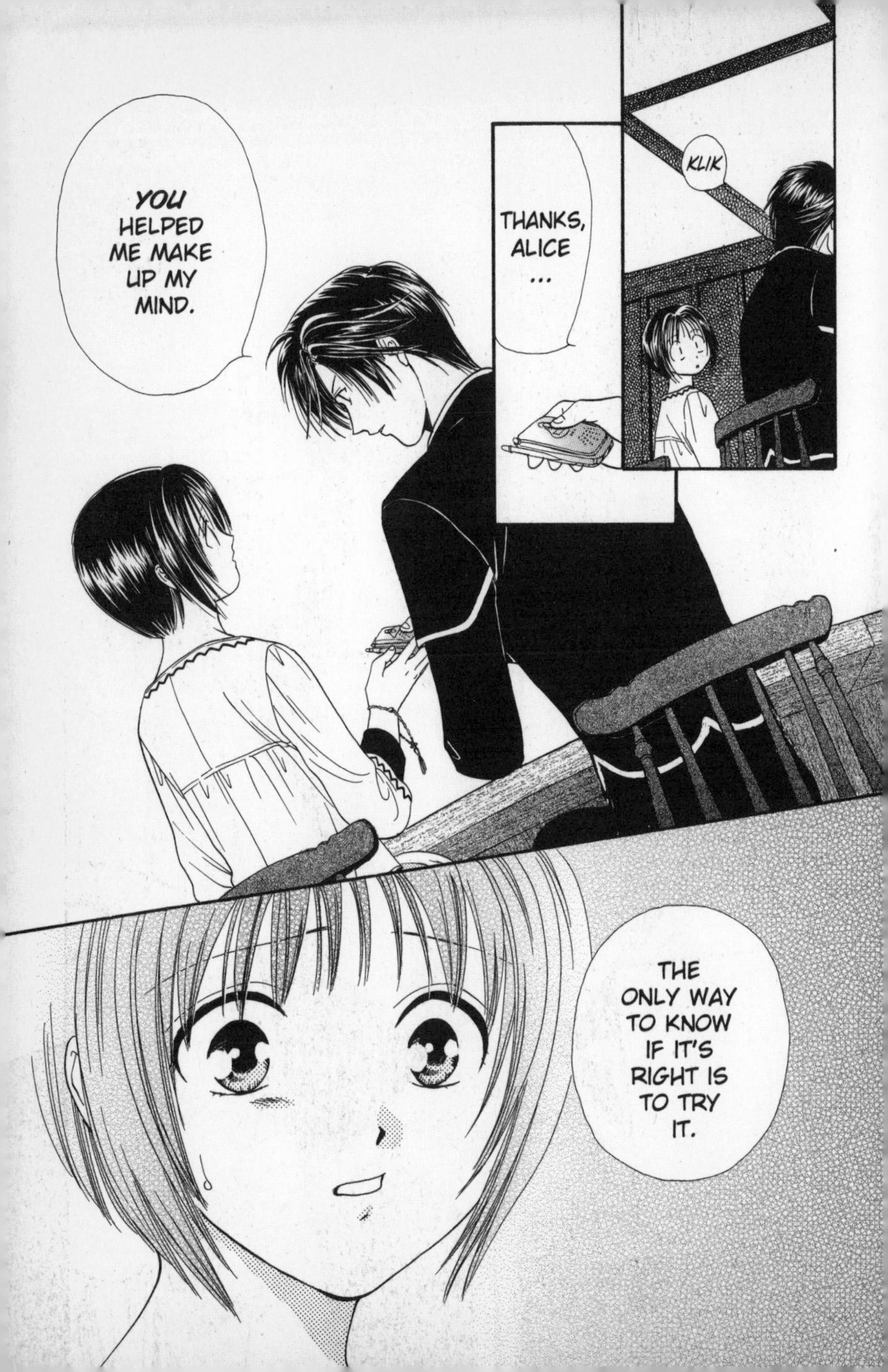
KLIK
THANKS, ALICE ...
YOU HELPED ME MAKE UP MY MIND.
THE ONLY WAY TO KNOW IF IT'S RIGHT IS TO TRY IT.

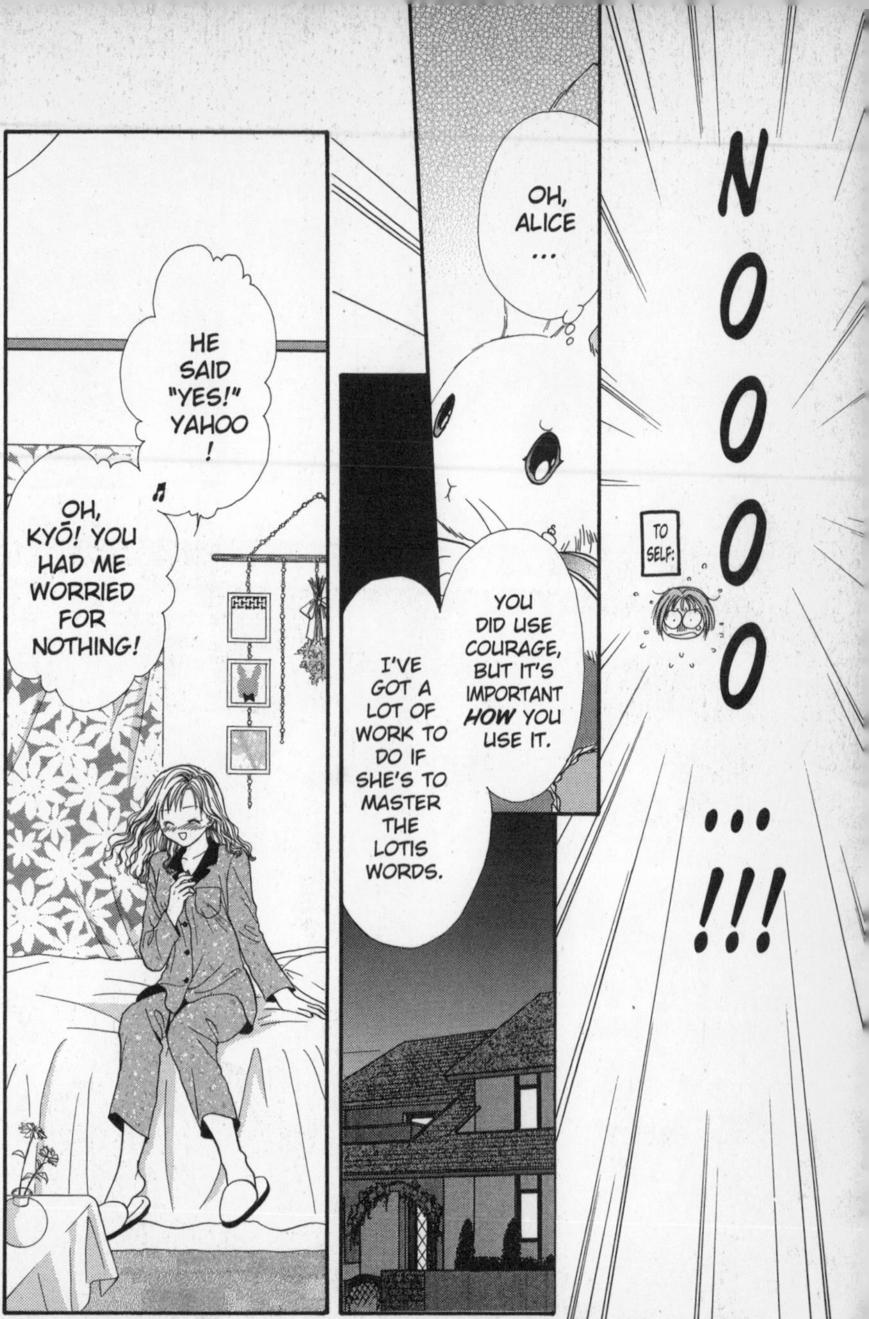
NOOOOO...!!!
TO SELF:
OH, ALICE ...
YOU DID USE COURAGE, BUT IT'S IMPORTANT HOW YOU USE IT.
I'VE GOT A LOT OF WORK TO DO IF SHE'S TO MASTER THE LOTIS WORDS.
HE SAID "YES!" YAHOO!
OH, KYŌ! YOU HAD ME WORRIED FOR NOTHING!

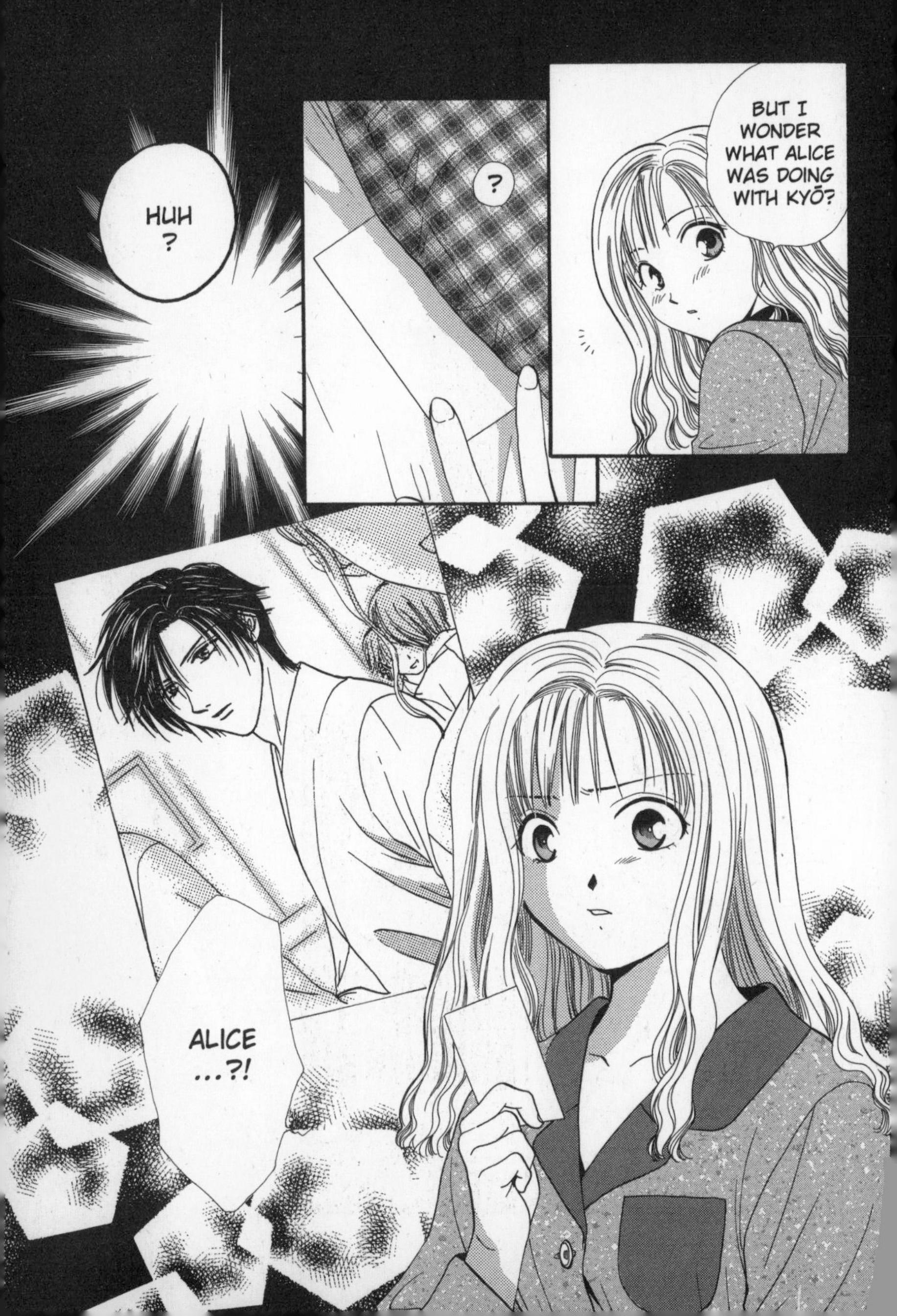
BUT I WONDER WHAT ALICE WAS DOING WITH KYŌ?
?
HUH ?
ALICE ...?!

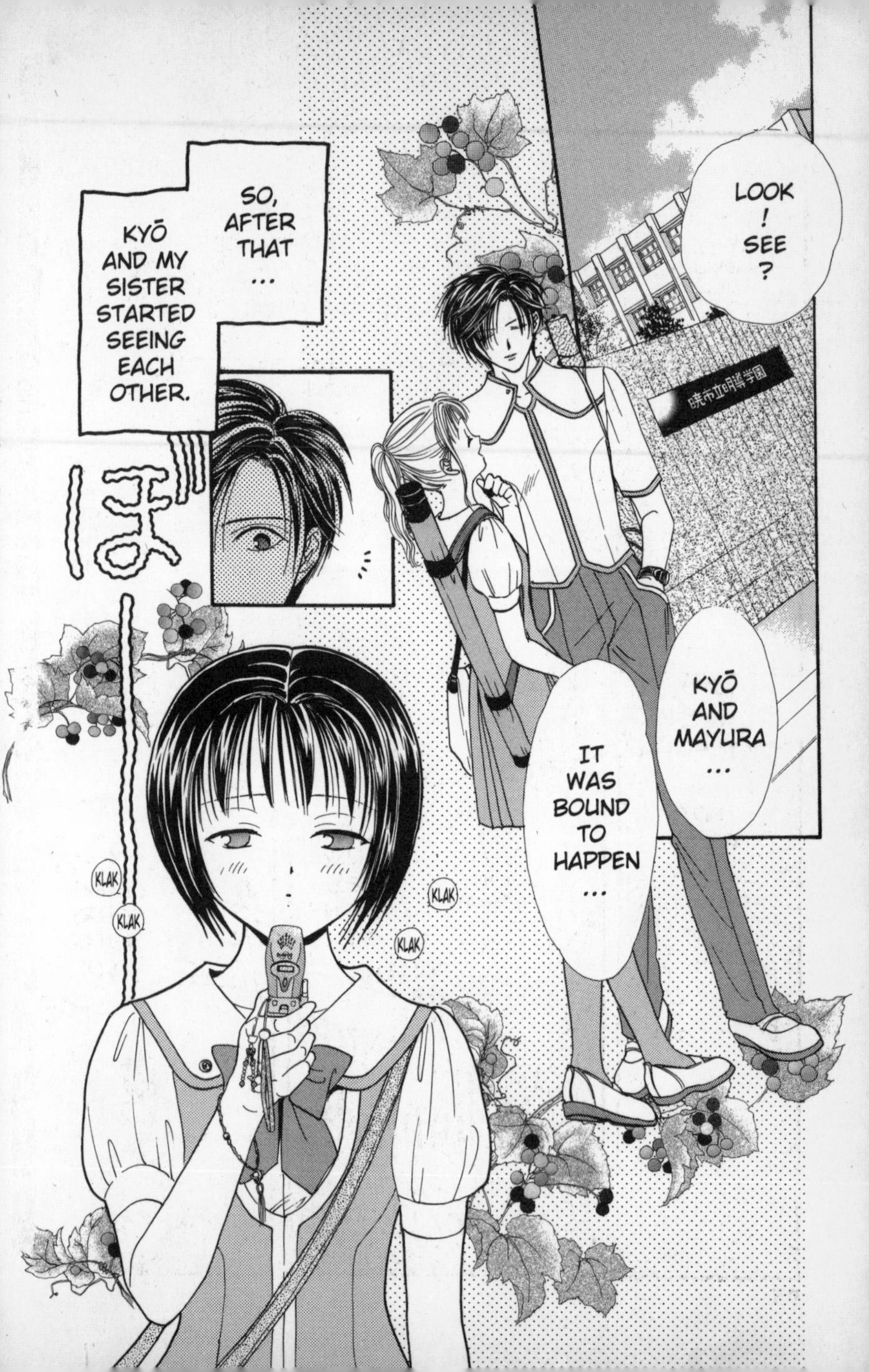

LOOK! SEE?
KYŌ AND MAYURA...
IT WAS BOUND TO HAPPEN...
SO, AFTER THAT...
KYŌ AND MY SISTER STARTED SEEING EACH OTHER.
...
KLAK
KLAK
KLAK
KLAK

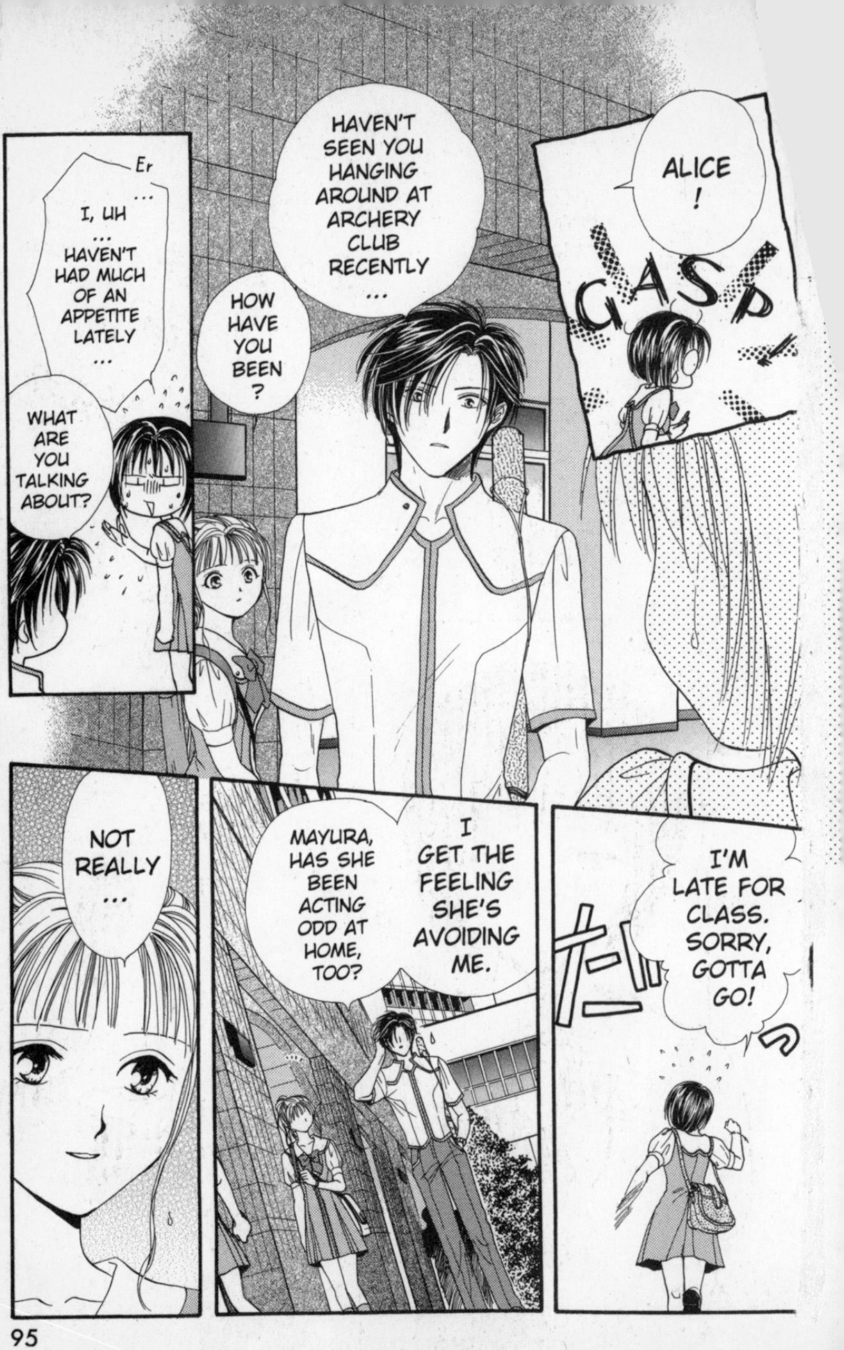
ALICE!
GASP!
HAVEN'T SEEN YOU HANGING AROUND AT ARCHERY CLUB RECENTLY ...
HOW HAVE YOU BEEN?
Er ... I, uh ... HAVEN'T HAD MUCH OF AN APPETITE LATELY ...
WHAT ARE YOU TALKING ABOUT?
I'M LATE FOR CLASS. SORRY, GOTTA GO!
I GET THE FEELING SHE'S AVOIDING ME.
MAYURA, HAS SHE BEEN ACTING ODD AT HOME, TOO?
NOT REALLY ...

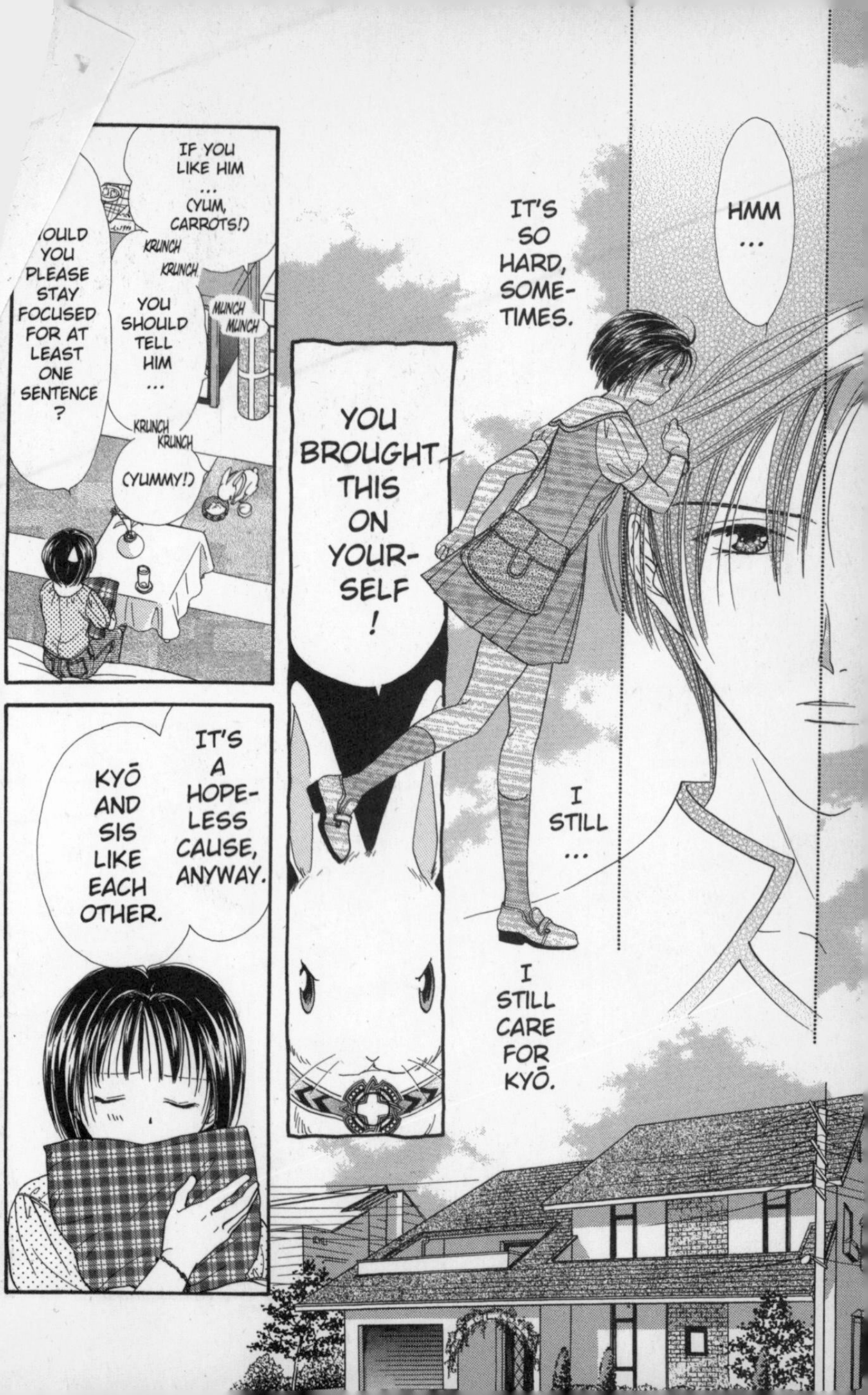
HMM ...
IT'S SO HARD, SOME-TIMES.
I STILL ...
I STILL CARE FOR KYŌ.
YOU BROUGHT THIS ON YOUR-SELF !
IF YOU LIKE HIM ... (YUM, CARROTS!)
KRUNCH KRUNCH
YOU SHOULD TELL HIM ...
MUNCH MUNCH
KRUNCH KRUNCH
(YUMMY!)
HOULD YOU PLEASE STAY FOCUSED FOR AT LEAST ONE SENTENCE ?
IT'S A HOPE-LESS CAUSE, ANYWAY.
KYŌ AND SIS LIKE EACH OTHER.

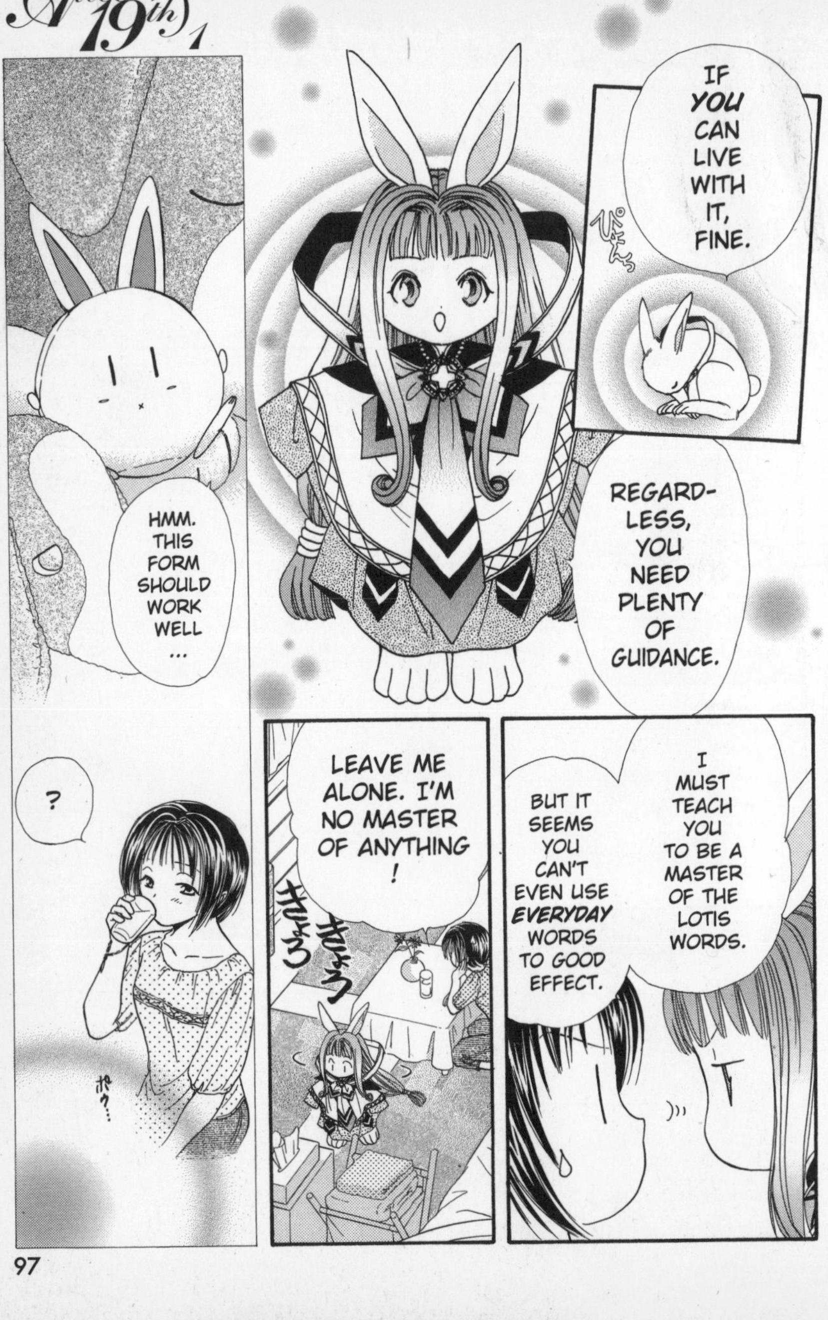
IF *YOU* CAN LIVE WITH IT, FINE.
REGARDLESS, YOU NEED PLENTY OF GUIDANCE.
HMM. THIS FORM SHOULD WORK WELL...
I MUST TEACH YOU TO BE A MASTER OF THE LOTIS WORDS.
BUT IT SEEMS YOU CAN'T EVEN USE *EVERYDAY* WORDS TO GOOD EFFECT.
LEAVE ME ALONE. I'M NO MASTER OF ANYTHING!
きょろ きょろ
?

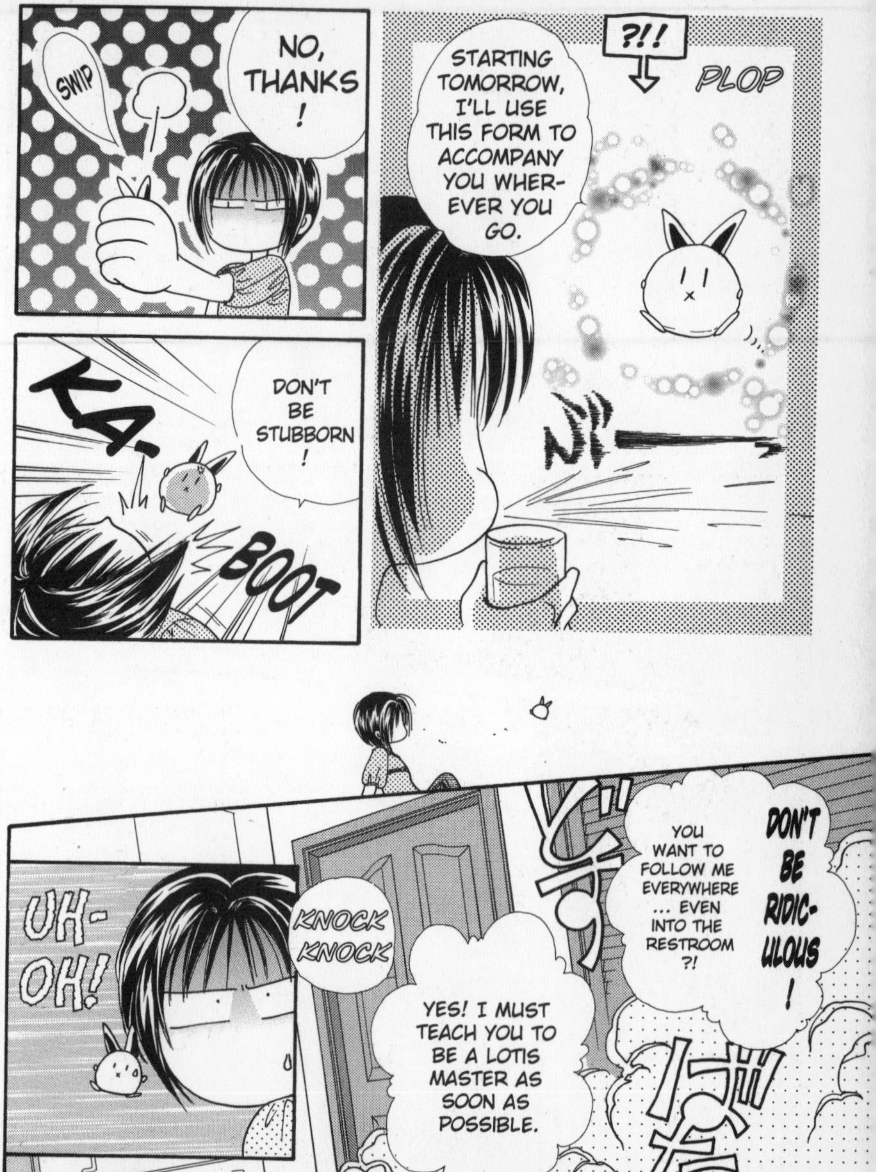
?!!
STARTING TOMORROW, I'LL USE THIS FORM TO ACCOMPANY YOU WHEREVER YOU GO.
PLOP
NO, THANKS!
SWIP
DON'T BE STUBBORN!
KA-
BOOT
DON'T BE RIDICULOUS!
YOU WANT TO FOLLOW ME EVERYWHERE ... EVEN INTO THE RESTROOM?!
YES! I MUST TEACH YOU TO BE A LOTIS MASTER AS SOON AS POSSIBLE.
KNOCK KNOCK
UH-OH!

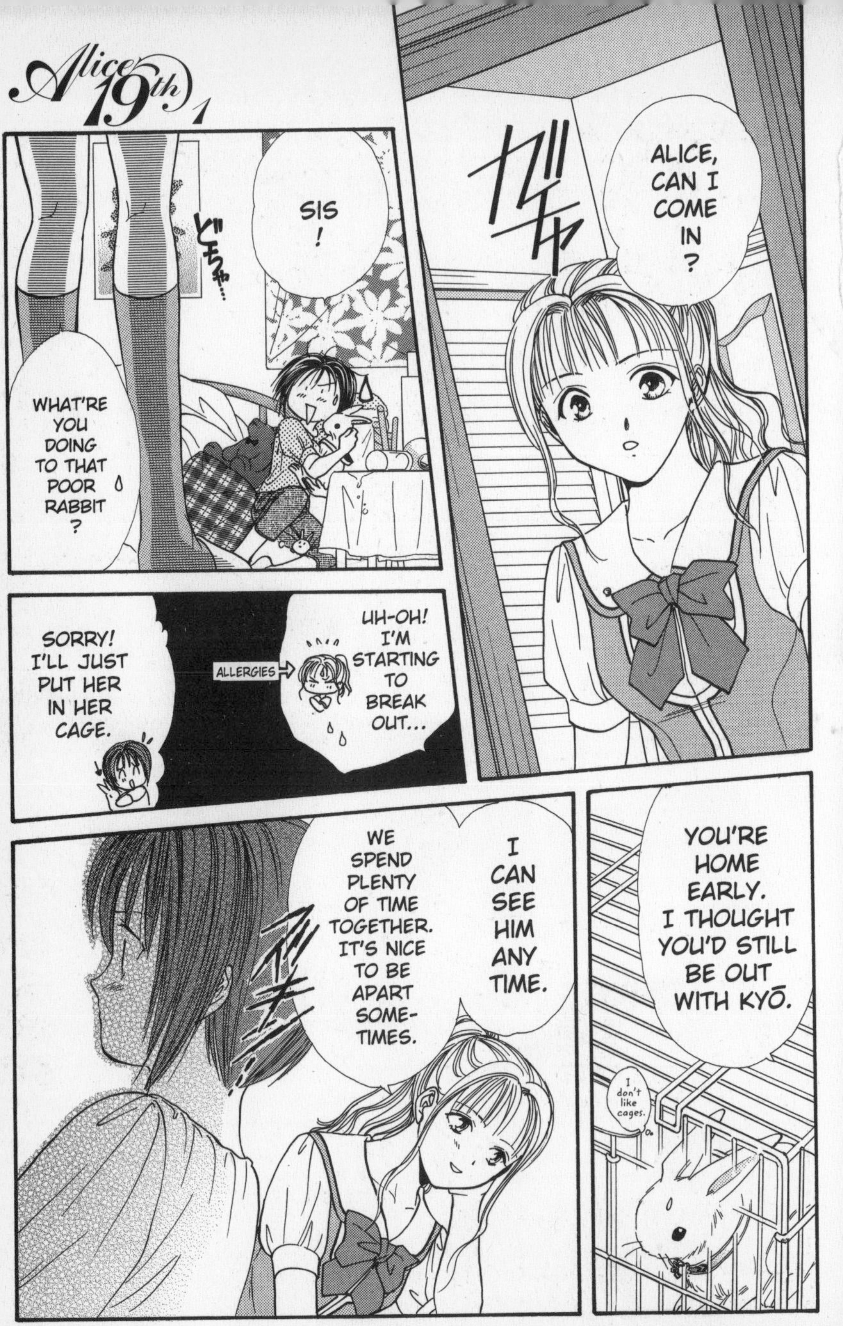
ガチャ
ALICE, CAN I COME IN?
SIS!
WHAT'RE YOU DOING TO THAT POOR RABBIT?
UH-OH! I'M STARTING TO BREAK OUT...
ALLERGIES
SORRY! I'LL JUST PUT HER IN HER CAGE.
YOU'RE HOME EARLY. I THOUGHT YOU'D STILL BE OUT WITH KYŌ.
I don't like cages.
I CAN SEE HIM ANY TIME.
WE SPEND PLENTY OF TIME TOGETHER. IT'S NICE TO BE APART SOMETIMES.

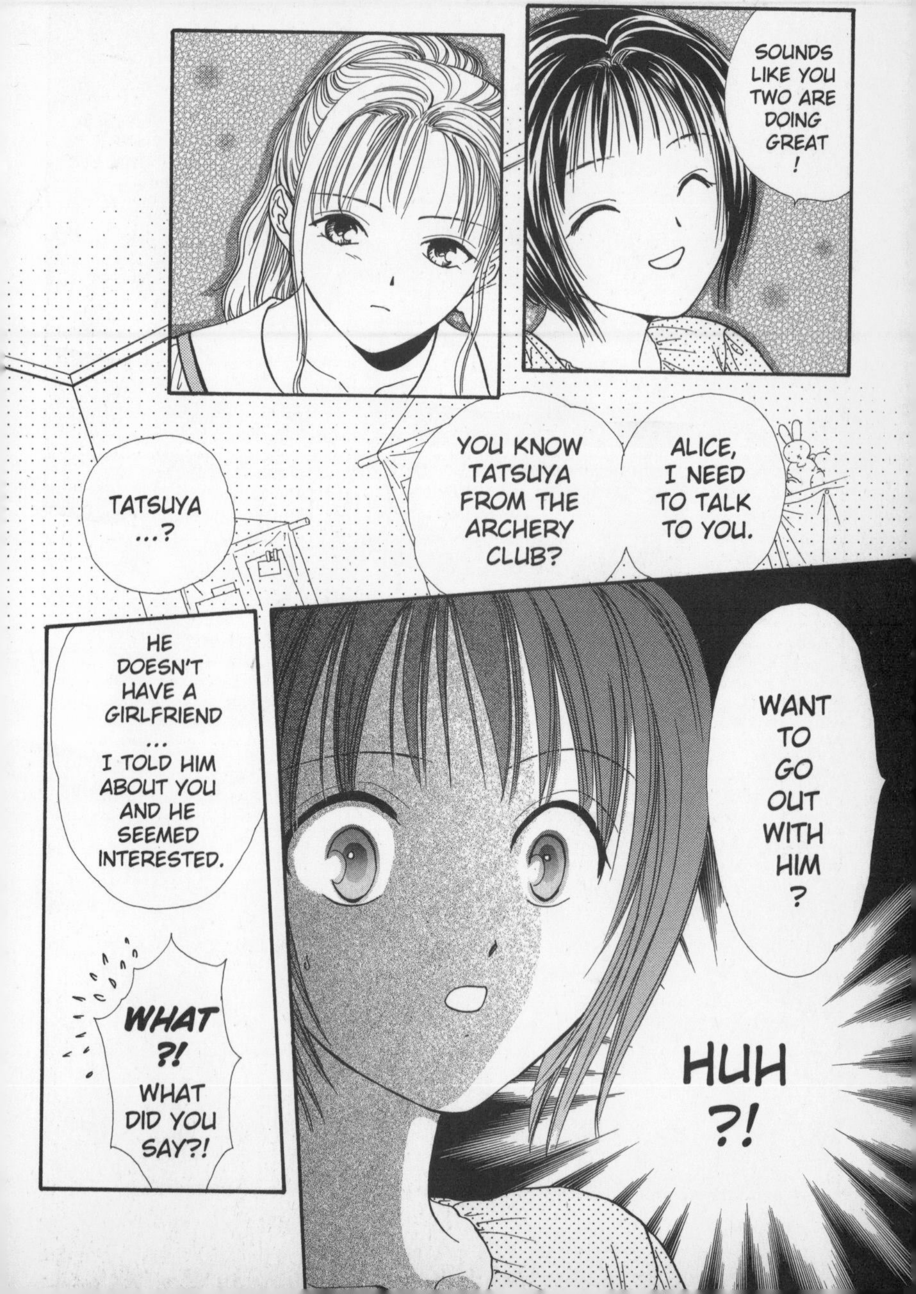
SOUNDS LIKE YOU TWO ARE DOING GREAT!
ALICE, I NEED TO TALK TO YOU.
YOU KNOW TATSUYA FROM THE ARCHERY CLUB?
TATSUYA...?
WANT TO GO OUT WITH HIM?
HUH?!
HE DOESN'T HAVE A GIRLFRIEND... I TOLD HIM ABOUT YOU AND HE SEEMED INTERESTED.
WHAT?! WHAT DID YOU SAY?!

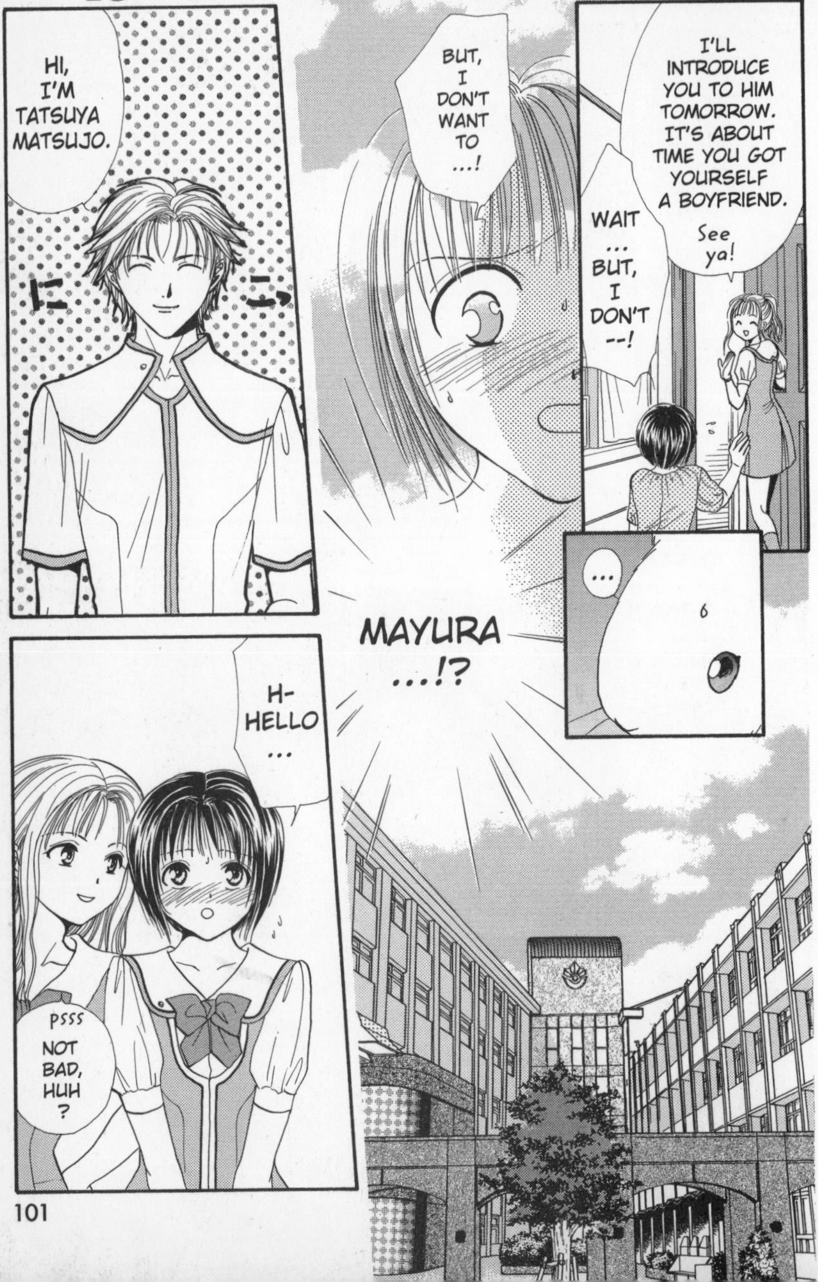
I'LL INTRODUCE YOU TO HIM TOMORROW. IT'S ABOUT TIME YOU GOT YOURSELF A BOYFRIEND.
See ya!
WAIT ... BUT, I DON'T --!
...
BUT, I DON'T WANT TO ...!
MAYURA ...!?
HI, I'M TATSUYA MATSUJO.
H-HELLO ...
PSSS NOT BAD, HUH ?

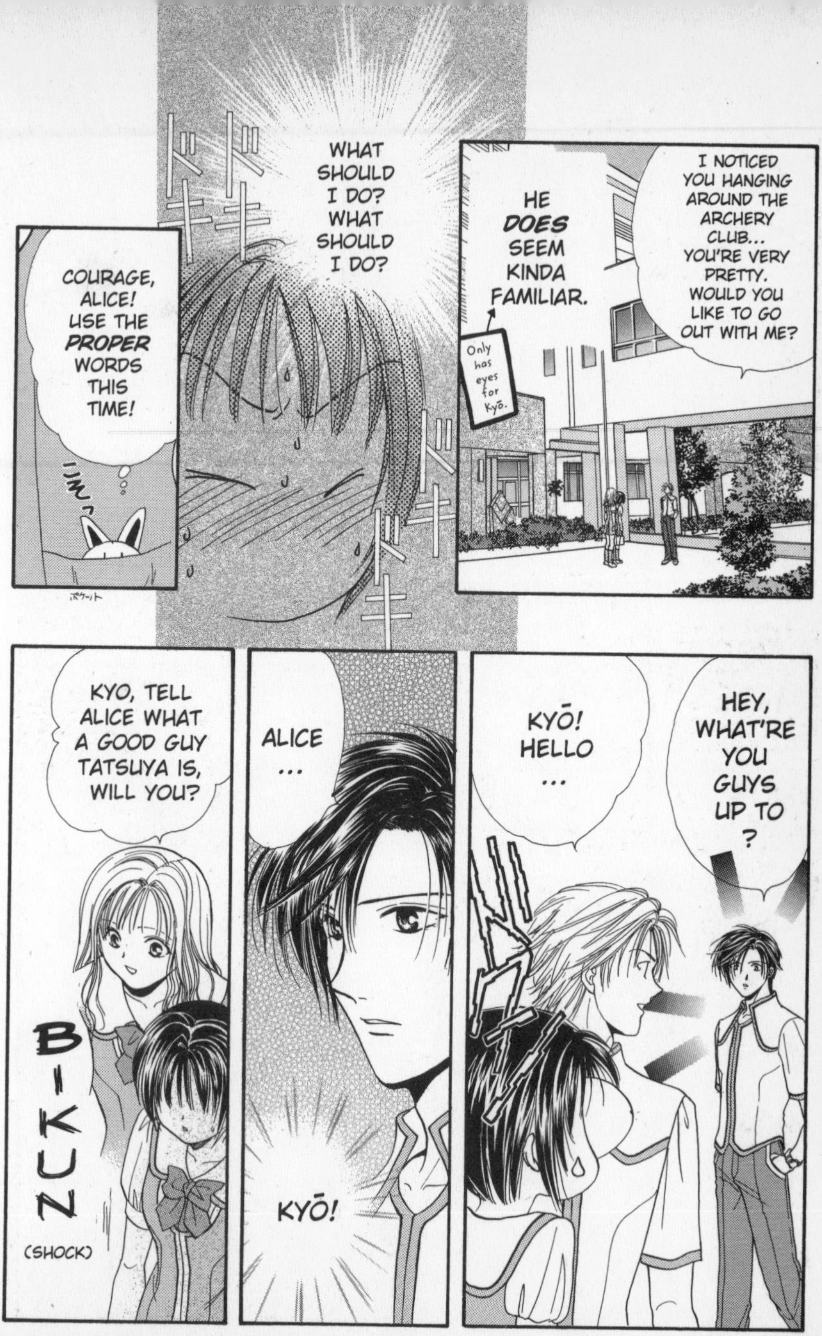
I NOTICED YOU HANGING AROUND THE ARCHERY CLUB... YOU'RE VERY PRETTY. WOULD YOU LIKE TO GO OUT WITH ME?
HE DOES SEEM KINDA FAMILIAR.
Only has eyes for Kyō.
WHAT SHOULD I DO? WHAT SHOULD I DO?
COURAGE, ALICE! USE THE PROPER WORDS THIS TIME!
HEY, WHAT'RE YOU GUYS UP TO ?
KYŌ! HELLO ...
ALICE ...
KYŌ!
KYO, TELL ALICE WHAT A GOOD GUY TATSUYA IS, WILL YOU?
B-I-KUN
(SHOCK)

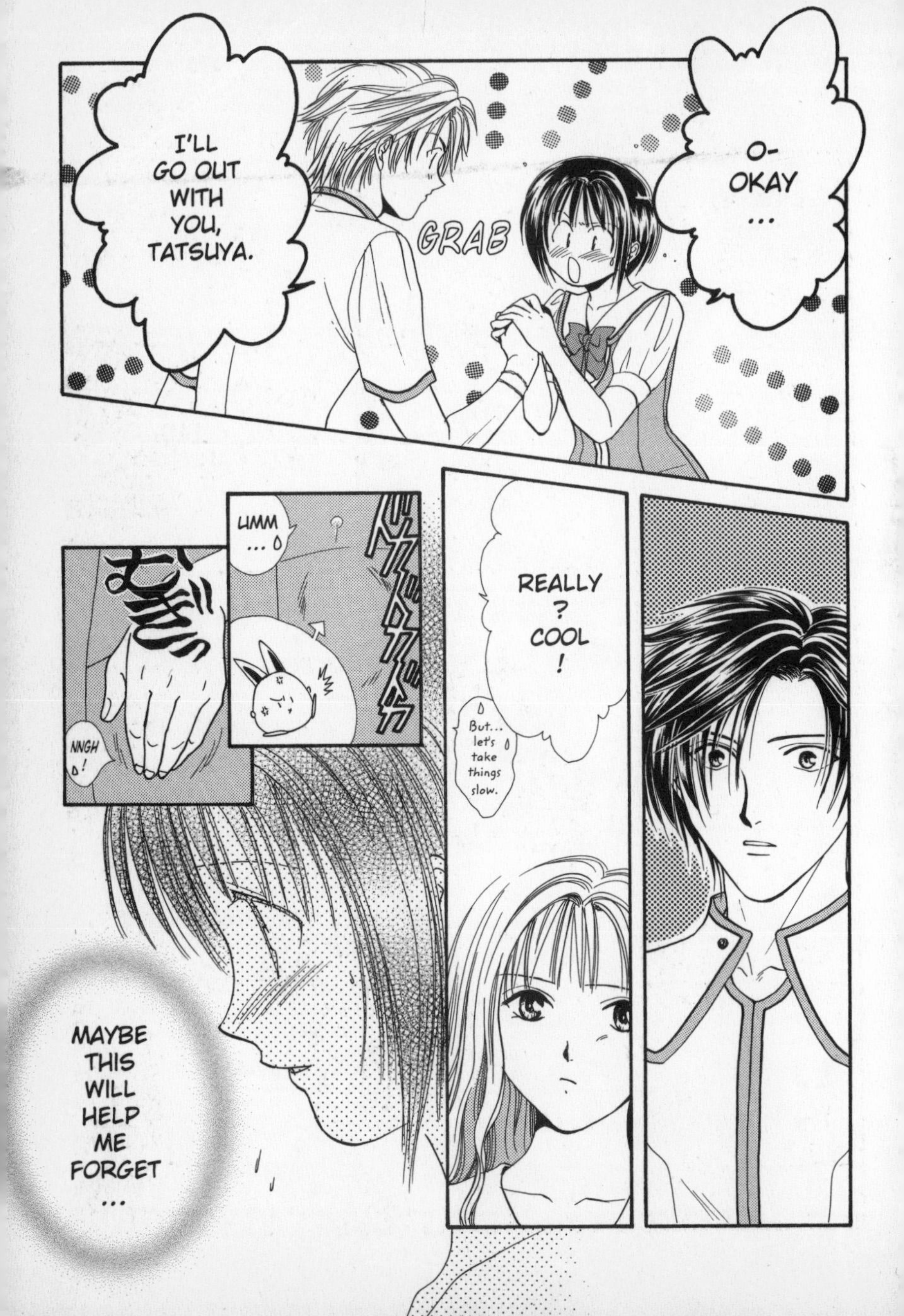
O-OKAY ...
I'LL GO OUT WITH YOU, TATSUYA.
GRAB
REALLY? COOL!
But... let's take things slow.
UMM ...
NNGH!
MAYBE THIS WILL HELP ME FORGET ...

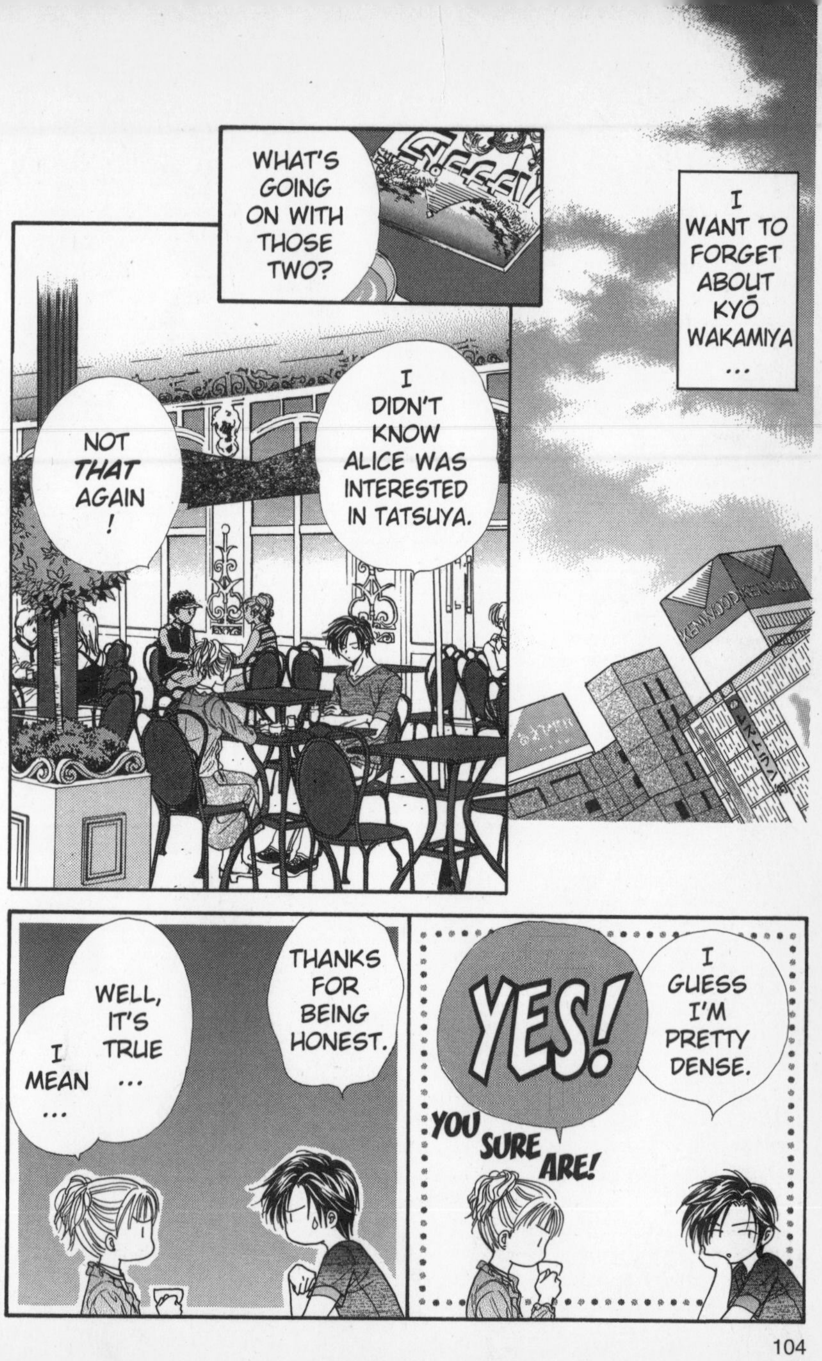
I WANT TO FORGET ABOUT KYŌ WAKAMIYA ...
WHAT'S GOING ON WITH THOSE TWO?
I DIDN'T KNOW ALICE WAS INTERESTED IN TATSUYA.
NOT *THAT* AGAIN !
I GUESS I'M PRETTY DENSE.
YES!
YOU SURE ARE!
THANKS FOR BEING HONEST.
WELL, IT'S TRUE ...
I MEAN ...

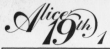

I never used a rabbit before, but it seemed so innocent and cute--just like my heroine. And the rabbit guide inspired the name, "Alice," as in "Alice in Wonderland." There's not much other connection, but they're both fantasy tales. When I thought of the name "Alice," it seemed so perfect that I never had a second thought. I've noticed that my heroines often have a name that includes a strong "A" sound. In Shishunki Miman Okotowari there was Asuka. In Fushigi Yugi there was Miaka and I used Aya in Ceres. The main character in Imadoki didn't have an "A", but there was a side character named Arisa. I think that names that have an "A" sound are cute. I use all kinds of names for my short stories, but there do happen to be a lot of "A" names.
I chose the sister's name, Mayura, right away. I intended to write Alice in kanji characters at first, but I wanted to differentiate their names. So, my editor suggested I use hiragana for Alice's name. I did however, agonize over the sisters' surname and also what to call Kyō. I wanted to create someone different from my other male characters. But it was difficult and I ended up looking at a lot of things before I came up with a name. I could have used a different kanji character, like the one for "capital," but I thought that the character for "to fulfill" seemed to fit his personality. While the story tends to have a Western feel, Kyō is a truly Japanese male. So, I've tried to make more aspects about him Japanese.

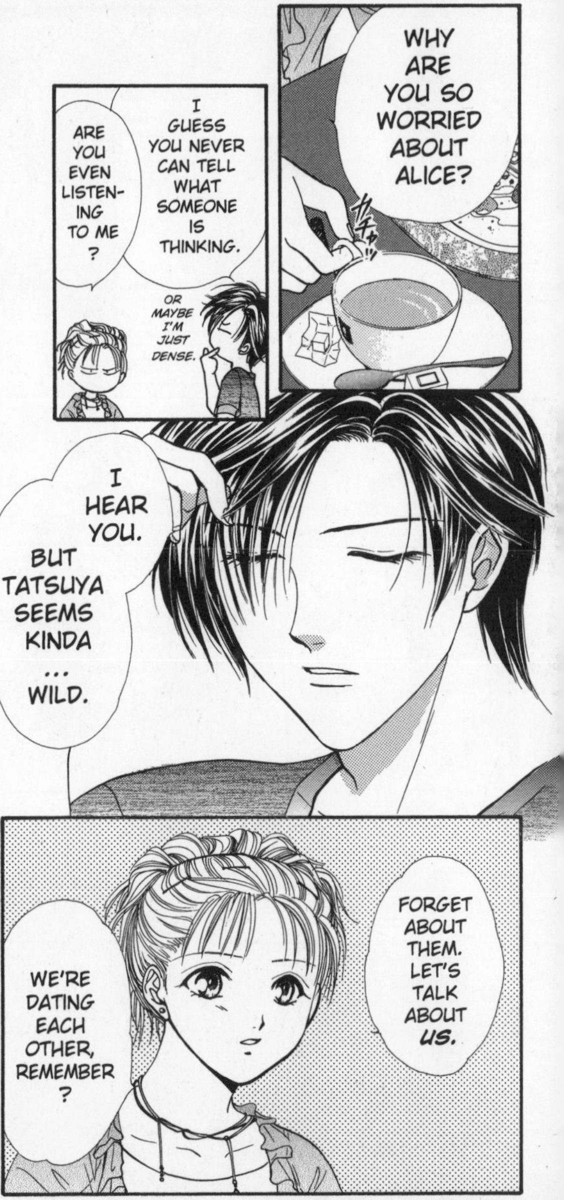
WHY ARE YOU SO WORRIED ABOUT ALICE?
I GUESS YOU NEVER CAN TELL WHAT SOMEONE IS THINKING.
ARE YOU EVEN LISTENING TO ME?
OR MAYBE I'M JUST DENSE.
I HEAR YOU.
BUT TATSUYA SEEMS KINDA ... WILD.
FORGET ABOUT THEM. LET'S TALK ABOUT US.
WE'RE DATING EACH OTHER, REMEMBER?

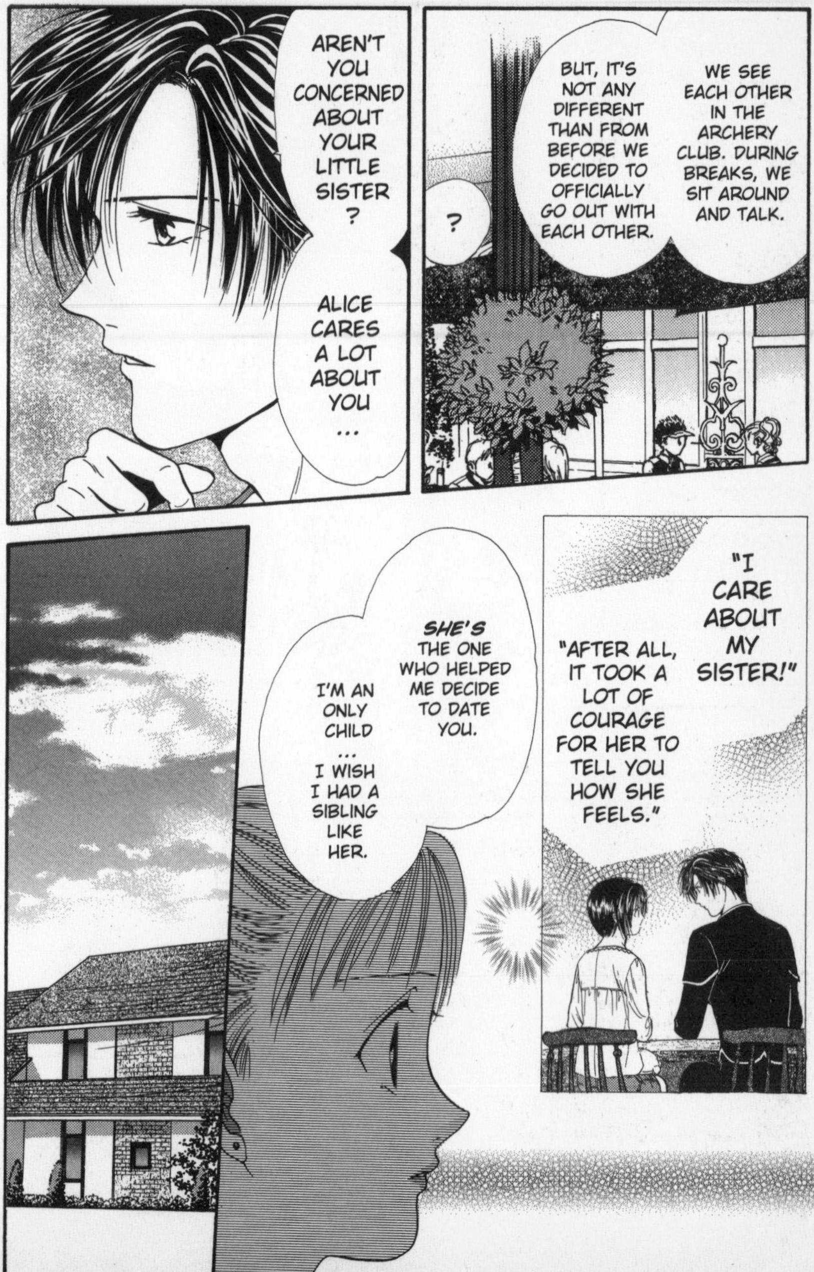
WE SEE EACH OTHER IN THE ARCHERY CLUB. DURING BREAKS, WE SIT AROUND AND TALK.
BUT, IT'S NOT ANY DIFFERENT THAN FROM BEFORE WE DECIDED TO OFFICIALLY GO OUT WITH EACH OTHER.
?
AREN'T YOU CONCERNED ABOUT YOUR LITTLE SISTER ?
ALICE CARES A LOT ABOUT YOU ...
"I CARE ABOUT MY SISTER!"
"AFTER ALL, IT TOOK A LOT OF COURAGE FOR HER TO TELL YOU HOW SHE FEELS."
SHE'S THE ONE WHO HELPED ME DECIDE TO DATE YOU.
I'M AN ONLY CHILD ... I WISH I HAD A SIBLING LIKE HER.

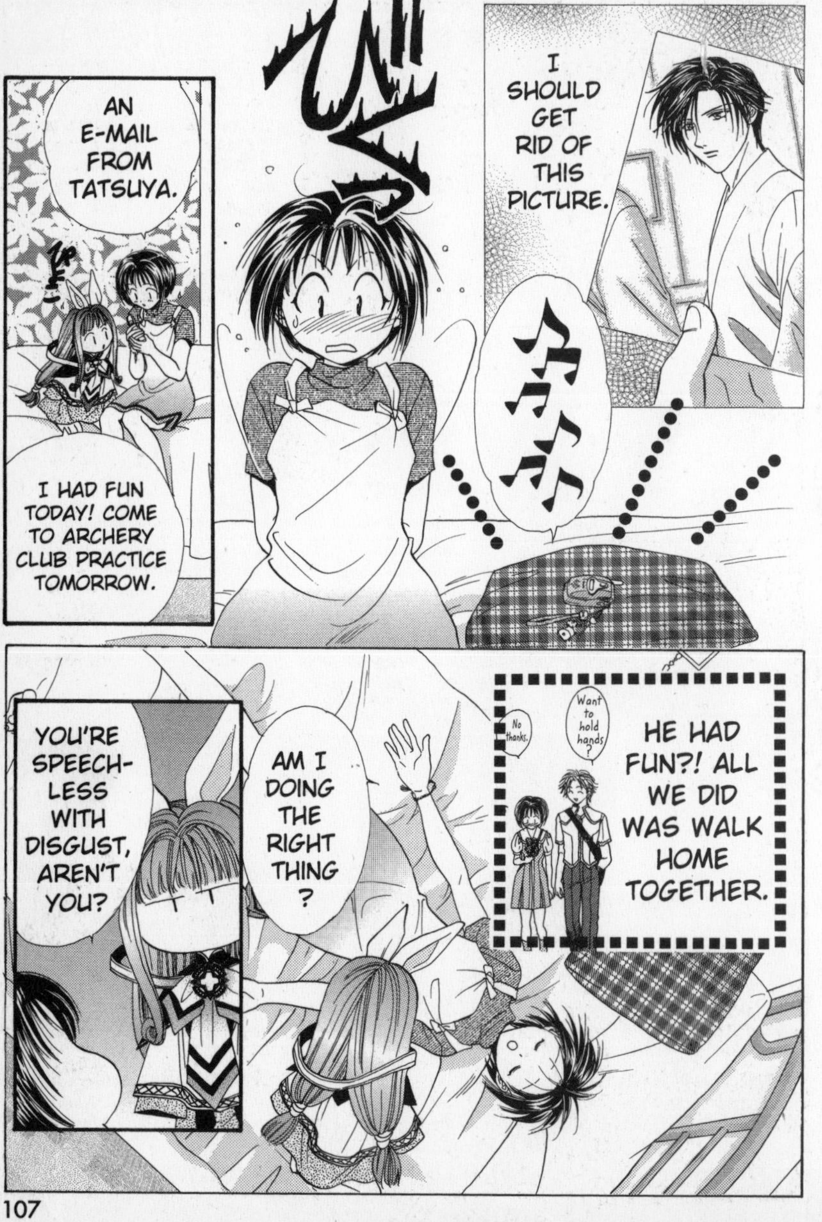
I SHOULD GET RID OF THIS PICTURE.
AN E-MAIL FROM TATSUYA.
I HAD FUN TODAY! COME TO ARCHERY CLUB PRACTICE TOMORROW.
HE HAD FUN?! ALL WE DID WAS WALK HOME TOGETHER.
Want to hold hands?
No thanks.
AM I DOING THE RIGHT THING?
YOU'RE SPEECH-LESS WITH DISGUST, AREN'T YOU?

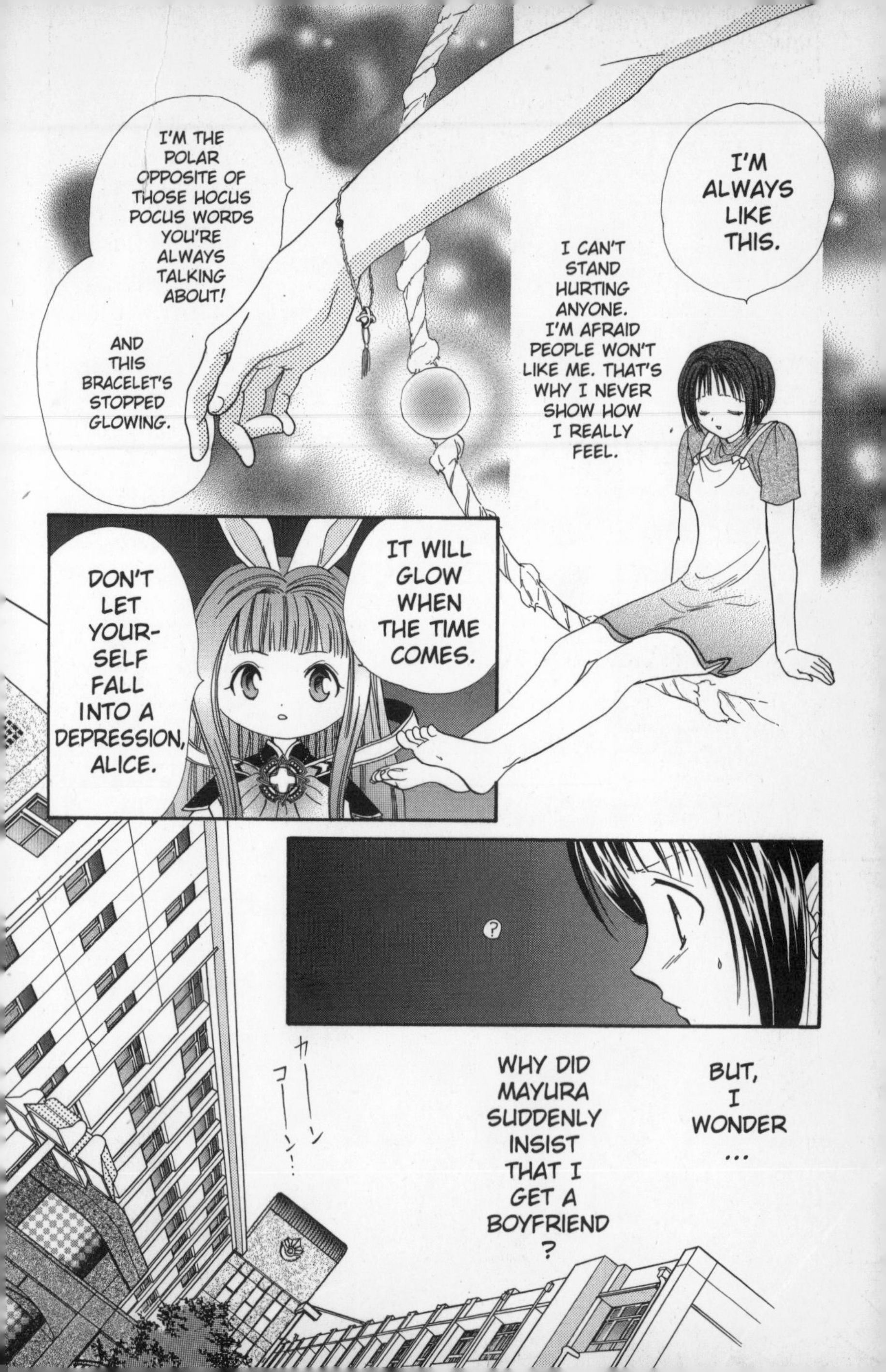
I'M ALWAYS LIKE THIS.
I CAN'T STAND HURTING ANYONE. I'M AFRAID PEOPLE WON'T LIKE ME. THAT'S WHY I NEVER SHOW HOW I REALLY FEEL.
I'M THE POLAR OPPOSITE OF THOSE HOCUS POCUS WORDS YOU'RE ALWAYS TALKING ABOUT!
AND THIS BRACELET'S STOPPED GLOWING.
IT WILL GLOW WHEN THE TIME COMES.
DON'T LET YOURSELF FALL INTO A DEPRESSION, ALICE.
?
BUT, I WONDER...
WHY DID MAYURA SUDDENLY INSIST THAT I GET A BOYFRIEND?
カーン コーン!!

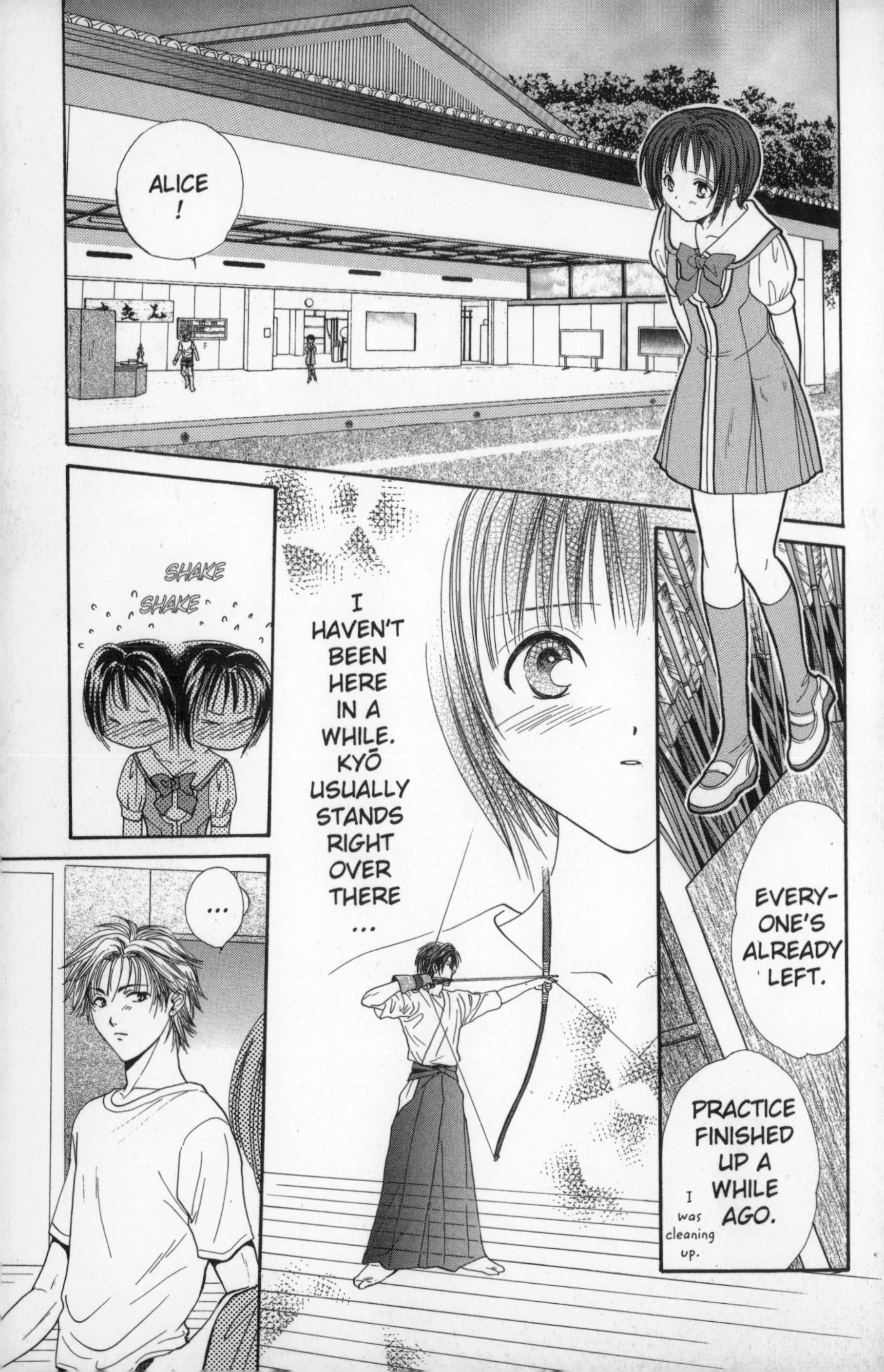
ALICE!
EVERY-ONE'S ALREADY LEFT.
PRACTICE FINISHED UP A WHILE AGO.
I was cleaning up.
I HAVEN'T BEEN HERE IN A WHILE. KYŌ USUALLY STANDS RIGHT OVER THERE...
SHAKE SHAKE
...

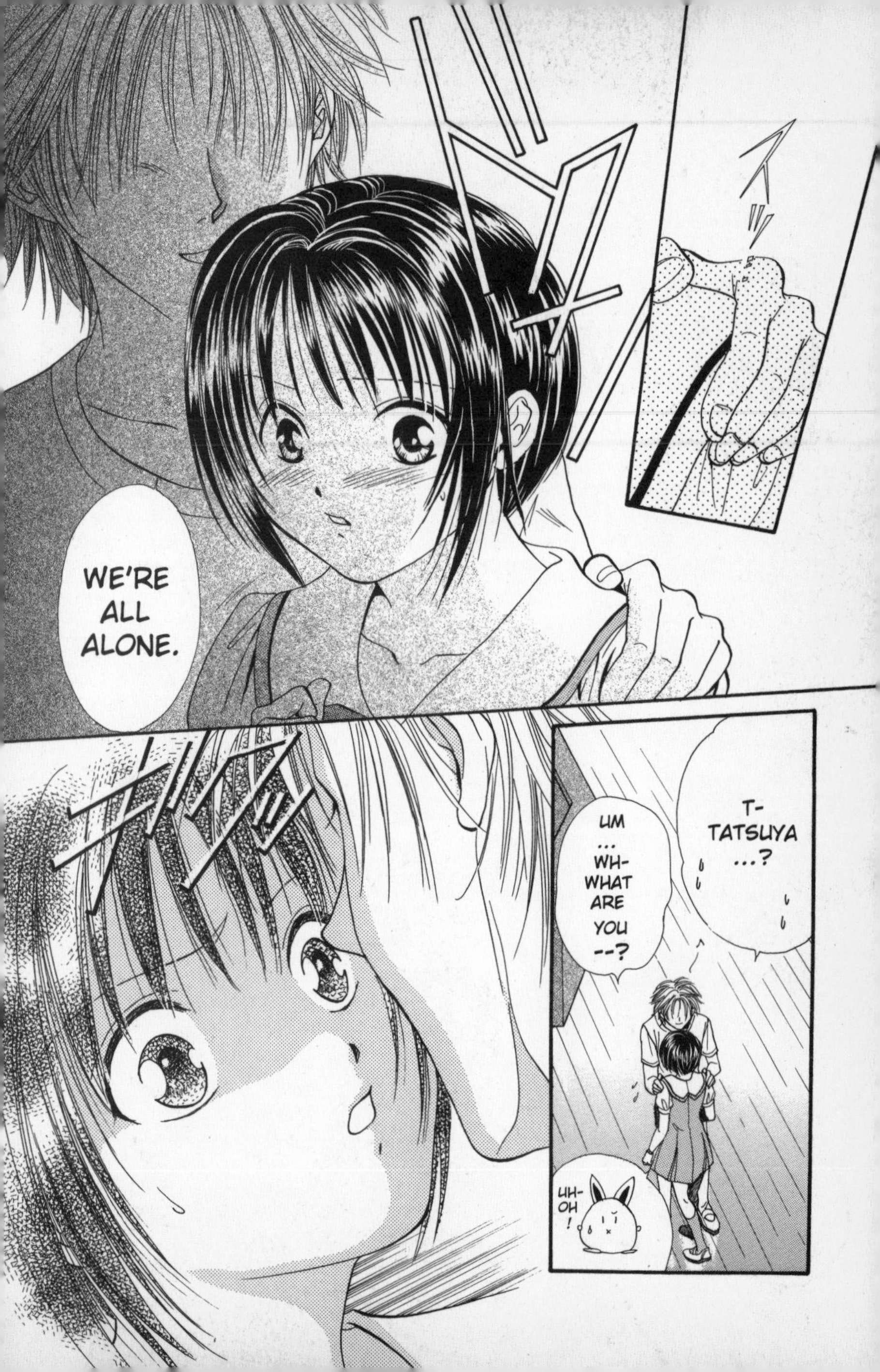
WE'RE ALL ALONE.
T-TATSUYA ...?
UM ... WH-WHAT ARE YOU --?
UH-OH!

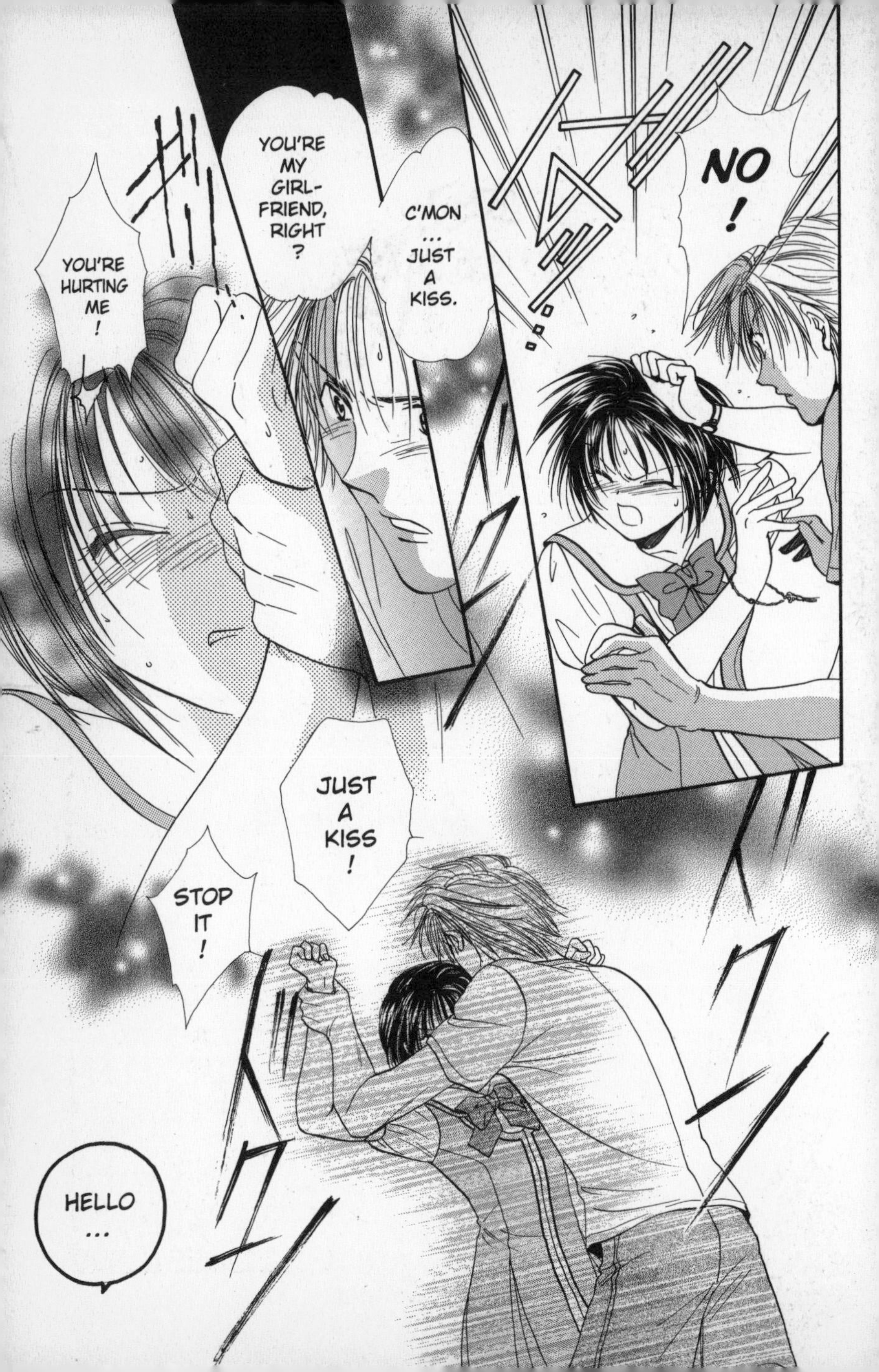
NO!
YOU'RE MY GIRL-FRIEND, RIGHT?
C'MON ... JUST A KISS.
YOU'RE HURTING ME!
JUST A KISS!
STOP IT!
HELLO ...

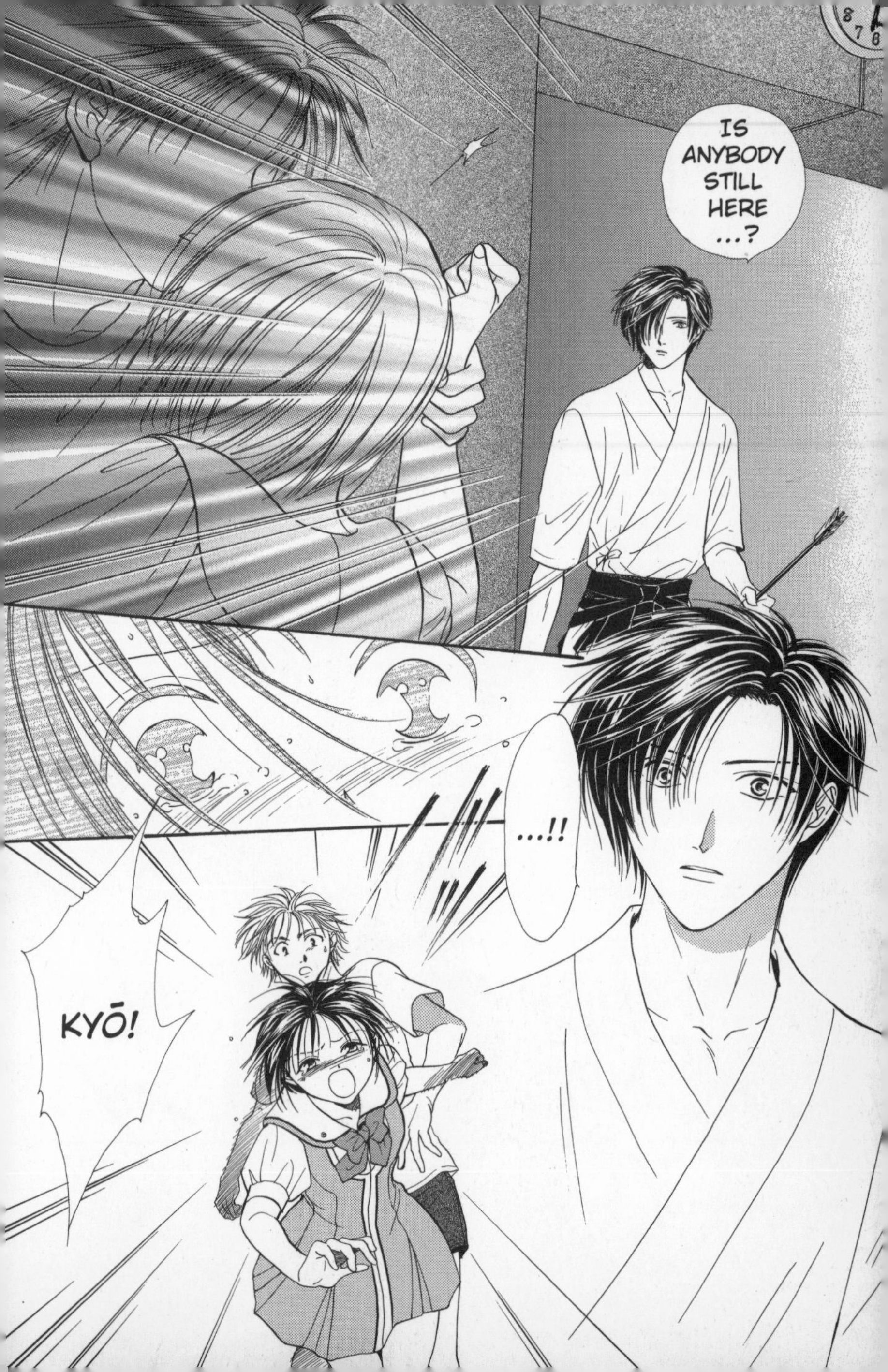
IS ANYBODY STILL HERE ...?
...!!
KYŌ!

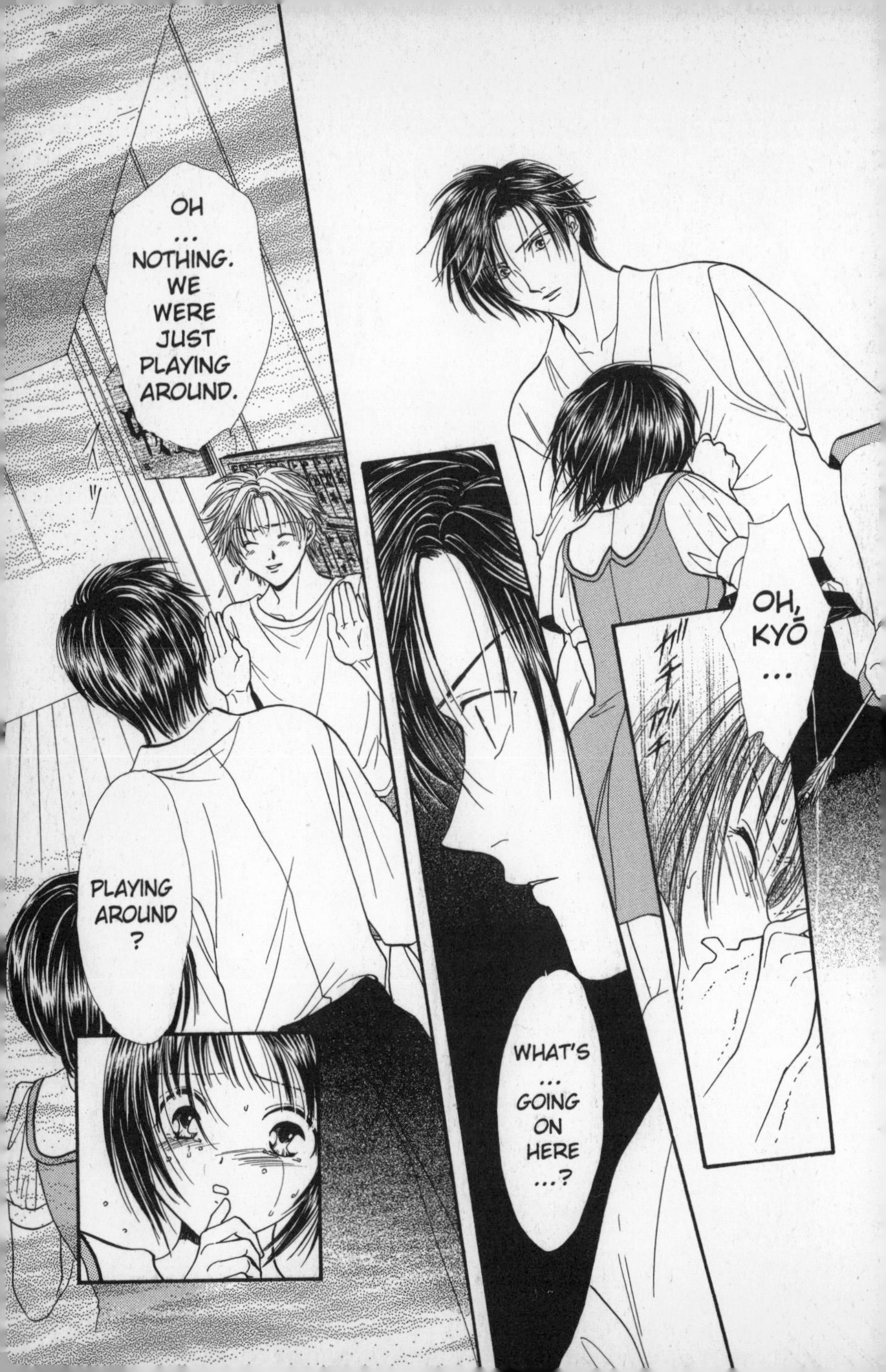
OH, KYŌ ...
ガチガチ
WHAT'S ... GOING ON HERE ...?
OH ... NOTHING. WE WERE JUST PLAYING AROUND.
PLAYING AROUND?

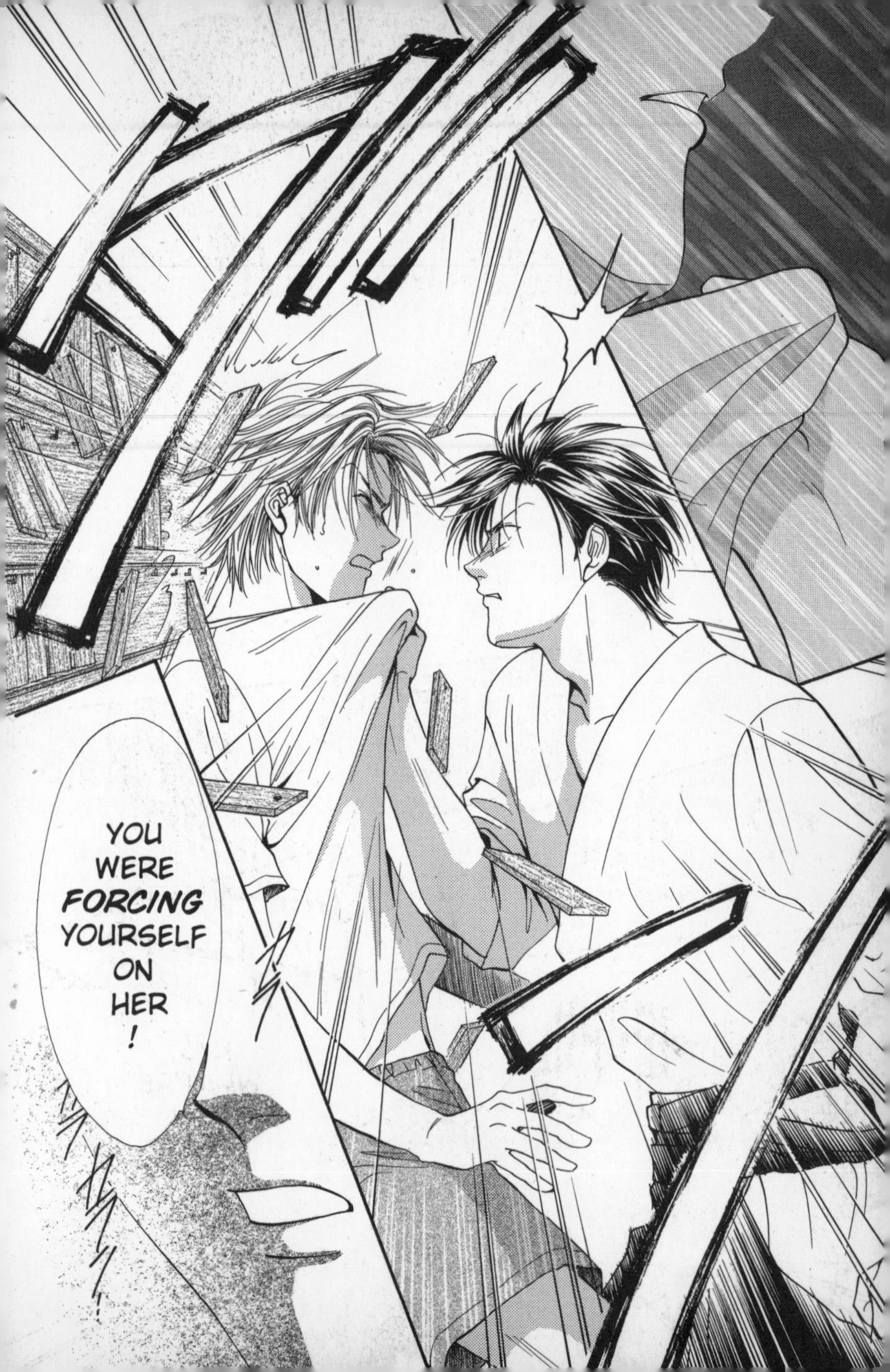
YOU WERE *FORCING* YOURSELF ON HER!

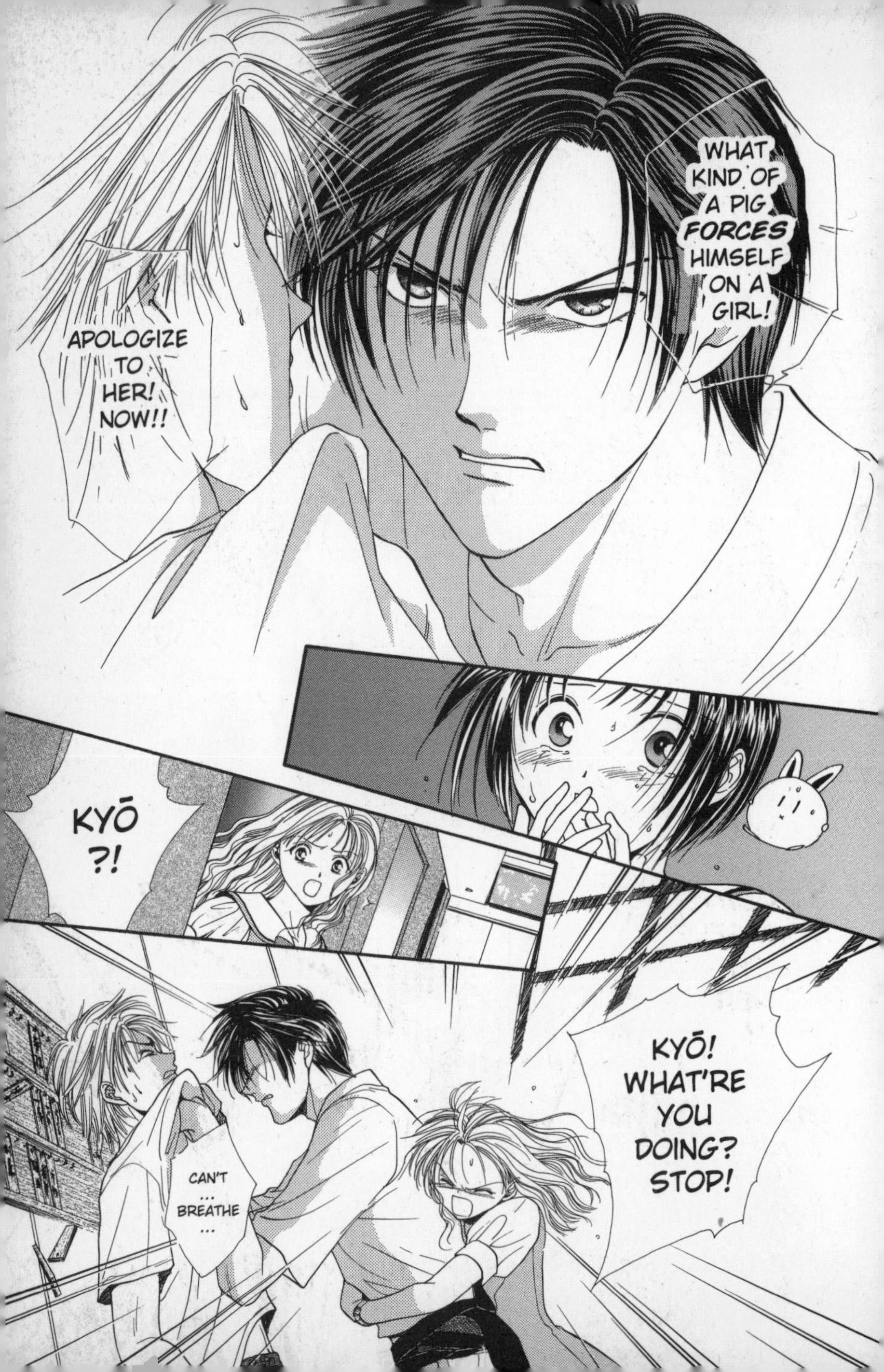
WHAT KIND OF A PIG FORCES HIMSELF ON A GIRL!
APOLOGIZE TO HER! NOW!!
KYŌ ?!
KYŌ! WHAT'RE YOU DOING? STOP!
CAN'T ... BREATHE ...

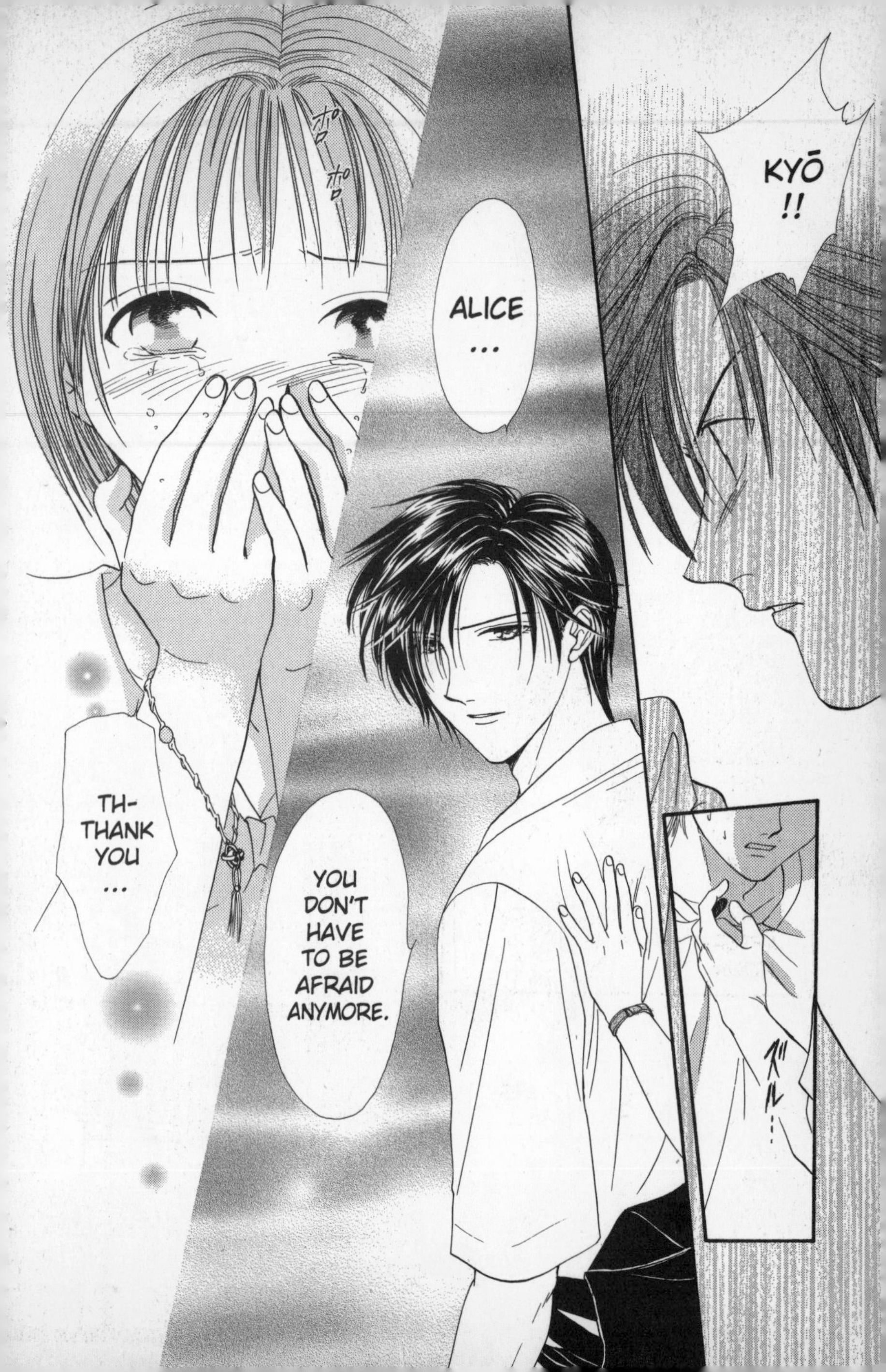
KYŌ !!
ズル…
ALICE ...
YOU DON'T HAVE TO BE AFRAID ANYMORE.
TH-THANK YOU ...

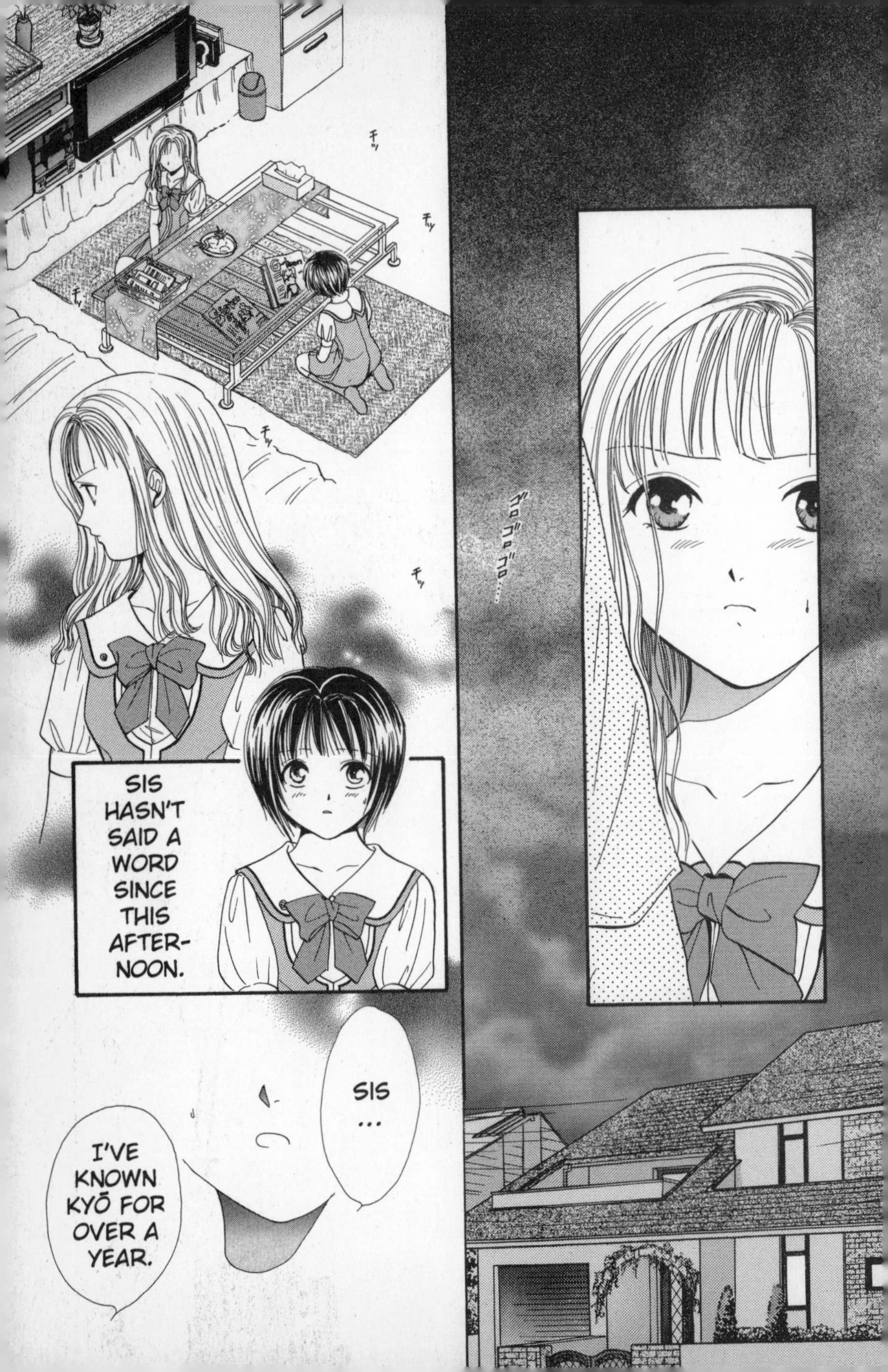
ゴロゴロゴロ…
チッ
チッ
チッ
チッ
チッ
SIS HASN'T SAID A WORD SINCE THIS AFTERNOON.
SIS...
I'VE KNOWN KYŌ FOR OVER A YEAR.

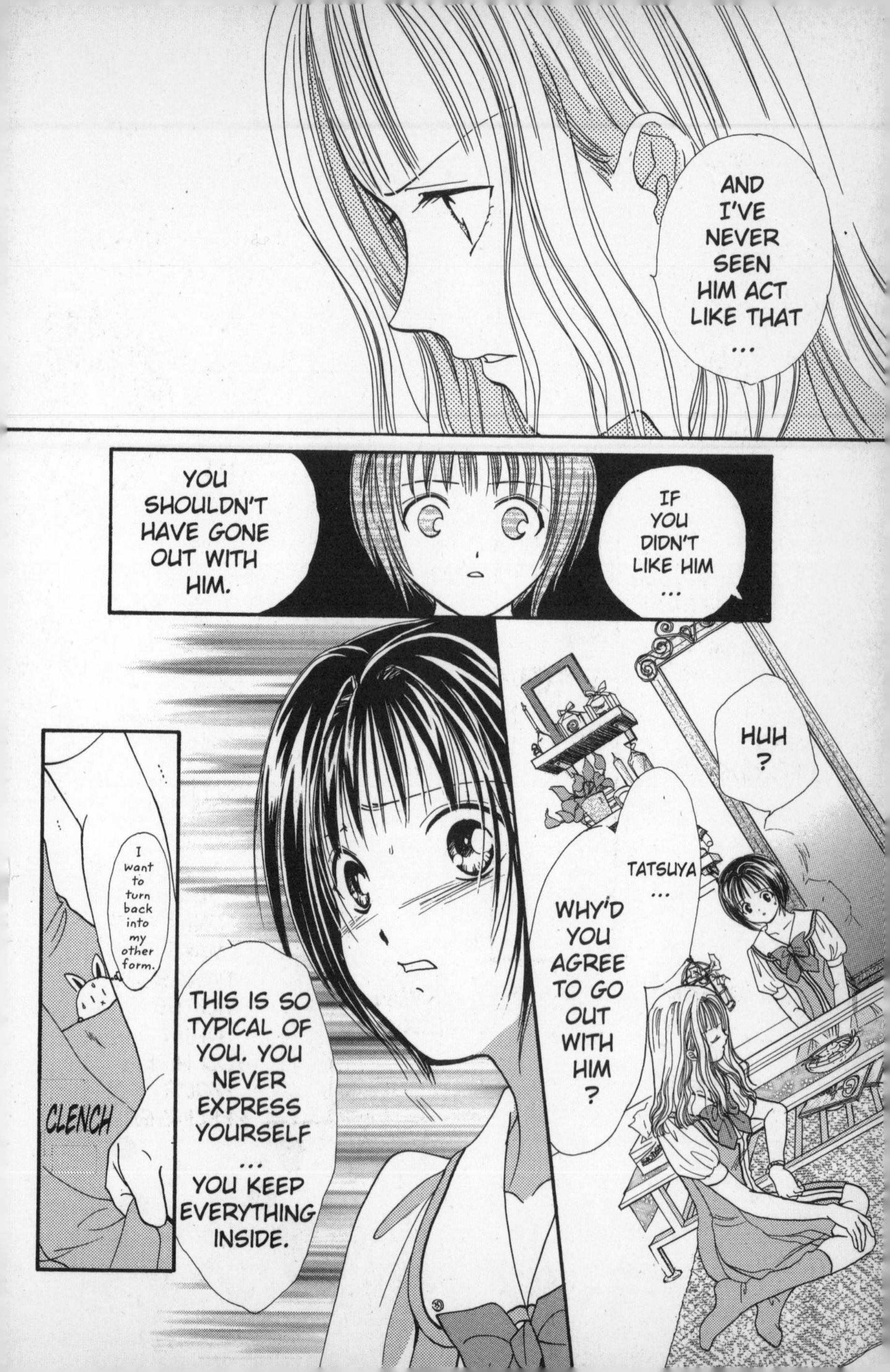
AND I'VE NEVER SEEN HIM ACT LIKE THAT ...
IF YOU DIDN'T LIKE HIM ...
YOU SHOULDN'T HAVE GONE OUT WITH HIM.
HUH ?
TATSUYA ...
WHY'D YOU AGREE TO GO OUT WITH HIM ?
THIS IS SO TYPICAL OF YOU. YOU NEVER EXPRESS YOURSELF ... YOU KEEP EVERYTHING INSIDE.
I want to turn back into my other form.
CLENCH

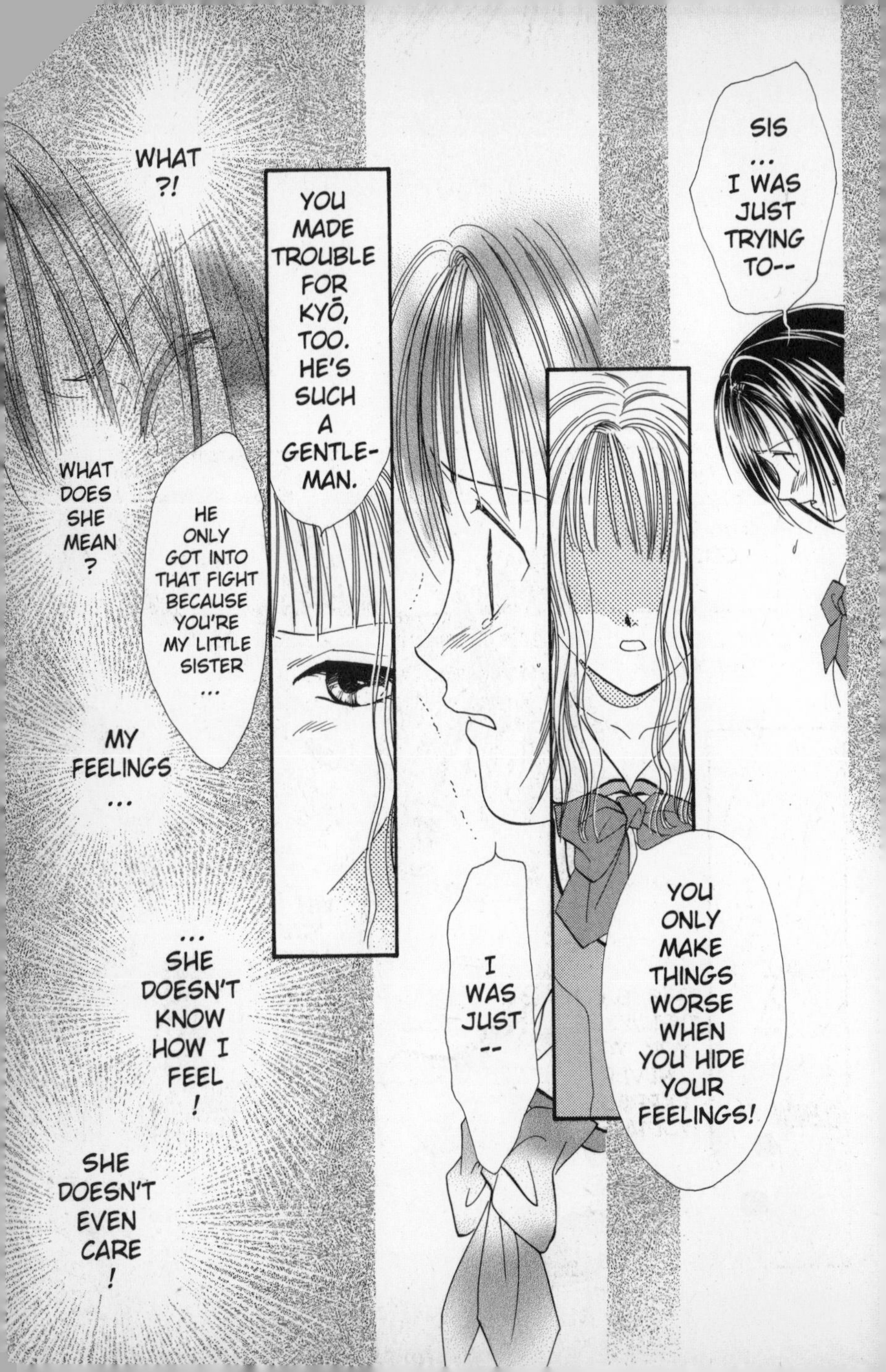
SIS ... I WAS JUST TRYING TO--
YOU ONLY MAKE THINGS WORSE WHEN YOU HIDE YOUR FEELINGS!
I WAS JUST --
YOU MADE TROUBLE FOR KYŌ, TOO. HE'S SUCH A GENTLE-MAN.
HE ONLY GOT INTO THAT FIGHT BECAUSE YOU'RE MY LITTLE SISTER ...
WHAT ?!
WHAT DOES SHE MEAN ?
MY FEELINGS ...
... SHE DOESN'T KNOW HOW I FEEL !
SHE DOESN'T EVEN CARE !

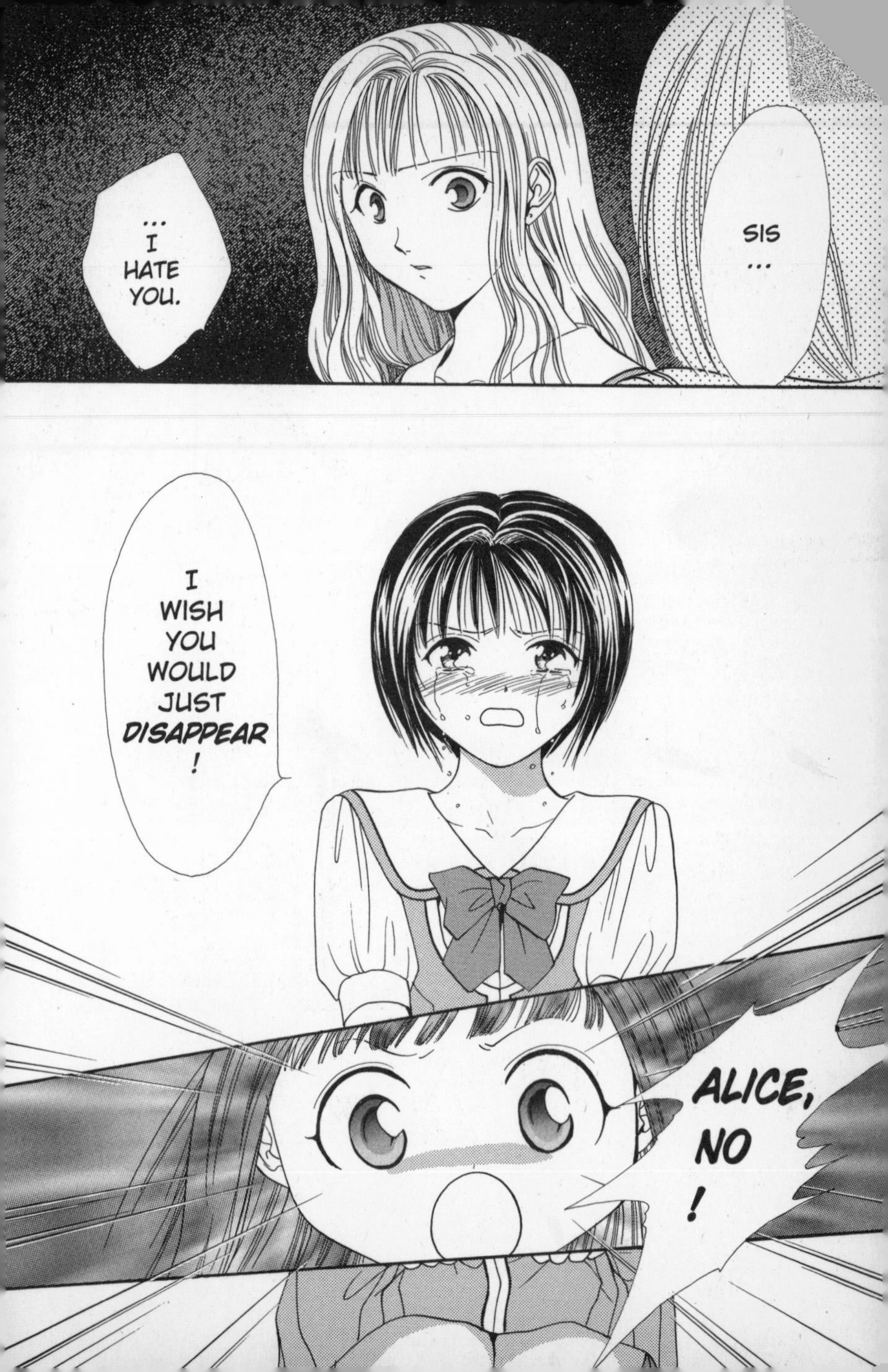
SIS ...
... I HATE YOU.
I WISH YOU WOULD JUST DISAPPEAR!
ALICE, NO!

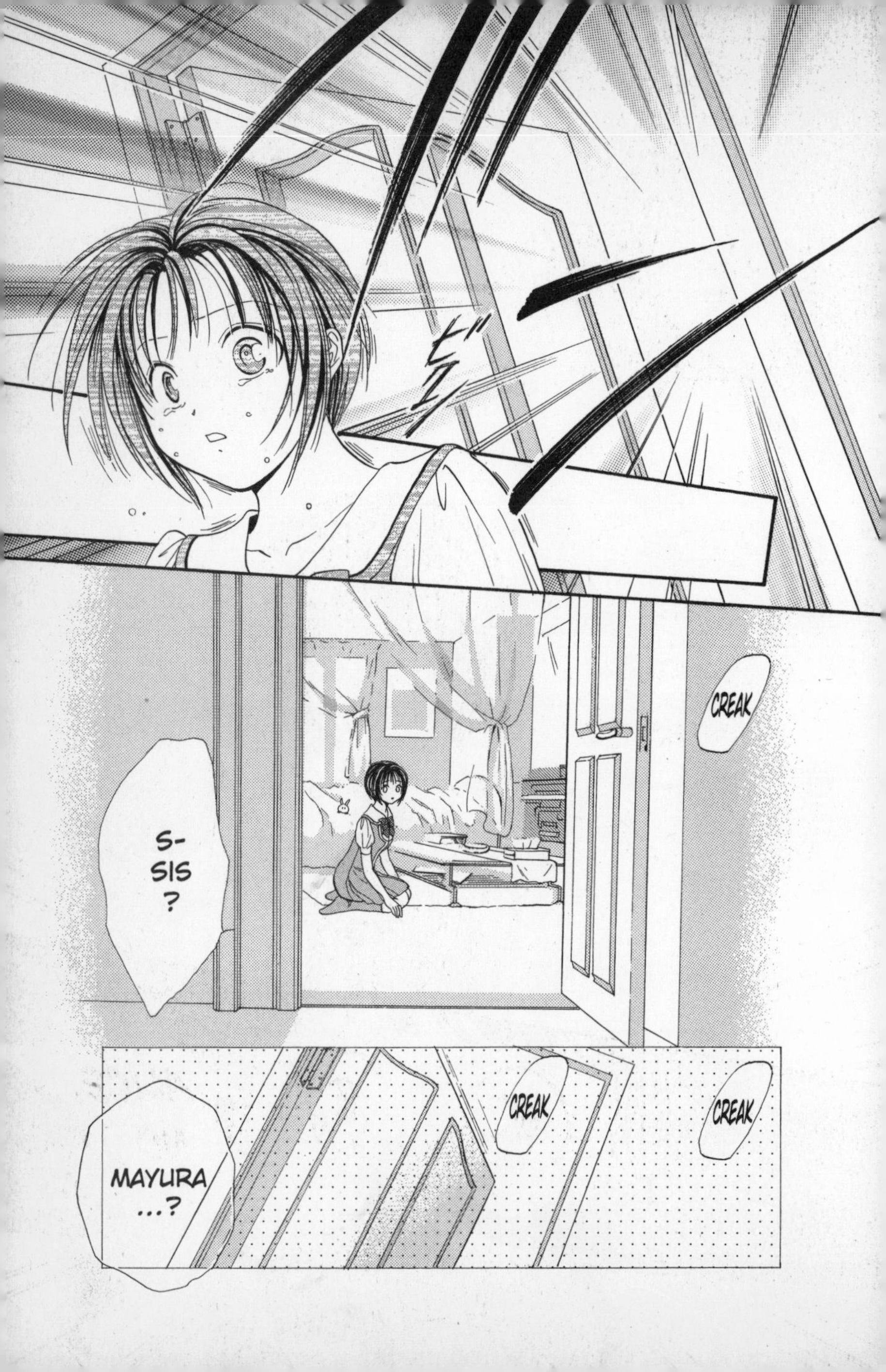
CREAK
S-SIS?
CREAK
CREAK
MAYURA...?

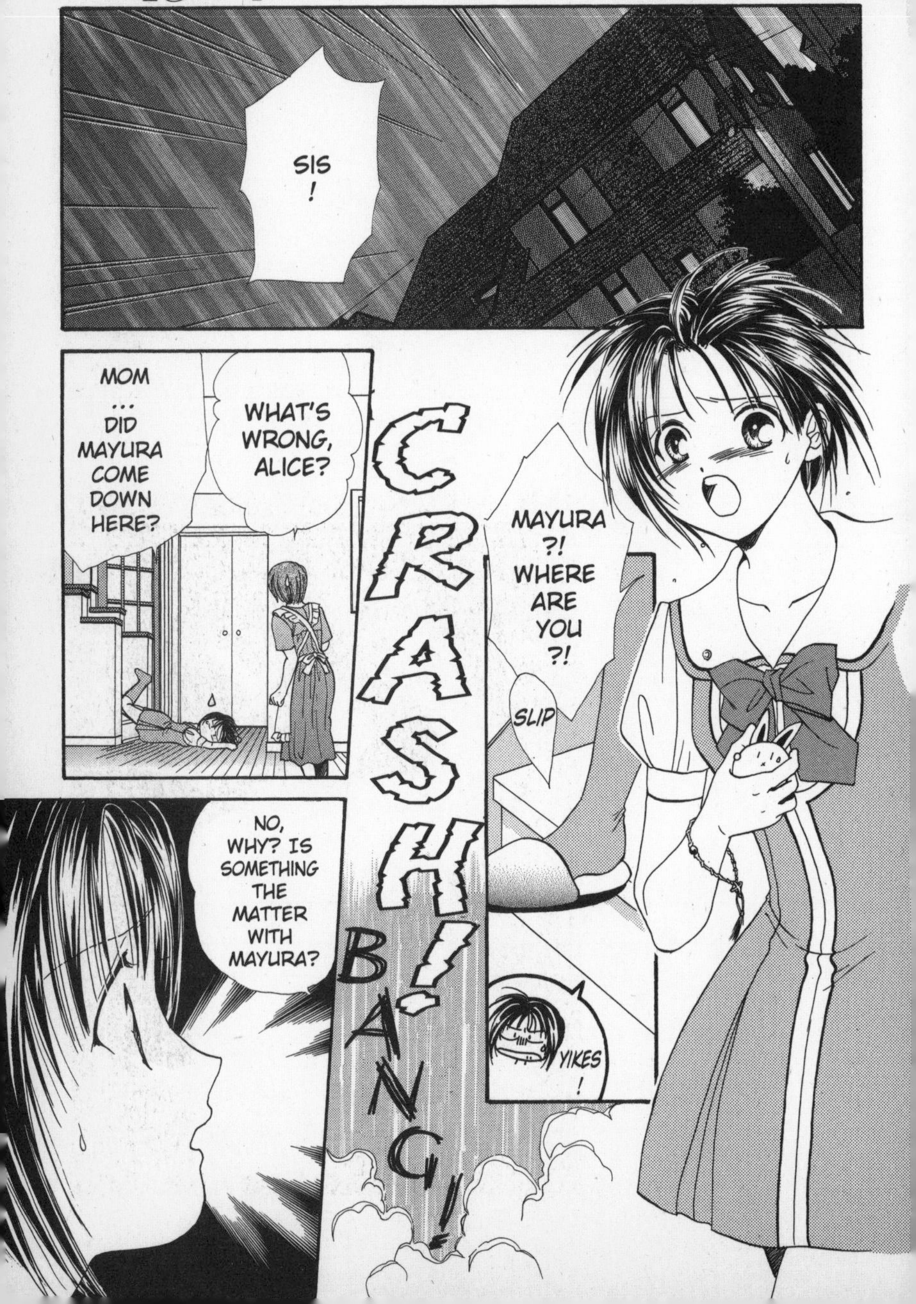
SIS!
MAYURA?! WHERE ARE YOU?!
SLIP
YIKES!
CRASH! BANG!
WHAT'S WRONG, ALICE?
MOM... DID MAYURA COME DOWN HERE?
NO, WHY? IS SOMETHING THE MATTER WITH MAYURA?

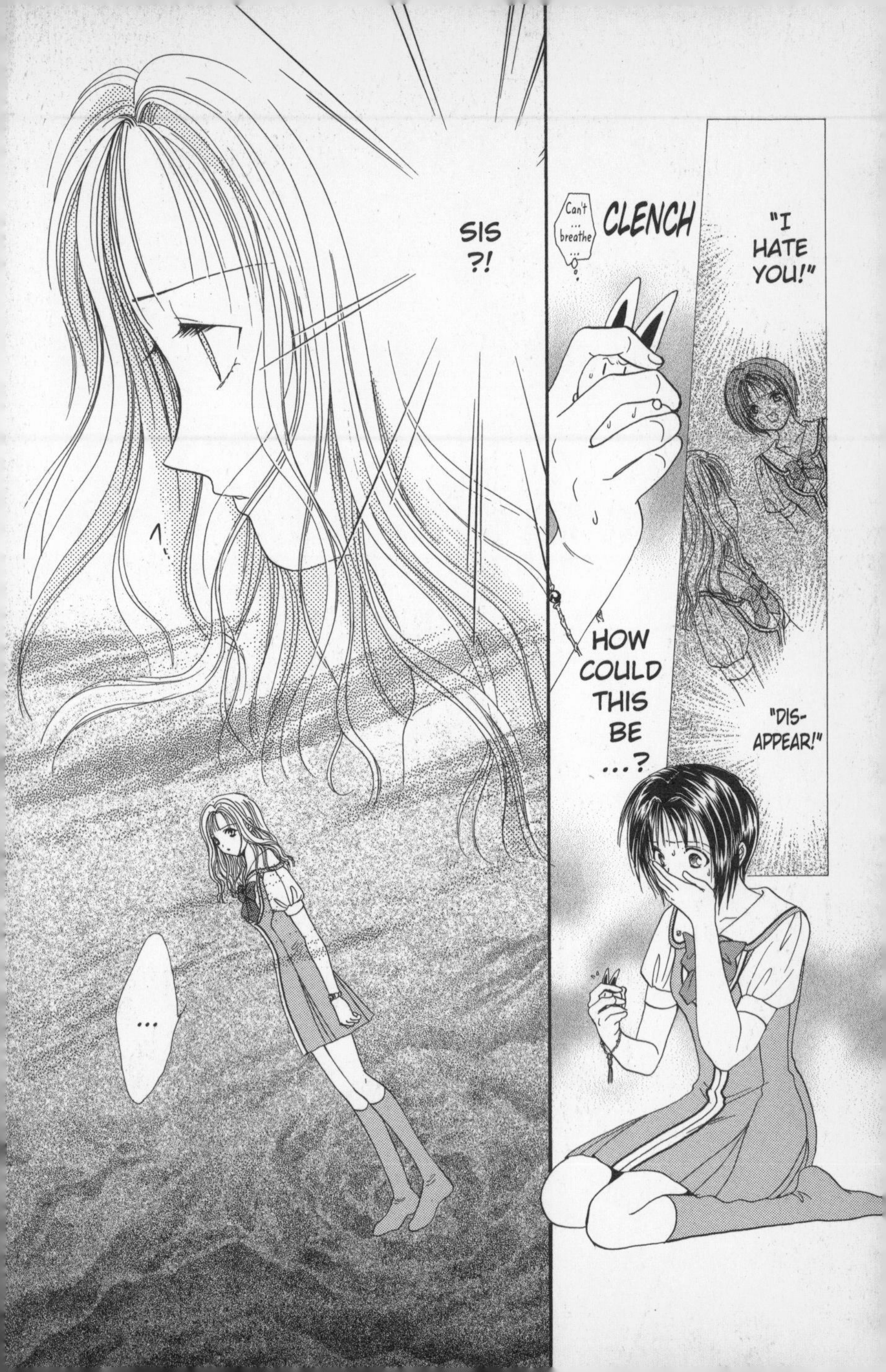
"I HATE YOU!"
"DIS-APPEAR!"
Can't ... breathe ...
CLENCH
HOW COULD THIS BE ...?
SIS ?!
...

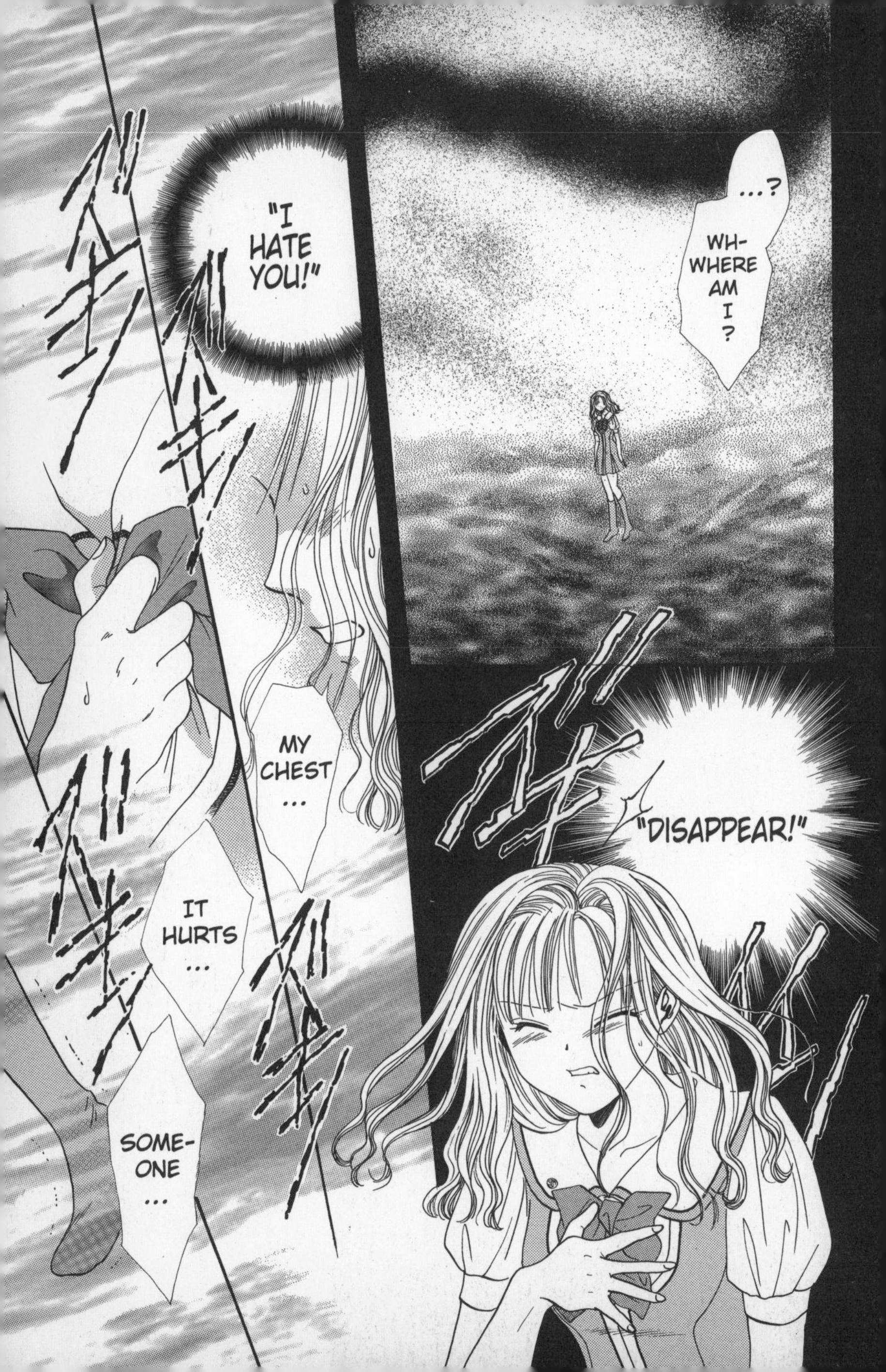
...?
WH-WHERE AM I?
"DISAPPEAR!"
"I HATE YOU!"
MY CHEST ...
IT HURTS ...
SOME-ONE ...

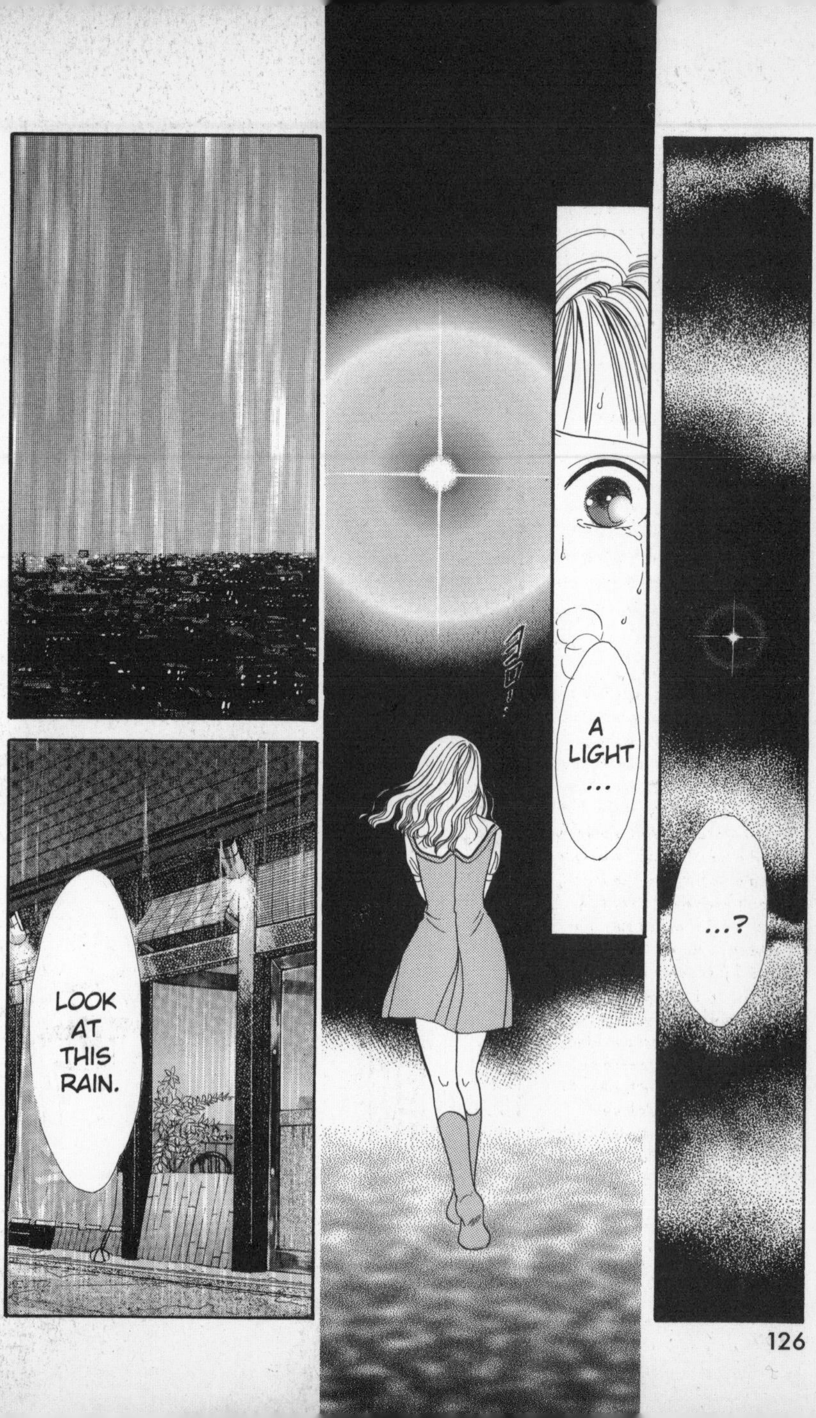
...?
A LIGHT ...
LOOK AT THIS RAIN.

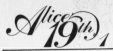

And so, archery is featured in this story! Later, Kyō also uses other martial arts, including kendo. But I really wanted to focus on archery. I'm surprised how many of you readers like archery, too. And many of you said you want to try it out. When I was in my teens, I loved the "look" of archery. So masculine! And those black hakama trousers were really cool. Archery is such a spiritual sport. Speaking of hakama trousers, red ones have the opposite effect of black. I've heard that red stimulates sexuality. And those shrine maidens wear red hakama... Forbidden fruit! I think the color black, is calming. It's rather stoic. And I love black school uniforms. (The look is a bit different this time, but it's still black.) Guys look really cool in long black coats, like Keanu Reeves in the Matrix! While I worked all night, a friend of mine watched that movie over and over. She said, "Watching Keanu satisfies me so much, I don't even need to eat!" I didn't get it until I saw him myself! (Wowee!) So with Kyō, I just combined many of the traits I prefer in men. My ideal was Tôya from Ceres. (He's also a dressed in black type.) But Kyō is more of a normal guy. A writer has to love her heroine's love-interest, or the stories won't feel engaging. But it's not good if all the men in the stories are alike. That's why I was really glad when people wrote in and said that the men in Alice 19th are different! But it's still me creating it.

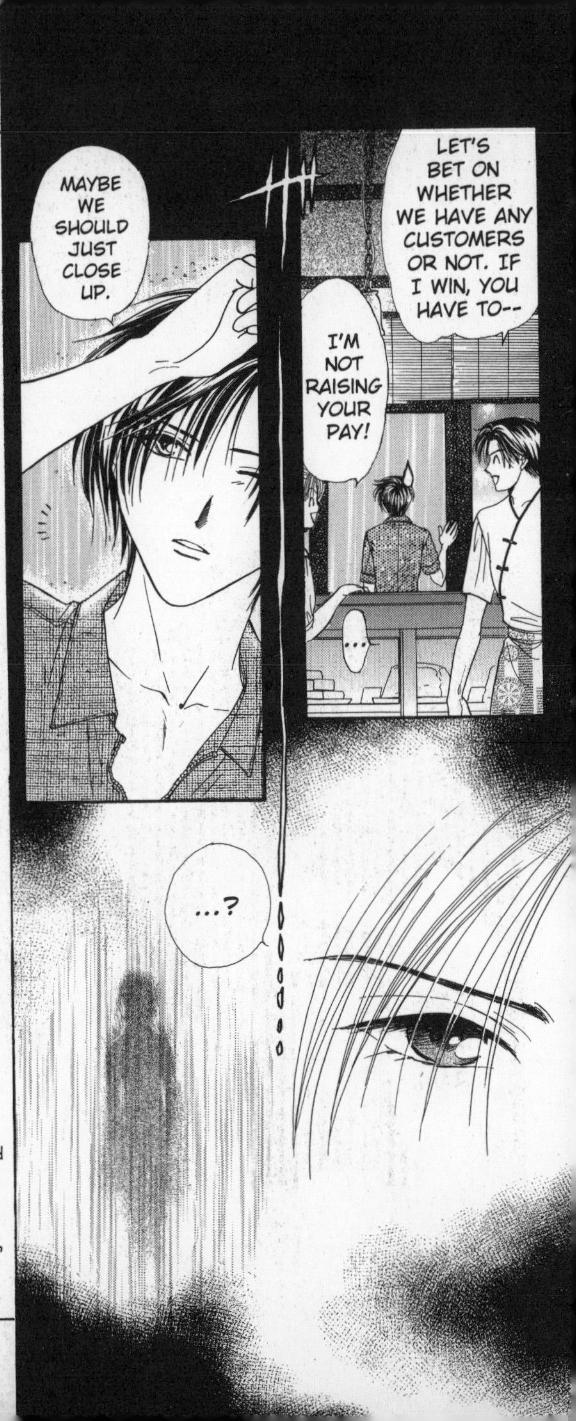
LET'S BET ON WHETHER WE HAVE ANY CUSTOMERS OR NOT. IF I WIN, YOU HAVE TO--
I'M NOT RAISING YOUR PAY!
...
MAYBE WE SHOULD JUST CLOSE UP.
...?

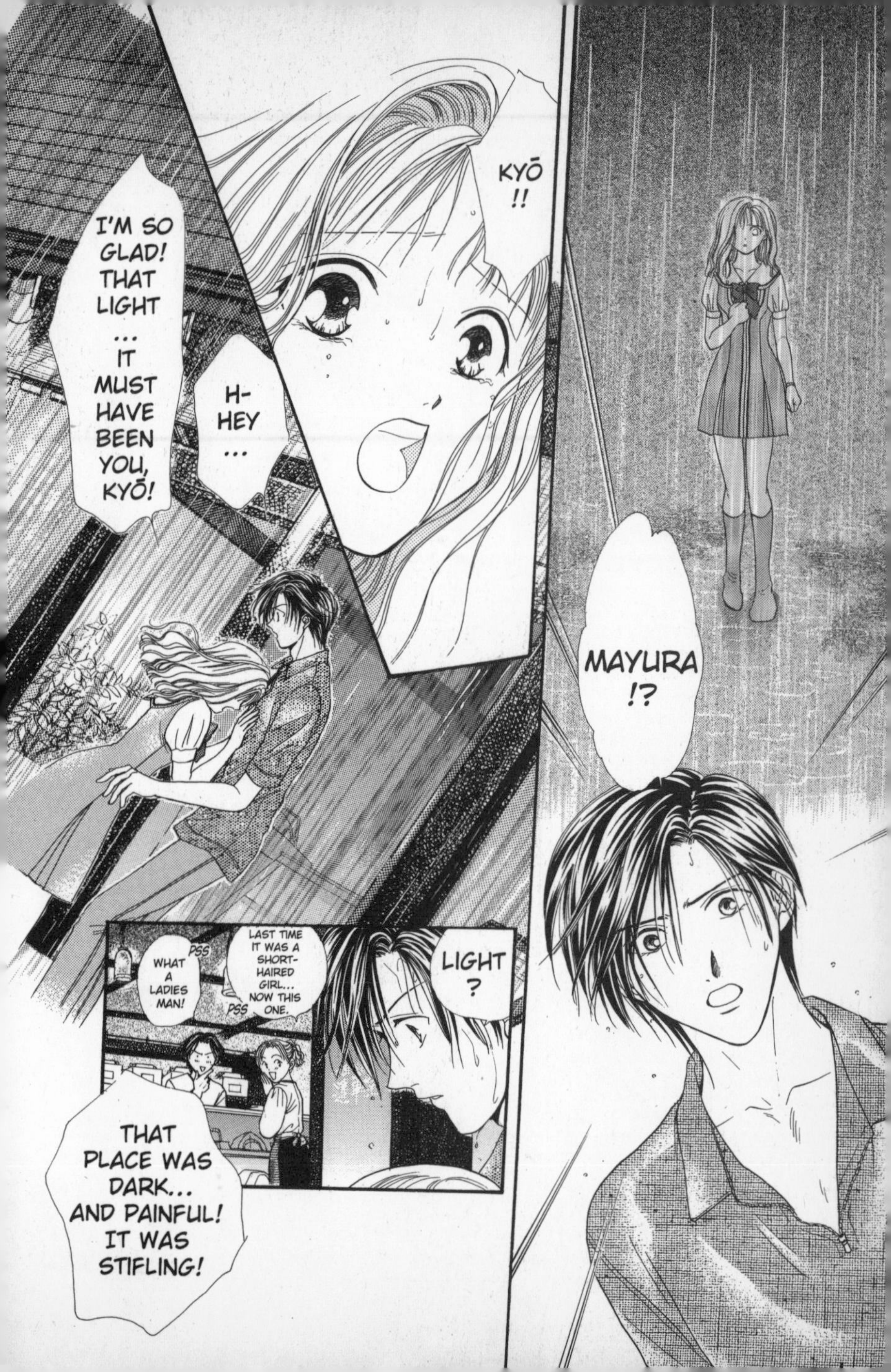
MAYURA !?
KYŌ !!
I'M SO GLAD! THAT LIGHT ... IT MUST HAVE BEEN YOU, KYŌ!
H-HEY ...
LIGHT ?
LAST TIME IT WAS A SHORT-HAIRED GIRL... NOW THIS ONE.
PSS
WHAT A LADIES MAN!
PSS
THAT PLACE WAS DARK... AND PAINFUL! IT WAS STIFLING!

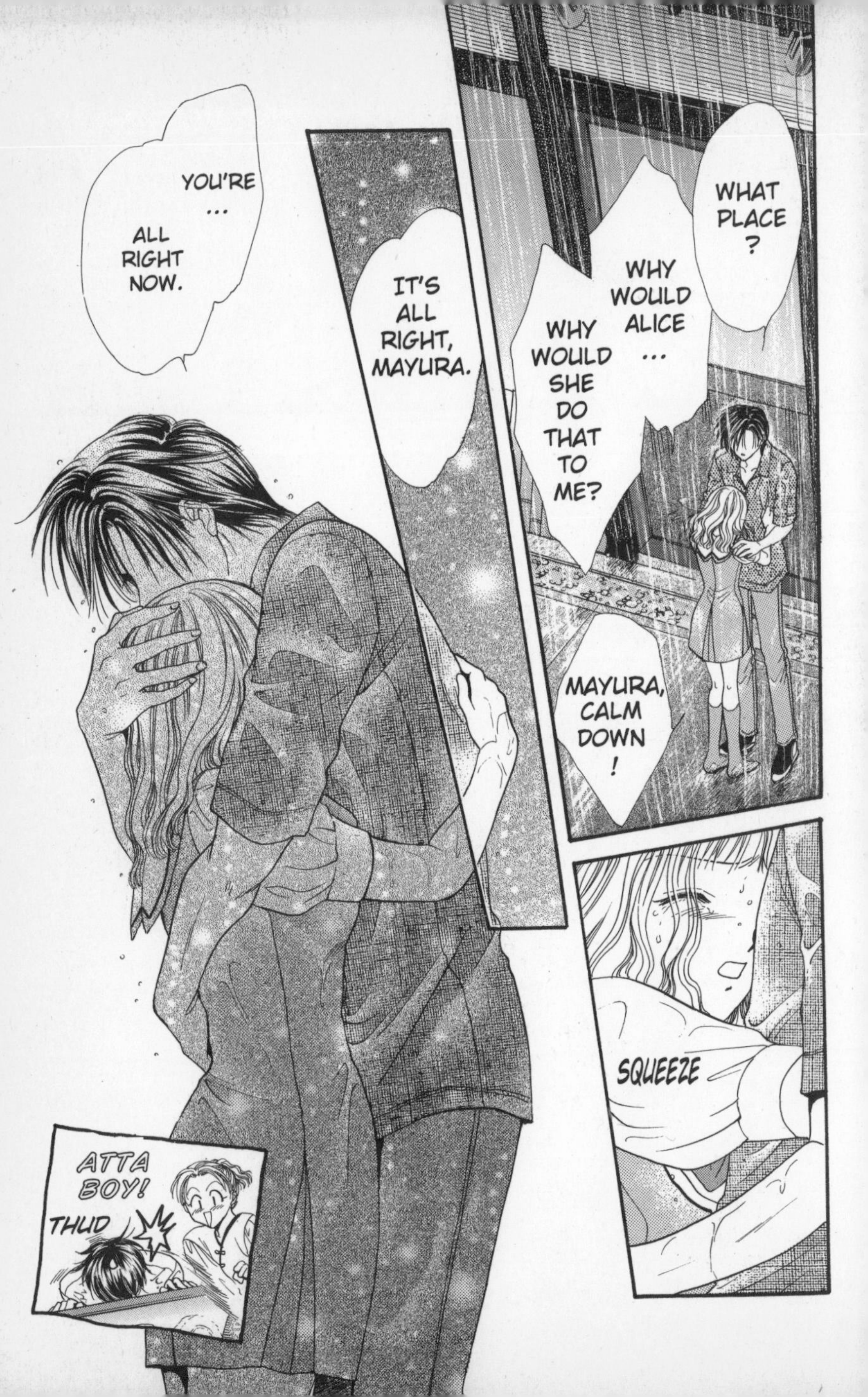
WHAT PLACE?
WHY WOULD ALICE ...
WHY WOULD SHE DO THAT TO ME?
MAYURA, CALM DOWN!
SQUEEZE
IT'S ALL RIGHT, MAYURA.
YOU'RE ... ALL RIGHT NOW.
ATTA BOY!
THUD

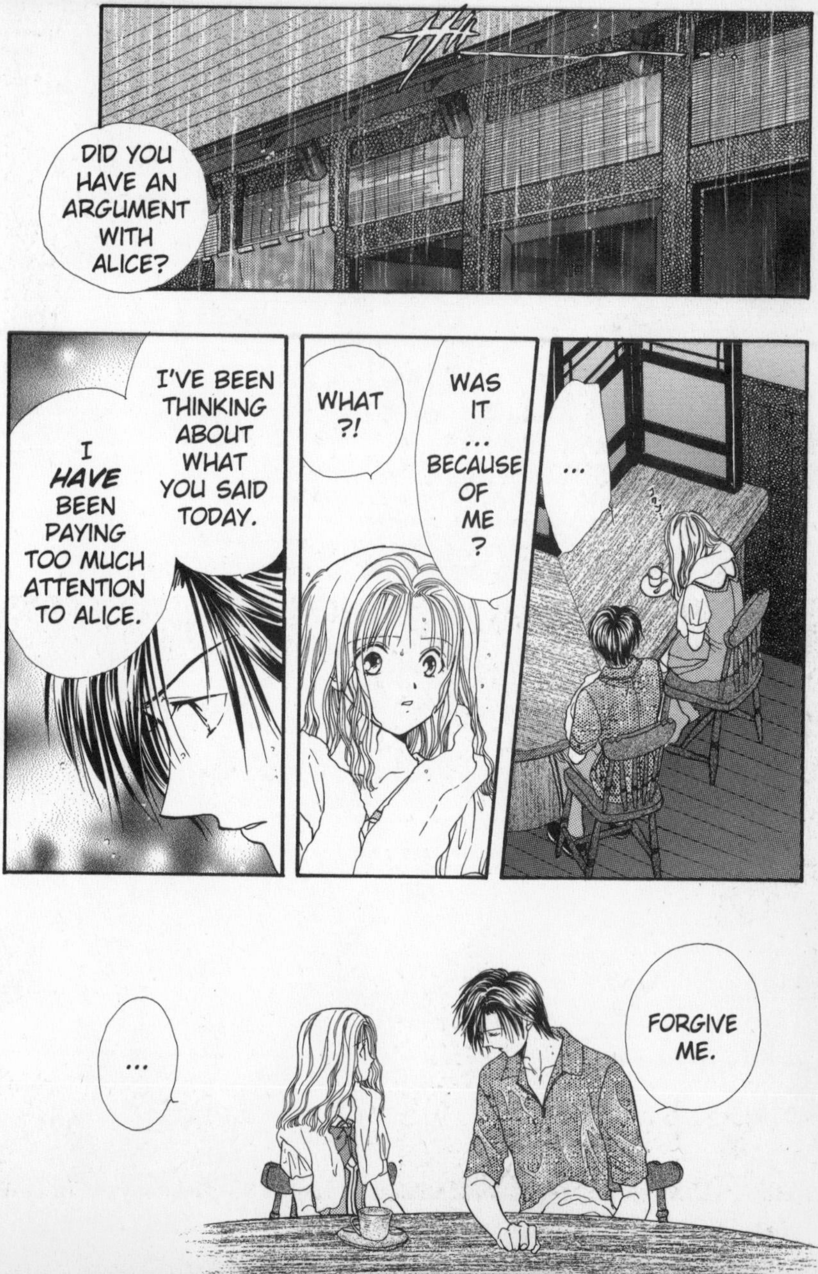
DID YOU HAVE AN ARGUMENT WITH ALICE?
...
WAS IT ... BECAUSE OF ME ?
WHAT ?!
I'VE BEEN THINKING ABOUT WHAT YOU SAID TODAY.
I *HAVE* BEEN PAYING TOO MUCH ATTENTION TO ALICE.
FORGIVE ME.
...

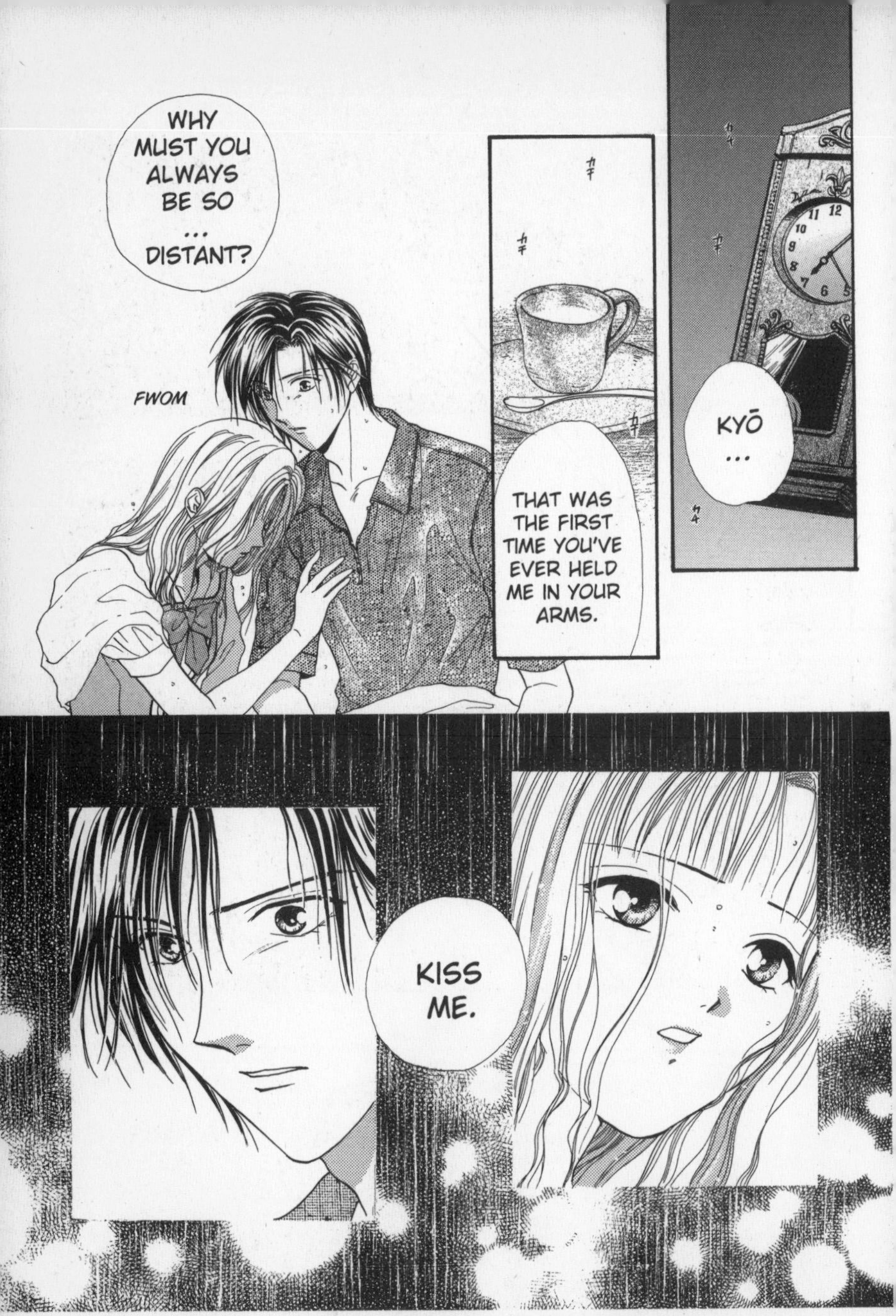
KYŌ ...
THAT WAS THE FIRST TIME YOU'VE EVER HELD ME IN YOUR ARMS.
WHY MUST YOU ALWAYS BE SO ... DISTANT?
FWOM
KISS ME.

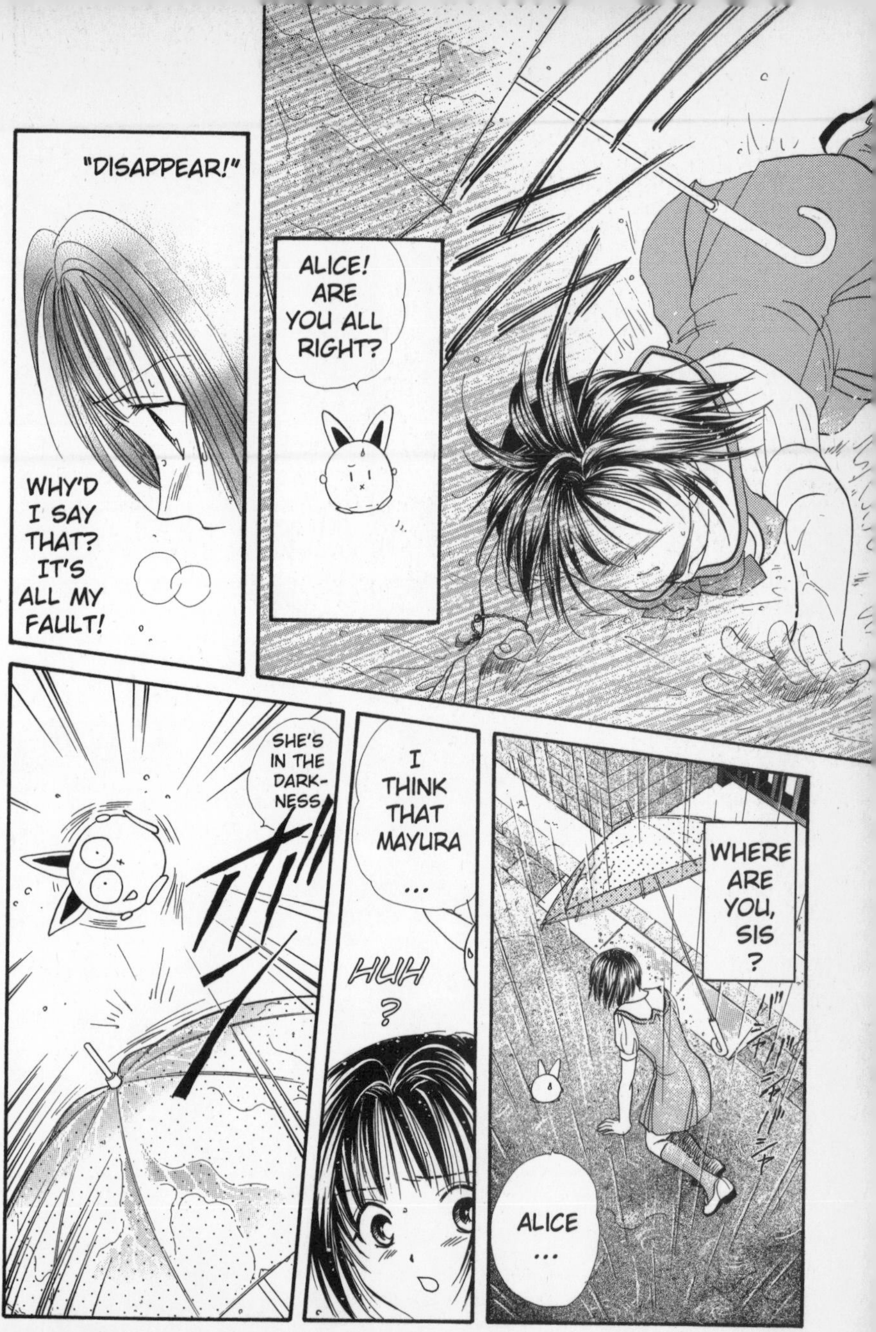
ALICE! ARE YOU ALL RIGHT?
"DISAPPEAR!"
WHY'D I SAY THAT? IT'S ALL MY FAULT!
WHERE ARE YOU, SIS?
ALICE ...
I THINK THAT MAYURA ...
HUH ?
SHE'S IN THE DARKNESS.

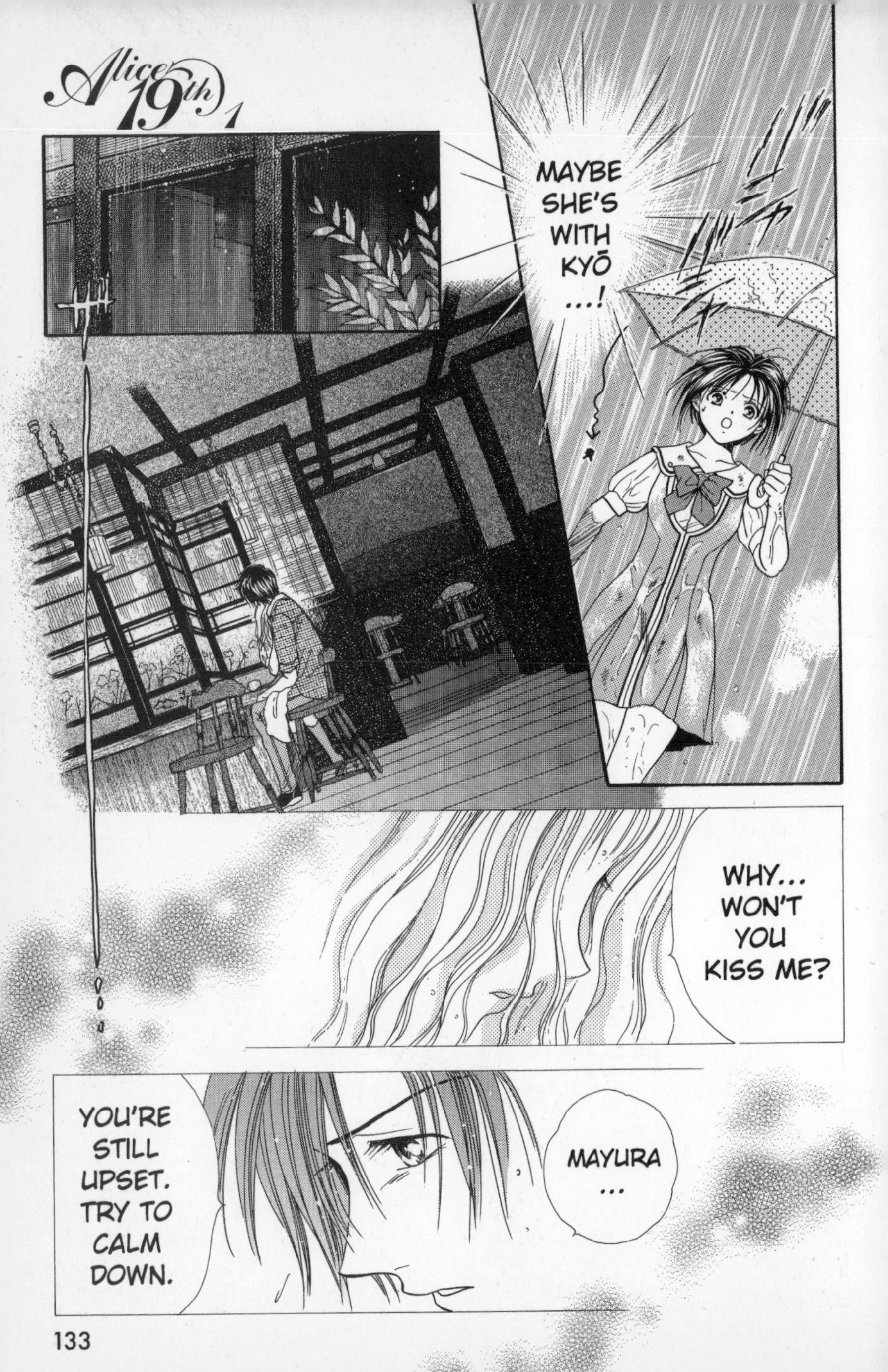
MAYBE SHE'S WITH KYŌ ...!
WHY... WON'T YOU KISS ME?
MAYURA ...
YOU'RE STILL UPSET. TRY TO CALM DOWN.

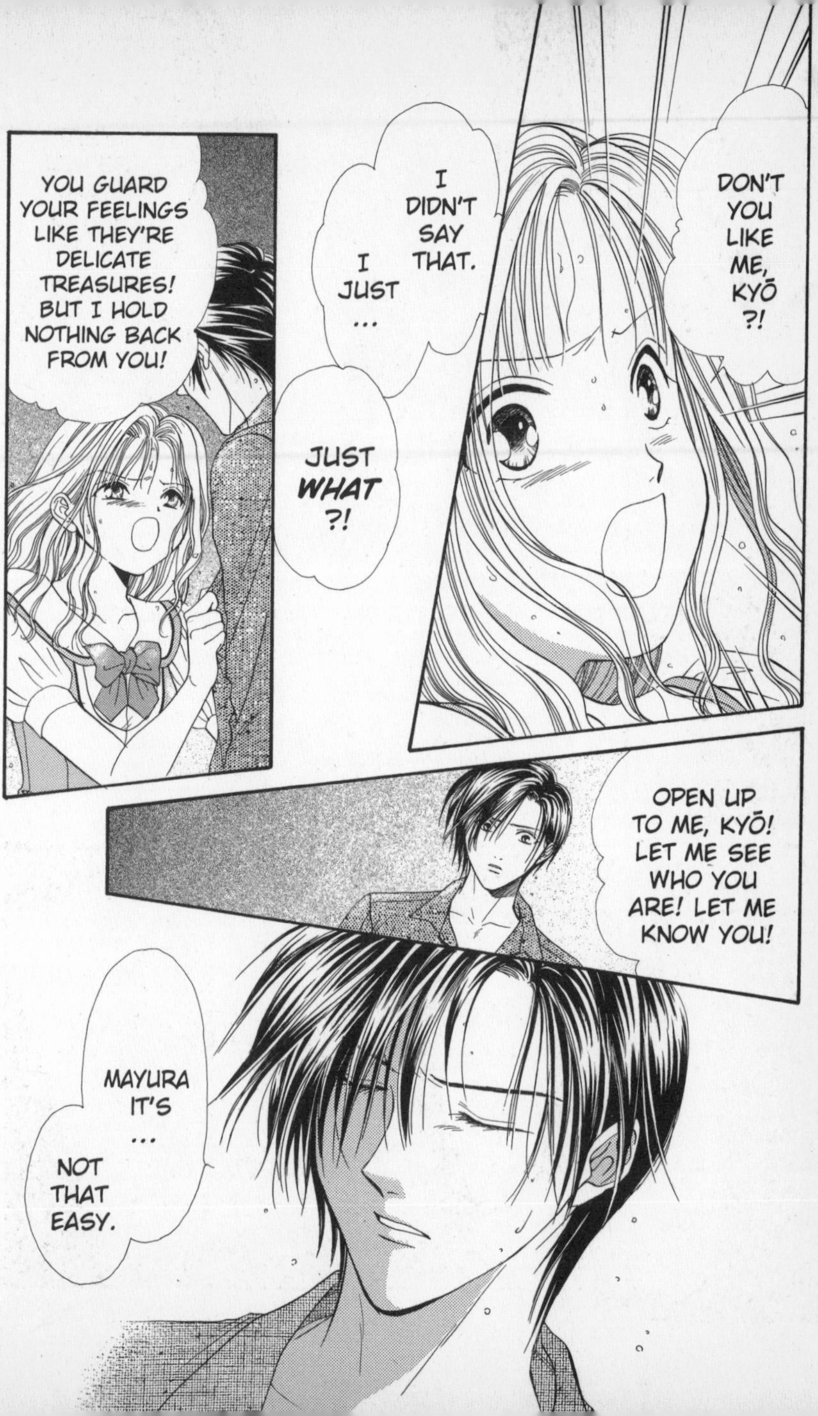
DON'T YOU LIKE ME, KYŌ?!
I DIDN'T SAY THAT.
I JUST ...
JUST *WHAT*?!
YOU GUARD YOUR FEELINGS LIKE THEY'RE DELICATE TREASURES! BUT I HOLD NOTHING BACK FROM YOU!
OPEN UP TO ME, KYŌ! LET ME SEE WHO YOU ARE! LET ME KNOW YOU!
MAYURA IT'S ...
NOT THAT EASY.

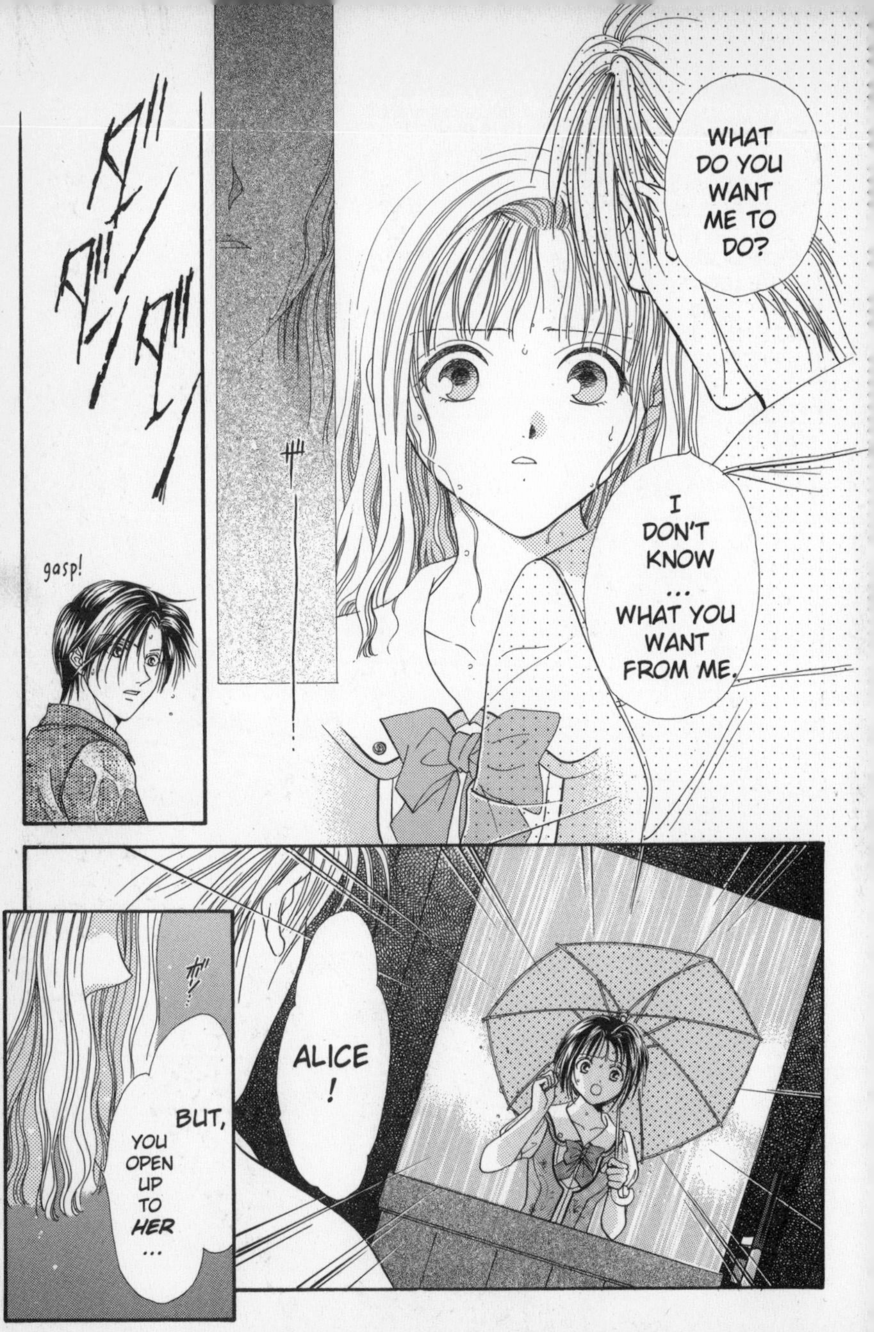
WHAT DO YOU WANT ME TO DO?
I DON'T KNOW ... WHAT YOU WANT FROM ME.
gasp!
ALICE!
BUT, YOU OPEN UP TO *HER* ...

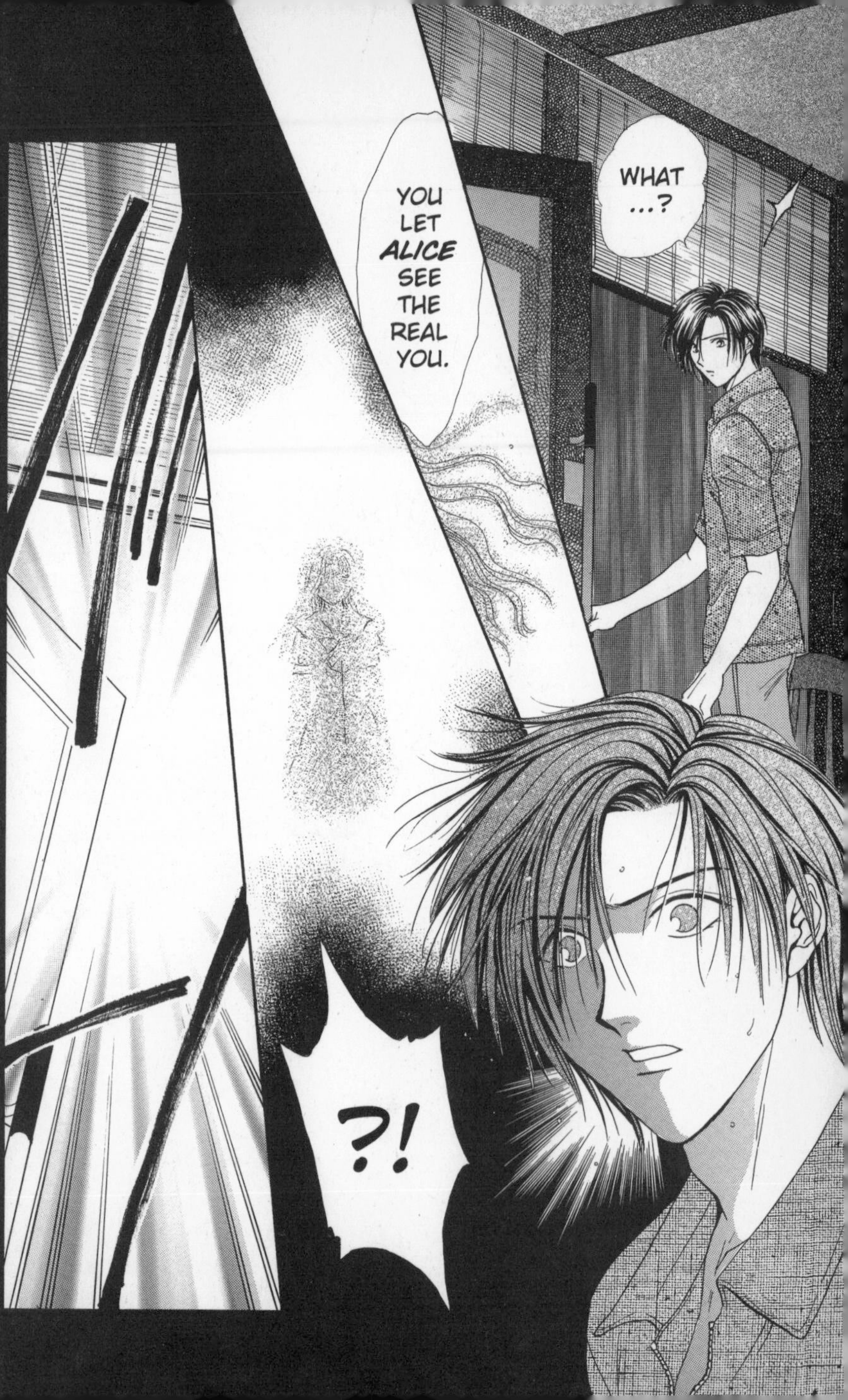
WHAT ...?
YOU LET ALICE SEE THE REAL YOU.
?!

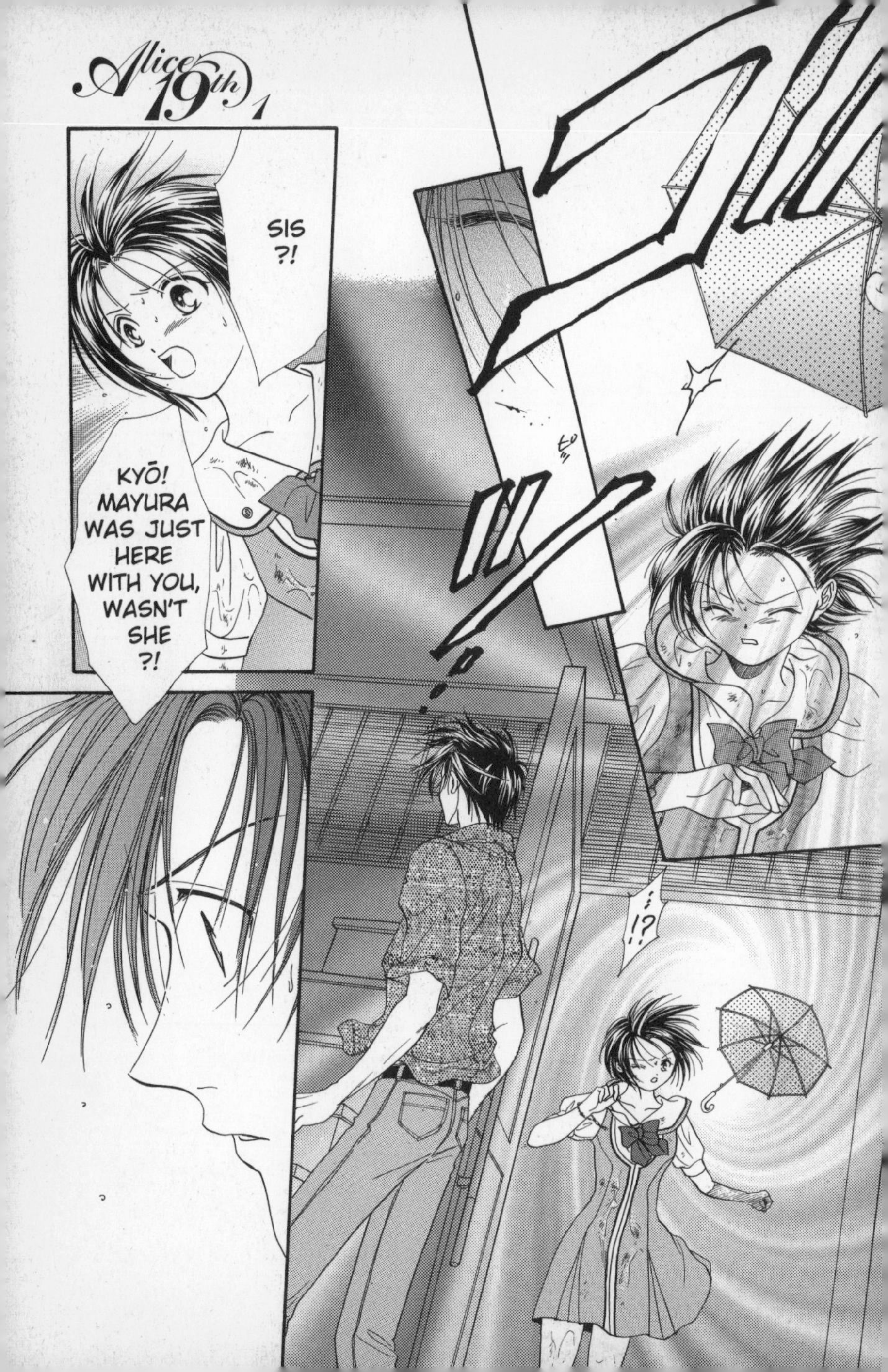
SIS ?!
KYŌ! MAYURA WAS JUST HERE WITH YOU, WASN'T SHE ?!
!?

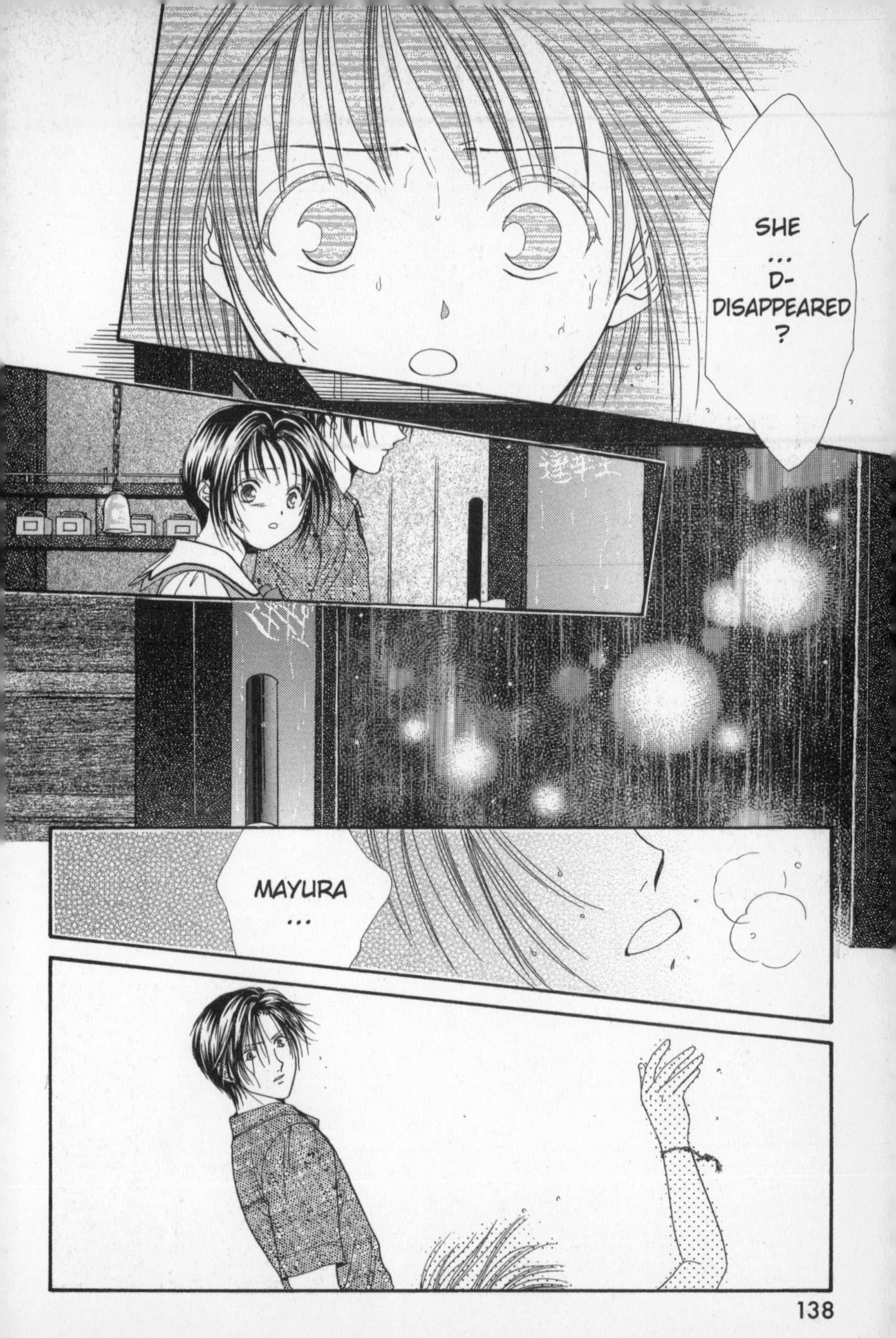
SHE ... D-DISAPPEARED?
MAYURA ...

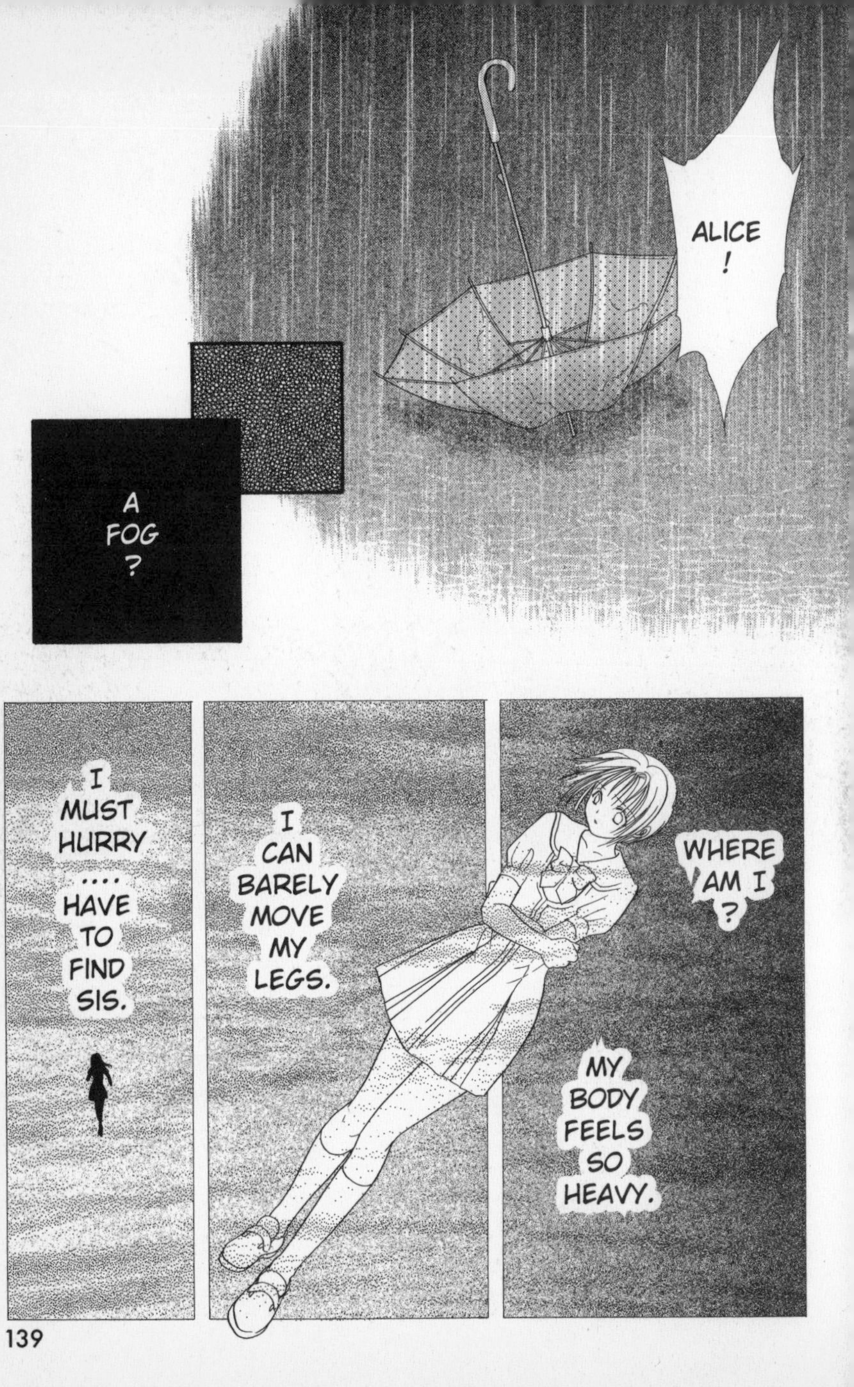
ALICE!
A FOG?
WHERE AM I?
MY BODY FEELS SO HEAVY.
I CAN BARELY MOVE MY LEGS.
I MUST HURRY .... HAVE TO FIND SIS.

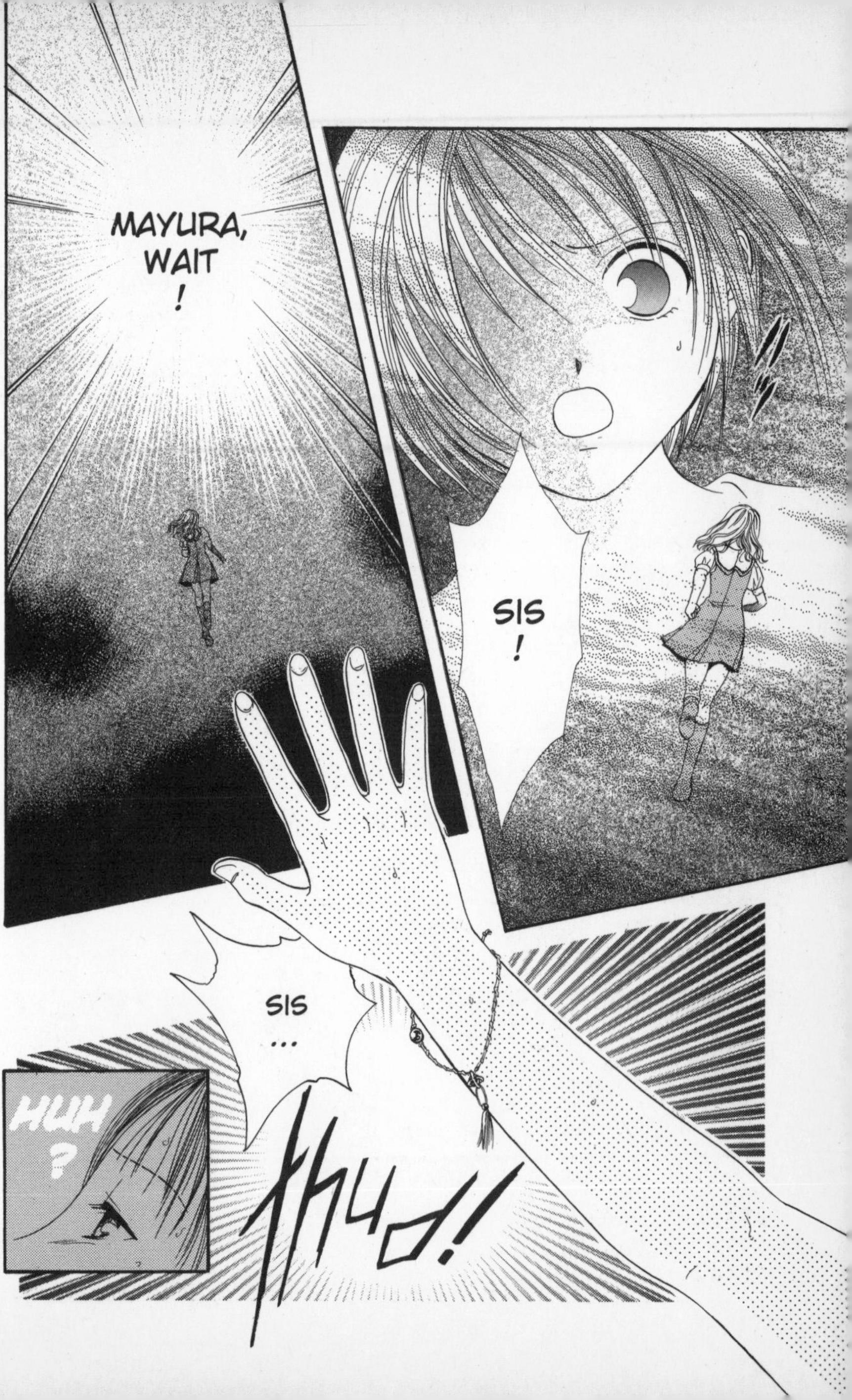
SIS!
MAYURA, WAIT!
SIS...
thud!
HUH?

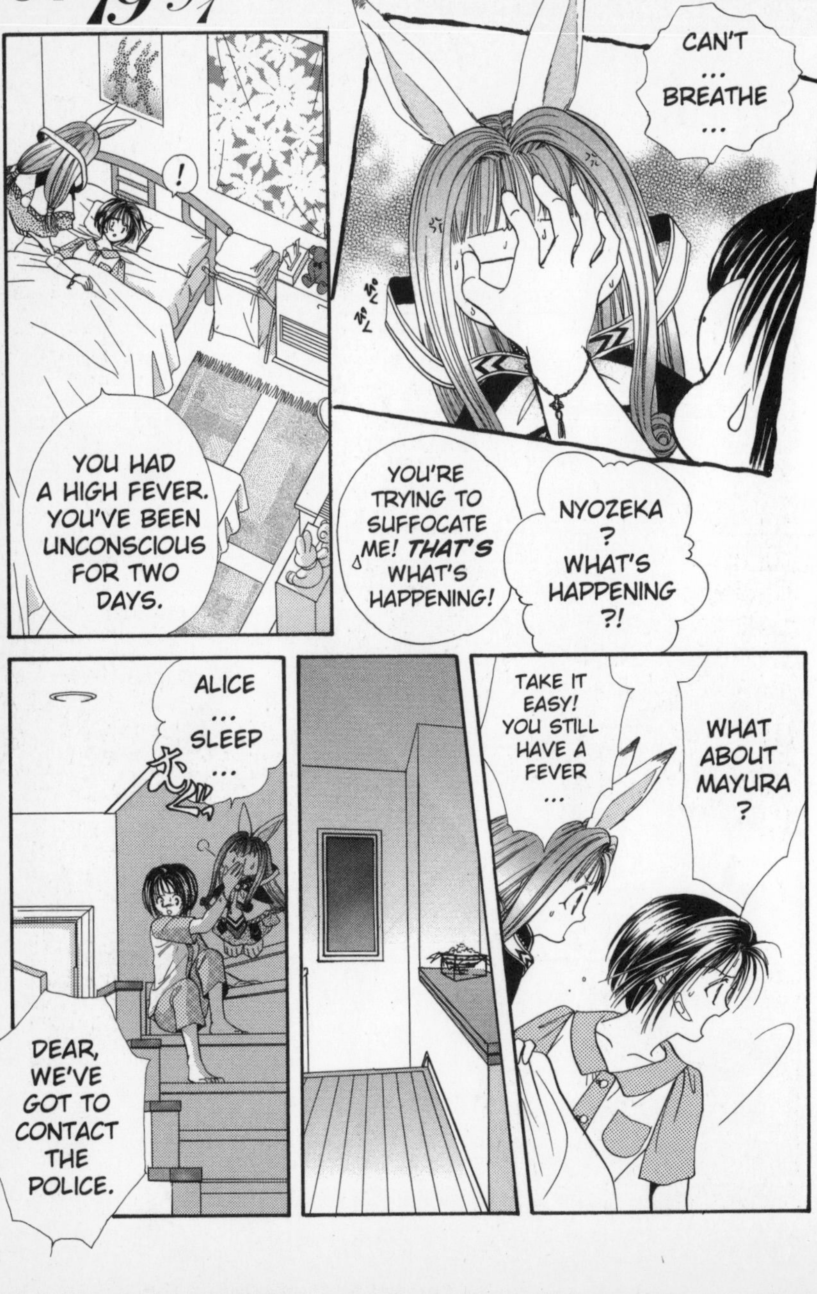
CAN'T ... BREATHE ...
NYOZEKA ? WHAT'S HAPPENING ?!
YOU'RE TRYING TO SUFFOCATE ME! THAT'S WHAT'S HAPPENING!
!
YOU HAD A HIGH FEVER. YOU'VE BEEN UNCONSCIOUS FOR TWO DAYS.
WHAT ABOUT MAYURA ?
TAKE IT EASY! YOU STILL HAVE A FEVER ...
ALICE ... SLEEP ...
DEAR, WE'VE GOT TO CONTACT THE POLICE.

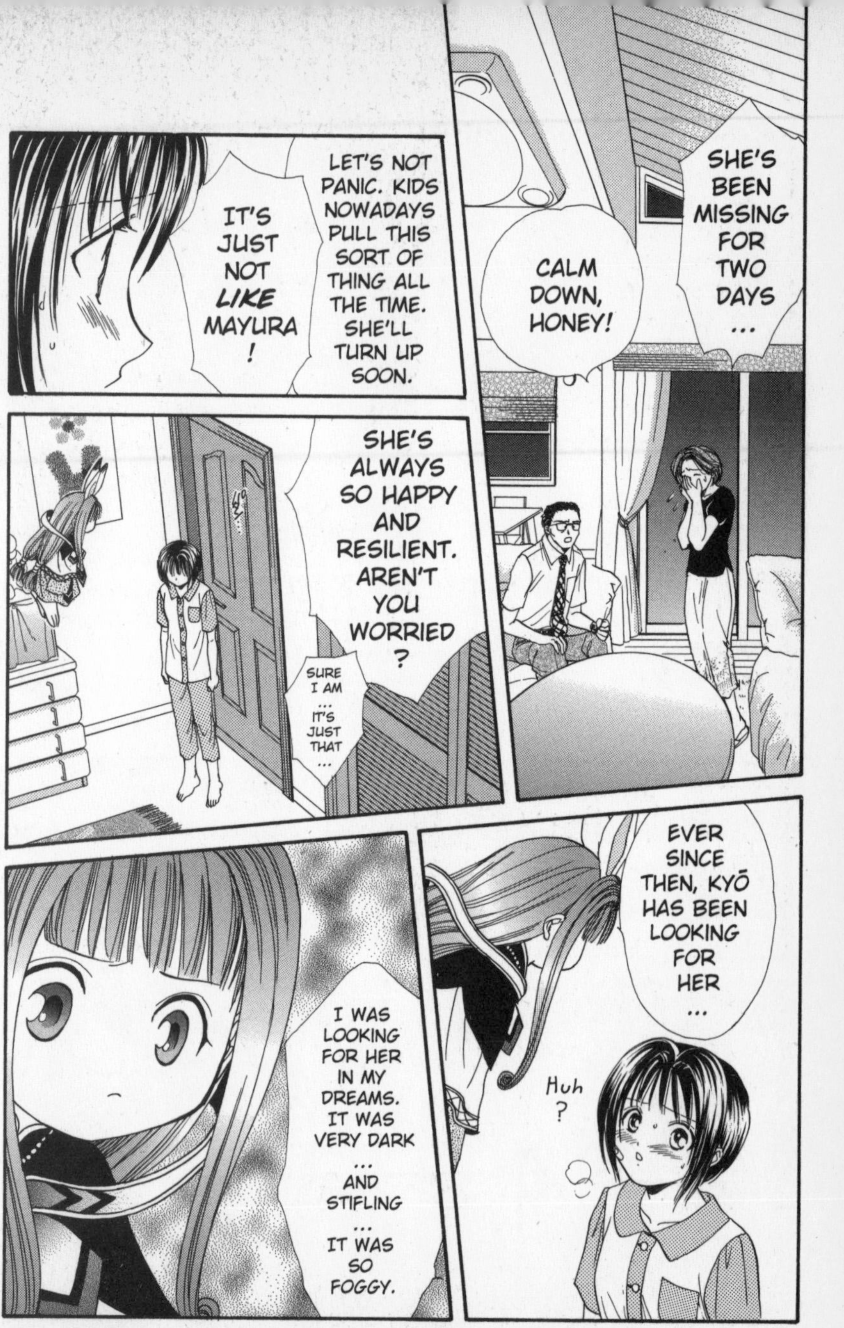
SHE'S BEEN MISSING FOR TWO DAYS ...
CALM DOWN, HONEY!
LET'S NOT PANIC. KIDS NOWADAYS PULL THIS SORT OF THING ALL THE TIME. SHE'LL TURN UP SOON.
IT'S JUST NOT *LIKE* MAYURA!
SHE'S ALWAYS SO HAPPY AND RESILIENT. AREN'T YOU WORRIED?
SURE I AM ... IT'S JUST THAT ...
EVER SINCE THEN, KYŌ HAS BEEN LOOKING FOR HER ...
Huh?
I WAS LOOKING FOR HER IN MY DREAMS. IT WAS VERY DARK ... AND STIFLING ... IT WAS SO FOGGY.

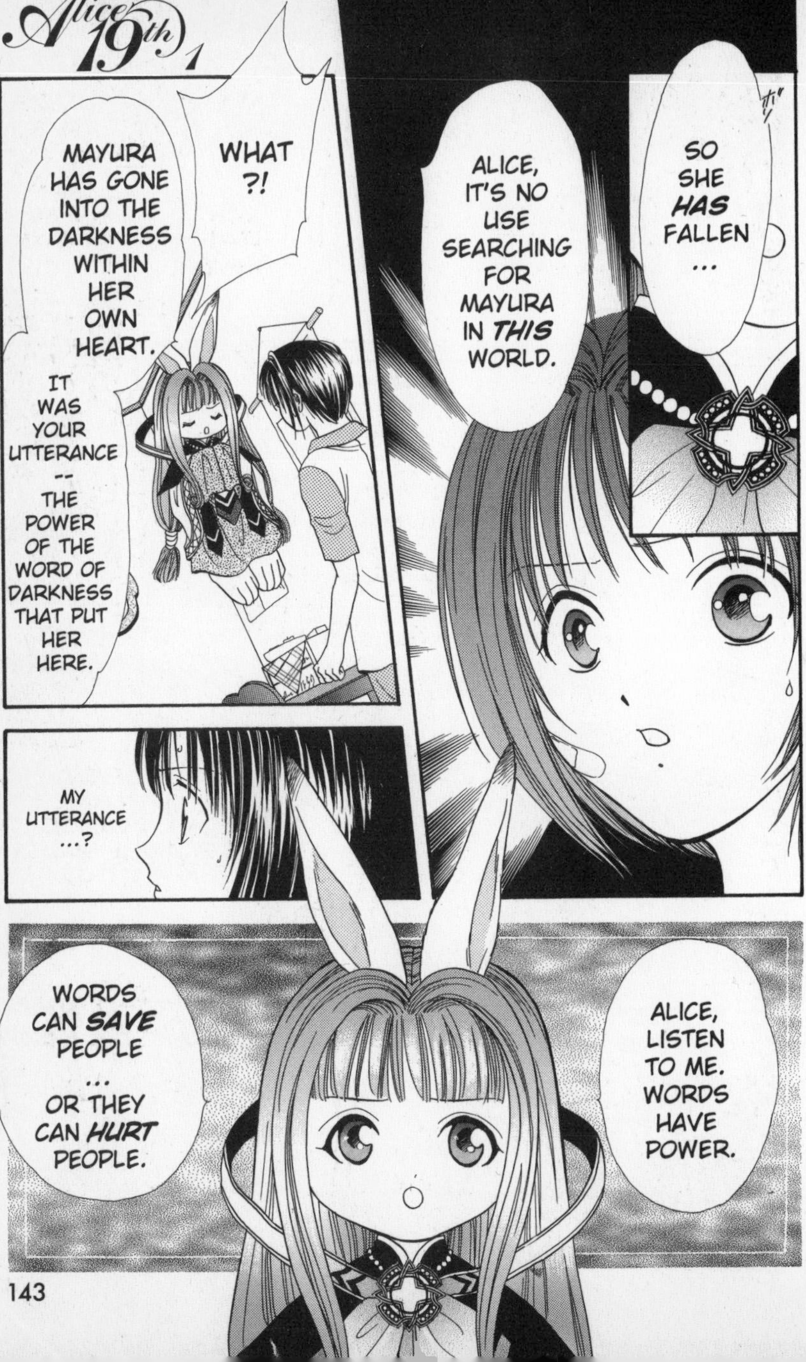
SO SHE *HAS* FALLEN ...
ALICE, IT'S NO USE SEARCHING FOR MAYURA IN *THIS* WORLD.
WHAT ?!
MAYURA HAS GONE INTO THE DARKNESS WITHIN HER OWN HEART.
IT WAS YOUR UTTERANCE -- THE POWER OF THE WORD OF DARKNESS THAT PUT HER HERE.
MY UTTERANCE ...?
ALICE, LISTEN TO ME. WORDS HAVE POWER.
WORDS CAN *SAVE* PEOPLE ... OR THEY CAN *HURT* PEOPLE.

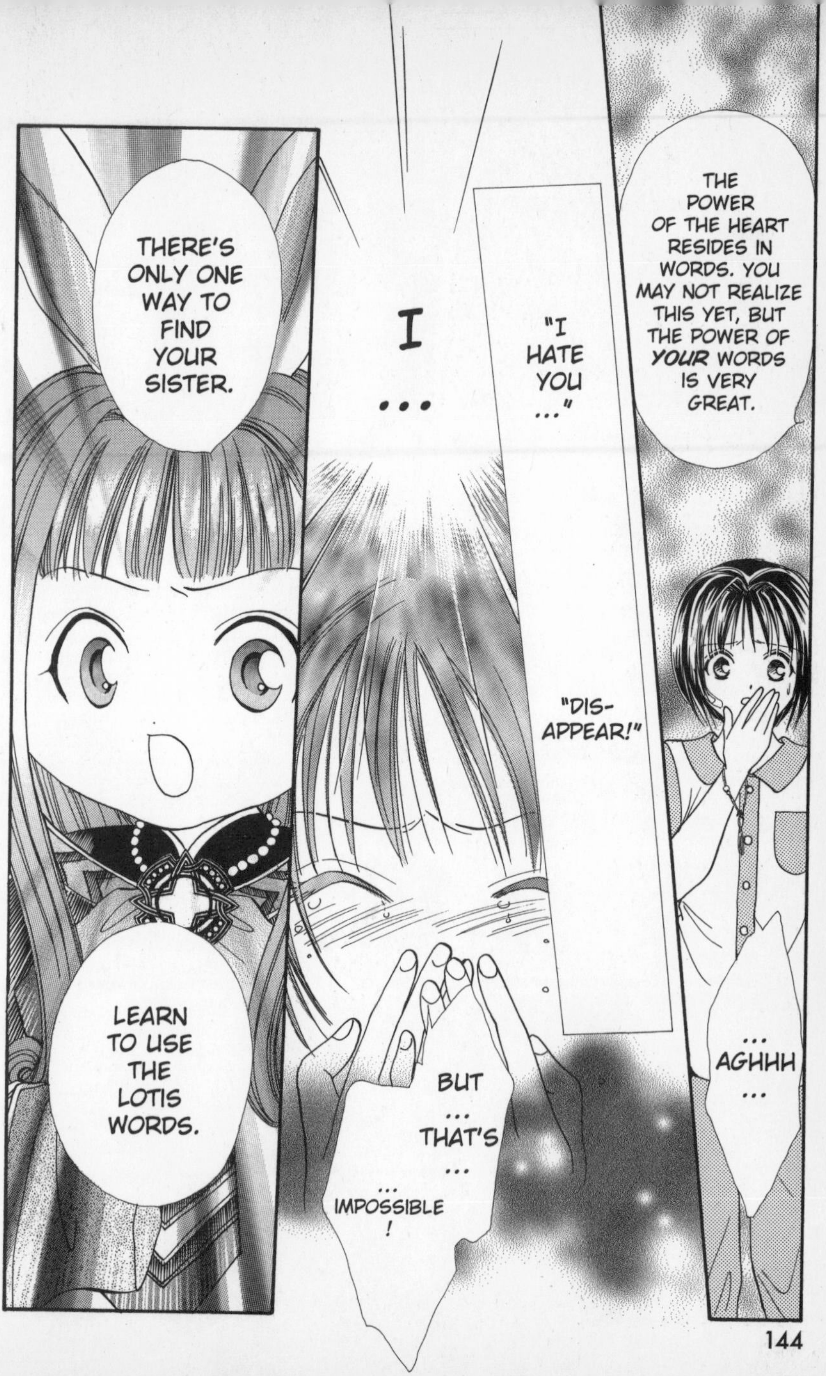
THE POWER OF THE HEART RESIDES IN WORDS. YOU MAY NOT REALIZE THIS YET, BUT THE POWER OF *YOUR* WORDS IS VERY GREAT.
... AGHHH ...
I ...
"I HATE YOU ..."
"DIS- APPEAR!"
BUT ... THAT'S ...
... IMPOSSIBLE !
THERE'S ONLY ONE WAY TO FIND YOUR SISTER.
LEARN TO USE THE LOTIS WORDS.

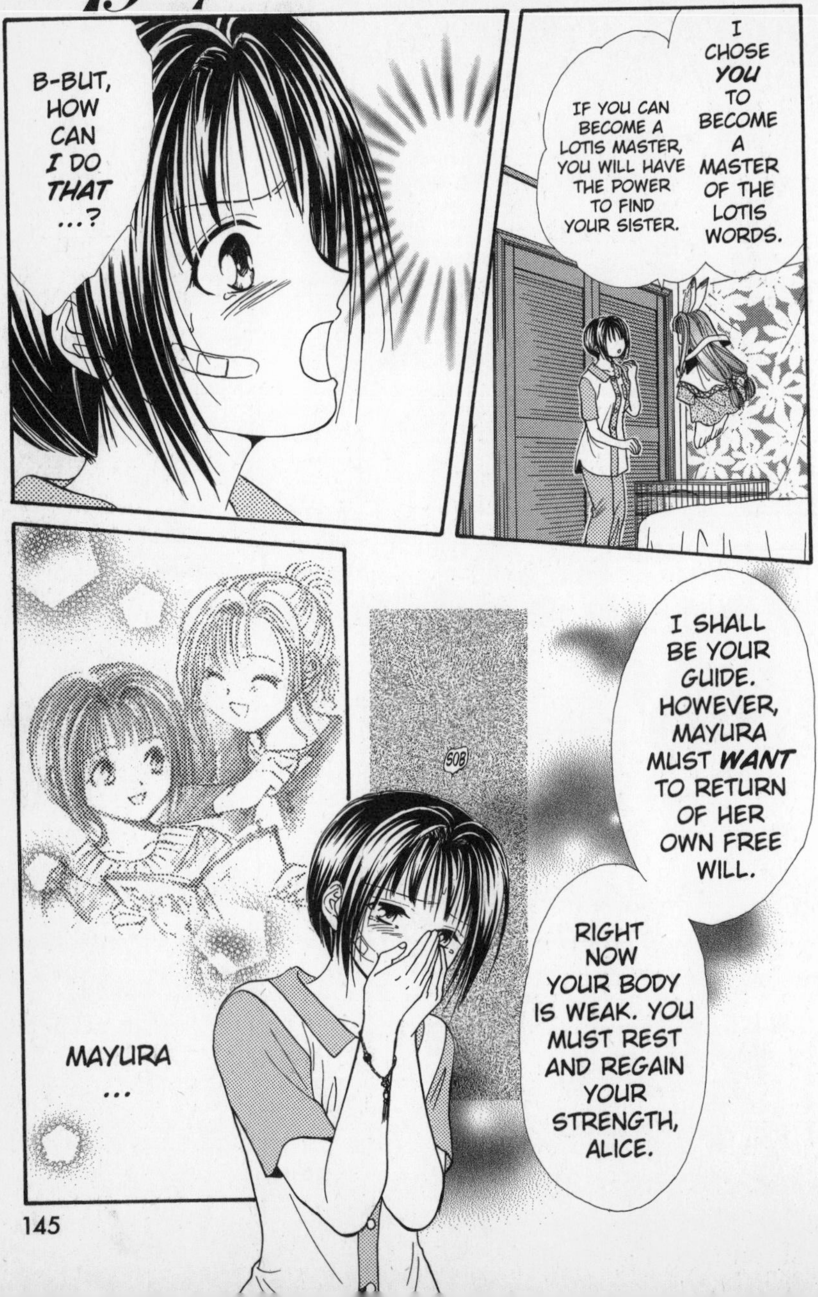
I CHOSE YOU TO BECOME A MASTER OF THE LOTIS WORDS.
IF YOU CAN BECOME A LOTIS MASTER, YOU WILL HAVE THE POWER TO FIND YOUR SISTER.
B-BUT, HOW CAN I DO THAT ...?
I SHALL BE YOUR GUIDE. HOWEVER, MAYURA MUST WANT TO RETURN OF HER OWN FREE WILL.
RIGHT NOW YOUR BODY IS WEAK. YOU MUST REST AND REGAIN YOUR STRENGTH, ALICE.
SOB
MAYURA ...

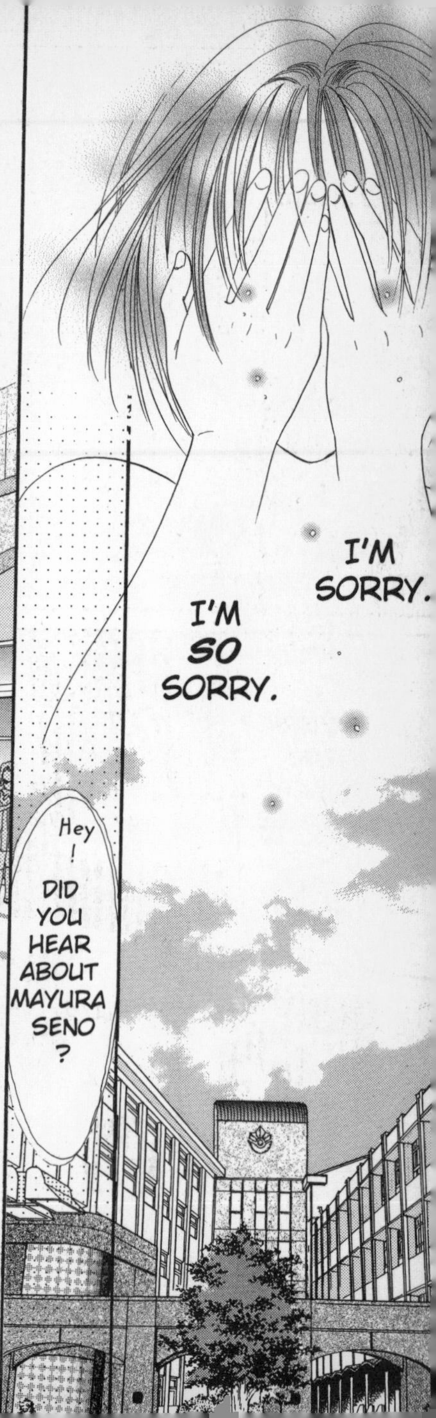
I'M SORRY.
I'M SO SORRY.
Hey! DID YOU HEAR ABOUT MAYURA SENO?

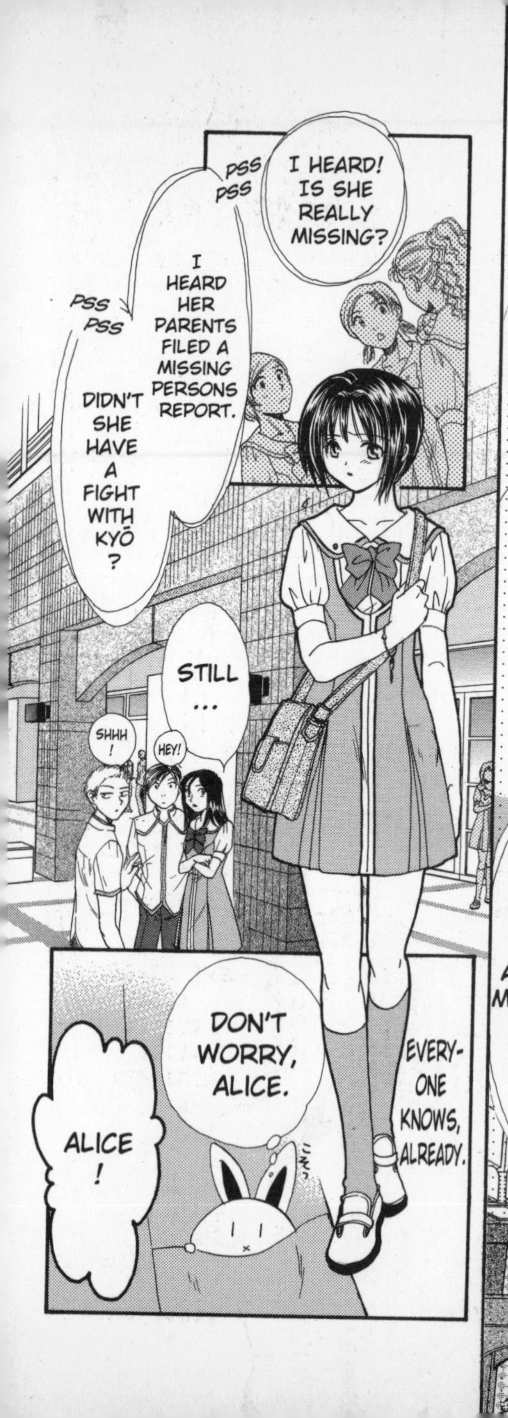
I HEARD! IS SHE REALLY MISSING?
PSS PSS
I HEARD HER PARENTS FILED A MISSING PERSONS REPORT.
PSS PSS
DIDN'T SHE HAVE A FIGHT WITH KYŌ?
STILL...
HEY!
SHHH!
EVERY-ONE KNOWS, ALREADY.
DON'T WORRY, ALICE.
ALICE!

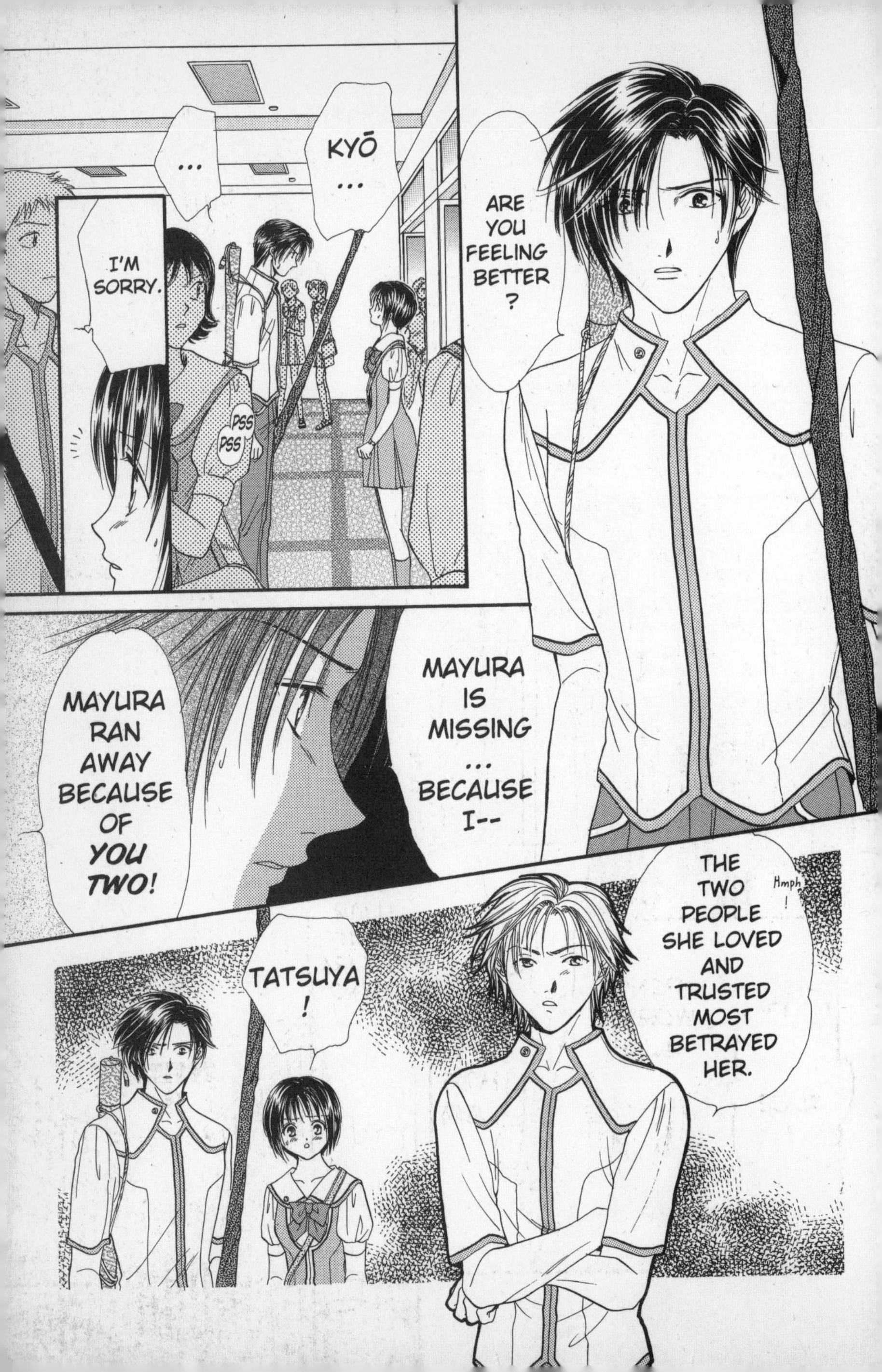
ARE YOU FEELING BETTER ?
KYŌ ...
...
I'M SORRY.
PSS PSS
MAYURA IS MISSING ... BECAUSE I--
MAYURA RAN AWAY BECAUSE OF *YOU TWO*!
THE TWO PEOPLE SHE LOVED AND TRUSTED MOST BETRAYED HER.
Hmph !
TATSUYA !

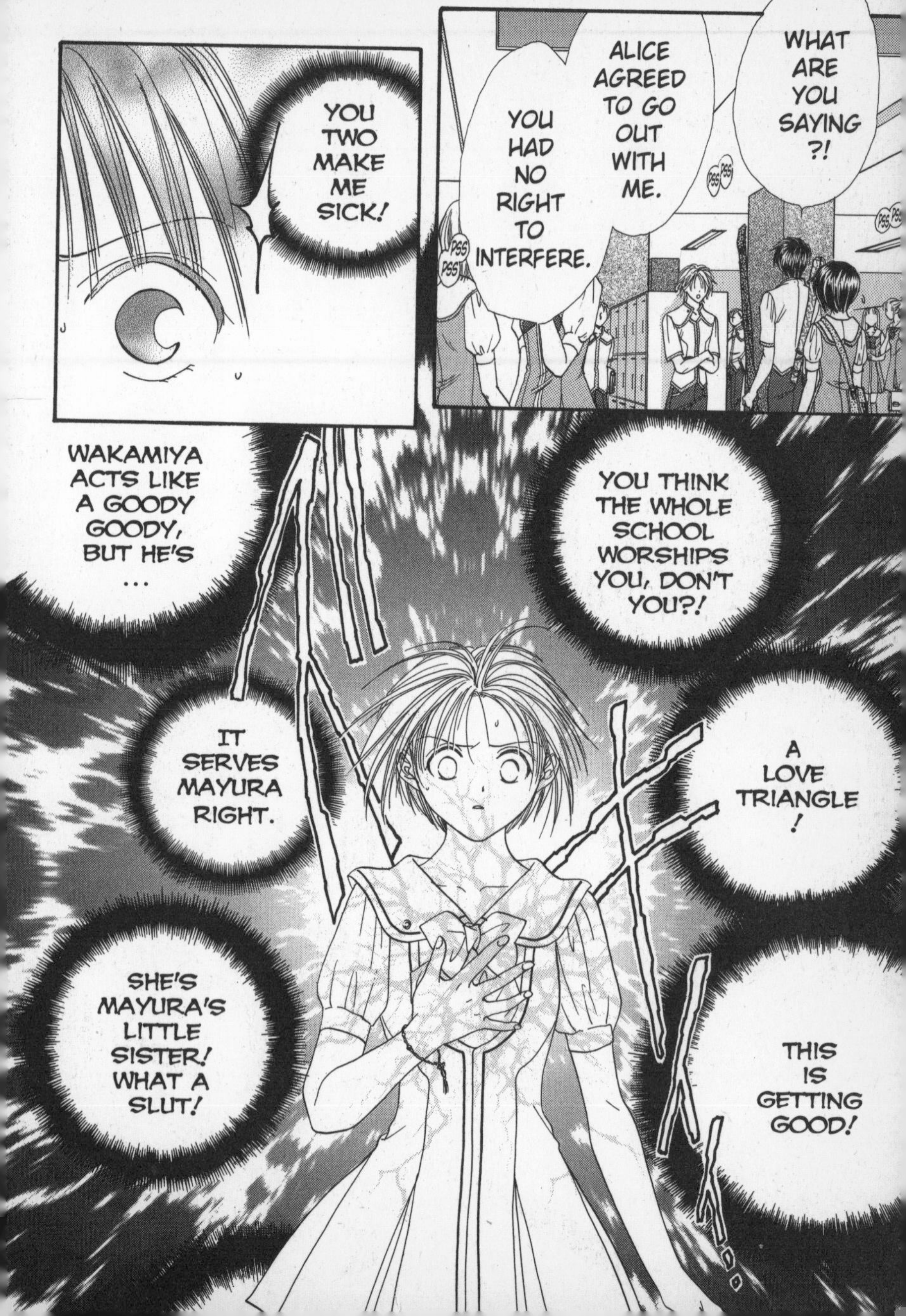
WHAT ARE YOU SAYING?!
ALICE AGREED TO GO OUT WITH ME.
YOU HAD NO RIGHT TO INTERFERE.
PSS PSS
PSS PSS
PSS PSS
YOU TWO MAKE ME SICK!
YOU THINK THE WHOLE SCHOOL WORSHIPS YOU, DON'T YOU?!
WAKAMIYA ACTS LIKE A GOODY GOODY, BUT HE'S ...
A LOVE TRIANGLE!
IT SERVES MAYURA RIGHT.
THIS IS GETTING GOOD!
SHE'S MAYURA'S LITTLE SISTER! WHAT A SLUT!

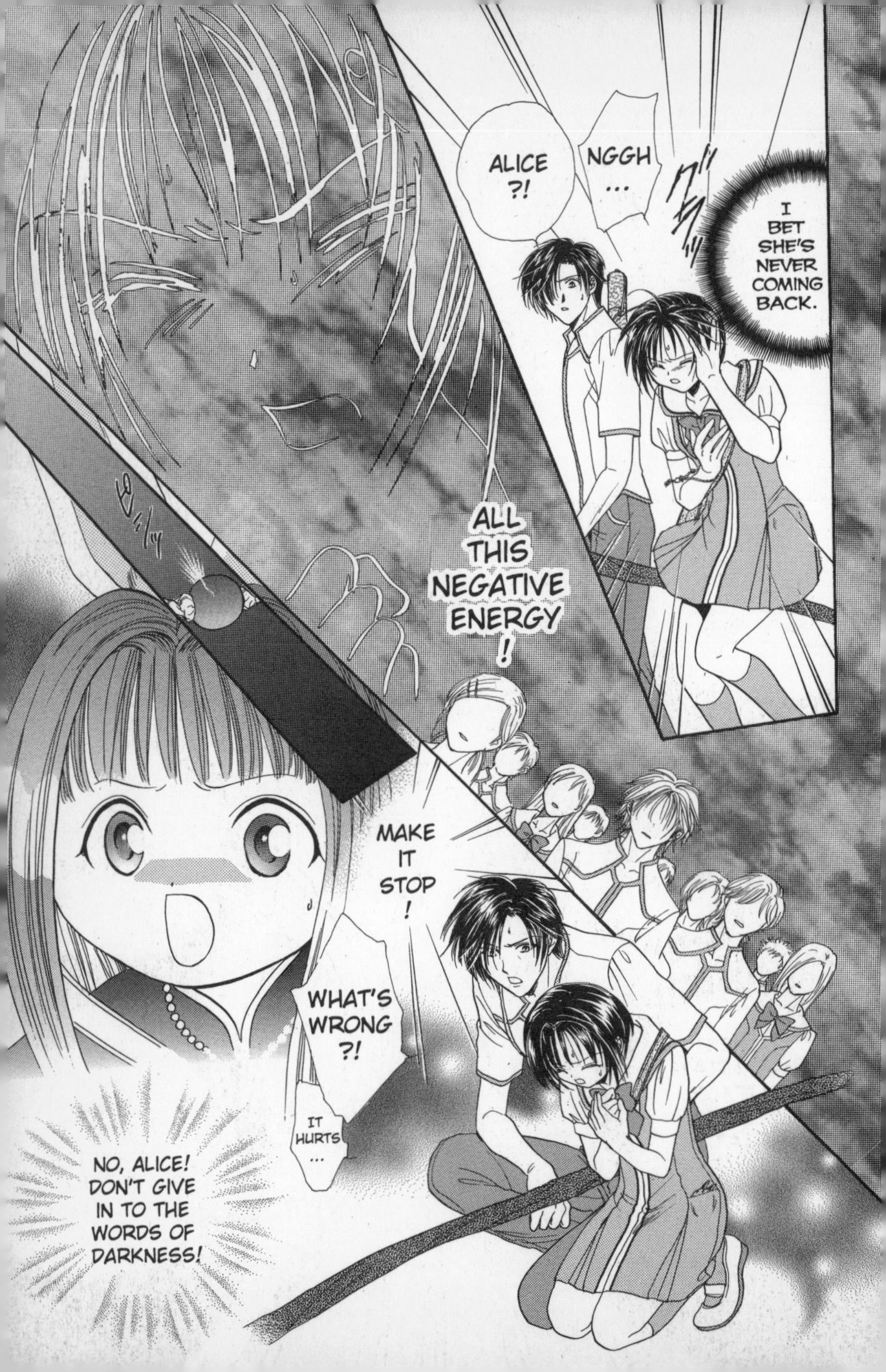
I BET SHE'S NEVER COMING BACK.
NGGH ...
ALICE ?!
ALL THIS NEGATIVE ENERGY !
MAKE IT STOP !
WHAT'S WRONG ?!
IT HURTS ...
NO, ALICE! DON'T GIVE IN TO THE WORDS OF DARKNESS!

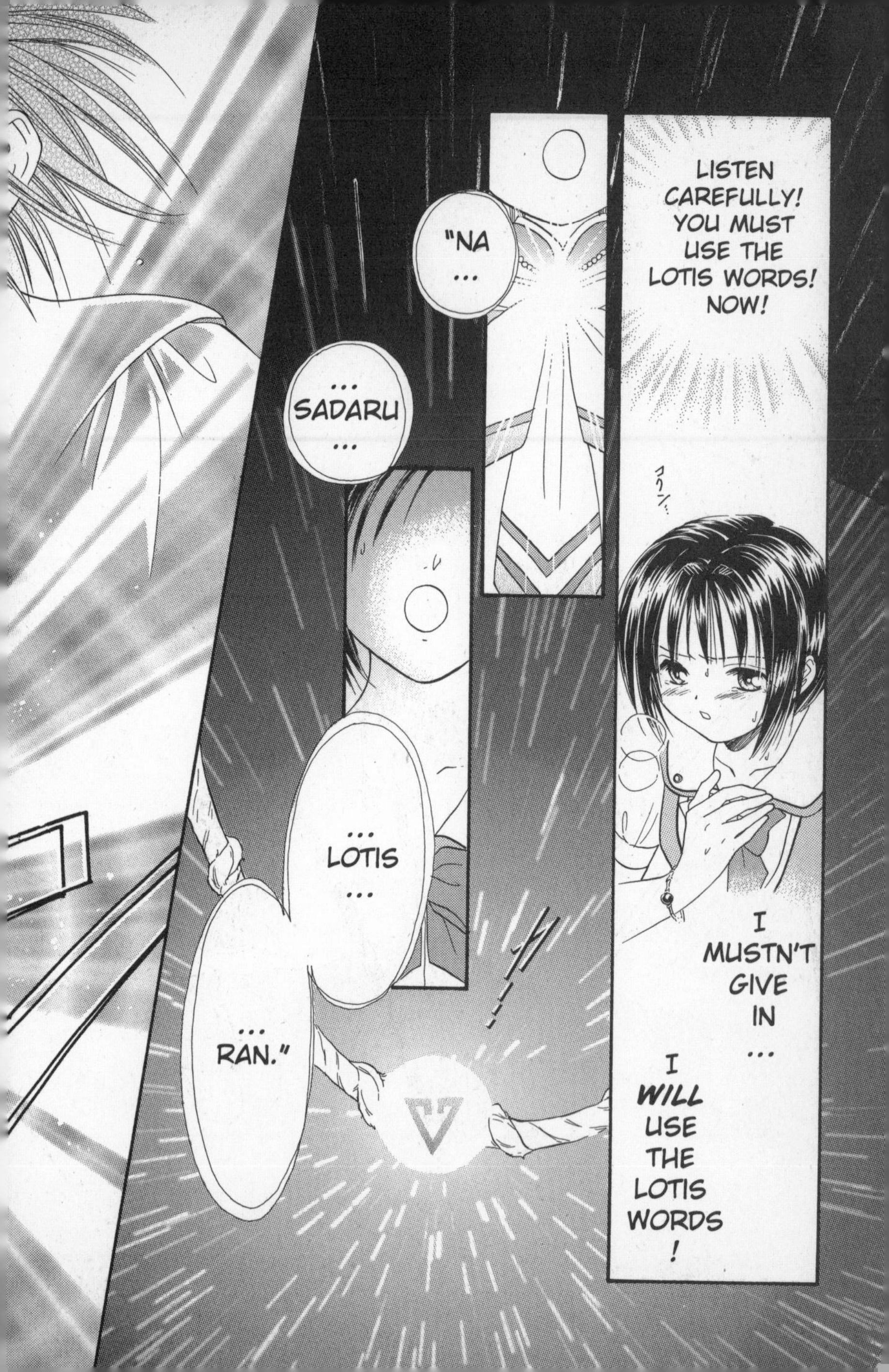
LISTEN CAREFULLY! YOU MUST USE THE LOTIS WORDS! NOW!
I MUSTN'T GIVE IN ...
I WILL USE THE LOTIS WORDS!
"NA ...
... SADARU ...
... LOTIS ...
... RAN."

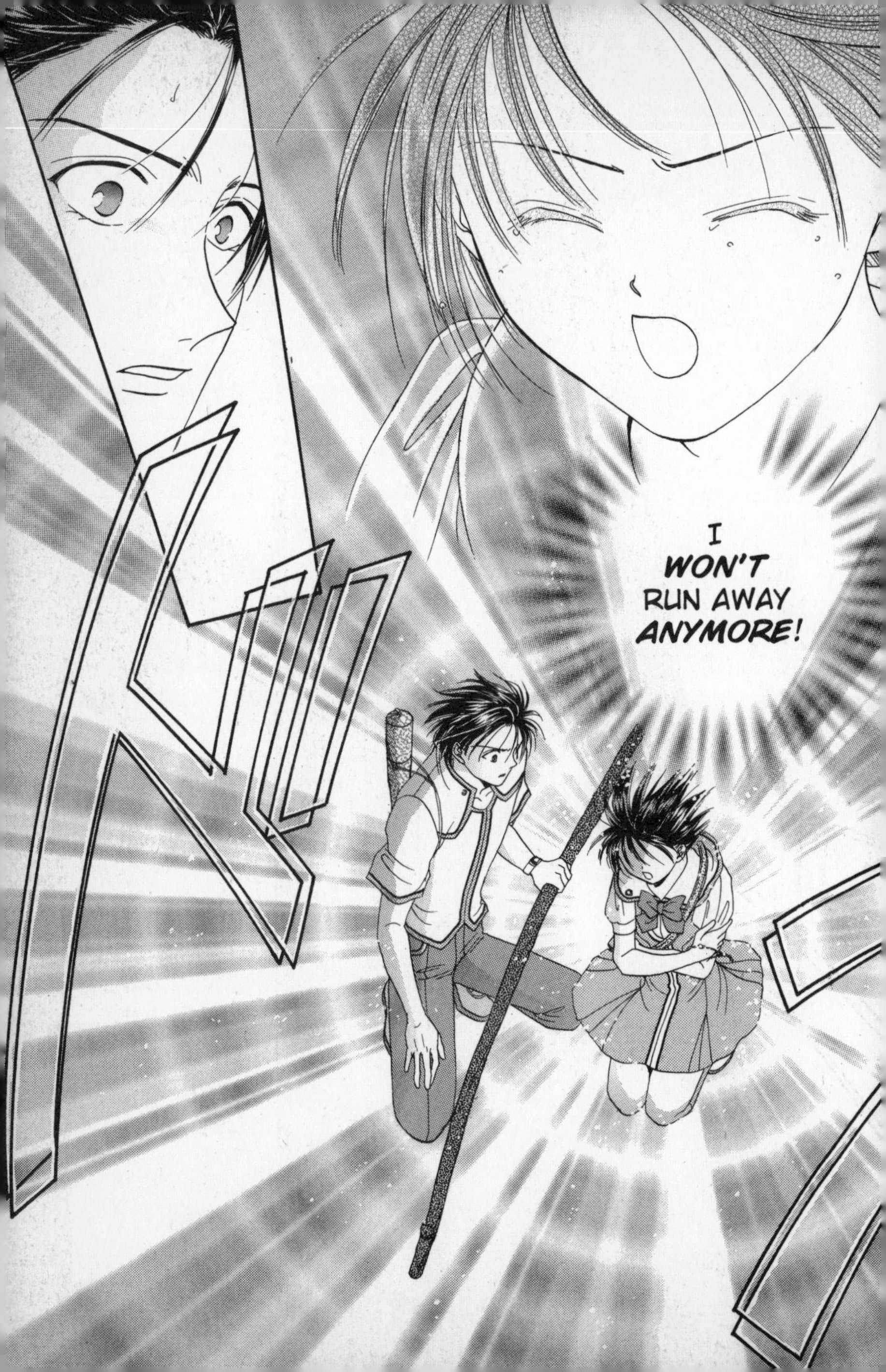
I WON'T RUN AWAY ANYMORE!

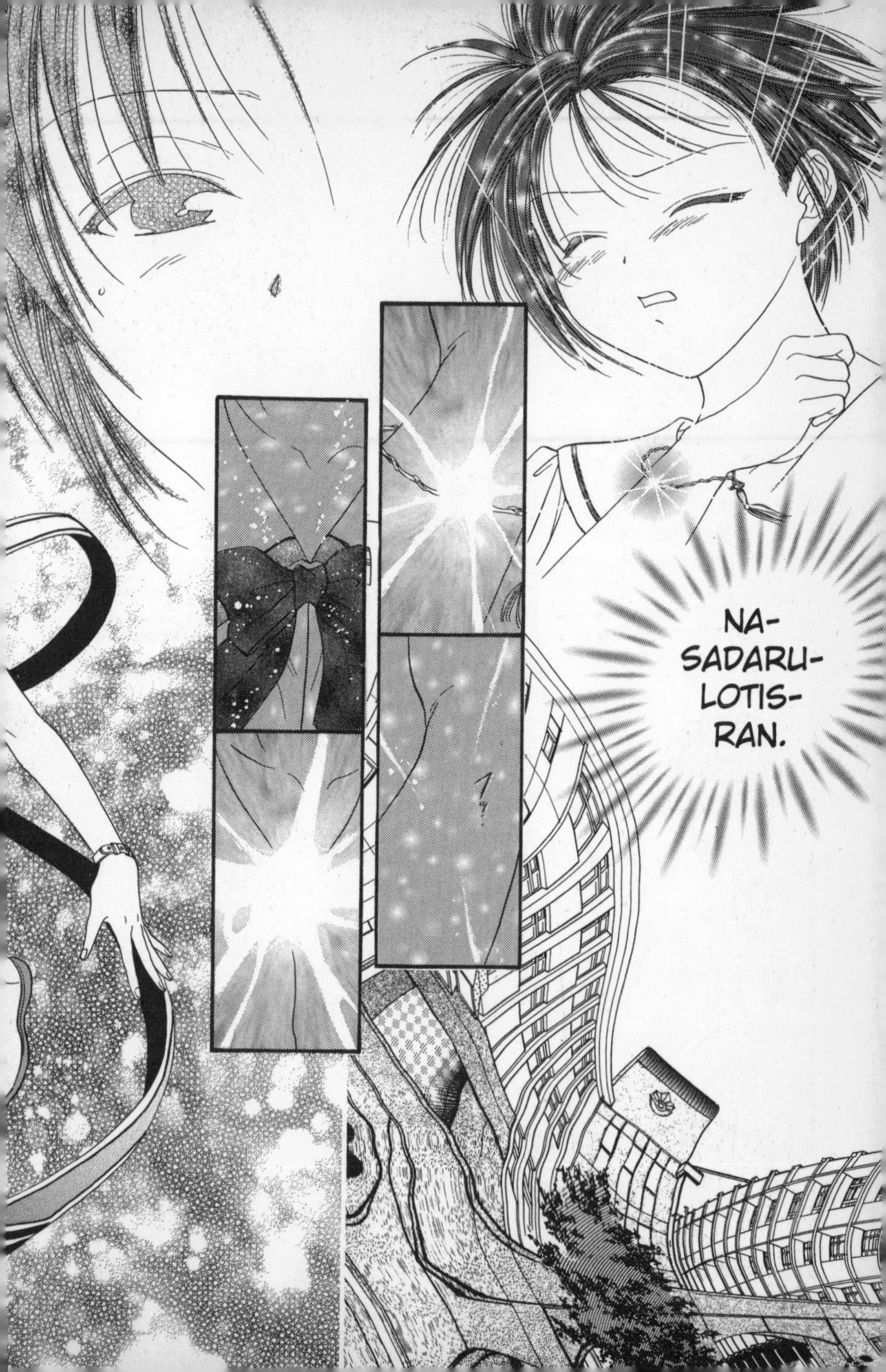
NA-
SADARU-
LOTIS-
RAN.

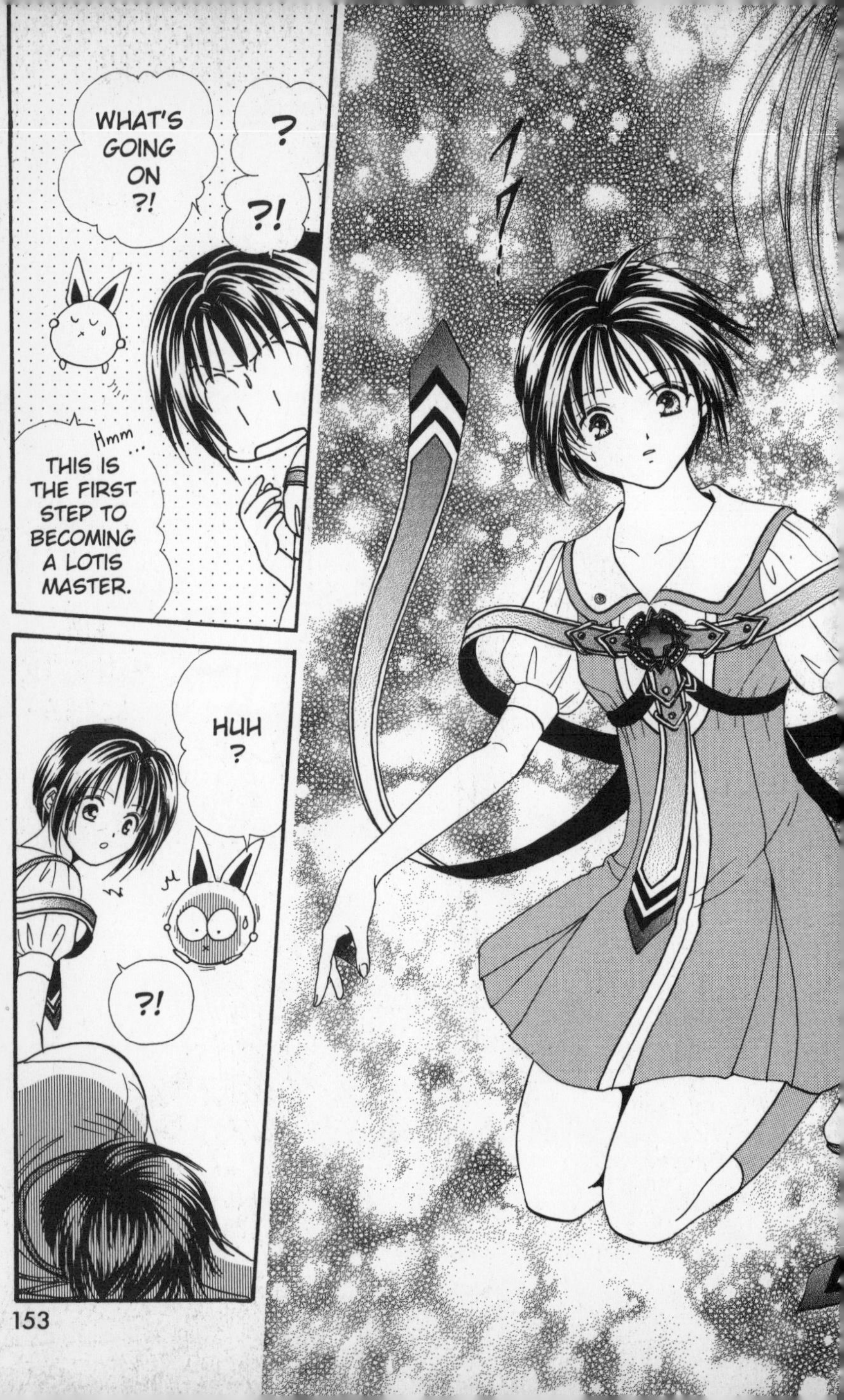
?
?!
WHAT'S GOING ON ?!
Hmm...
THIS IS THE FIRST STEP TO BECOMING A LOTIS MASTER.
HUH ?
?!

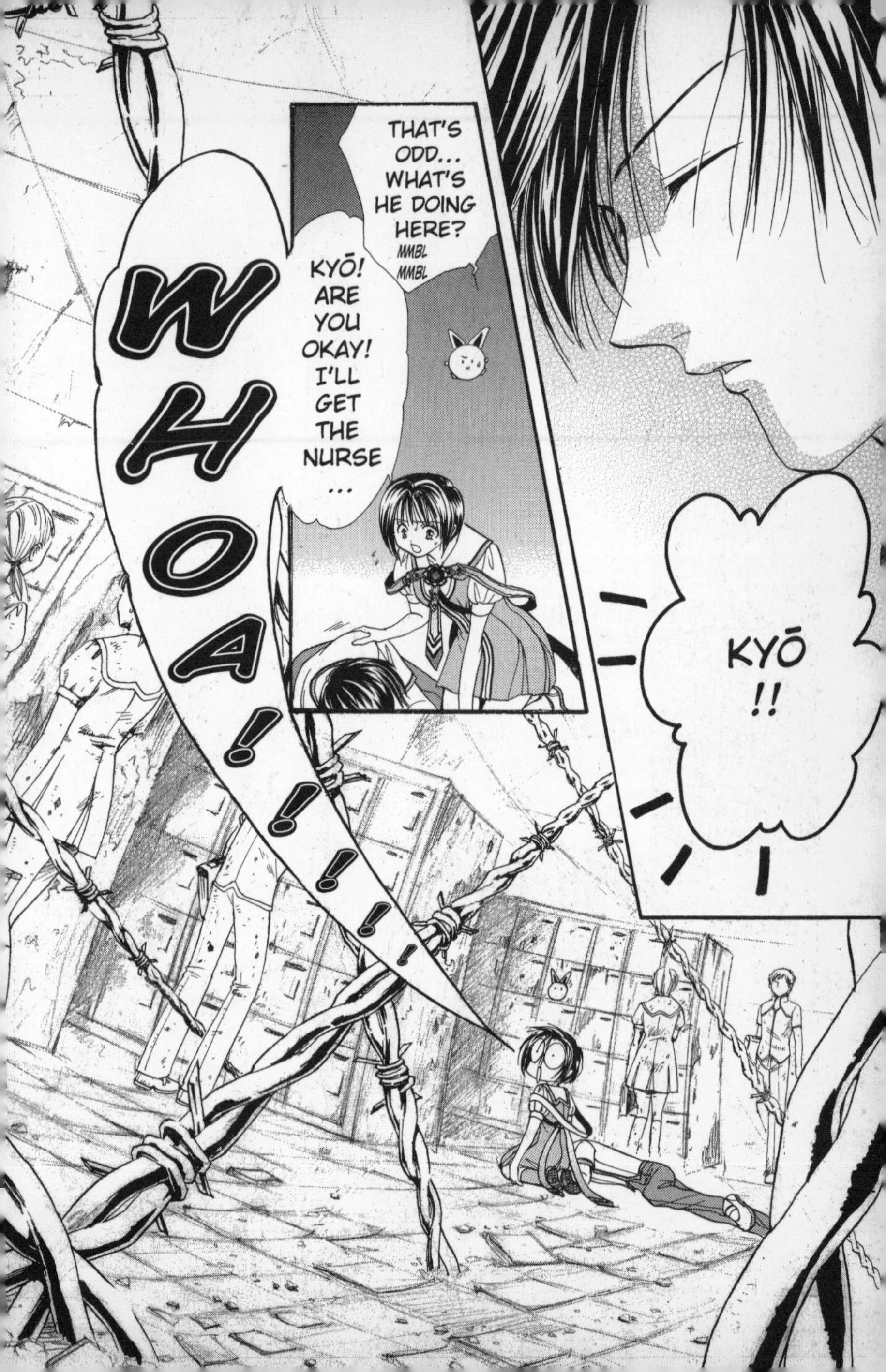
KYŌ !!
THAT'S ODD... WHAT'S HE DOING HERE?
MMBL MMBL
KYŌ! ARE YOU OKAY! I'LL GET THE NURSE ...
WHOA!!!!!!

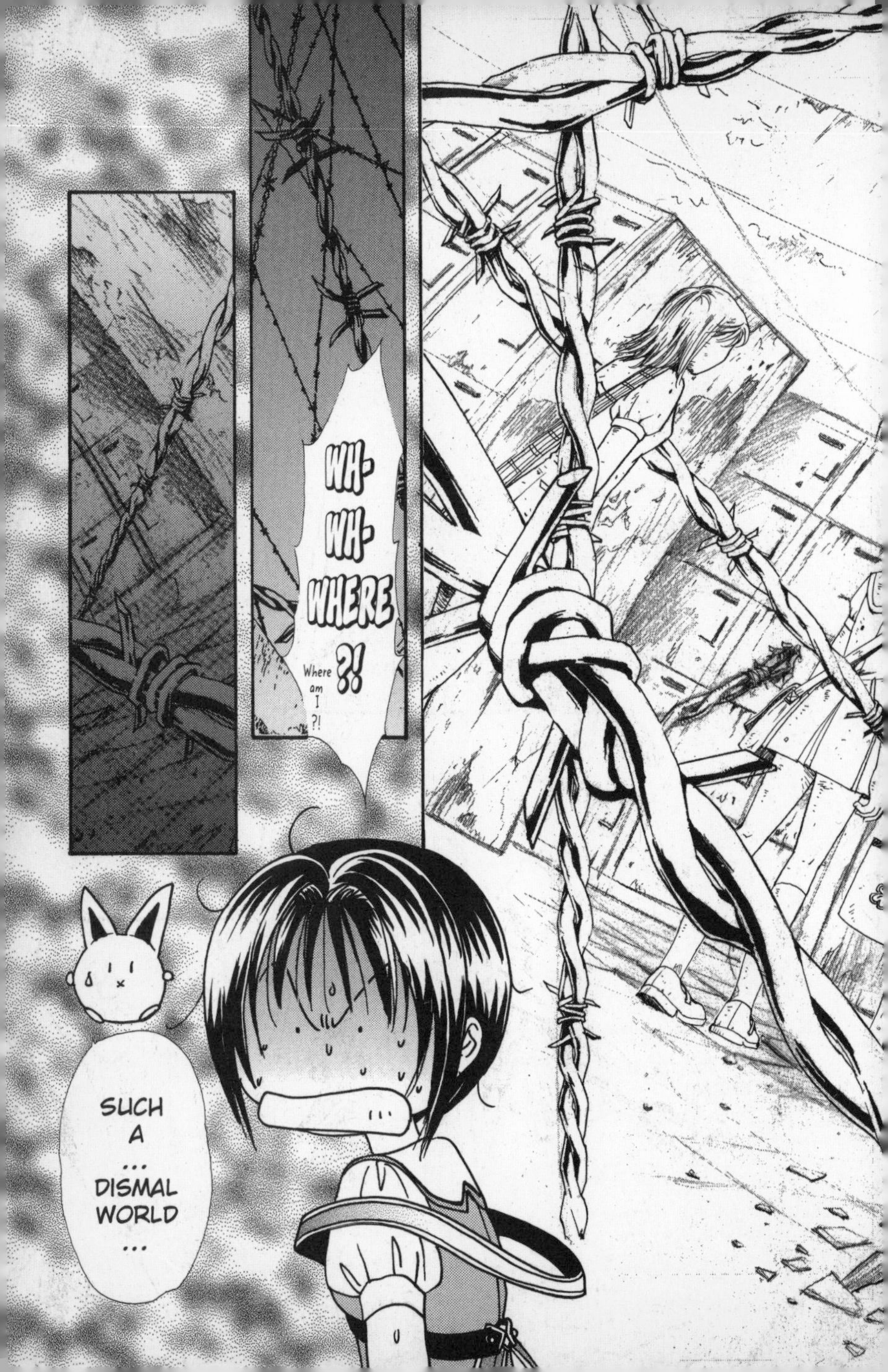
WH-WH-WHERE?!
Where am I?!
SUCH A ... DISMAL WORLD ...

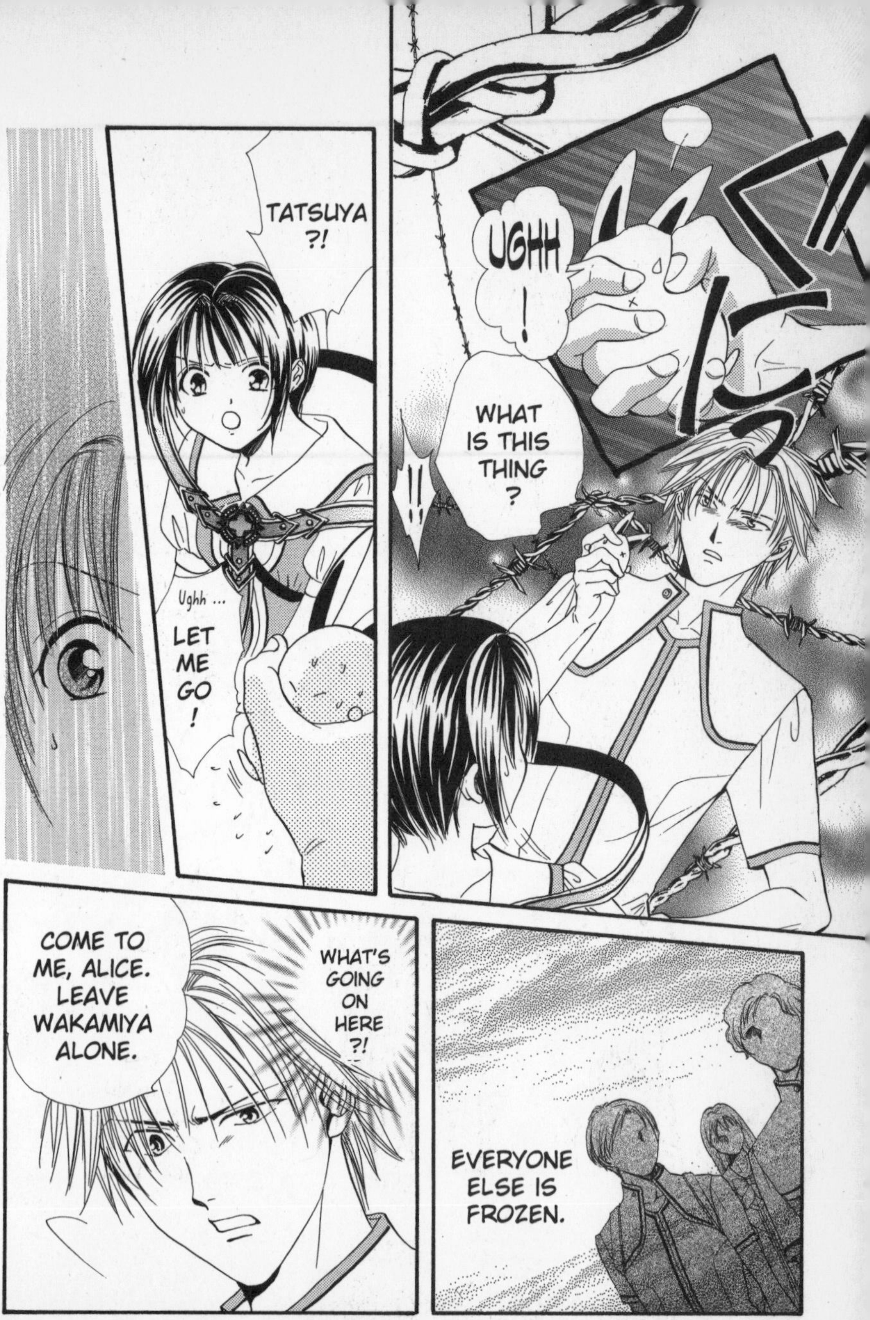
UGHH !
WHAT IS THIS THING ?
!!
TATSUYA ?!
Ughh ...
LET ME GO !
EVERYONE ELSE IS FROZEN.
WHAT'S GOING ON HERE ?!
COME TO ME, ALICE. LEAVE WAKAMIYA ALONE.

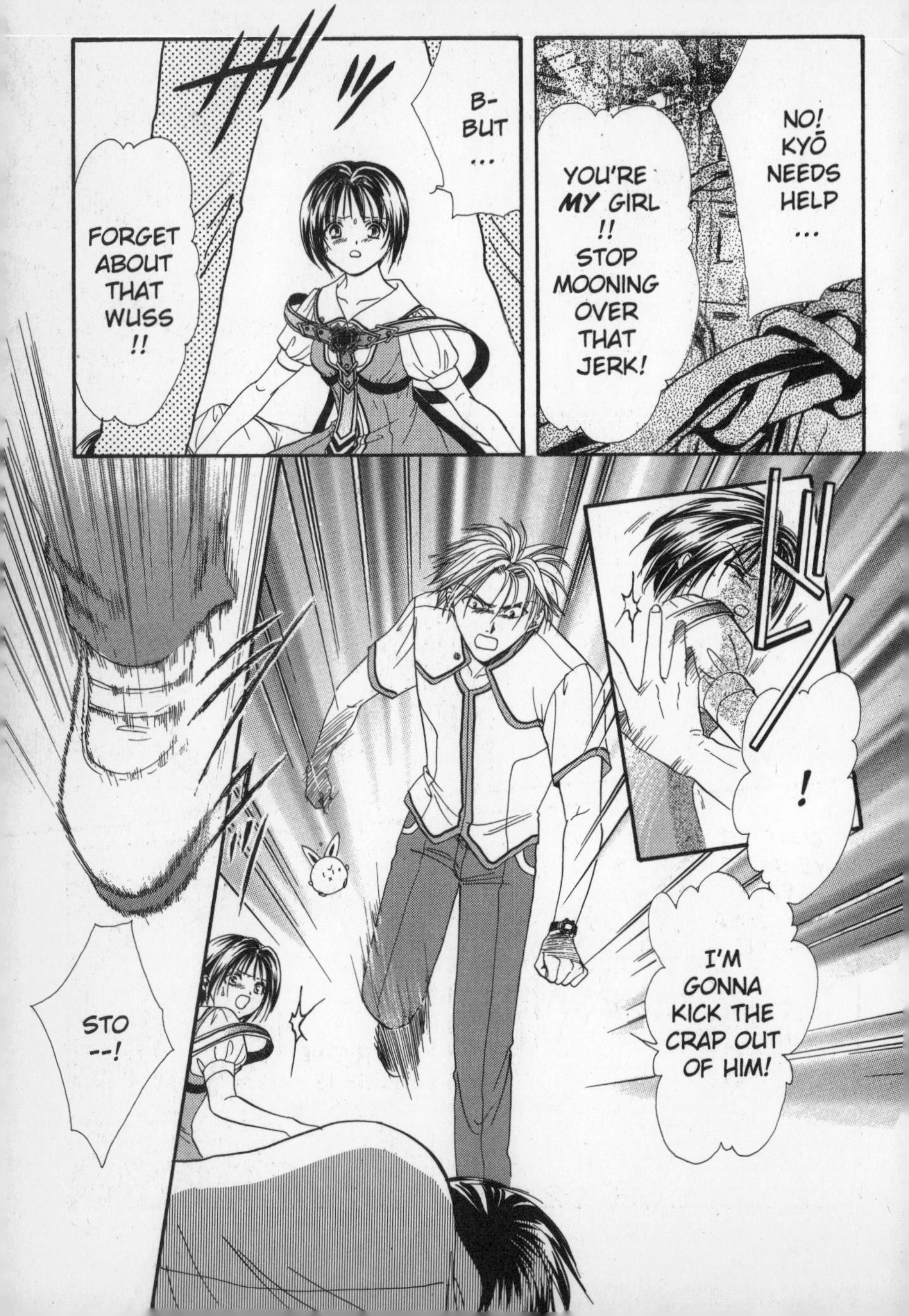
NO! KYŌ NEEDS HELP ...
YOU'RE *MY* GIRL !! STOP MOONING OVER THAT JERK!
B- BUT ...
FORGET ABOUT THAT WUSS !!
!
I'M GONNA KICK THE CRAP OUT OF HIM!
STO --!

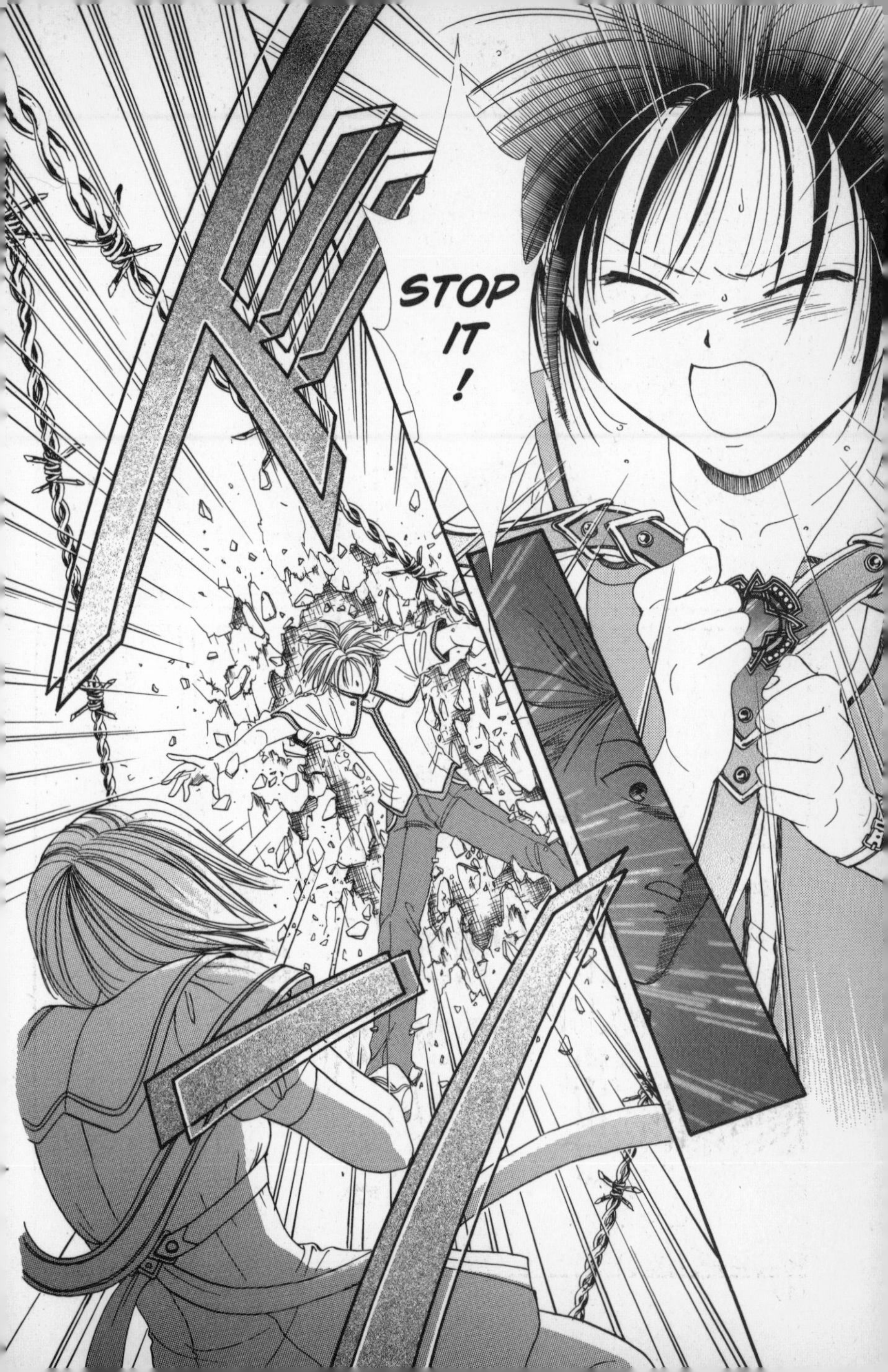
STOP IT!

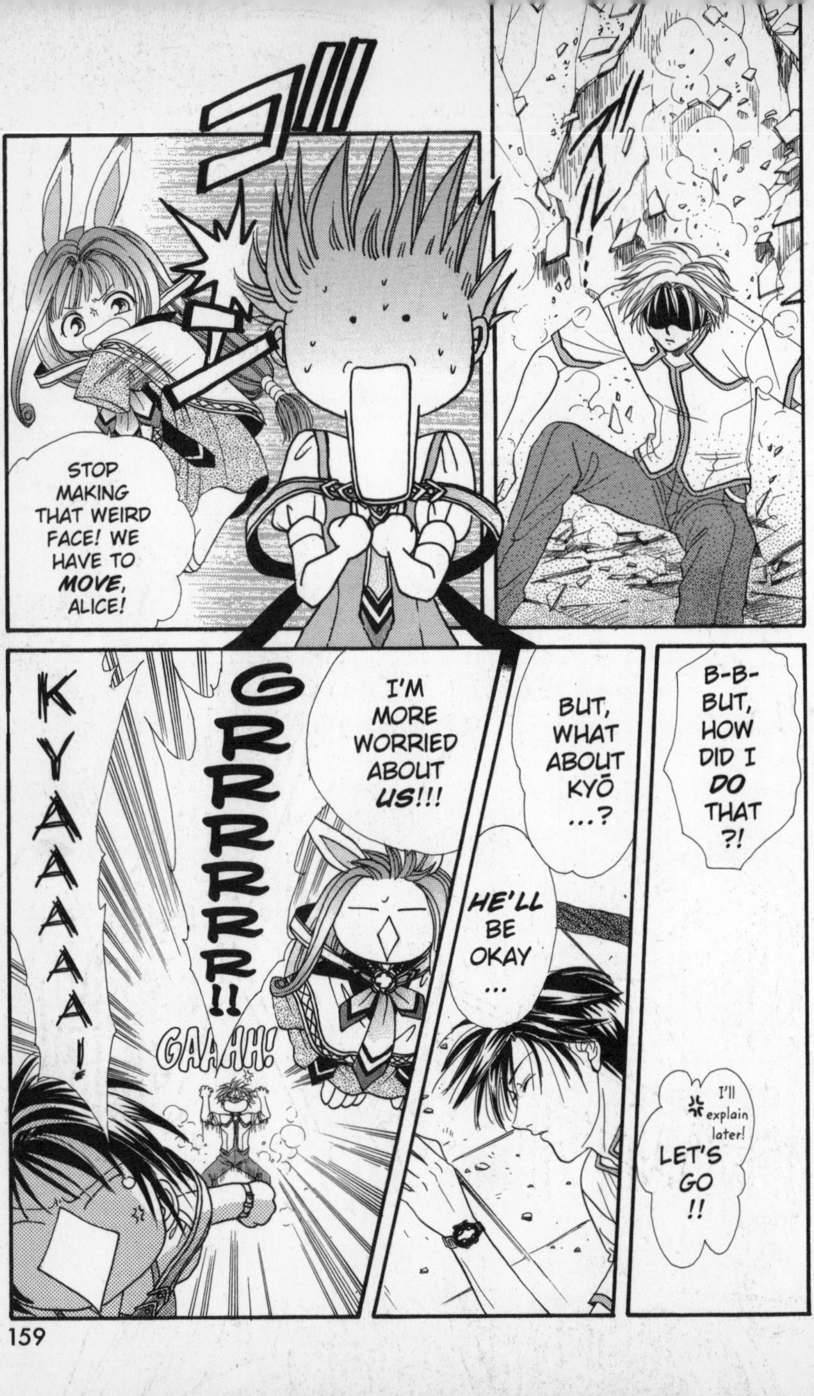
STOP MAKING THAT WEIRD FACE! WE HAVE TO *MOVE*, ALICE!
B-B-BUT, HOW DID I *DO* THAT?!
I'll explain later!
LET'S GO!!
BUT, WHAT ABOUT KYŌ...?
*HE'LL* BE OKAY...
I'M MORE WORRIED ABOUT *US*!!!
GRRRRRR!!
KYAAAAA!
GAAAH!

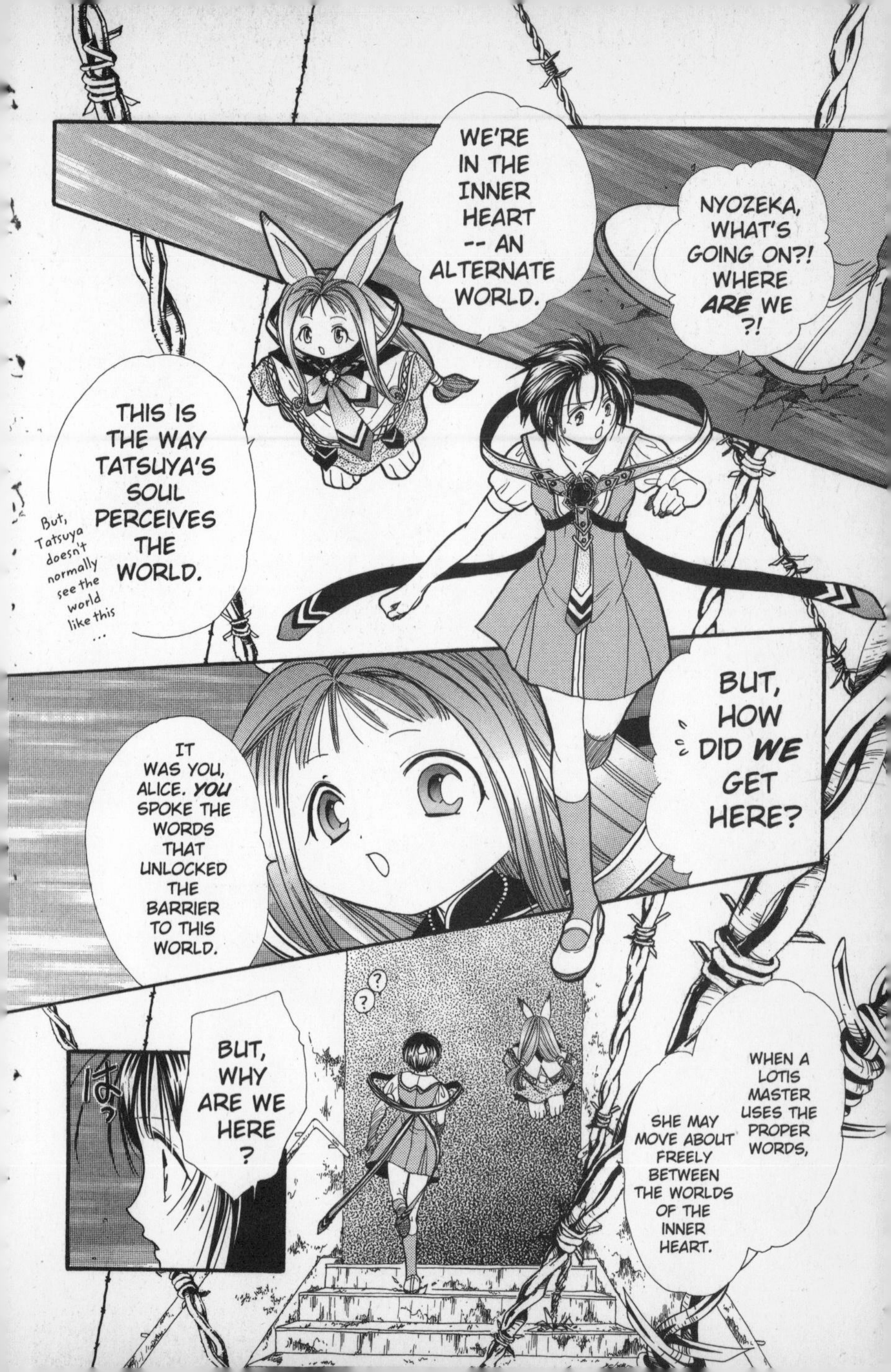
NYOZEKA, WHAT'S GOING ON?! WHERE *ARE* WE ?!
WE'RE IN THE INNER HEART -- AN ALTERNATE WORLD.
THIS IS THE WAY TATSUYA'S SOUL PERCEIVES THE WORLD.
But, Tatsuya doesn't normally see the world like this ...
BUT, HOW DID *WE* GET HERE?
IT WAS YOU, ALICE. *YOU* SPOKE THE WORDS THAT UNLOCKED THE BARRIER TO THIS WORLD.
WHEN A LOTIS MASTER USES THE PROPER WORDS,
SHE MAY MOVE ABOUT FREELY BETWEEN THE WORLDS OF THE INNER HEART.
?
?
BUT, WHY ARE WE HERE ?
はっ

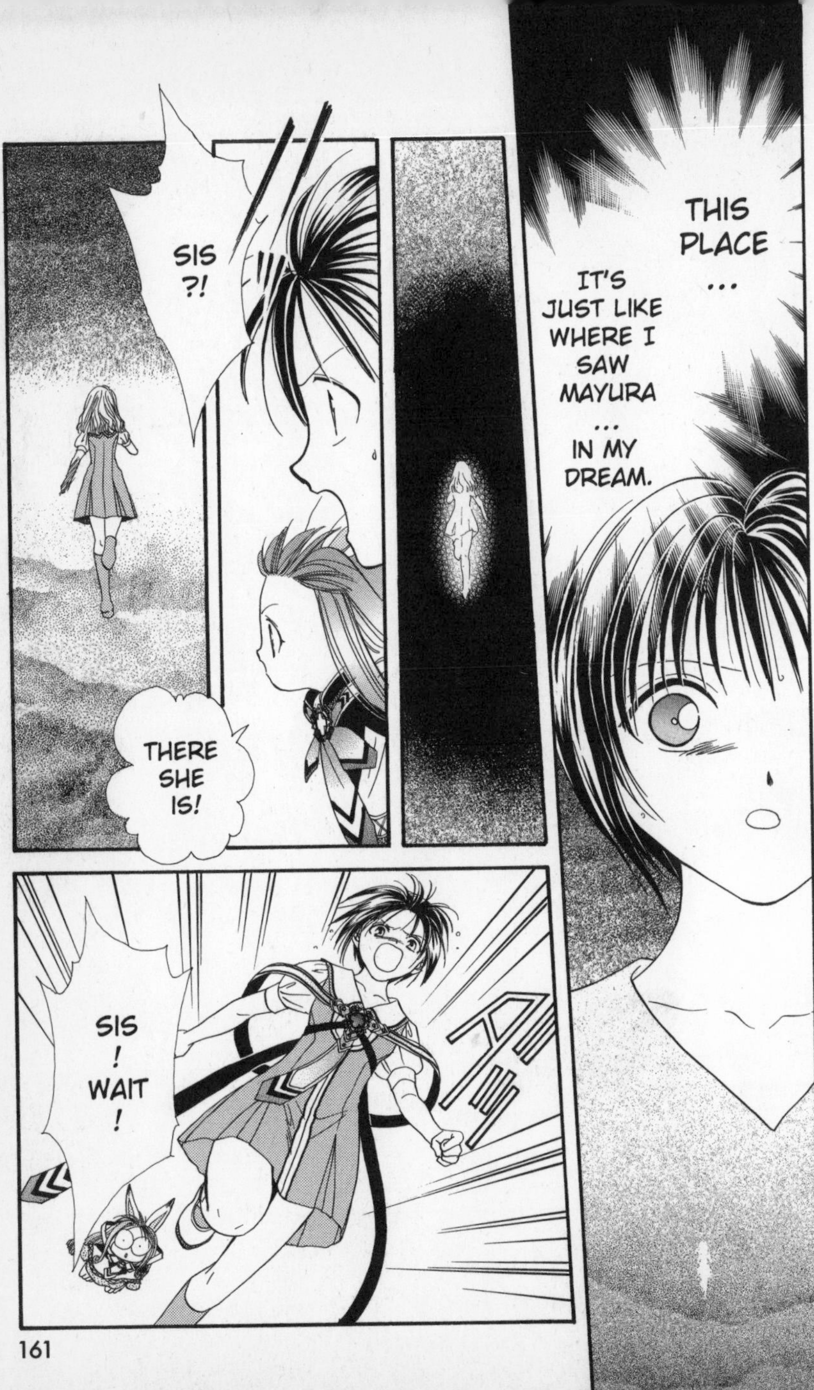
THIS PLACE ...
IT'S JUST LIKE WHERE I SAW MAYURA ... IN MY DREAM.
SIS ?!
THERE SHE IS!
SIS ! WAIT !

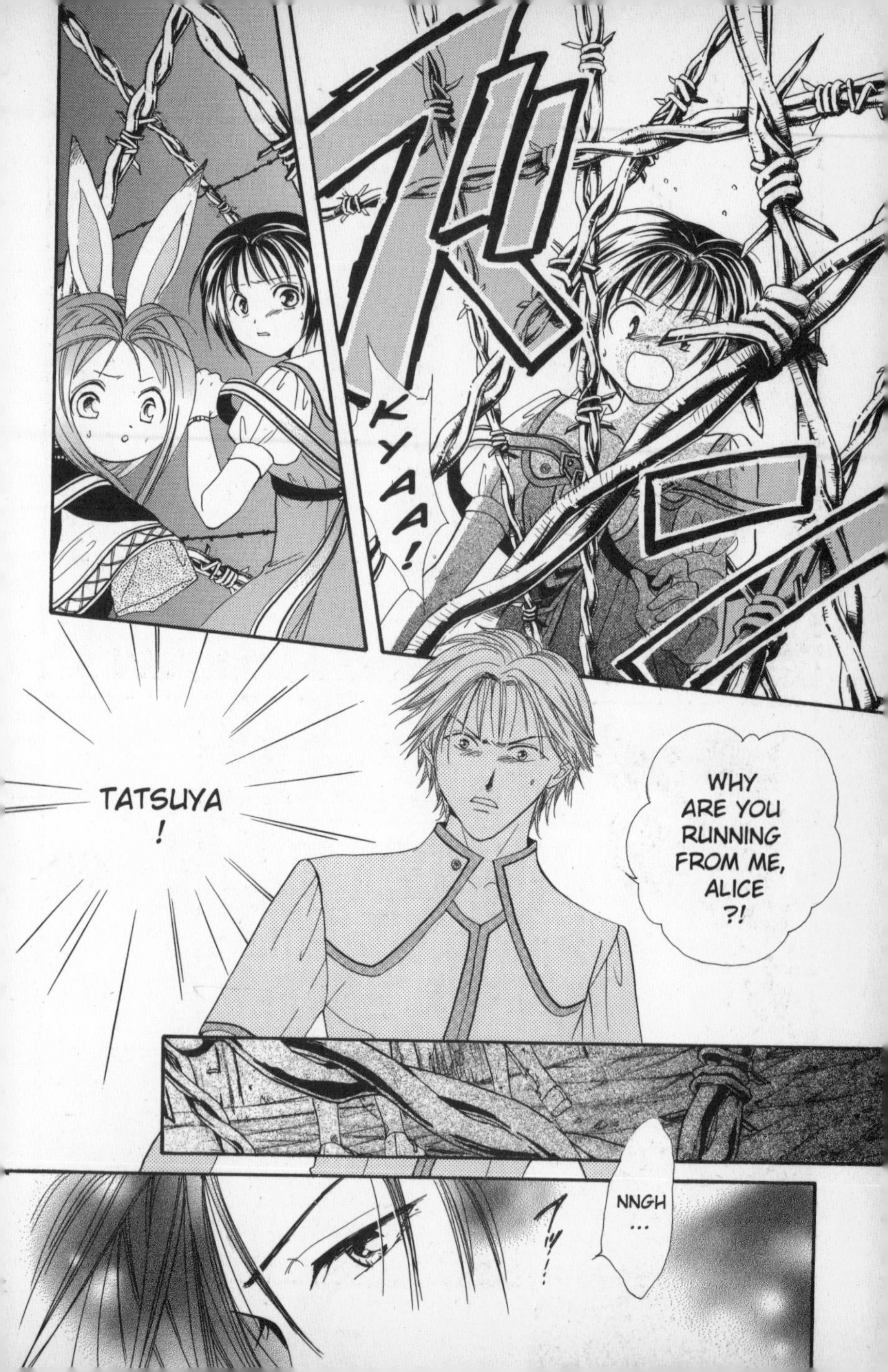
KYAA!
WHY ARE YOU RUNNING FROM ME, ALICE?!
TATSUYA!
NNGH...

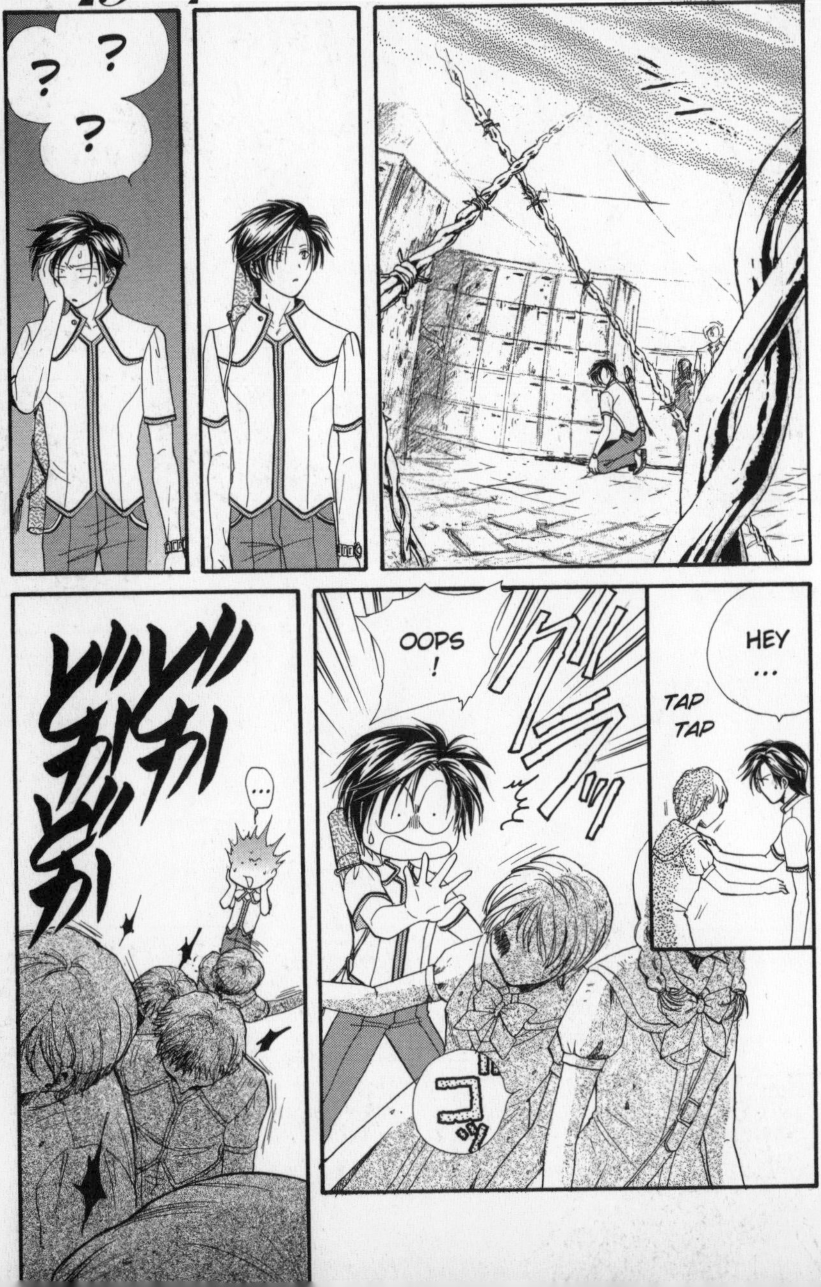
? ? ? ?
HEY ...
TAP TAP
OOPS !
...

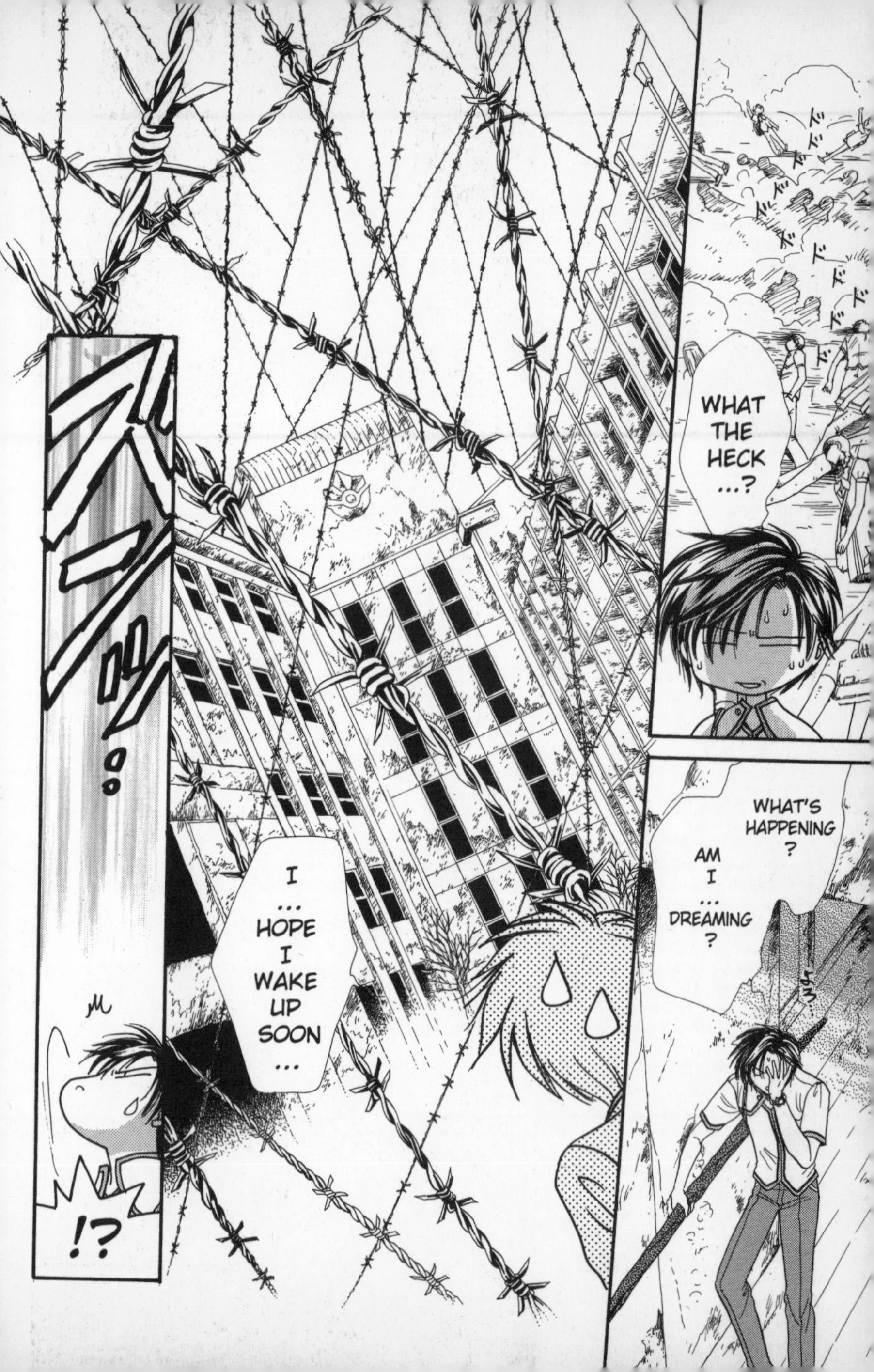
WHAT THE HECK ...?
WHAT'S HAPPENING? AM I ... DREAMING?
I ... HOPE I WAKE UP SOON ...
!?

Wow! The first volume is almost over! In the next, I'll write about more characters, including biographical info. In keeping with the Western feel of Alice 19th, the illustration gallery has girls with lace and frills instead of contemporary fashions. Myself, I can't wear frilly clothes, but girls like that kind of stuff, right? A world of pink houses and pink dresses! I loved them when I was a little girl. I used to swear I'd never wear pants. Where did I go wrong?

But as we grow into adults, we're able to accept things more fully. A few years ago, I was a real Tomboy, but lately, I've come to embrace my feminine side. And I wear mostly long skirts. (This supposedly lengthens the body.) I miss the old me, that used to speak in a gruff and masculine way. I get a lot of letters from girls who use this masculine language, and I can really relate to them.

Now then, the Western style of this story is in part intended to change my "Watase creates Chinese/Asian influenced manga" image. This image was created by works like Fushigi Yûgi. Speaking of, there are going to be so many things coming out relating to FY—everything from a book of cell art, a kanzenban (complete edition) of the manga, some outside story novels, another OAV series, and well, there's too much to mention here. Check for info in Shôjo Comics. I think there will also be info in the graphic novels, DVDs and-- oh, well, probably the best place for information is Shôjo Comics. If you're interested, please check there. I'll be working hard on my illustrations!

See ya in the next volume!!

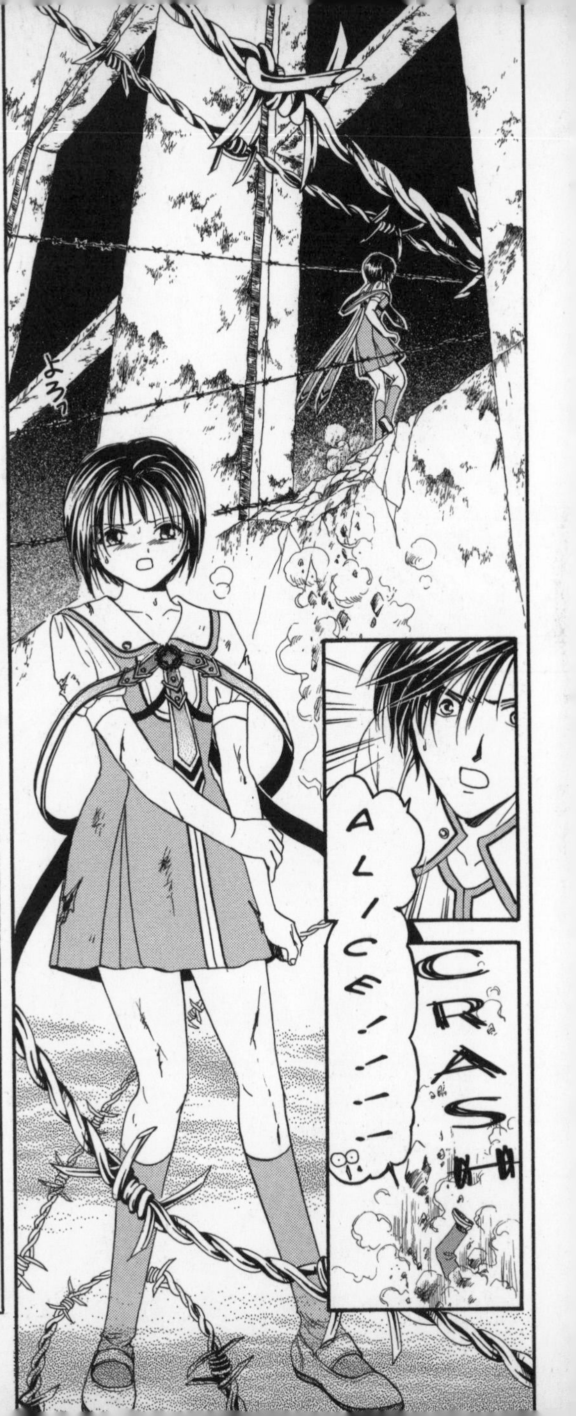
ALICE!!!!
CRASH
よろっ

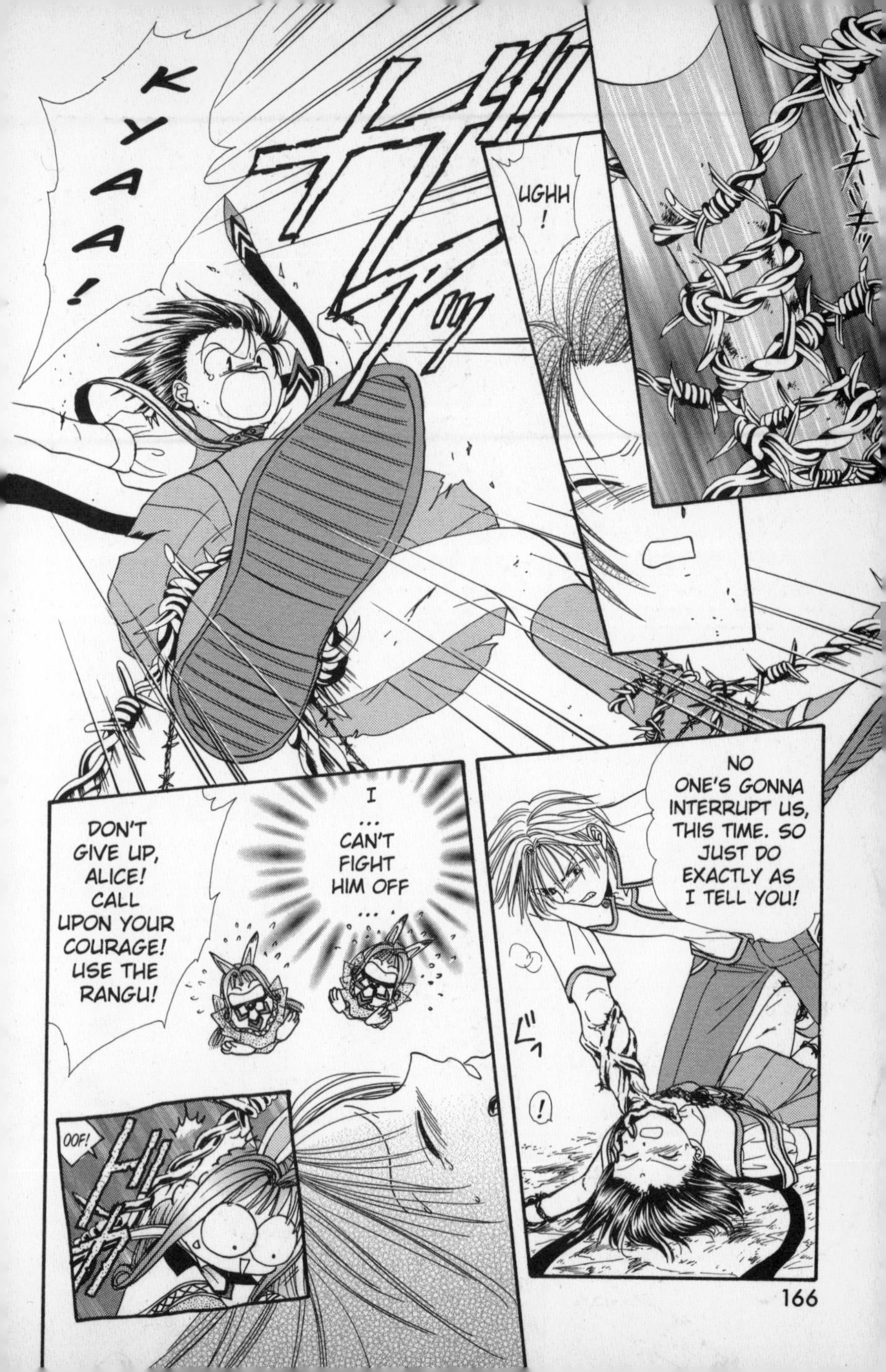
UGHH !
KYAAA!
NO ONE'S GONNA INTERRUPT US, THIS TIME. SO JUST DO EXACTLY AS I TELL YOU!
!
I ... CAN'T FIGHT HIM OFF ...
DON'T GIVE UP, ALICE! CALL UPON YOUR COURAGE! USE THE RANGU!
OOF!

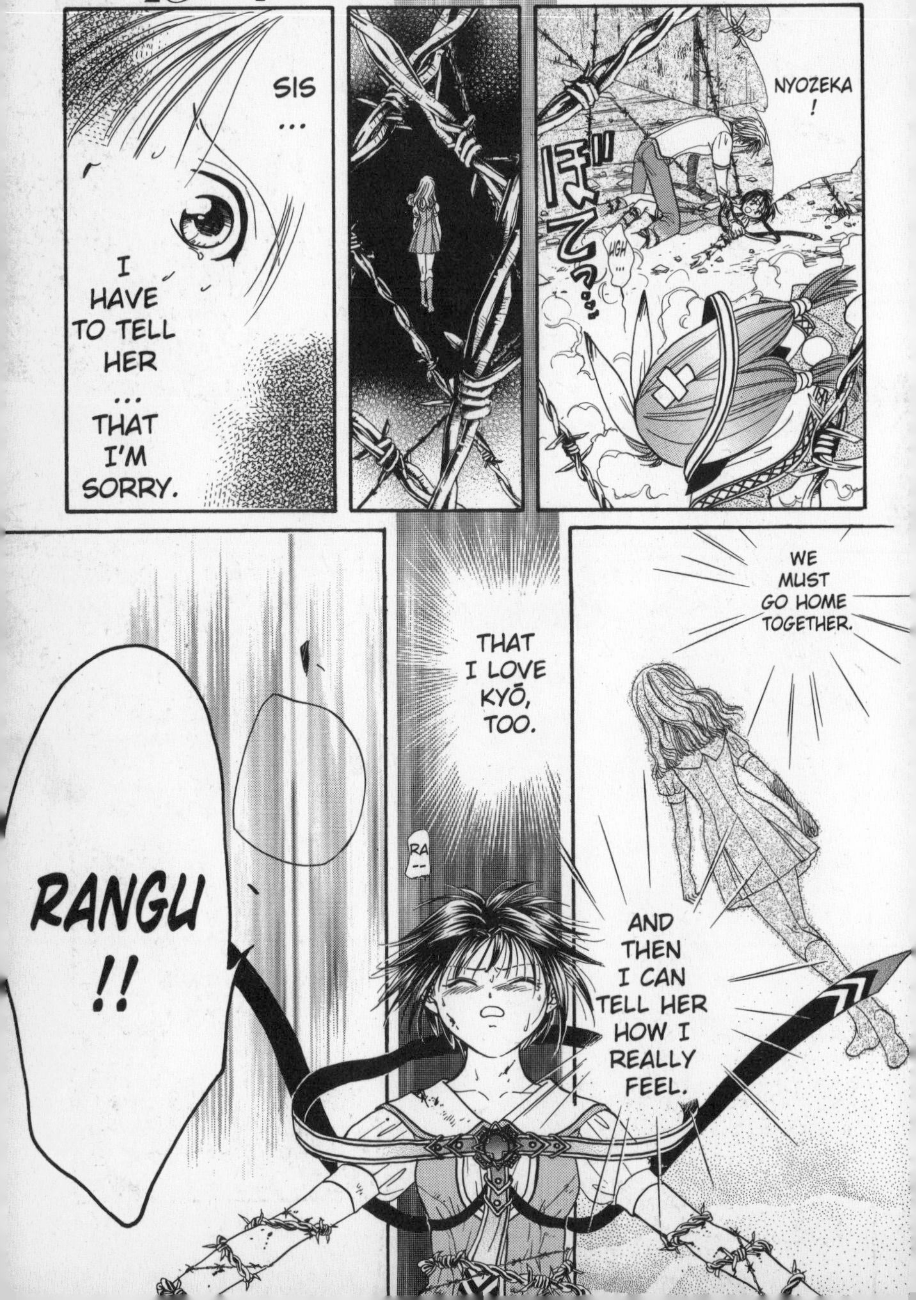
NYOZEKA!
UGH...
SIS...
I HAVE TO TELL HER... THAT I'M SORRY.
WE MUST GO HOME TOGETHER.
THAT I LOVE KYŌ, TOO.
AND THEN I CAN TELL HER HOW I REALLY FEEL.
RA--
RANGU!!

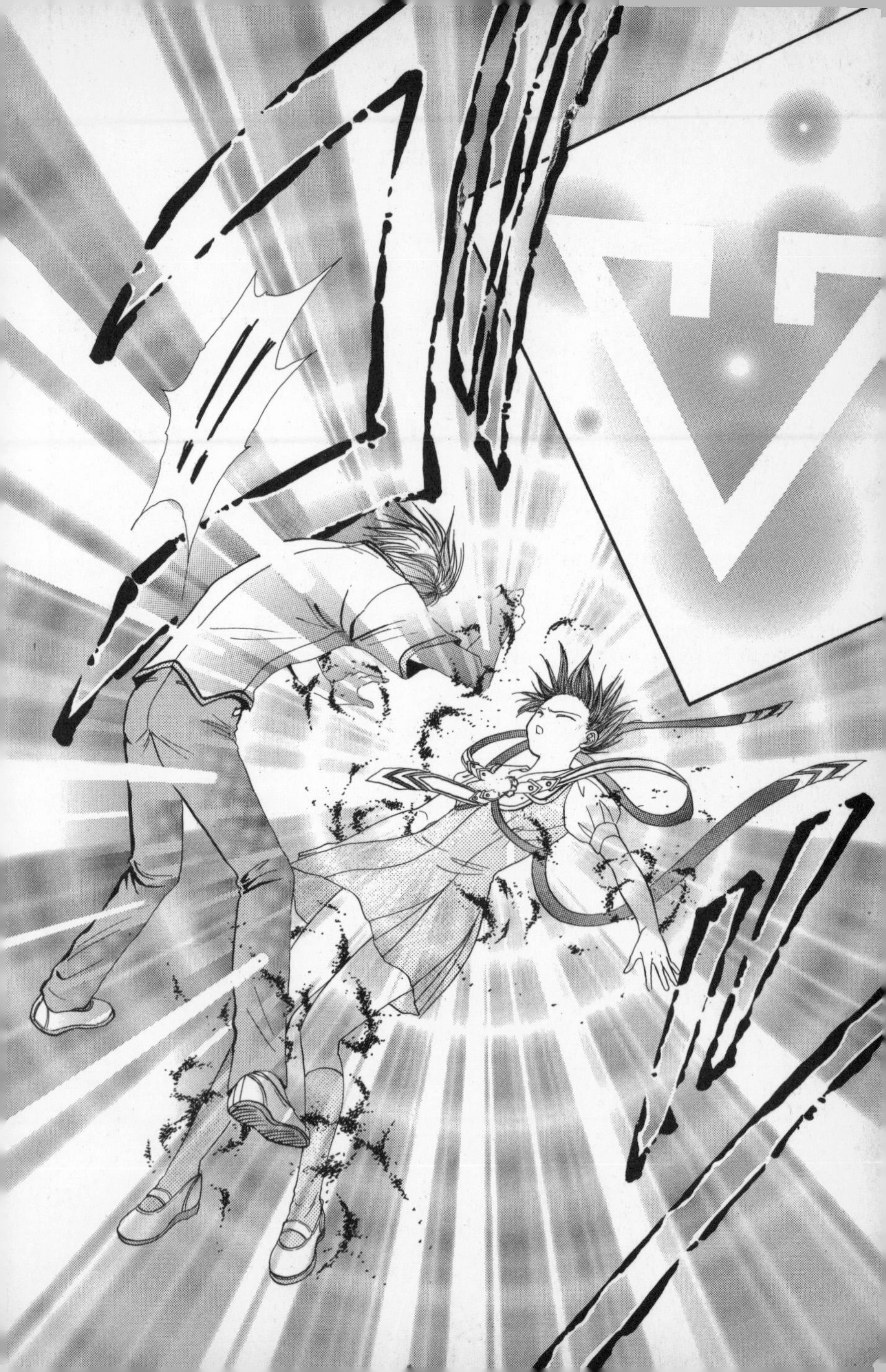

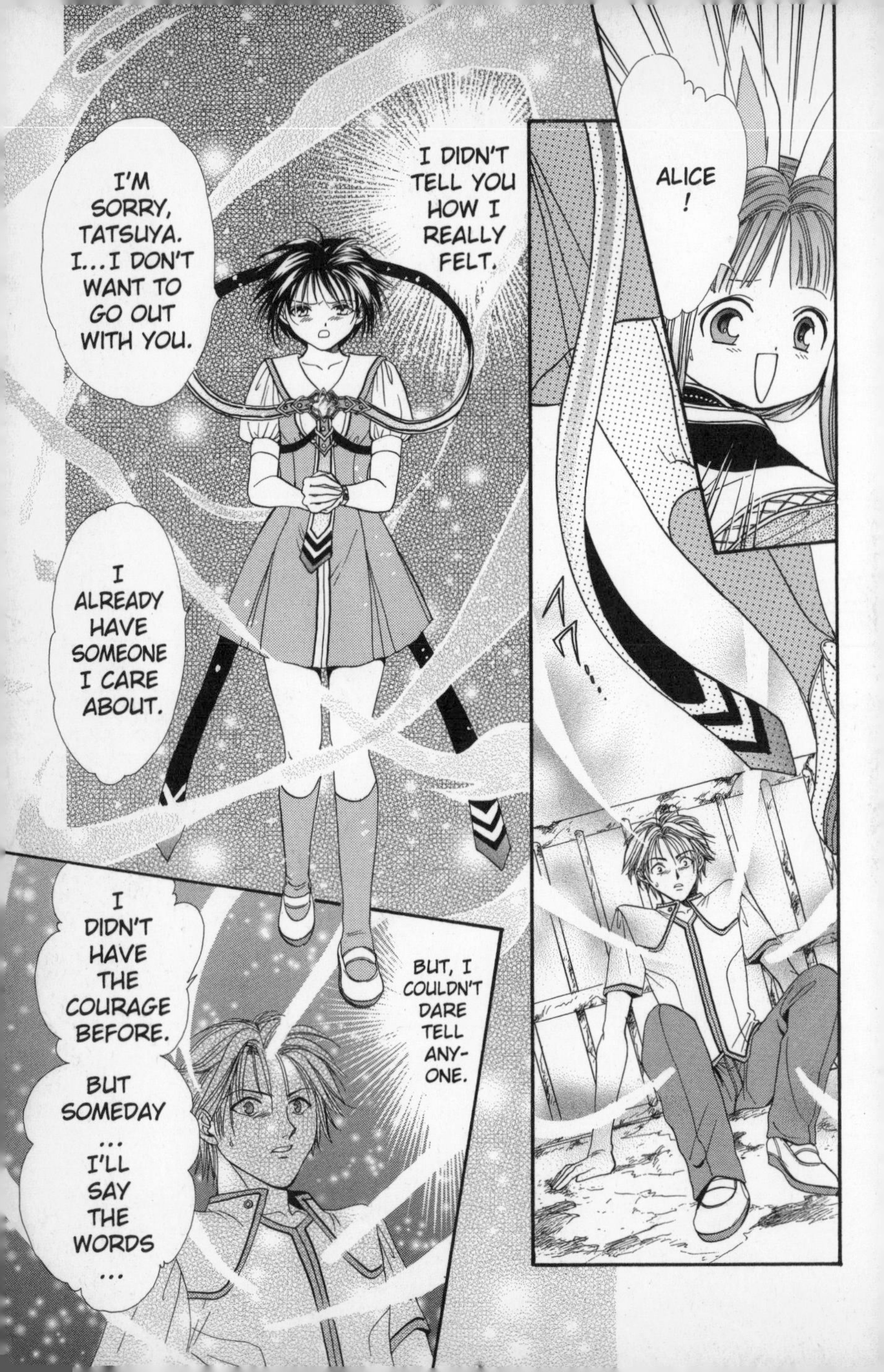
ALICE!
I DIDN'T TELL YOU HOW I REALLY FELT.
I'M SORRY, TATSUYA. I...I DON'T WANT TO GO OUT WITH YOU.
I ALREADY HAVE SOMEONE I CARE ABOUT.
BUT, I COULDN'T DARE TELL ANYONE.
I DIDN'T HAVE THE COURAGE BEFORE.
BUT SOMEDAY ... I'LL SAY THE WORDS ...

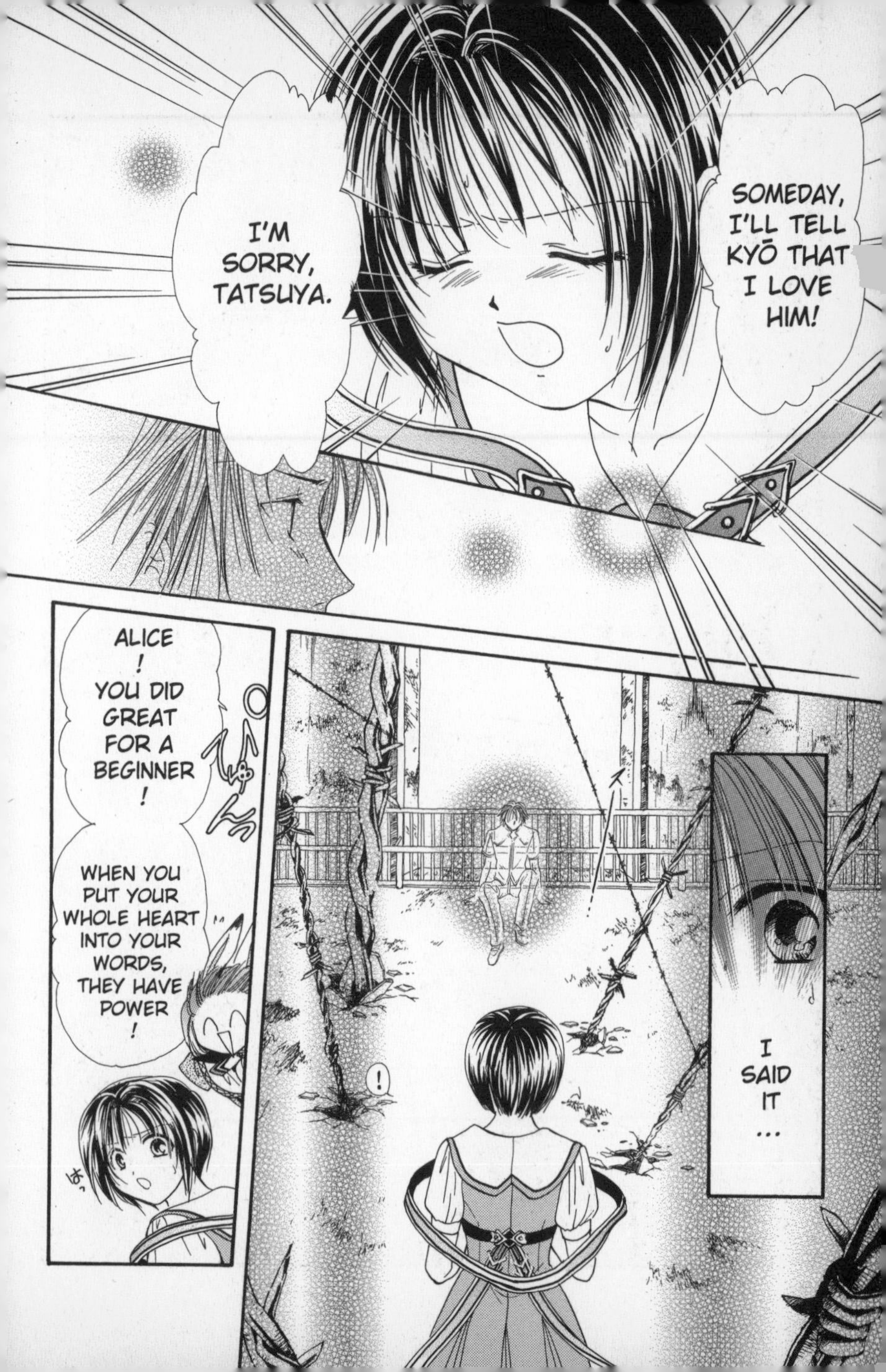
SOMEDAY, I'LL TELL KYŌ THAT I LOVE HIM!
I'M SORRY, TATSUYA.
I SAID IT ...
!
ALICE! YOU DID GREAT FOR A BEGINNER!
WHEN YOU PUT YOUR WHOLE HEART INTO YOUR WORDS, THEY HAVE POWER!

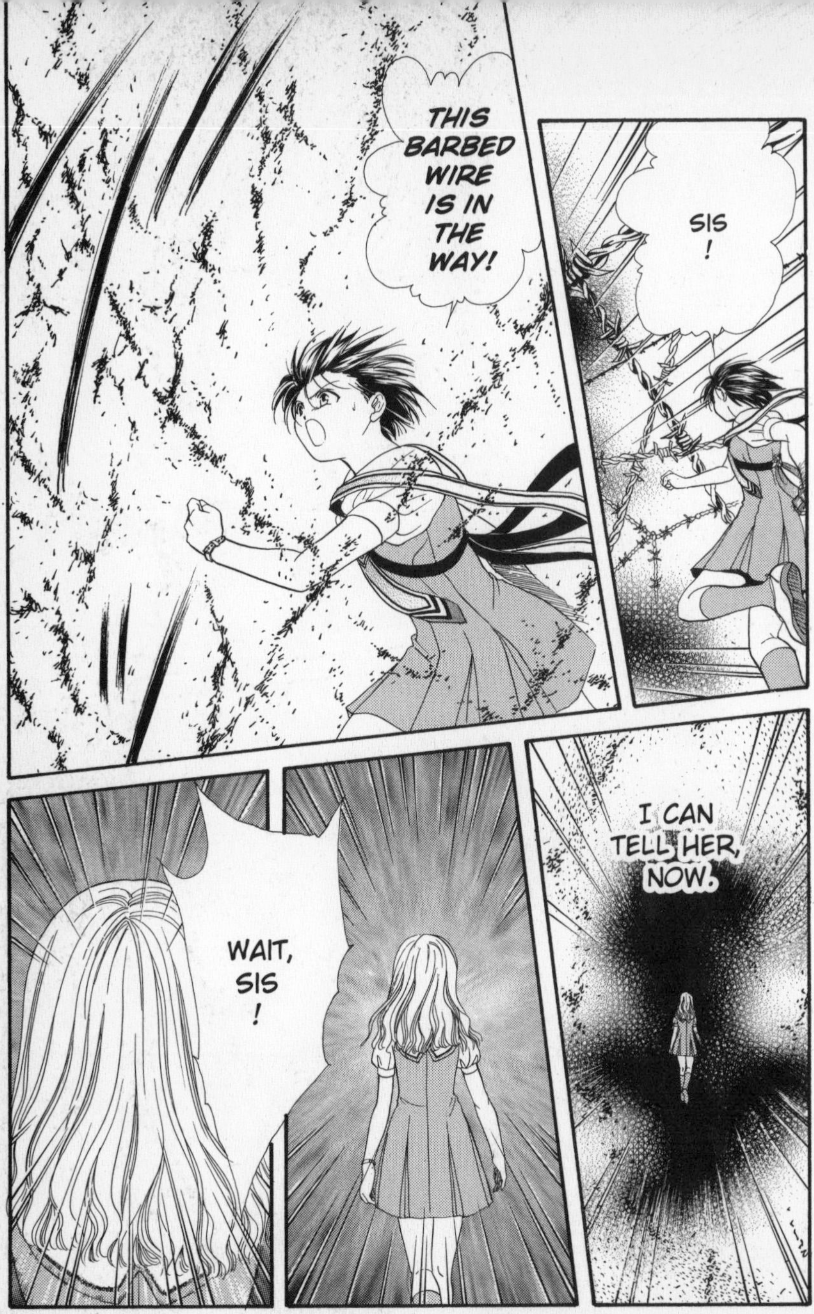
SIS!
THIS BARBED WIRE IS IN THE WAY!
I CAN TELL HER, NOW.
WAIT, SIS!

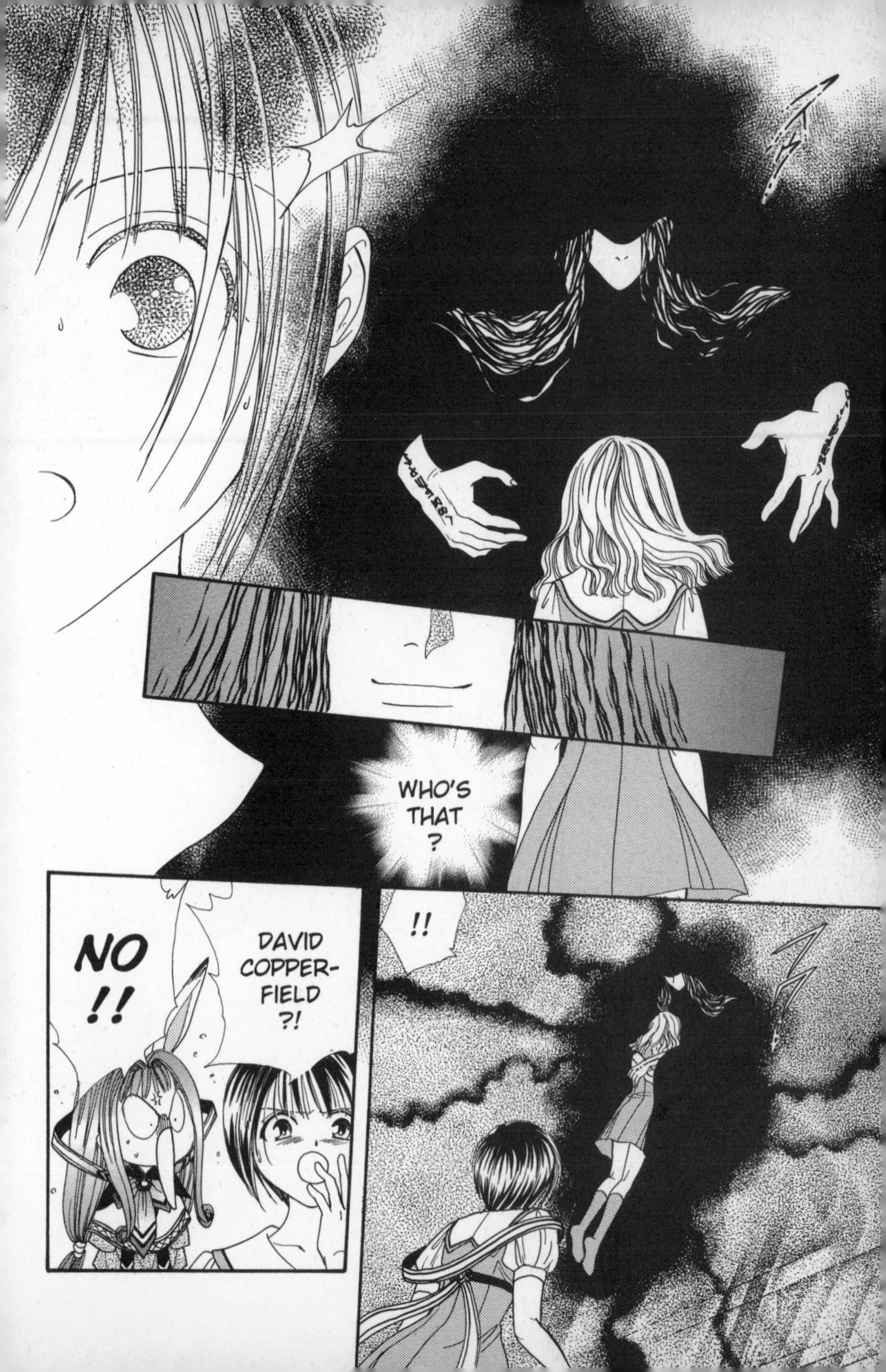
WHO'S THAT?
!!
DAVID COPPER-FIELD ?!
NO !!

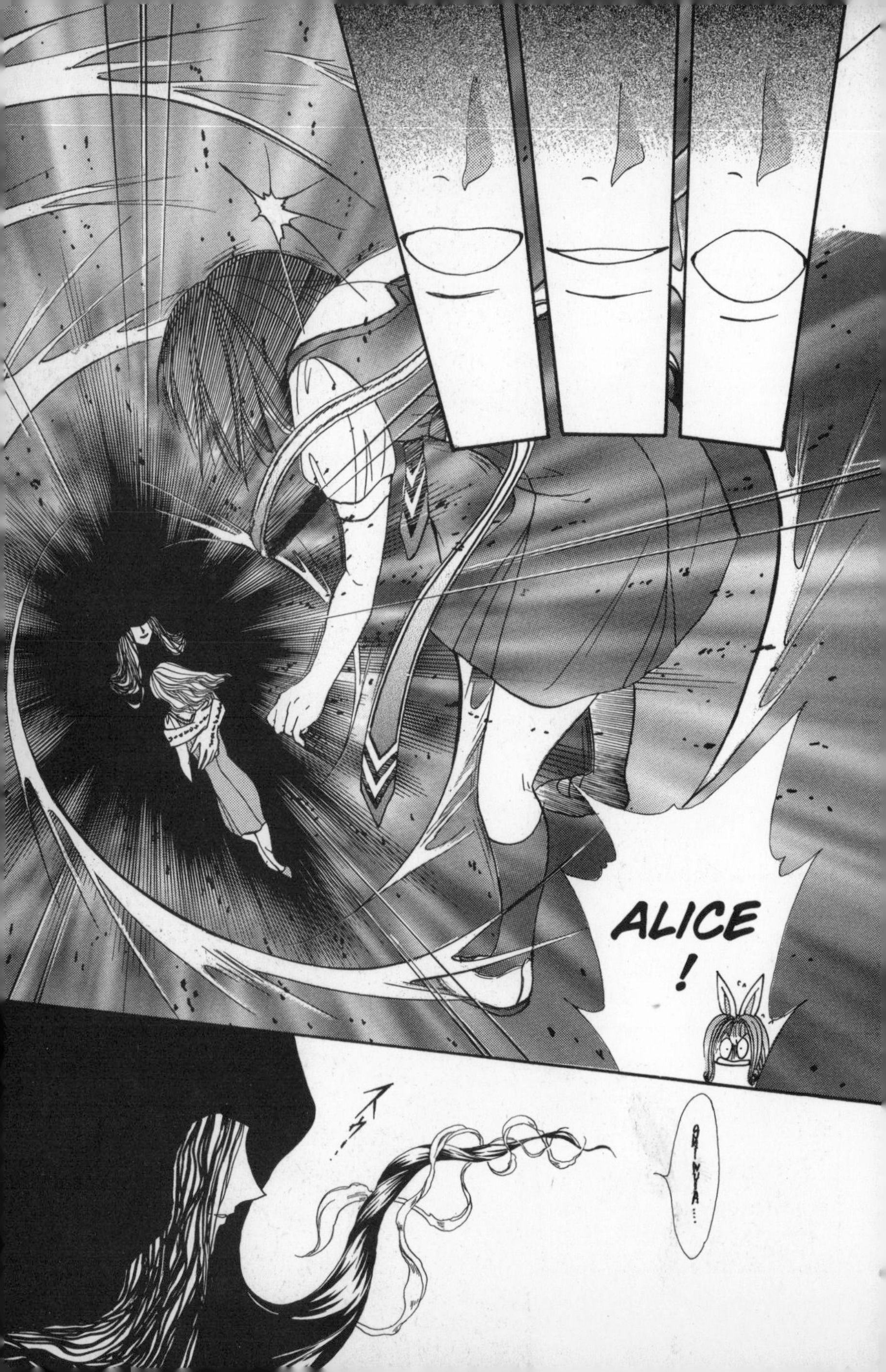
ALICE !
ORINVIA...

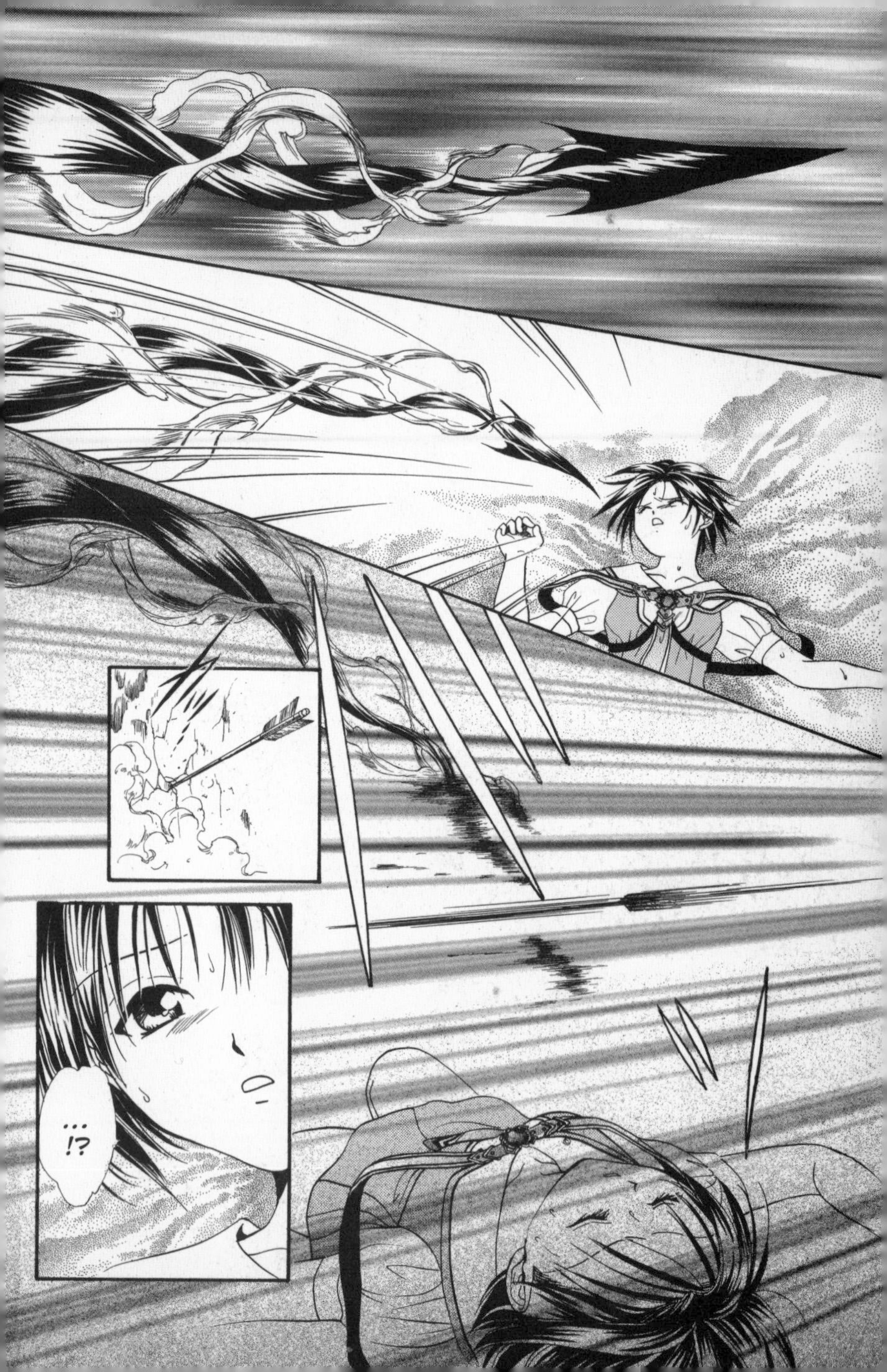
...!?

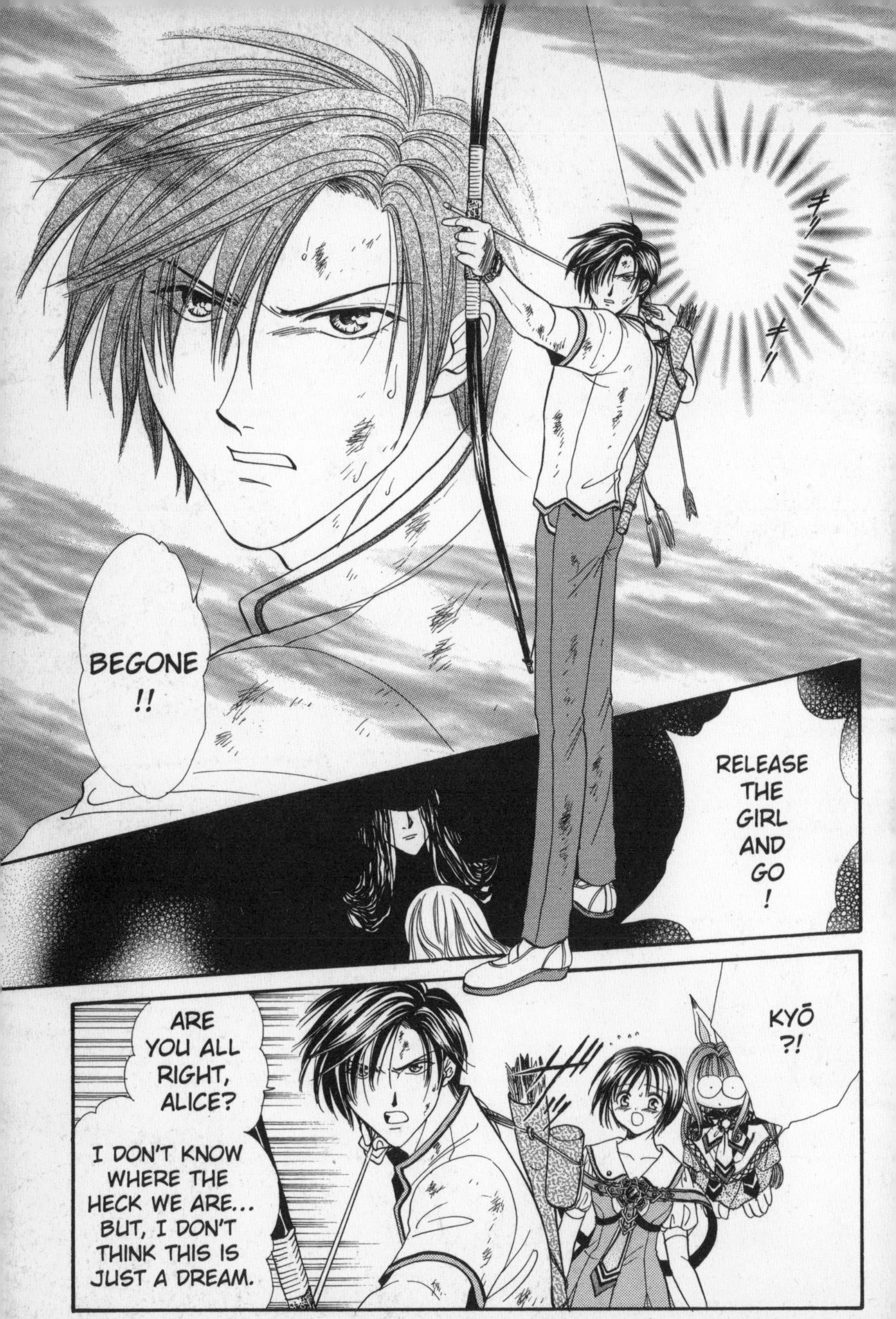
キリ キリ キリ
BEGONE !!
RELEASE THE GIRL AND GO !
KYŌ ?!
ARE YOU ALL RIGHT, ALICE?
I DON'T KNOW WHERE THE HECK WE ARE... BUT, I DON'T THINK THIS IS JUST A DREAM.

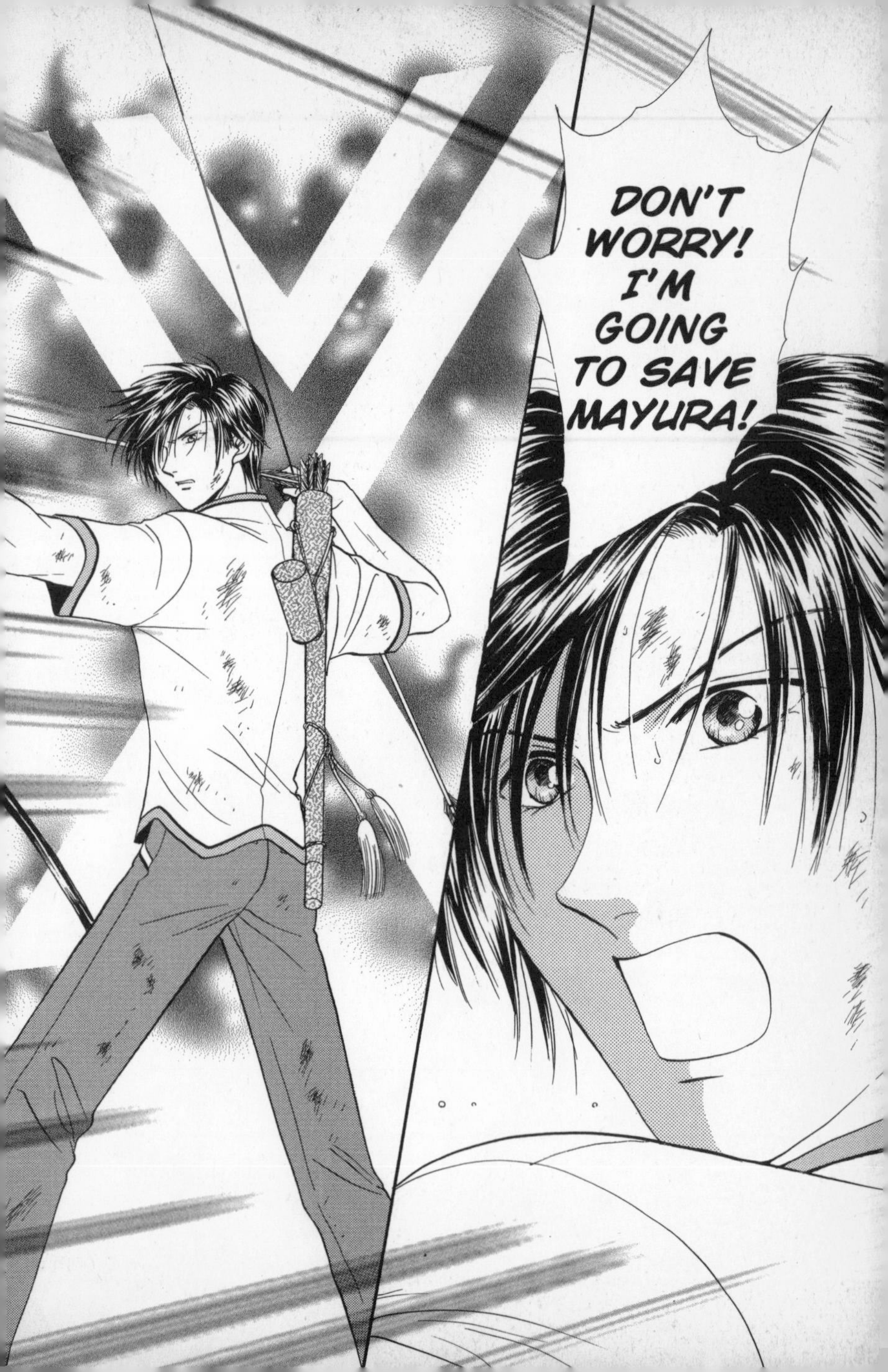
DON'T WORRY! I'M GOING TO SAVE MAYURA!

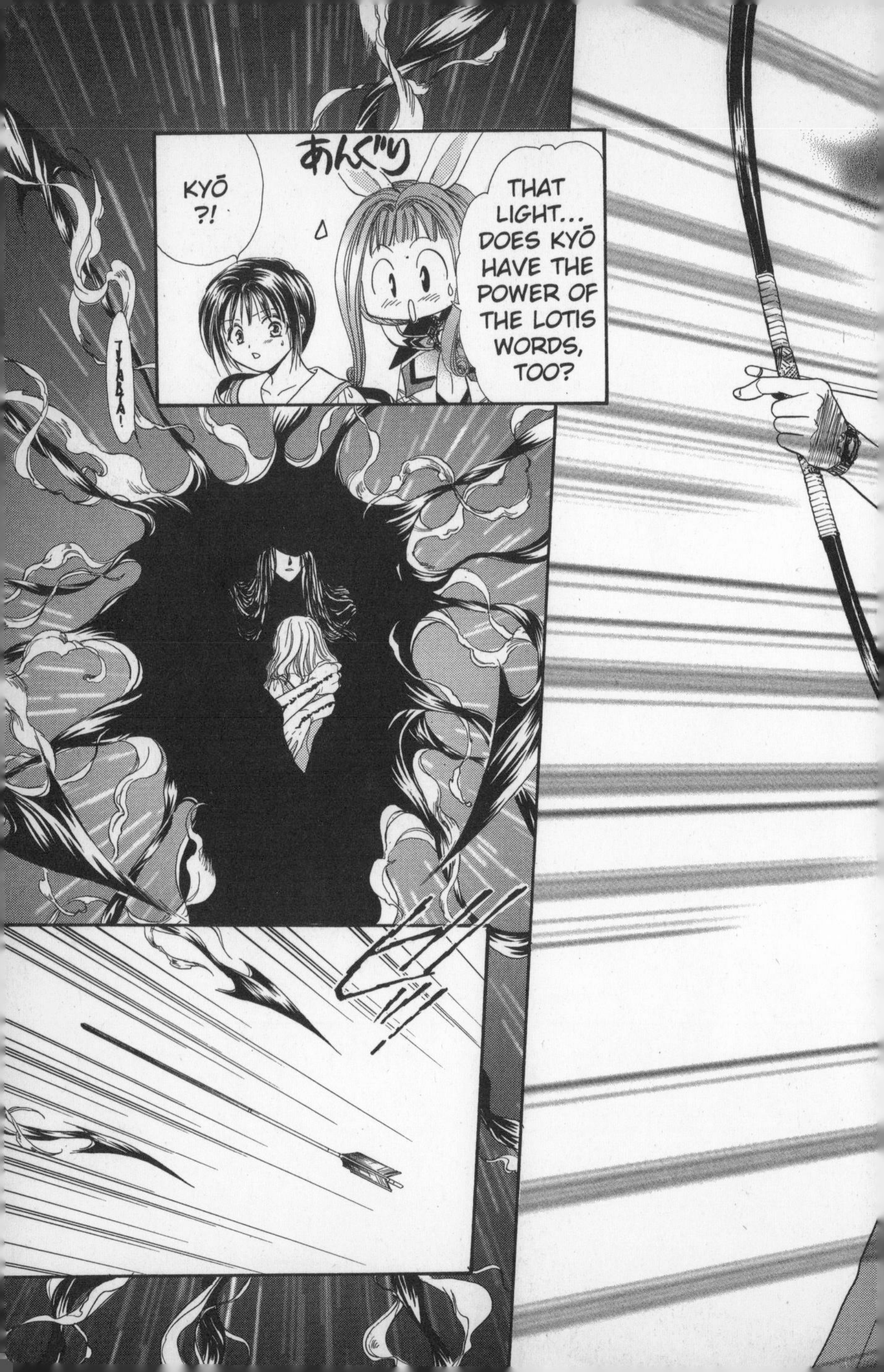
THAT LIGHT... DOES KYŌ HAVE THE POWER OF THE LOTIS WORDS, TOO?
あんぐり
KYŌ ?!

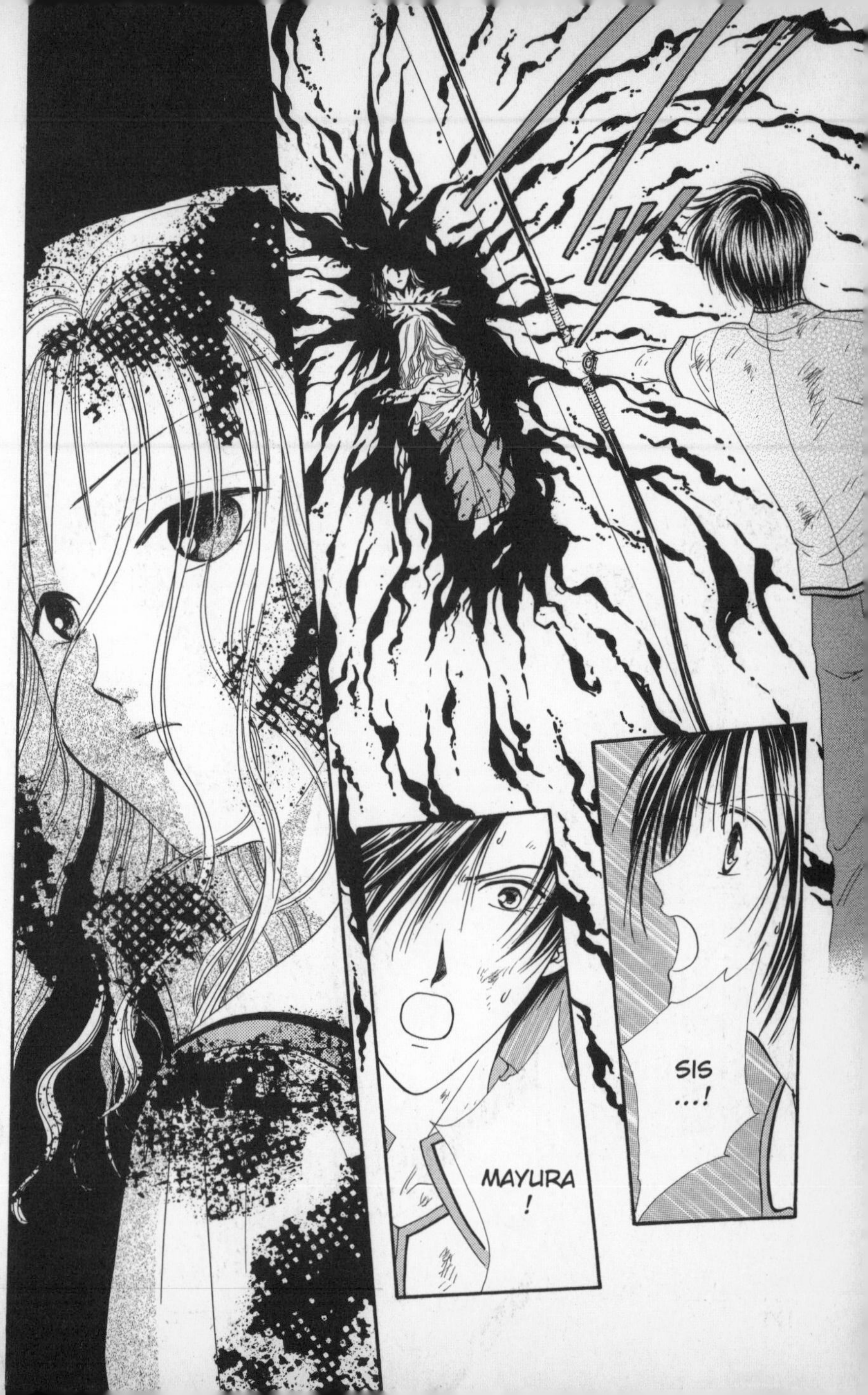
SIS ...!
MAYURA !

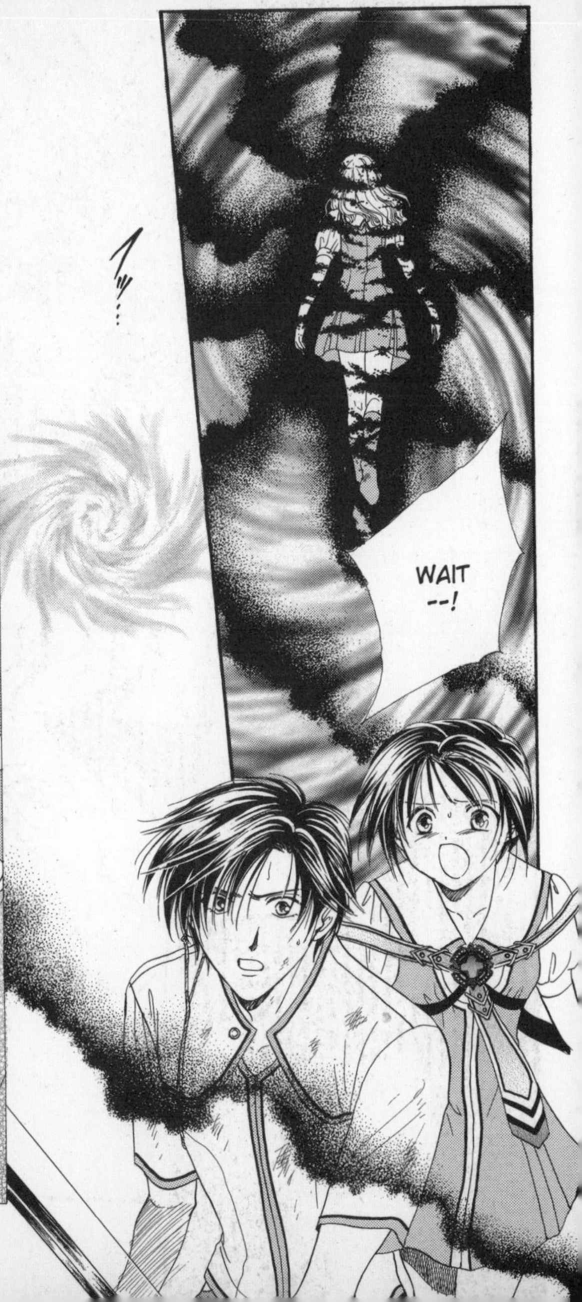
WAIT
--!
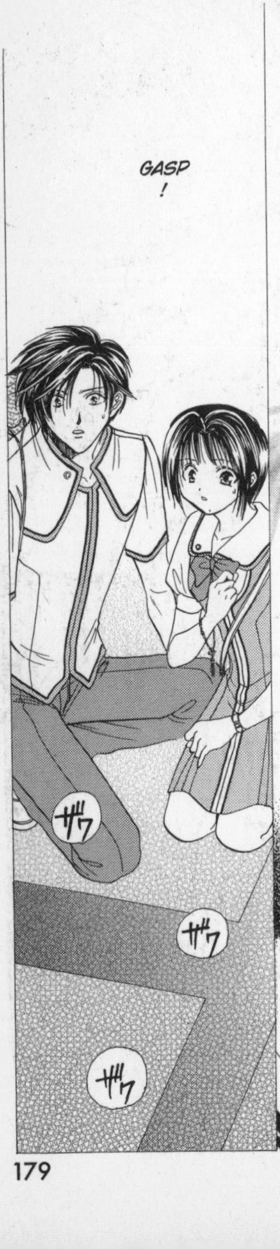
GASP
!
ザワ
ザワ
ザワ

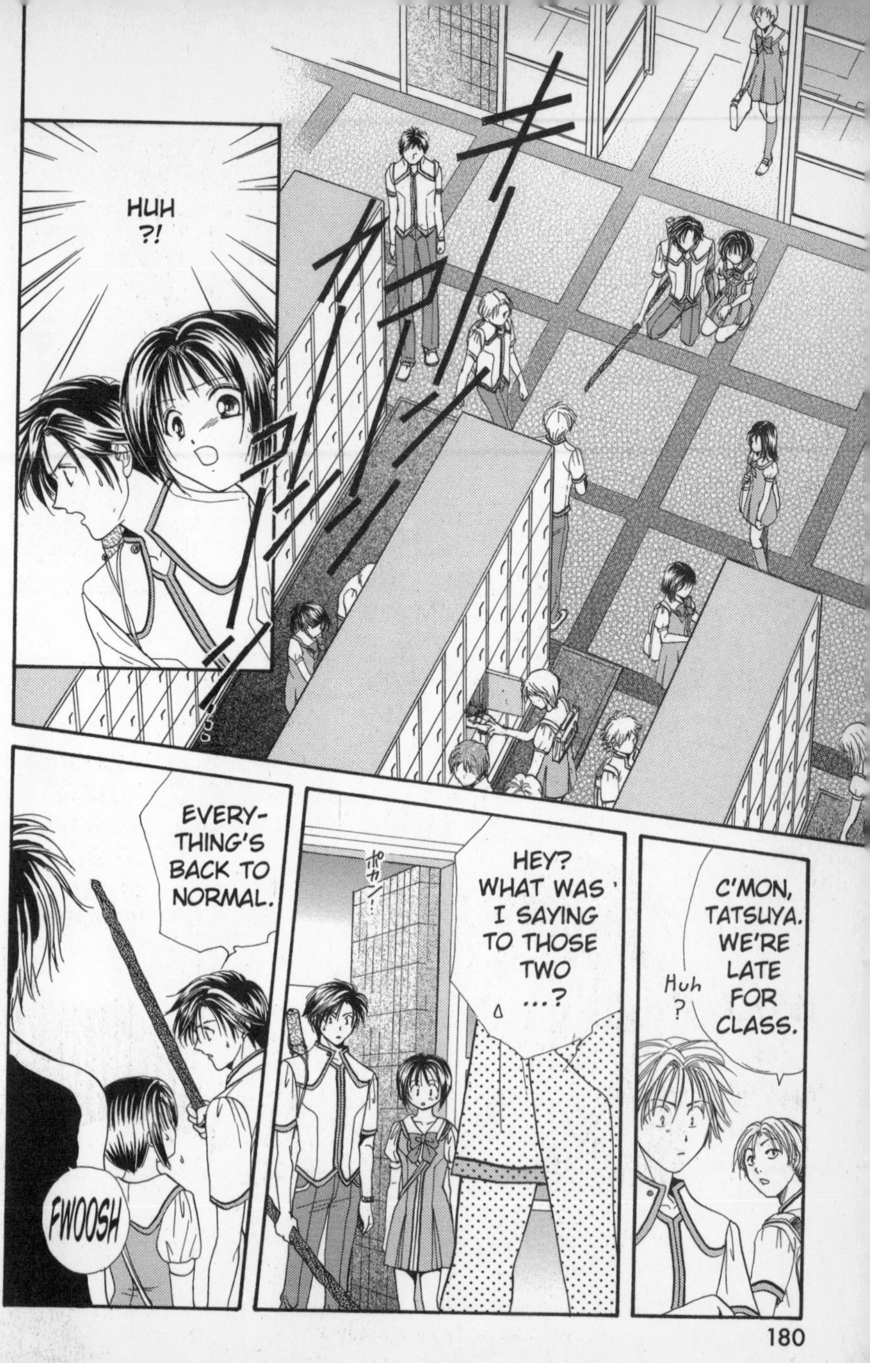
HUH ?!
C'MON, TATSUYA. WE'RE LATE FOR CLASS.
Huh ?
HEY? WHAT WAS I SAYING TO THOSE TWO ...?
EVERY-THING'S BACK TO NORMAL.
FWOOSH

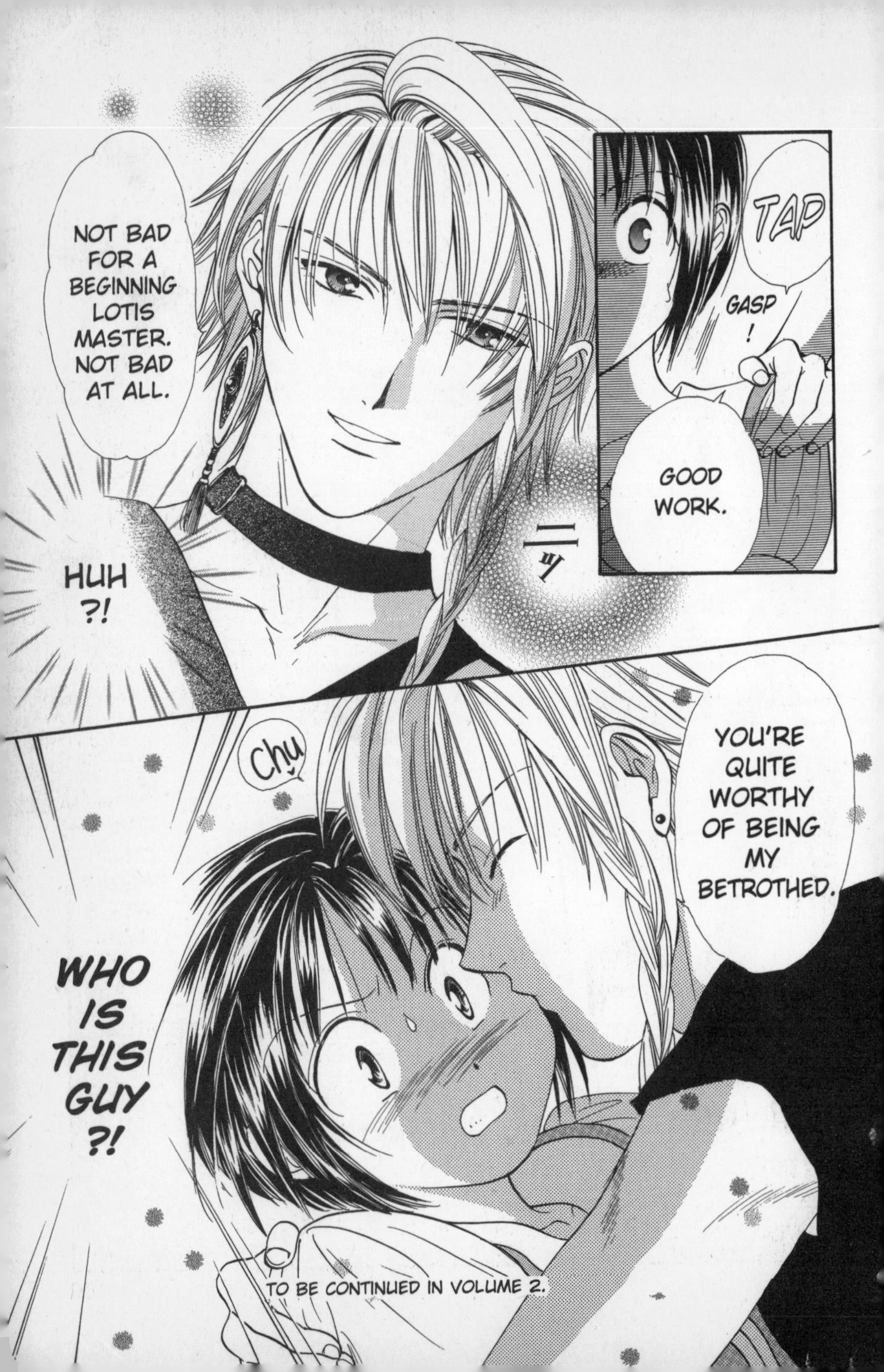
TAP
GASP !
GOOD WORK.
NOT BAD FOR A BEGINNING LOTIS MASTER. NOT BAD AT ALL.
HUH ?!
YOU'RE QUITE WORTHY OF BEING MY BETROTHED.
Chu
WHO IS THIS GUY ?!
TO BE CONTINUED IN VOLUME 2.

# ILLUSTRATION GALLERY

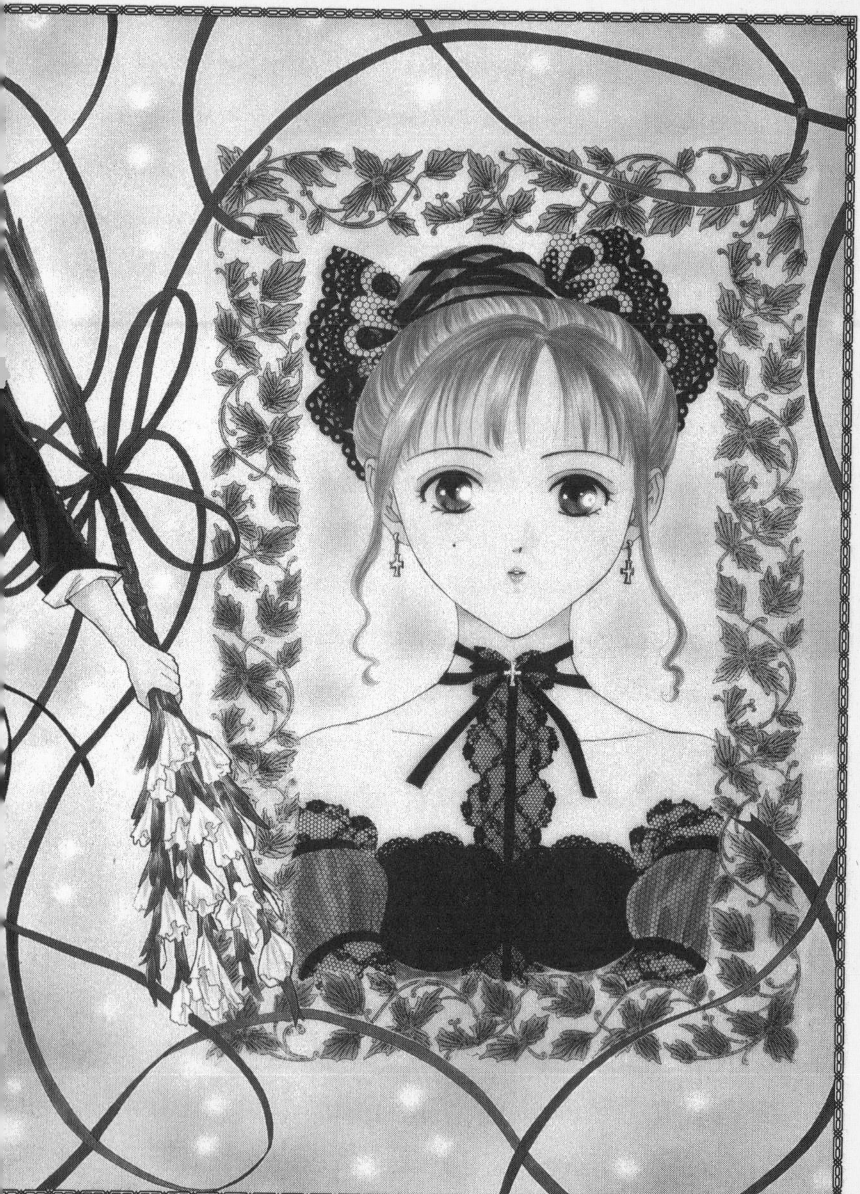

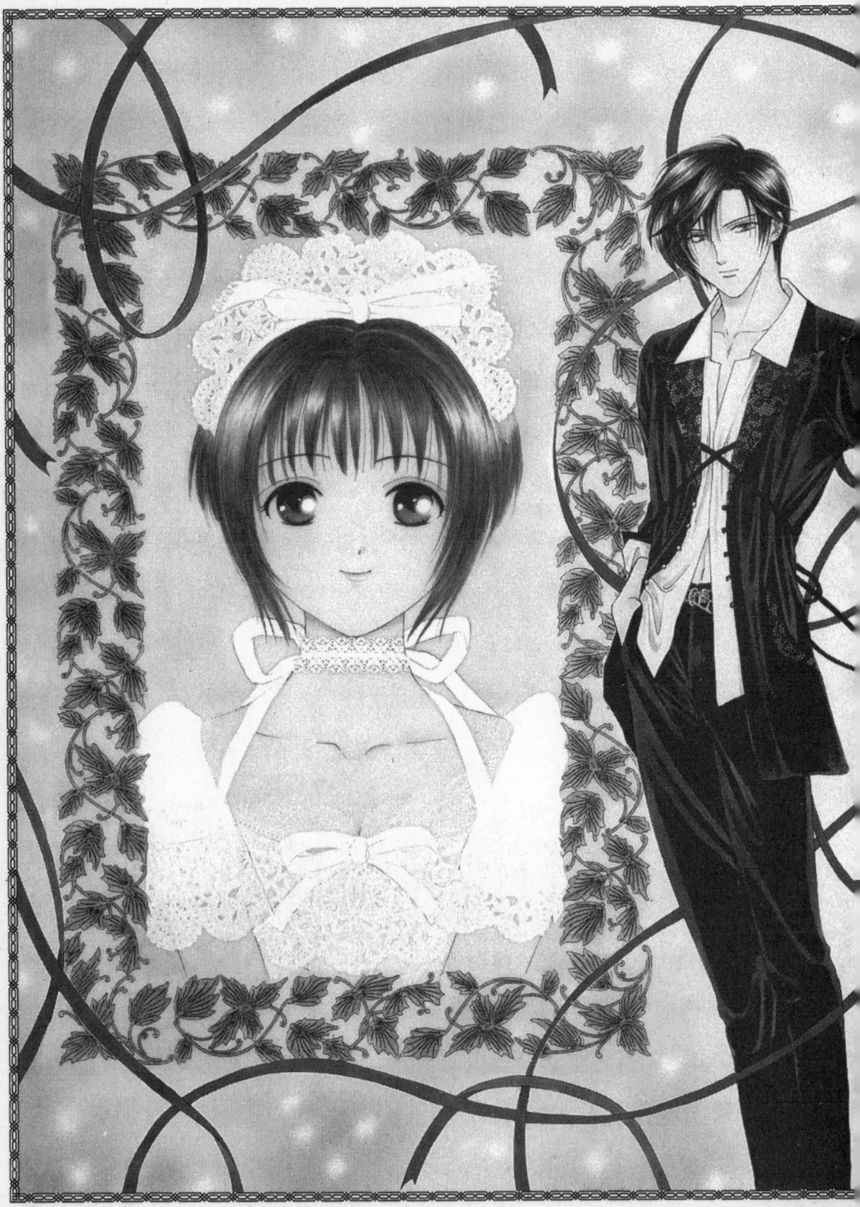

# About the Author:

Yû Watase was born on March 5 in a town near Osaka, and she was raised there before moving to Tokyo to follow her dream of creating manga. In the decade since her debut short story, *Pajama de Ojama* ("An Intrusion in Pajamas"), she has produced more than 50 compiled volumes of short stories and continuing series. Perhaps most well known for her smash-hit fantasy / romance stories *Fushigi Yûgi: The Mysterious Play* and *Ceres Celestial Legend*, her latest work, *Appare Jipangu*, is set in the Edo Period about a girl who cures people of their sadness and is currently being serialized in *Shôjo Comic*. Ms. Watase loves science fiction, fantasy and comedy.

If you enjoyed this manga, then you won't want to miss these other titles by the same author!

©1992 Yuu Watase / Shogakukan.

**Fushigi Yûgi:** A girl from modern times is magically transported to the Universe of the Four Gods—a magical world based on ancient Chinese legend. Another fantasy love triangle extravaganza brought to you by Yû Watase! More hunky male characters, more of Yû Watase's great artwork, and another intense storyline!

©1997 Yuu Watase / Shogakukan

**Ceres Celestial Legend:** Aya Mikage thinks she's just a normal girl in high school until she discovers that she can transform into a vastly powerful "celestial maiden" named Ceres.... But Ceres has a vendetta against Aya's family and is out for revenge! And because of the manifestation of Ceres, Aya's own family is out to kill her!

# Glossary of Sound Effects, Signs, and other Miscellaneous Notes

Each entry includes: the location, indicated by page number and panel number (so 3.1 means page 3, panel number 1); the phonetic romanization of the original Japanese; and our English "translation"—we offer as close an English equivalent as we can.

29.3——FX: Fushigi na usa usa
(Strange bunny)

30.4——FX: Tan! (thock! Arrow striking)

31.2——FX: Kasha (photo appears)

31.3——FX: Pako (whack)

32.4——FX: Poko (whack)

33.2——FX: Poko (whap)

33.3——FX: Pako (whack)

33.4——FX: Pako (whack)

33.6——FX: Hyu (whizz)

34.2——FX: Bin! (thwizz!)

35.1——FX: Zuka zuka (stomp stomp)

37.2——FX: Zukin! (heartbreak)

37.4——FX: Ta (footstep)

38.4——FX: Ban! (bam! bursting into room)

40.5——FX: Kin kon (school bell)

43.1——FX: Pita (come to stop)

44.1——FX: Dokun dokun (heart pounding)

44.3——FX: Dokun dokun (heart pounding)

44.4——FX: Dokun (heart pounding)

46.3——FX: Peko (bow)

53.3——FX: Go! (blam!)

5.2——FX: Kachi kachi kachi (click)

9.1——FX: Chi chi chi (chirp chirp chirp)

10.1——Cell phone:Tuesday, May 8—7:15 am

10.2——FX: Gyo (shock)

10.5——FX: Gaba! (wakes with a start)

11.1——FX: Dota dota dota (dashing around)

12.5——FX: Bata bata bata
(frantic dashing around)

13.3——FX: Batan (slam)

13.4——FX: Kachi kachi (clicking cell phone)
FX: Kachi kachi kachi
(clicking cell phone)

14.2——FX: Chika (click—traffic light change)

16.2——FX: Zaa (whoosh voices heard)

22.3——FX: Zu za za!
(frantically trying to get up)

23.1——FX: Ba (flash)

23.4——FX : Buroror : (vrooom)
FX : Paaa (honk)

27.1——FX: Piku (twitch)

27.2——FX: Ba! (snatch!)

28.1——FX: Pa paaa (honk)
FX: Paaa (honk)

28.2——FX: Gakkushi (disappointment)

58.2—FX: Zawa (creepy sound)

59.3—FX: Po! (lights appear)

60.1—FX: Pa (poof)

61.2—FX: Pa (poof! switch back)

62.3—FX: Zukin! (shock)

64.3—FX: Da! (running away)

64.4—FX: Ha... (sigh)

65.5—FX: Gacha (door opening)

67.1—FX: Ban (door bursts open)

67.2—FX: Gabah! (hug)

67.4—FX: Dota (fall on floor)

69.3—FX: Zuki! (heart breaking)

72.1—FX: Patan (fwump)

72.2—FX: Bori bori (chomp chomp)

73.3—FX: Kasa (clutching photo)

74.1—FX: Kara (Opens door)

74.2—FX: Gaba! (jumps up)

80.1—FX: Don (shock)

81.1—FX: Doki doki (heart beating)
FX: Doki (heart beating)

82.1—shop window: Rengado Cafe

83.4—FX: Gan (shock)

84.2—FX: Gashan! (crash!)
FX: Dotabata (panic attack)

84.3—FX: Zukin (heart breaking)

85.3—FX: Doku doku doku (pounding heart)

86.4—FX: Kachi kachi kachi kachi kachi (tick-tock sound)

88.2—FX: Kachi kachi kachi kachi kachi (tick-tock sound)

89.2—FX: Su! (swish)

89.4—FX: Doki (surprise)

94.1—sign: Akatsuki Shiritsu Meido Gakuen (name of high school)

94.2—FX: Bo (daze)

95.4—FX: Da! (dash)

97.1—FX: Pyon (hop)

97.4—FX: Kyoro kyoro (looking around)

97.5—FX: Po (confusion)

98.1—FX: Bu (spew)

98.5—FX: Dosu bata (bam slam)

99.1—FX: Gacha (door opens)

99.2—FX: Docha (fear)

99.5—FX: Zukin (shock)

101.4—FX: Niko (smile)

102.2—FX: Doki doki (nervous)

102.3—FX: Koso (peeking)

102.4—FX: Dokun (eye ball popping shock)

102.6—FX: Bikun (shock)

103.4—FX: Doka doka doka (struggling)

103.5—FX: Mugi (squeeze)

105.1—FX: Kacha (cup rattling)

107.2—FX: Biku (shock)

107.3—FX: Pyoko (peek)

108.5—FX: Kan kon (school chime)

110.2—FX: Dokun (panic)

110.4—FX: Giku (panic)

111.1 —FX: Ba! (slap)

111.4—FX: Gii (squeeze)

111.5—FX: Dokun dokun dokun
(ba-bump ba-bump)

112.4—FX: Ba (dash)

113.3—FX: Gachi Gachi (trembling)

113.5—FX: Su (fwup)

114.2—FX: Gun (crunch)

114.3—FX: Kara karan (crash)

116.2—FX: Zuru (letting go)

117.1 —FX: Goro goro goro (thunder)

117.2 —FX: Chi chi chi chi chi (tic toc)

121.1 —FX: Gun (fwoosh)
FX: Bikun (fwoosh)

125.2-125.5–FX: Zukin (panic)

126.3—FX: Yoro (sparkle)

127.2—FX: Za (rain)

130.1 —FX: Za (rain)

130.2—FX: Kokun (fwump)

131.1-131.2–FX: Kachi kachi kachi (tic toc)

132.1 —FX: Basha (splash)

132.4—FX: Basha basha basha
(splash splash splash)

132.6—FX: Bon! (bop)

133.1 —FX: Basha basha (splash)

133.3—FX: Zaaa (rain)

135.2—FX: Zaa! (rain)

135.3—FX: Dan dan dan (running)

135.5—FX: Boso (snf)

136.4—FX: Ban (slam)

137.1 —FX: Go! (roar)

140.1 —FX: Ha (gasp)

141.1 —FX: Piku piku (twitch twitch)

141.6—FX: Mugu (muffle)

142.3—FX: Patan (door shuts)

146.4—FX: Koso (hide)

148.3—FX: Zuki (shock)

149.1 —FX: Gura (shock)

150.1 —FX: Kokun (thinking)

150.2—FX: Kaa (shine)

151.2—FX: Don (bam!)

152.3—FX: Fu (fwom)

153.1 —FX: Fuwa (floating)

156.1 —FX: Guni (squeeze)

157.2 —FX: Za! (swoosh)

157.3—FX: Don (shove)

157.4—FX: Shu! (fwoosh)

158.2—FX: Don! (bam!)

174.3 —FX: Ba! (bam)

174.4 —FX: Kaa! (thud)

175.1 —FX: Kiri kiri kiri (pulling of bow)

175.3 —FX: Za! (swoosh)

177.2 —FX: Anguri (surprise)

177.3 —FX: Bii! (ping)

178.1 —FX: Ba! (swoosh)

179.2 —FX: Fuu! (zap)

179.3 —FX: Zawa zawa zawa (swish)

180.1 —FX: Kin kon kan kon (school chime)

180.4 —FX: Pokan (huh)

181.2 —FX: Ni (smile)

159.1 —FX: Zuru (crumble)

159.2 —FX: Gon (bonk)

160.6 —FX: Ha (gasp)

161.3 —FX: Ha (gasp)

161.4 —FX: Da! (dash)

162.1 —FX: Zun! (smash)

162.5 —FX: Fuu! (noticing something)

163.1 —FX: Sheen (silence)

163.5 —FX: Gura! (falling)

163.5 —FX: Go (falling over)

163.6 —FX: Doka doka doka (falling people)

164.1 —FX: Don don don (falling people)

164.2 —FX: Yoro (fwom)

164.4 —FX: Zuun! (swoosh)

166.1 —FX: Gi gi (twisting metal)

166.3 —FX: Zaa! (fwoosh)

166.4 —FX: Gu! (choking

166.6 —FX: Doka (bonk)

167.1 —FX: Bote (plop)

168.1 —FX: Go! (roar)

169.1 —FX: Fuwaa! (swoosh)

170.4 —FX: Pyun (leap)

170.4 —FX: Ha (gasp)

171.2 —FX: Ba (fwoosh)

172.1 —FX: Su (fwom)

173.2 —FX: Suuu (swish)

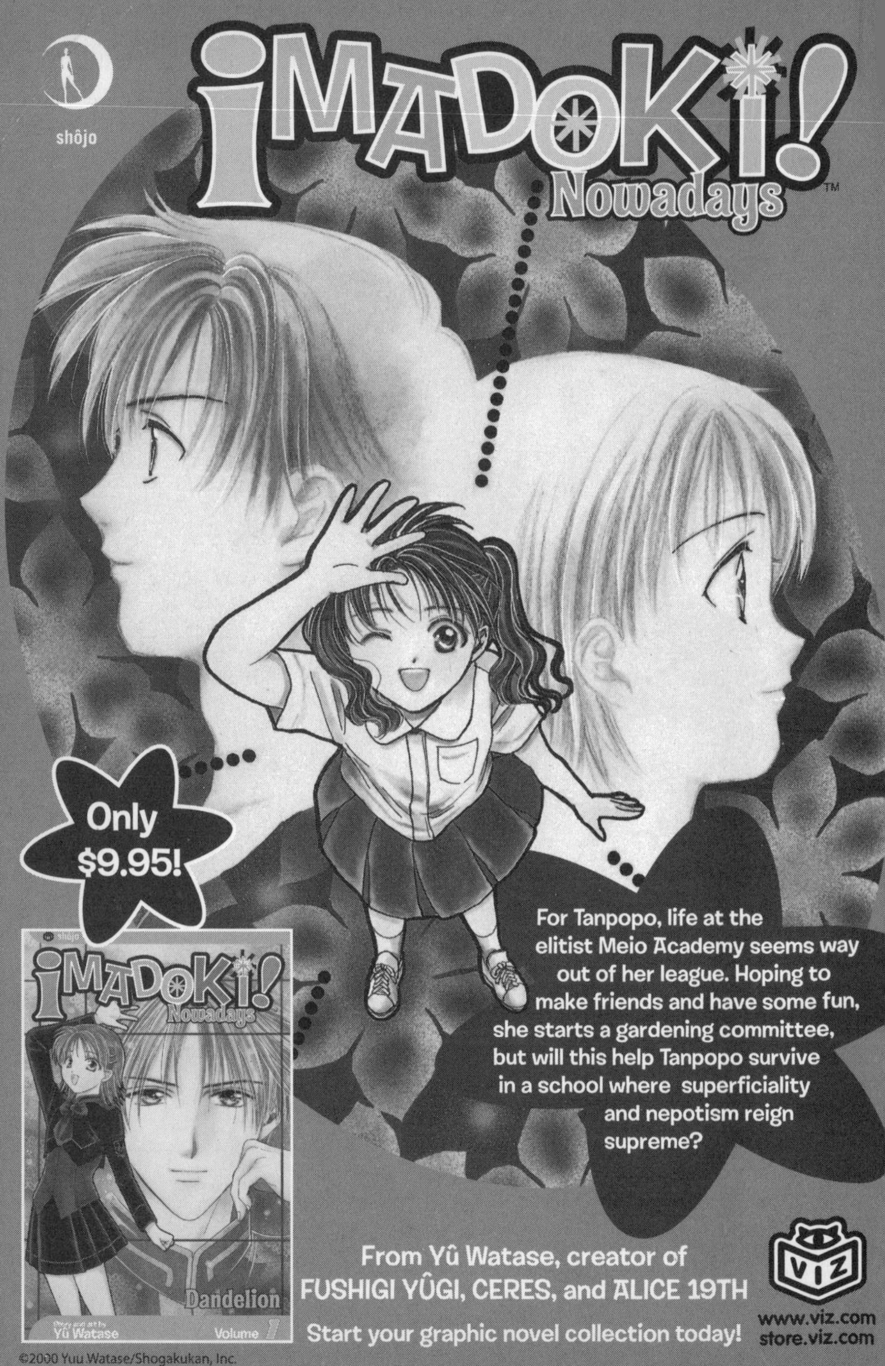
shôjo
IMADOKI! Nowadays™
Only $9.95!
For Tanpopo, life at the elitist Meio Academy seems way out of her league. Hoping to make friends and have some fun, she starts a gardening committee, but will this help Tanpopo survive in a school where superficiality and nepotism reign supreme?
IMADOKI! Nowadays
Dandelion
Story and art by Yû Watase
Volume 1
From Yû Watase, creator of FUSHIGI YÛGI, CERES, and ALICE 19TH
Start your graphic novel collection today!
VIZ
www.viz.com
store.viz.com

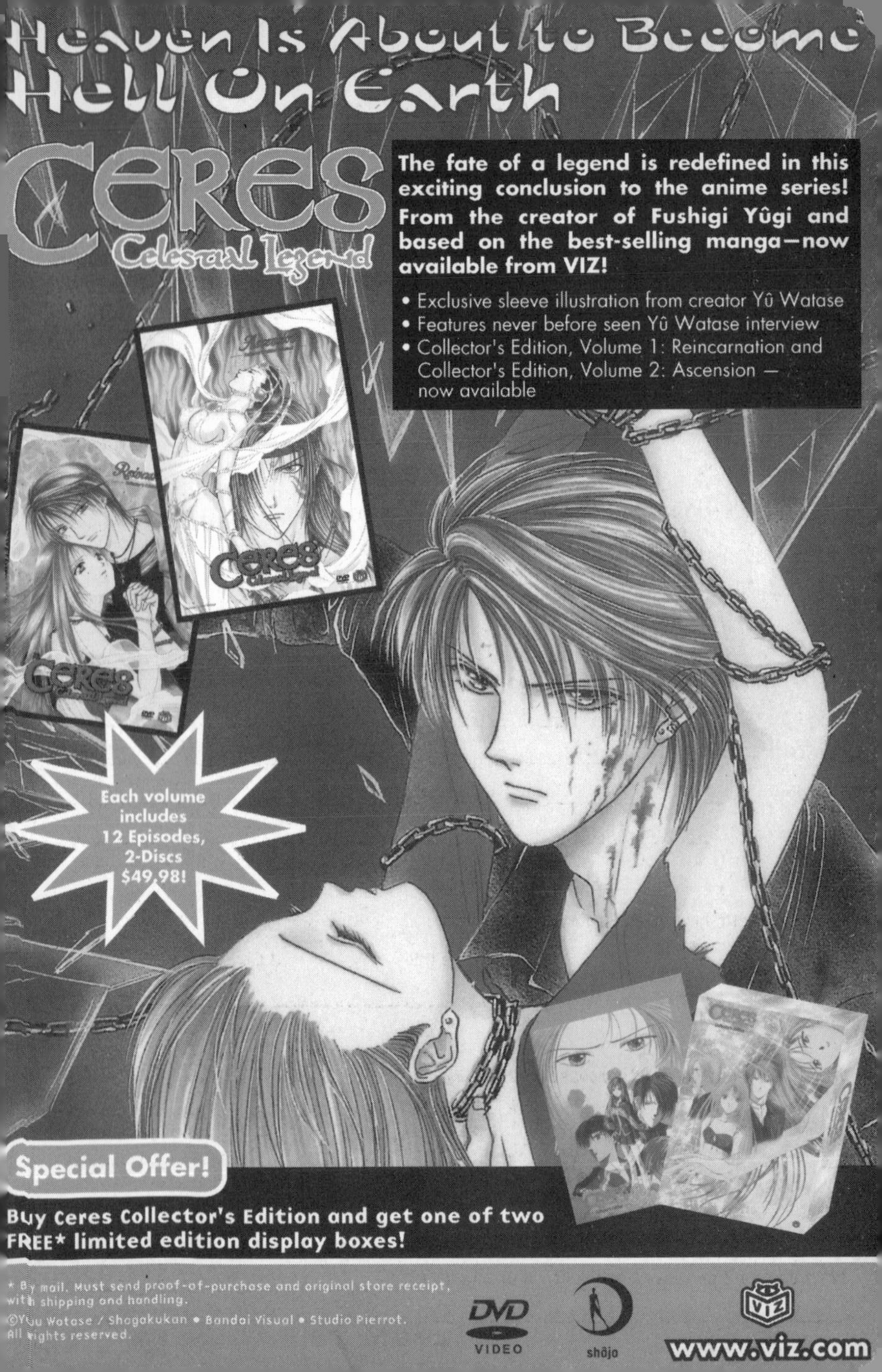
Heaven Is About to Become Hell On Earth
Ceres Celestial Legend
The fate of a legend is redefined in this exciting conclusion to the anime series! From the creator of Fushigi Yûgi and based on the best-selling manga—now available from VIZ!
• Exclusive sleeve illustration from creator Yû Watase
• Features never before seen Yû Watase interview
• Collector's Edition, Volume 1: Reincarnation and Collector's Edition, Volume 2: Ascension — now available
Each volume includes 12 Episodes, 2-Discs $49.98!
Special Offer!
Buy Ceres Collector's Edition and get one of two FREE* limited edition display boxes!
* By mail. Must send proof-of-purchase and original store receipt, with shipping and handling.
©Yuu Watase / Shogakukan • Bandai Visual • Studio Pierrot. All rights reserved.
DVD VIDEO
shōjo
VIZ
www.viz.com

**How many anime and/or manga titles have you purchased in the last year? How many were VIZ titles?** **(please check one from each column)**

| ANIME | MANGA | VIZ |
|---|---|---|
| ☐ None | ☐ None | ☐ None |
| ☐ 1-4 | ☐ 1-4 | ☐ 1-4 |
| ☐ 5-10 | ☐ 5-10 | ☐ 5-10 |
| ☐ 11+ | ☐ 11+ | ☐ 11+ |

**I find the pricing of VIZ products to be:** **(please check one)**

☐ Cheap ☐ Reasonable ☐ Expensive

**What genre of manga and anime would you like to see from VIZ?** **(please check two)**

☐ Adventure ☐ Comic Strip ☐ Science Fiction ☐ Fighting

☐ Horror ☐ Romance ☐ Fantasy ☐ Sports

**What do you think of VIZ's new look?**

☐ Love It ☐ It's OK ☐ Hate It ☐ Didn't Notice ☐ No Opinion

**Which do you prefer?** **(please check one)**

☐ Reading right-to-left

☐ Reading left-to-right

**Which do you prefer?** **(please check one)**



☐ Sound effects in English

☐ Sound effects in Japanese with English captions

☐ Sound effects in Japanese only with a glossary at the back

**THANK YOU! Please send the completed form to:**

NJW Research
42 Catharine St.
Poughkeepsie, NY 12601

**All information provided will be used for internal purposes only. We promise not to sell or otherwise divulge your information.**

# COMPLETE OUR SURVEY AND LET US KNOW WHAT YOU THINK!

☐ Please do NOT send me information about VIZ products, news and events, special offers, or other information.

☐ Please do NOT send me information from VIZ's trusted business partners.

**Name:** _____

**Address:** _____

**City:** _____ **State:** _____ **Zip:** _____

**E-mail:** _____

☐ Male  ☐ Female   **Date of Birth** (mm/dd/yyyy): ___ / ___ / ___   ( Under 13? Parental consent required )

## What race/ethnicity do you consider yourself? (please check one)

☐ Asian/Pacific Islander        ☐ Black/African American       ☐ Hispanic/Latino

☐ Native American/Alaskan Native   ☐ White/Caucasian          ☐ Other: _____

## What VIZ product did you purchase? (check all that apply and indicate title purchased)

☐ DVD/VHS _____

☐ Graphic Novel _____

☐ Magazines _____

☐ Merchandise _____

## Reason for purchase: (check all that apply)

☐ Special offer           ☐ Favorite title            ☐ Gift

☐ Recommendation          ☐ Other _____

## Where did you make your purchase? (please check one)

☐ Comic store            ☐ Bookstore               ☐ Mass/Grocery Store

☐ Newsstand              ☐ Video/Video Game Store   ☐ Other: _____

☐ Online (site: _____ )

## What other VIZ properties have you purchased/own? _____

_____